Speaking of GENDER

edited by
ELAINE SHOWALTER

ROUTLEDGE · NEW YORK & LONDON

First published in 1989 by
Routledge
An imprint of Routledge, Chapman and Hall, Inc.
29 West 35 Street
New York, NY 10001

Published in Great Britain by
Routledge
11 New Fetter Lane
London EC4P 4EE

Library of Congress Cataloging in Publication Data

Speaking of gender / [edited by] Elaine Showalter
     p.   cm.
   ISBN 0-415-90026-3   ISBN 0-415-90027-1 (pbk.)
   1. English literature—History and criticism. 2. Sex role in
literature. 3. Feminism and literature. 4. English literature–
–History and criticism—Theory, etc. 5. American literature–
–History and criticism—Theory, etc.   I. Showalter, Elaine.
PR408.S49S64 1988
820'.9'352042—dc19   88-20936

British Library Cataloguing in Publication Data

Speaking of gender.
   1. English literature—Critical studies
   I. Showalter, Elaine, *1941–*
   820.9

ISBN 0-415-90026-3
ISBN 0-415-90027-1 Pbk

Contents

Acknowledgments

Thanks to Deborah Smith for reseasrch assistance in the preparation of this book. Permission to reprint essays has been granted by the following:

Carol L. Barash, "Virile Womanhood: Olive Schreiner's Narratives of a Master Race," from *Women's Studies International Forum*, 9 (1986): 333–40; by permission of Pergamon Journals, Ltd.

Christopher Craft, " 'Kiss Me With Those Red Lips': Gender and Inversion in Bram Stoker's *Dracula*," from *Representations* 8 (Fall 1984): 107–33; by permission of the Regents of the University of California.

Susan Stanford Friedman, "Creativity and the Childbirth Metaphor: Gender Difference in Literary Discourse," from *Feminist Studies* 13, no. 1 (1987): 49–82; by permission of the publisher Feminist Studies, Inc., c/o Women's Studies Program, University of Maryland, College Park, MD 20742.

Elliot L. Gilbert, "The Female King: Tennyson's Arthurian Apocalypse," from *PMLA* 98 (1983): 863–78; by permission of the Modern Language Association of America.

Sandra M. Gilbert, "Soldier's Heart: Literary Men, Literary Women, and the Great War," from *Signs* 8 (1983): 422–50; by permission of the author.

Barbara Johnson, "Gender Theory and the Yale School," from *Rhetoric and Form: Deconstruction at Yale*, ed. and with an introduction by Robert Con Davis and Ronald Schiefer. Copyright © 1985 by the University of Oklahoma Press.

David Leverenz, "The Politics of Emerson's Man-making Words," from *PMLA* 10, (January 1986): 38–56; by permission of the Modern Language Association of America.

D.A. Miller, "*Cage aux folles:* Sensation and Gender in Wilkie Collins's *The Woman in White*," from *The Nineteenth Century British Novel*, ed. Jeremy Hawthorn, London: Edward Arnold, 1986, pp. 95–124; by permission of the author and Edward Arnold Publishers.

Phyllis Rackin, "Androgyny, Mimesis, and the Marriage of the Boy Heroine on the English Renaissance Stage," *PMLA* 102 (January 1987): 29–41; by permission of the Modern Language Association of America.

Patrocinio P. Schweickart, "Reading Ourselves: Toward a Feminist Theory of Reading," from *Gender and Reading*, Baltimore: Johns Hopkins University Press, 1986, pp. 31–62; by permission of The Johns Hopkins University Press.

Susan Schweik, "Writing War Poetry Like a Woman," from *Critical Inquiry* 13 (Spring 1987): 532–56; by permission of the University of Chicago Press.

Peter Schwenger, "The Masculine Mode," from *Critical Inquiry* 5 (Summer 1979): 621–33; by permission of the University of Chicago Press.

Eve Kosofsky Sedgwick, "The Beast in the Closet: James and the Writing of Homosexual Panic," from Ruth Yeazell, ed., *Sex, Politics, and Science in the Nineteenth-Century Novel: Selected Papers from the English Institute*, Baltimore: Johns Hopkins University Press, 1986, pp. 147–186; by permission of The Johns Hopkins University Press.

Valerie Smith, "Gender Theory and Afro-American Criticism," copyright 1988, by permission of the author.

Speaking of GENDER

1

Introduction: The Rise of Gender

Elaine Showalter

Talking About Gender

One of the most striking changes in the humanities in the 1980s has been the rise
of gender as a category of analysis. In December 1987, a reporter visiting the
annual convention of the American Historical Association in Washington, DC was
impressed by the proliferation of topics dealing with gender, from "Sex, Gender,
and the Constitution," to "The Homosexual Experience in Modern Germany." "You
can't do anything now without making reference to gender," the conservative
historian Gertrude Himmelfarb lamented. "You can't talk about the Austro-Hun-
garian Empire without talking about gender."[1] A Hapsburg or a Himmelfarb seeking
a conference where gender was not part of the program would have found no refuge
at the Modern Language Association either, for gender has changed the shape of
literary conversation as well. In the wake of feminist criticism, gender has become
recognized as "a crucial determinent in the production, circulation, and con-
sumption of literary discourse."[2] You can't discuss Donne or Byron, the Elizabethan
stage or the modernist poem, the films of F.W. Murnau or *The Texas Chainsaw
Massacre*, without talking about gender.

What do we talk about when we talk about gender? To begin with, all speech
is necessarily talk about gender, since in every language gender is a grammatical
category, and the masculine is the linguistic norm.[3] Even in English, a language
in which only nouns referring to human beings and animals are formally gendered
(in contrast to languages such as French or German in which all nouns, including
inanimate objects, places, and concepts have gender as well), the masculine form
is generic, universal, or unmarked, while the feminine form is marked by a suffix
or some other variant. We can call either Sylvia Plath or Robert Lowell a "poet",
but we can not call Lowell a "poetess" except as an insult. Furthermore, as Monique
Wittig has observed, language usage is the site of a covert struggle for gender
meanings: "One must understand that men are not born with a faculty for the
universal, and that women are not all reduced at birth to the particular. The
universal has been, and is, continually at every moment, appropriated by men."[4]

Secondly, within Anglo-American feminist discourse, the term "gender" has
been used for the past several years to stand for the social, cultural, and psycho-

logical meaning imposed upon biological sexual identity; indeed, the problematization of gender relations, according to the theorist Jane Flax, is "the single most important advance in feminist theory."[5] Thus "gender" has a different meaning than the term "sex," which refers to biological identity as female or male, or "sexuality," which is the totality of an individual's sexual orientation, preference, and behavior. While a traditional view would hold that sex, gender, and sexuality are the same—that a biological male, for example, "naturally" acquires the masculine behavioral norms of his society, and that his sexuality "naturally" evolves from his hormones—scholarship in a number of disciplines shows that concepts of masculinity vary widely within various societies and historical periods, and that sexuality is a complex phenomenon shaped by social and personal experience. The contemporary phenomenon of transsexual operations, in which individuals undergo surgery and hormonal treatment in order to adjust their anatomical sex to their experiential sense of gender and sexuality, is one illustration of the social pressures to conform to gender codes. Even a successful transsexual like the journalist Jan Morris has wondered whether she would have bothered to change sex, "if society had allowed me to live in the gender I preferred."[6]

Thirdly, talking about gender means talking about both women and men. Gender theory began to develop during the early 1980s in feminist thought in the fields of history, anthropology, philosophy, psychology, and natural science, marking a shift from the women-centered investigations of the 1970s, such as women's history, gynocriticism, and psychology of women, to the study of gender relations involving both women and men. Such a shift, some feminist scholars argued, would ultimately have a more radically transformative impact on the disciplines than studies of women, which too easily could be ghettoized, leaving disciplinary structures and practices intact. In "Anthropology and the Study of Gender" (1981), for example, Judith Shapiro argued that the goal of feminist research ought not to be a focus on "women," but rather the integration of "the study of gender differences into the central pursuits of the social sciences." The real objective, she argued, was to make it "as impossible for social scientists to avoid dealing with gender in their studies of social differentiation as it is for them to avoid dealing with such things as rank, class, and kinship."[7] In the natural sciences, Evelyn Fox Keller, Ruth Bleier, and Donna Haraway asked "how much of the nature of science is bound up with the idea of masculinity, and what would it mean for science if it were otherwise?"[8] In the field of history, Natalie Davis, Joan Kelley-Gadol, and Gerda Lerner were raising similar questions. The aim of feminist history, Davis observed, is "to understand the significance of the sexes, of gender groups in the historical past. Our goal is to discover the range in sex roles and in sexual symbolism in different societies and periods, to find out what meaning they had and how they functioned to maintain the social order or to promote its change."[9]

The introduction of gender into the field of literary studies marks a new phase in feminist criticism, an investigation of the ways that all reading and writing, by men as well as by women, is marked by gender. Talking about gender, moreover, is a constant reminder of the other categories of difference, such as race and class, that structure our lives and texts, just as theorizing gender emphasizes the parallels between feminist criticism and other forms of minority discourse. As Cora Kaplan eloquently notes, "a feminist literary criticism that privileges gender in isolation from other forms of social determination offers us a similarly partial reading of the role played by sexual difference in literary discourse, a reading bled dry of its most troubling and contradictory meanings."[10]

Gender is far, however, from reaching a state of consensus. While most feminist scholars agree on the distinction between sex and gender, and the need to explore masculinity as well as femininity, and homosexuality as well as heterosexuality, there is vigorous intellectual debate about the construction of gender, and the way it should be used by scholars and critics. The editors of the journal *Signs* find that "gender is an analytic concept whose meanings we work to elucidate, and a subject matter we proceed to study as we try to define it."[11] The terms "gender" and "sexual difference," for example, are often used interchangeably in feminist writing, as in Cora Kaplan's statement above; yet, strictly speaking, they derive from different theoretical perspectives. The term "sexual difference" comes out of the discourses of poststructuralism and psychoanalysis, and originates with the question of difference in language, subjectivity, and identity. Thus the organizers of the 1986 Conference on Sexual Difference at the University of Southampton (England) announced that their "trajectory followed from questions posed to and raised by poststructuralist theory," (although the by-standers at the Southampton station who watched conference participants queue up for the Sexual Difference minibus may have thought that quite another trajectory was under way.) Critics working under the rubric of "sexual difference" make use of Freudian and post-Freudian accounts of the construction of gendered subjectivities, relying heavily on the work of Jacques Lacan. They believe that gender is primarily constructed through the acquisition of language, rather than through social ascription or cultural practice. The speaking subject must enter the symbolic system ruled by the Law of the Father, and marked by the signifier of the phallus and the castration complex. In taking up a linguistic position as "he" or "she" in relation to the symbolic, the subject learns to be gendered. Thus to deconstruct language is to deconstruct gender; to subvert the symbolic order is to subvert sexual difference.

For those materialist critics who prefer the term "gender," however, talking about "sexual difference" implies both a belief in the inevitability of the social relations between the sexes, and a downgrading of history and social process in favor of psychic and linguistic determinants. As the historian Joan W. Scott notes, "The theory tends to universalize the categories and relationship of male and female. . . . The phallus is the only signifier; the process of constructing the gendered subject is, in the end, predictable because always the same."[12] Marxist-feminist critics point out that gender does not exist independently or in a social and political vacuum, but is always shaped within ideological frameworks. "Masculinity and femininity," writes Cora Kaplan, "do not appear in cultural discourse, anymore than they do in mental life, as pure binary forms at play. They are always, already, ordered and broken up through other social and cultural terms, other categories of difference,"[13] such as homophobia, class divisions, and racial hierarchies. Thus gender should not be treated as a an isolated category within a purely psychoanalytic framework, but should rather be seen as part of a process of social construction.

Furthermore, gender is not only a question of *difference*, which assumes that the sexes are separate and equal; but of *power*, since in looking at the history of gender relations, we find sexual assymetry, inequality, and male dominance in every known society. As the lawyer and feminist theoretician Catherine MacKinnon has forcefully maintained, to tread gender as sexual difference rather than sexual hierarchy "obscures and legitimizes the way gender is imposed by force." The concept of sexual difference, according to MacKinnon, "hides that force behind a static description of gender as a biological or mythic or semantic partition, engraved, inscribed or inculcated by god, nature, society (agents unspecified), the unconscious, the cosmos."[14] Feminist scholars with a materialist or Marxist orientation analyze the ways that gender ideology is inscribed, represented, and reproduced in a variety of cultural practices, including literature, the mass media, film, and popular culture.[15]

Gender and Feminist Criticism

Gender has always been a significant term in feminist criticism, but, until recently, in practice it referred primarily to women and to women's writing. Gynocriticism, the feminist study of women's writing, assumes that all writing by women is marked by gender; as Alicia Ostriker notes, "writers necessarily articulate gendered experience, just as they necessarily articulate the spirit of a nationality, an age, a language."[16] Although feminist critics recognize that the meaning of gender needs to be interpreted within a variety of historical, national, racial, and sexual contexts, they maintain that women writers are not free to renounce or transcend their gender entirely. As Sandra Gilbert asks, "If a writer is a woman who has been raised as a woman—and I daresay only a very few biologically anomalous human females have not been raised as women—how can her sexual identity be split off from her literary energy? Even a denial of her femininity . . . would surely be significant to an understanding of the dynamics of her aesthetic creativity."[17] Women can differentiate their positions from any number of stereotypes of femininity, and define themselves also in terms of being black, lesbian, South African, or working-class; but to deny that they are affected by being women at all is self-delusion or self-hatred, the legacy of centuries of denigration of women's art.

A second assumption of gynocriticism is that women's writing is always "bi-textual," in dialogue with both masculine and feminine literary traditions.[18] Gender relations are thus seen as inscribed in every female text, in the sense that women's writing necessarily takes place within, rather than outside, a dominant male discourse, through acts of "revision, appropriation, and subversion."[19] Women's literary and critical texts are both double-voiced discourses, inevitably and continually engaged with patrilineal and matrilineal sources.

At the beginning of this decade, however, few feminist critics were analyzing *men's* writing as a gendered discourse, rather than as patriarchal or sexist. Although the London-based Marxist-Feminist Literature Collective, for example, had argued as early as 1977 that "all subjects are gendered and . . . all literary discourse is gender-specific,"[20] they too had investigated only the female subject and women's literary texts. While feminist critics declared that no art or criticism was gender-free, in practice they usually treated art by men as free from gender constructions, apart from its problematic or misogynistic representations of women.

In an essay in *SIGNS* in 1981, Myra Jehlen argued that feminist criticism should also draw attention to the gender of male discourse. By developing a history of women's writing, she pointed out, feminist criticism had demonstrated that the assumed universality of the literary canon was a patriarchal myth, and that what was usually called "literature" was in fact "men's writing." Given this discovery, Jehlen maintained, the agenda for an "aggressive" feminist criticism was a "radical comparativism," in which texts by male and female authors working within the same historical conditions and genres are set against each other to reveal the "contingency of the dominant male tradition."[21]

Jehlen's call for radical comparativism was premature since we had no body of criticism that explored the issues of gender in male authors as gynocriticism had done for female authors; it was far too early and dangerous to give up the demanding task of reconstructing women's literary heritage, a heritage still unfamiliar to many scholars, in exchange for a one-sided comparativism. Nevertheless, Jehlen's essay appeared at the beginning of a renewed feminist interest in reading male texts, not as documents of sexism and misogyny, but as inscriptions of gender, and "renditions of sexual difference."[22] The terminology of "gender" began to appear in comparative feminist studies of such themes as cross-dressing and metaphoric transvestism;[23] in collections such as *The Poetics of Gender;* and in articles and books about the male canon.[24] Some of the most significant work was being carried out by feminist Shakespeareans like Coppèlia Kahn, Linda Bamber, and Madelon Gohlke, who studied metaphors of masculinity in the plays. As of the late 1980s, this revisionary process has had important effects on work within several periods of English and American literature, especially the eighteenth century, the Romantic period, the fin de siècle, and modernism.

From Male Feminism to Gender Theory

In the early 1980s the intellectual and political relations between feminist critics and their male colleagues were much more strained than in the fields of social history or symbolic anthropology. While there were many well-known male historians specializing in women's history, and many anthropologists working on kinship, sexuality, and gender, feminist literary criticism was still regarded—or disregarded—as a subject beneath the intellectual notice of male theorists, even those who saw themselves as radicals. Several books on contemporary literary theory that appeared around 1980 left out any mention of feminist criticism at all; and women who specialized in other forms of critical theory, as Barbara Johnson points out in her essay here on "Gender Theory and the Yale School," were ignored and marginalized, even when they dutifully suppressed the feminine in their own texts. "As every feminist critic knows," Sandra Gilbert lamented in 1980, "most of our male colleagues don't come to our talks, don't read our essays and books, don't in fact concede that we exist as thinkers, teachers, and writers who are part of a significant intellectual movement."[25]

Nevertheless, the impact of feminist criticism and theory on the profession of literary studies could not be ignored forever, and early in the 1980s a number of prominent male critics and theorists took up the question of feminist literary theory. Few male literary critics at this time, however, perceived masculinity as a subject within feminist thought; unlike femininity, it seemed "natural, transparent, and unproblematic,"[26] for, as Jane Flax points out, "in a wide variety of cultures and discourses, men tend to be seen as free from or not determined by gender relations."[27] Thus for this first wave of "male feminists," the call to develop an awareness of gender was initially heard not as an invitation to think about masculinity, but rather as a challenge to "master" feminist criticism and to correct what they saw as its shortcomings and flaws.

In a review of some of the first books by "male feminists" in 1983, I asked whether genuine self-transformation or merely intellectual appropriation was under way; after all, mastery of the feminine has long been a stance of masculine authority; and from *Fanny Hill* to Benny Hill, some men have achieved enormous skill and success in female impersonation. Until men questioned their own reading practices, I thought, male feminism was just a form of critical cross-dressing, a version of the transvestite films of that year like "Tootsie," which made female masquerade a way to take over women's newly-acquired power. In order to make a genuine contribution to feminist theory, I argued, male theorists must confront "what might be implied by reading as a man, and with a questioning or surrender of paternal privileges."[28] Similar demands for men to "develop a consciousness of their own gender," to "write a masculine discourse and affirm that they are doing so,"[29] came from feminist theorists in England, Germany, and France.

But when they were asked to write or read as *men*, male critics drew a blank. As Stephen Heath admitted in an essay on "Male Feminism" (1984), "men have been trained simply to read, they have the acquired neutrality of domination, theirs is the security of indifference—it is women who are different, the special case."[30] The taboos against this sort of male self-analysis were so strong that as one theorist suggested, "masculinity imagines itself poorly, or imagines itself, at most, only by feminizing itself."[31] For men to discuss masculinity was already to diminish or threaten their own manliness, since in terms of social conditioning, as Peter Schwenger points out in "The Masculine Mode," for a man "to think about masculinity is to become less masculine oneself. . . . The real man thinks about practical matters rather than abstract ones and certainly does not brood upon himself or the nature of his sexuality."[32]

Thus many feminist critics worried that male critics would appropriate, penetrate, or exploit feminist discourse for professional advantage, without accepting the risks and challenges of investigating masculinity, or analyzing their own critical practice. Some "male feminism" looked a lot like the old misogyny dressed up in Woolf's clothing, even when critics couched their attacks in the fashionable terminology of "essentialism," rather than in the cruder language of overt sexism. At the same time, male critics were perturbed by the "ingratitude" and intransigence of feminist critics, who did not seem to greet their well-intended efforts with the enthusiasm they had expected.

Some of these controversies were vividly demonstrated in the debates and often bitter exchanges of the 1980s that took place between "male feminists" and feminist critics at conferences, in journals, and in the book *Men in Feminism* (1987). The Australian critic K.K. Ruthven, for example, angered many feminist critics by his assertion that "the female 'problematic' is too important to be left in the hands of anti-intellectual feminists," and that it should be carried on by politically neutral "men who make a living from talking about books."[33] As Meaghan Morris objected, "men have no business in feminism, when they've nothing *but* business therein.[34] When Larry Lipking proposed a woman's "poetics of abandonment," Joan DeJean retorted that he was not responding to a deficiency in feminist literature or theory, but rather attempting to "consign strong female critics to abandonment, out of . . . a fear that unless female theorists are cast off, critical sons may have an increasingly difficult time proving their legitimacy."[35] In an essay about male gender anxieties in the poems of Wallace Stevens, Frank Lentricchia excoriated Sandra Gilbert and Susan Gubar at length for their "essentialist humanism" and "sexist" views of patriarchy, citing the "persuasive deflation of a number of major American and French feminist literary reputations" in Toril Moi's *Sexual/Textual Politics,* and declaring that "a younger wave of feminists . . . are at the verge of open revolt against their mothers." Lentricchia's vicarious pleasure at this "deflation," and his obviously eager anticipation of a postfeminist "revolt" against major feminist reputations, Gilbert and Gubar responded, were the real motives of his essay,[36] rather than the question of gender itself.

Nevertheless, by the mid-1980s, serious inquiries into masculine modes of creativity, interpretation and representation began to develop in a number of contexts outside the star wars of literary theory: in the writing of a generation of male critics influenced by feminist critical practice; in Afro-American criticism and theory; in the work of the New Historicists; and most of all, in the emergent fields of men's studies and gay studies.[37] Books like Alfred Habegger's *Gender,*

Fantasy and Realism in American Literature (1982), and Joseph Boone's *Tradition Counter Tradition: Love and the Form of Fiction* (1987), explored the relations between gender and genre. Men's studies, which situates "masculinities as objects of study on a par with femininities, instead of elevating them to universal norms,"[38] began to look at men's writing as well as at sociological and historical problems. Work in gay literary criticism has also moved from the effort to define a gay literary sensibility to investigations of the connections between gender, masculinity, and homosexuality. A significant step in the development of gender criticism was Eve Kosofsky Sedgwick's book *Between Men: English Literature and Male Homosocial Desire* (1985). Sedgwick analyzed the inscriptions of male homosexuality in relation to class, race, and the gender system as a whole. Following on work by Freud, Levi-Strauss, René Girard, Gayle Rubin, and others, she focused on the exchange of women to mediate male bonding, and on the repressed bonds between male rivals in erotic triangles. By placing relationships between men along a continuum from the homosocial to homoerotic, and by studying the ways in which society exercised "secular power over male bonds," Sedgwick made it possible to look at the "the shape of the entire male homosocial spectrum and its effects on women;"[39] indeed, her work has been so influential that one can begin to speak of the Sedgwick School, or École d'Eve. As several gay critics have noted, Sedgwick's woman-centered and feminist work brought both homophobia and male homosexuality "to center stage in the discussion of the construction of gender."[40] While men's studies, gay studies, and feminist criticism have different politics and priorities, together they are moving beyond "male feminism" to raise challenging questions about masculinity in literary texts, questions that enable gender criticism to develop.[41]

Gender as a Category of Literary Analysis

The essays in this collection offer a cross-section of some of the most interesting new work in gender and literary criticism currently being produced in the United States; they specifically address the ways that critics have begun both to rethink literary theory in the light of gender, and to build gender theory into their critical practice. The first group of essays by Patrocinio Schweickart, Barbara Johnson, and Valerie Smith, explore and reconstruct the "gender subtexts" of three major contemporary critical movements, showing the covert inscriptions of gender ideology in reader-response criticism, the Yale School, and Afro-American criticism. Schweickart's essay, which won the Florence Howe Award for Outstanding Feminist Scholarship in 1984, raises the question of gender and reading from the perspective of the woman reader and the feminist reader and shows how talking about gender foregrounds the masculine constructs and assumptions of reader-response criticism. Johnson's essay, first presented at a conference in 1983 following the death of Paul de Man, is in a sense her own declaration of independence both from the Yale School, and from the gender-blindness of deconstructionist theory. Looking at the work of Geoffrey Hartman, de Man, Hillis Miller, Harold Bloom, and, in an ironic act of self-criticism, "Barbara Johnson", she shows how the "desire to deny difference" created blind-spots within deconstructive insights. Smith's essay, written especially for this volume, discusses the history of gender in Afro-American criticism, and the way it has been changed by black feminists.

The second group of essays show how reading gender can illuminate a wide variety of literary issues and texts. Susan Friedman and Peter Schwenger build on now-classic feminist literary theories to extend our awareness of masculinity and of gender difference in literary representation. In a dialog with Gilbert and Gubar's celebrated claim that the pen is a metaphorical penis, Friedman investigates the different ways male and female writers have used the metaphor of childbirth to describe literary creativity. Schwenger's pioneering essay on "The Masculine Mode" (1979), expanded in his book *Phallic Critiques: Masculinity and Twentieth-Century Literature* (1984), draws on theories of women's writing to hypothesize an *écriture masculine*, a literary style in men's writing which can be seen as a language of the male body. Considering male textuality from a different perspective in his essay on Emerson's "man-making words," David Leverenz both looks at metaphors of masculinity in Emerson's writing, and argues that his current high status with American male intellectuals and businessmen has come in part because he "inspires feeling of access to manly power."

New Historicist critics have used gender as one of the fundamental categories of cultural production. Phyllis Rackin analyzes the meanings of gender on the Renaissance stage where boys played women's parts, and where costume, transvestism, and role-playing highlighted changing conceptions of gender, and made the theatre a subversive arena of sexual authority. Following the New Historicist interest in the symbolic body of the ruler, and in the discourse of history itself as a site of power and resistance, Elliot Gilbert discusses Tennyson's Arthur as "the female king," whose lineage subverts patriarchal rule, and displays the "advantages and dangers of sexual role reversal."

While the New Historicists often focus on the Renaissance, and feminist criticism originally concentrated on the Victorian novel, gender criticism has found its ideal text-milieu in the *fin de siècle*, a period described by historians and writers as both a crisis in masculinity and an age of sexual anarchy. With the rise of the New Woman, and with the decline of patriarchal authority and imperialism, transformations of gender and genre are significant elements in literary practice. The essays here by D.A. Miller, Christopher Craft, Eve Sedgwick, and Carol Barash concentrate on English, American, and South African writers, although similar work has also been carried out on French and German texts. Craft and Miller give breathtaking readings of two popular late-Victorian novels of sensation, detection, and terror, *The Woman in White* and *Dracula*, showing how each inscribes myths of gender, sexual inversion, homoeroticism, and misogyny. In "The Beast in the Closet," Sedgwick investigates the "paranoid Gothic" as a major genre of gay writing, showing how homosexual panic is thematized in the short stories of Henry James in the figures of the bachelor, unspeakability, and the closet. While Craft, Miller, and Sedgwick focus on male writers, Carol Barash's essay on the South African writer Olive Schreiner shows how theorics of both gender and race can be used in feminist criticism. Barash looks at the contradictions between Schreiner's position as a feminist, and her colonialist and racist views of black and white motherhood.

The two final essays by Sandra Gilbert and Susan Schweik are both comparativist studies of differing representations of war experience in twentieth-century literature by women and men. Both come out of the realization that "war must be understood as a gendering activity, one that ritually marks the gender of all members of a society, whether or not they are combatants."[42] Gilbert provides a strikingly documented investigation of the radically different meanings of World War I to men who felt themselves becoming "no-men" and women who felt guiltily empowered. Schweik uses the World War II poems of Marianne Moore and Randall Jarrell to explore the ways in which the noncombatant poet became gendered as a feminine figure, and the ways in which Moore and Jarrell subvert gender categories in an American poetic tradition. Through an understanding of gender ideology, we can come to understand that for Moore to write war poetry "like a woman," (and, by analogy, for the feminist critic to read and write "like a woman") is a complex literary and social construct that also casts light on the construction of a masculine literary subject.

The appearance of this anthology may disturb some readers who worry that "gender studies" could be a pallid assimiliation of feminist criticism into the mainstream (or male stream), of English studies, a return to the old priorities and binary oppositions that will reinstate familiar male canons while crowding hard-won courses on women writers out of the curriculum. Others fear that talking about gender is a way for both male and female critics to avoid the political commitment of feminism. Still others raise the troubling possibility that gender will be isolated from issues of class and race. These are serious questions that must continue to concern us. But gender theory *can* be a significant and radical expansion of our work; the turn to gender, as June Howard points out, "need not be depoliticizing. Its consequences depend on what we choose to do, on the kind of theory and the kind of critical community we build."[43] I believe that the fundamental changes have now begun that make the formation of a strong critical community around the issue of gender a genuine and exciting possibility. While this community, like this book, will include critics who are male and female, black and white, gay, lesbian, and straight, its members can explore a range of gendered subjectivities and literatures besides their own.

Like other aspects of literary analysis, talking about gender without a commitment to dismantling sexism, racism, and homophobia, can degenerate into nothing more than a talk show, with men trying to monopolize the [post]feminist conversation. But as the essays in this book demonstrate, the genuine addition of gender as a "central problem in every text" read and taught, "whatever the era and whoever the author," could also move us a step further towards post-patriarchy.[44] That's a step worth trying to take together.

Notes

A note on the text: The essays in this book were originally published in journals and books with different policies of citation and editorial style. While all the footnotes have been checked for completeness, I have retained the reference style in which the essays were first written.

1. Richard Bernstein, "History Convention Reflects Change from Traditional to 'Gender' Studies," *New York Times*, January 9, 1988, p. 6.

2. K. K. Ruthven, *Feminist Literary Studies: An Introduction*, Cambridge: Cambridge U. Press, 1984, p. 9.

3. See Dennis Baron's lively study *Grammar and Gender*, New Haven: Yale U. Press, 1986, for an overview of gender in language.

4. Monique Wittig, "The Mark of Gender," in *The Poetics of Gender*, ed. Nancy K. Miller, New York: Columbia U. Press, 1986, p. 66.

5. Jane Flax, "Postmodernism and Gender Relations in Feminist Theory," *Signs*, 12 (Summer 1987): 627.

6. Jan Morris, *Conundrum*, New York: Harcourt Brace Jovanovich, 1974. See also Pat Caplan, ed., *The Cultural Construction of Sexuality*, London: Tavistock, 1987, and Jeffrey Weeks, *Sexuality and Its Discontents*, London: Routledge & Kegan Paul, 1985.

7. Judith Shapiro, "Anthropology and the Study of Gender" in *A Feminist Perspective in the Academy*, ed. Elizabeth Langland and Walter Gove, Chicago: U. of Chicago Press, 1981, p. 112. See also Sherry B. Ortner and Harriet Whitehead, *Sexual Meanings: The Cultural Construction of Gender and Sexuality*, Cambridge: Cambridge U. Press, 1981.

8. Evelyn Fox Keller, *Reflections on Gender and Society*, New Haven: Yale U. Press, 1985, p. 3.

9. Natalie Z. Davis, "Women's History in Transition: The European Case," *Feminist Studies* 3 (1976): 90.

10. Cora Kaplan, *Sea Changes: Culture and Feminism*, London: Verso, 1986, p. 148.

11. "Within/and Without: Women, Gender, and Theory," *Signs*, 12 (Summer 1987): 619.

12. Joan Wallach Scott, "Gender: A Useful Category of Historical Analysis: *American Historical Review* 91 (November 1986): 1068.

13. Kaplan, *Sea Changes*, p. 148.

14. Catherine MacKinnon, *Feminism Unmodified*, Cambridge: Harvard University Press, 1987, p. 32.

15. See Michèle Barrett, *Women's Oppression Today: Problems in Marxist Feminist Analysis*, London: Verso, 1980; and Teresa de Lauretis, *Technologies of Gender*, Bloomington: Indiana U. Press, 1987.

16. Alicia Suskin Ostriker, *Stealing the Language: The Emergence of Women's Poetry in America*, Boston: Beacon Press, 1986, p. 9.

17. Sandra Gilbert, "Feminist Criticism in the University: An Interview," in *Criticism in the University*, ed. Gerald Graft and Reginald Gibbons, Evanston: Northwestern U. Press, 1985, p. 117.

18. The term "bitextual" comes from Naomi Schor, "Dreaming Dissymmetry: Barthes, Foucault, and Sexual Difference," in *Men in Feminism*, ed. Alice Jardine and Paul Smith, London & New York: Methuen, 1987, p. 110.

19. Elizabeth Abel, "Introduction," *Writing and Sexual Difference*, ed. Abel, Chicago: U. of Chicago Press, 1982, p. 2.

20. Marxist-Feminist Literature Collective, "Women's Writing: *Jane Eyre, Shirley, Villette, Aurora Leigh*," in *Ideology & Consciousness* 3 (Spring 1978): 47.

21. Myra Jehlen, "Archimedes and the Paradox of Feminist Criticism," *Signs* 6 (Summer 1981): See also Judith Spector, "Gender Studies: New Directions for Feminist Criticism," *College English* 43 (April 1981): 374–78.

22. Elizabeth Abel, "Introduction," *Writing and Sexual Difference*, p. 2.

23. See, for example, Sandra Gilbert, "Costumes of the Mind: Transvestism as Metaphor in Modern Literature, in *Writing and Sexual Difference*, pp. 193–220; and Susan J. Wolfson, " 'Their She Condition': Cross-Dressing and the Politics of Gender in *Don Juan*," *ELH* (1987): 585–617.

24. See, for example, Sheila Macleod, *Lawrence's Men and Women*, London: Heinemann, 1985; Margaret Ferguson, Maureen Quilligan, and Nancy J. Vickers, eds., *Rewriting the Renaissance*, Chicago: U. of Chicago Press, 1986; and Janet Batsleer et al., *Rewriting English: Cultural Politics of Gender and Class*, London: Metho 1985.

25. Sandra M. Gilbert, "What Do Feminist Critics Want?" in *The New Feminist Criticism*, ed. Elaine Showalter, New York: Pantheon, 1985, p. 37.

26. Catherine MacKinnon, "Feminism, Marxism, Method, and the State," *Signs* 7 (Spring 1982): 537.

27. Flax, "Postmodernism and Gender Relations," p. 629.

28. Elaine Showalter, "Critical Cross-Dressing: Male Feminists and the Woman of the Year," reprinted in *Men and Feminism*, pp. 116–132.

29. Gisela Ecker, "Introduction," to *Feminist Aesthetics*, ed. Ecker, trans. Harriet Anderson, London: Women's Press, 1985; and Luce Irigaray, interview with Elaine Hoffman Baruch and Lucianne Serrano, *Women Writers Talking*, ed. Janet Todd, London: Holmes and Meier, 1984, p. 243.

30. Stephen Heath, "Male Feminism," reprinted in *Men in Feminism*, p. 27.

31. Philippe Lacoue-Labarthe: quoted in Frank Lentricchia, "Patriarchy Against Itself—The Young Manhood of Wallace Stevens," *Critical Inquiry* 13 (Summer 1987): 742.

32. Peter Schwenger, "The Masculine Mode," reprinted in this volume.

33. Ruthven, *Feminist Literary Studies*, pp. 8, 10.

34. Meaghan Moris, "in any event . . . ," in *Men in Feminism*, p. 180.

35. See Lipking, "Aristotle's Sister: A Poetics of Abandonment," *Critical Inquiry* 10 (September 1983), and Joan DeJean, "Fictions of Sappho," *Critical Inquiry* (Summer 1987): 805.

36. See Frank Lentricchia, "Patriarchy Against Itself," and Gilbert and Gubar, "The Man on the Dump versus the United Dames of America; or, What Does Frank Lentricchia Want?", *Critical Inquiry* 14 (Winter 1988): 386–406.

37. Among this group of critics one might cite Andrew Ross, Henry Louis Gates, Houston Baker, Melvin Dixon, Stephen Heath, Joseph Kestner, Charles Bernheimer, Alan Sinfield, Louis Montrose, Jonathan Dollimore, Peter Stallybrass, Uli Knoepflmacher, Lee Mitchell, Wayne Koestenbaum, Lee Edelman, Michael Cadden, Richard Dellamora, and Ed Cohen, in addition to those whose work is included in this book.

38. Harry Brod, "Themes and Theses of Men's Studies," in *The Making of Masculinities: The New Men's Studies,* ed. Brod, Boston: Allen & Unwin, 1987, p. 2.

39. Eve Kosofsky Sedgwick, *Between Men: English Literature and Homosocial Desire,* New York: Columbia U. Press, 1985, p. 88.

40. See Richard Dellamora, "Masculine Desire and the Question of the Subject," paper delivered at MLA December 1987, and Craig Owens, "Outlaws: Gay Men in Feminism," *Men in Feminism,* p. 231.

41. For one recent feminist critique of men's studies, see Lois Banner, "Margaret Mead, Men's Studies, and Feminist Scholarship," *ASA Newsletter,* 11, March 1988: "I do not think that men's studies is analogous to women's studies, and I think that the use of the term incorrectly implies that it is. Once before in the 20th century the 'woman-centered' analysis was coopted by an emphasis on gender and the family, and I think that it could be coopted again. I think it is time for all of us to use the term 'feminist.' This term encompasses the rest: thus we have the feminist study of women, of men, and of gender." (p. 4) See also Janet M. Todd, *Feminist Literary History,* London: Polity Press, who wonders whether the rise of gay studies means that "feminism has had its place in the liberal sun and should move over to leave the victim's space for a greater (male) victim, the homosexual." (p. 118)

42. Margaret R. Higonnet, et al., ed. *Between the Lines: Gender and the Two World Wars,* New Haven: Yale U. Press, p. 4.

43. June Howard, "Feminist Differings: Recent Surveys of Feminist Literary Theory and Criticism," *Feminist Studies* 14 (Spring 1988): 187.

44. See Jerrold E. Hogle, "Teaching the Politics of Gender in Literature," in *Changing Our Minds: Feminist Transformations of Knowledge,* ed. Susan Hardy Aiken, et al.; Albany: State U. of New York Press, 1988, p. 99. The term "post-patriarchy" is from Toril Moi, "Introduction," *French Feminist Thought,* ed, Moi, London: Basil Blackwell, 1987, p. 12.

GENDER SUBTEXTS

2

Reading Ourselves: Toward a
Feminist Theory of Reading

Patrocinio P. Schweickart

Three Stories of Reading

A. Wayne Booth begins his Presidential Address to the 1982 MLA Convention by considering and rejecting several plausible myths that might enable us "to dramatize not just our inescapable plurality but the validity of our sense that [as teachers and scholars of literature and composition] we belong together, somehow working on common ground." At last he settles on one story that is "perhaps close enough to our shared experience to justify the telling."[1]

Once upon a time there was a boy who fell in love with books. When he was very young he heard over and over the legend of his great-grandfather, a hardworking weaver who so desired knowledge that he figured out a way of working the loom with one hand, his legs, and his feet, leaving the other hand free to hold a book, and worked so steadily in that crooked position that he became permanently crippled. The boy heard other stories about the importance of reading. Salvation, he came to believe, was to be found in books. When he was six years old, he read *The Wizard of Oz*—his first *real* book—and was rewarded by his Great-Aunt Manda with a dollar.

When the boy grew up, he decided to become a teacher of "litcomp." His initiation into the profession was rigorous, and there were moments when he nearly gave up. But gradually, "there emerged from the trudging a new and surprising love, a love that with all my previous reading I had not dreamed of: the love of skill, of craft, of getting clear in my mind and then in my writing what a great writer had got right in his work" (Booth, p. 315). Eventually, the boy, now grown, got his doctorate, and after teaching for thirteen years in small colleges, he returned to his graduate institution to become one of its eminent professors.

Booth caps his narration by quoting from *The Autobiography of Malcolm X*. It was in prison that Malcolm learned to read:

> For the first time I could pick up a book and now begin to understand what the book way saying. Anyone who has read a great deal can imagine the new world that opened. Let me tell you something: from then until I left that

17

prison, in every free moment I had, if I was not reading in the library, I was reading on my bunk. . . . [M]onths passed without my even thinking about being imprisoned. In fact, up to then, I never had been so truly free in my life. (As quoted by Booth, p. 317)

"Perhaps," says Booth, "when you think back now on my family's story about great-grandfather Booth, you will understand why reading about Malcolm X's awakening speaks to the question of where I got my 'insane love' [for books]" (p. 317).

B. When I read the Malcolm X passage quoted in Booth's address, the ellipsis roused my curiosity. What, exactly, I wondered, had been deleted? What in the original exceeded the requirements of a Presidential Address to the MLA? Checking, I found the complete sentence to read: "Between Mr. Muhammad's teachings, my correspondence, my visitors—usually Ella and Reginald—and my reading, months passed without my even thinking about being imprisoned."[2] Clearly, the first phrase is the dissonant one. The reference to the leader of the notorious Black Muslims suggests a story of reading very different from Booth's. Here is how Malcolm X tells it. While serving time in the Norfolk Prison Colony, he hit on the idea of teaching himself to read by copying the dictionary.

In my slow, painstaking, ragged handwriting, I copied into my tablet everything on that first page, down to the punctuation marks. . . . Then, aloud, to myself, I read back everything I'd written on the tablet. . . . I woke up the next morning thinking about these words. . . . That was the way I started copying what eventually became the entire dictionary. (p. 172)

After copying the dictionary, Malcolm X began reading the books in the prison library. "No university would ask any student to devour literature as I did when this new world opened to me, of being able to read and *understand*" (p. 173). Reading had changed the course of his life. Years later, he would reflect on how "the ability to read awoke inside me some long dormant craving to be mentally alive" (p. 179).

What did he read? What did he understand? He read Gregor Mendel's *Findings in Genetics* and it helped him to understand "that if you started with a black man, a white man could be produced; but starting with a white man, you never could produce a black man—because the white chromosome is recessive. And since no one disputes that there was but one Original Man, the conclusion is clear" (p. 175). He read histories, books by Will Durant and Arnold Toynbee, by W. E. B. du Bois and Carter G. Woodson, and he saw how "the glorious history of the black man" had been "bleached" out of the history books written by white men.

[His] eyes opened gradually, then wider and wider, to how the world's white men had indeed acted like devils, pillaging and raping and bleeding and draining the whole world's non-white people. . . . I will never forget how shocked I was when I began reading about slavery's total horror. . . . The world's most monstrous crime, the sin and the blood on the white man's hands, are almost impossible to believe. (p. 175)

He read philosophy—the works of Schopenhauer, Kant, Nietzsche, and Spinoza—and he concluded that the "whole stream of Western Philosophy was now wound up in a cul-de-sac" as a result of the white man's "elaborate, neurotic necessity to hide the black man's true role in history" (p. 180). Malcolm X read voraciously, and book after book confirmed the truth of Elijah Muhammad's teachings. "It's a crime, the lie that has been told to generations of black men and white both. . . . Innocent black children growing up, living out their lives, dying of old age—and all of their lives ashamed of being black. But the truth is pouring out of the bag now" (p. 181).

Wayne Booth's story leads to the Crystal Ballroom of the Biltmore Hotel in Los Angeles, where we attend the protagonist as he delivers his Presidential Address to the members of the Modern Language Association. Malcolm X's love of books took him in a different direction, to the stage of the Audubon Ballroom in Harlem, where, as he was about to address a mass meeting of the Organization of Afro-American Unity, he was murdered.

C. As we have seen, an ellipsis links Wayne Booth's story of reading to Malcolm X's. Another ellipsis, this time not graphically marked, signals the existence of a third story. Malcolm X's startling reading of Mendel's genetics overlooks the most rudimentary fact of human reproduction: whether you start with a black man or a white man, without a woman, you get *nothing*. An excerpt from Virginia Woolf's *A Room of One's Own* restores this deleted perspective.[3]

The heroine, call her Mary, says Woolf, goes to the British Museum in search of information about women. There she discovers to her chagrin that woman is, "perhaps, the most discussed animal in the universe?"

Why does Samuel Butler say, "Wise men never say what they think of women"? Wise men never say anything else apparently. . . . Are they capable of education or incapable? Napoleon thought them incapable. Dr. Johnson thought the opposite. Have they souls or have they not souls? Some savages say they have none. Others, on the contrary, maintain that women are half divine and worship them on that account. Some sages hold that they are shallower in the brain; others that they are deeper in the consciousness. Goethe honoured them; Mussolini despises them. Wherever one looked men thought about women and thought differently. (pp. 29–30)

Distressed and confused, Mary notices that she has unconsciously drawn a picture in her notebook, the face and figure of Professor von X. engaged in writing his monumental work, *The Mental, Moral, and Physical Inferiority of the Female Sex*.

"His expression suggested that he was labouring under some emotion that made him jab his pen on the paper as if he were killing some noxious insect as he wrote, but even when he had killed it that did not satisfy him; he must go on killing it. . . . A very elementary exercise in psychology . . . showed me . . . that the sketch of the angry professor had been made in anger" (pp. 31–32).

Nothing remarkable in that, she reflects, given the provocation. But "How explain the anger of the professors?. . . . For when it came to analysing the impression left by these books, . . . there was [an] element which was often present and could not immediately be identified. Anger, I called it. . . . To judge from its odd effects, it was anger disguised and complex, not anger simple and open" (p. 32).

Disappointed with essayists and professors, Mary turns to historians. But apparently women played no significant role in history. What little information Mary finds is disturbing: "Wife-beating," I read, "was a recognised right of man, and was practised without shame by high as well as low" (p. 44). Oddly enough, literature presents a contradictory picture.

> If women had no existence save in the fiction written by men, one would imagine her a person of the utmost importance; very various; heroic and mean; splendid and sordid; infinitely beautiful and hideous in the extreme; as great as a man, some think even greater. But this is woman in fiction. In fact, as Professor Trevelyan points out, she was locked up, beaten and flung about the room. (p. 45)

At last, Mary can draw but one conclusion from her reading. Male professors, male historians, and male poets can not be relied on for the truth about women. Woman herself must undertake the study of woman. Of course, to do so, she must secure enough money to live on and a room of her own.

Booth's story, we recall, is told within the framework of a professional ritual. It is intended to remind us of "the loves and fears that inform our daily work" and of "what we do when we are at our best," to show, if not a unity, then enough of a "center" to shame us whenever we violate it." The principal motif of the myth is the hero's insane love for books, and the way this develops with education and maturity into "critical understanding," which Booth defines as the synthesis of thought and passion which should replace, "on the one hand, sentimental and uncritical identifications that leave minds undisturbed, and on the other, hypercritical negations that freeze or alienate" (pp. 317–18). Booth is confident that the experience celebrated by the myth is archetypal. "Whatever our terms for it, whatever our theories about how it happens or why it fails to happen more often, can we reasonably doubt the importance of the moment, at any level of study, when any of us—you, me, Malcolm X, may great-grandfather—succeeds in entering other minds, or 'taking them in,' as nourishment for our own?" (p. 318).

Now, while it is certainly true that something one might call "critical understanding" informs the stories told by Malcolm X and Virginia Woolf, these authors fill this term with thoughts and passions that one would never suspect from Booth's definition. From the standpoint of the second and third stories_of reading, Booth's story is utopian. The powers and resources of his hero are equal to the challenges he encounters. At each stage he finds suitable mentors. He is assured by the people around him, by the books he reads, by the entire culture, that he is right for the part. His talents and accomplishments are acknowledged and justly rewarded. In short, from the perspective of Malcolm X's and Woolf's stories, Booth's hero is fantastically privileged.

Utopian has a second meaning, one that is by no means pejorative, and Booth's story is utopian in this sense as well. In overlooking the realities highlighted by the stories of Malcolm X and Virginia Woolf, Booth's story anticipates what might be possible, what "critical understanding" might mean for *everyone*, if only we overcome the pervasive systemic injustices of our time.

Reader-Response Theory and Feminist Criticism

Reader-response criticism, as currently constituted, is utopian in the same two senses. The different accounts of the reading experience that have been put forth overlook the issues of race, class, and sex, and give no hint of the conflicts, sufferings, and passions that attend these realities. The relative tranquility of the tone of these theories testifies to the privileged position of the theorists. Perhaps, someday, when privileges have withered away or at least become more equitably distributed, some of these theories will ring true. Surely we ought to be able to talk about reading without worrying about injustice. But for now, reader-response criticism must confront the disturbing implications of our historical reality. Paradoxically, utopian theories that elide these realities betray the utopian impulses that inform them.

To put the matter plainly, reader-response criticism needs feminist criticism. The two have yet to engage each other in a sustained and serious way, but if the promise of the former is to be fulfilled, such an encounter must soon occur. Interestingly, the obvious question of the significance of gender has already been explicitly raised, and—this testifies to the increasing impact of feminist criticism as well as to the direct ideological bearing of the issue of gender on reader-response criticism—not by a feminist critic, but by Jonathan Culler, a leading theorist of reading: "If the experience of literature depends upon the qualities of a reading self, one can ask what difference it would make to the experience of literature and thus to the meaning of literature if this self were, for example, female rather than male. If the meaning of a work is the experience of a reader, what difference does it make if the reader is a woman?"[4]

Until very recently this question has not occurred to reader-response critics. They have been preoccupied with other issues. Culler's survey of the field is instructive here, for it enables us to anticipate the direction reader-response theory might take when it is shaken from its slumber by feminist criticism. According to Culler, the different models (or "stories") of reading that have been proposed are all organized around three problems. The first is the issue of control: Does the text control the reader, or vice versa? For David Bleich, Norman Holland, and Stanley Fish, the reader holds controlling interest. Readers read the poems they have made. Bleich asserts this point most strongly: the constraints imposed by the words on the page are "trivial," since their meaning can always be altered by "subjective action." To claim that the text supports this or that reading is only to "moralistically claim . . . that one's own objectification is more authoritative than someone else's."[5] At the other pole are Michael Riffaterre, Georges Poulet, and Wolfgang Iser, who acknowledge the creative role of the reader, but ultimately take the text to be the dominant force. To read, from this point of view, is to create the text according to *its* own promptings. As Poulet puts it, a text, when invested with a reader's subjectivity, becomes a "subjectified object," a "second self" that depends on the reader, but is not, strictly speaking, identical with "him." Thus, reading "is a way of giving way not only to a host of alien words, images and ideas, but also to the very alien principle which utters and shelters them. . . . I am on loan to another, and this other thinks, feels, suffers and acts within me."[6] Culler argues persuasively that, regardless of their ostensible theoretical commitments, the prevailing stories of reading generally vacillate between these reader-dominant and text-dominant poles. In fact, those who stress the subjectivity of the reader as against the objectivity of the text ultimately portray the text as determining the responses of the reader. "The more active, projective, or creative the reader is, the more she is manipulated by the sentence or by the author" (p. 71).

The second question prominent in theories of reading is closely related to the first. Reading always involves a subject and an object, a reader and a text. But what constitutes the objectivity of the text? What is "in" the text? What is supplied by the reader? Again, the answers have been equivocal. On the face of it, the situation seems to call for a dualistic theory that credits the contributions of both text and reader. However, Culler argues, a dualistic theory eventually gives way to a monistic theory, in which one or the other pole supplies everything. One might say, for instance, that Iser's theory ultimately implies the determinacy of the text and the authority of the author: "The author guarantees the unity of the work, requires the reader's creative participation, and through his text, prestructures the shape of the aesthetic object to be produced by the reader."[7] At the same time, one can also argue that the "gaps" that structure the reader's response are not built into the text, but appear (or not) as a result of the particular interpretive strategy employed by the reader. Thus, "there is no distinction between what the text gives and what the reader supplies; he supplies *everything*."[8] Depending on which aspects of the theory one takes seriously, Iser's theory collapses either into a monism of the test or a monism of the reader. The third problem identified by

Culler concerns the ending of the story. Most of the time stories of reading end happily. "Readers may be manipulated and misled, but when they finish the book their experience turns into knowledge . . . as though finishing the book took them outside the experience of reading and gave them mastery of it" (p. 79). However, some critics—Harold Bloom, Paul de Man, and Culler himself—find these optimistic endings questionable, and prefer instead stories that stress the impossibility of reading. If, as de Man says, rhetoric puts "an insurmountable obstacle in the way of any reading or understanding," then the reader "may be placed in impossible situations where there is no happy issue, but only the possibility of playing out the roles dramatized in the text" (Culler, p. 81).

Such have been the predominant preoccupations of reader-response criticism during the past decade and a half. Before indicating how feminist critics could affect the conversation, let me consider an objection. A recent and influential essay by Elaine Showalter suggests that we should not enter the conversation at all. She observes that during its early phases, the principal mode of feminist criticism was "feminist critique," which was counter-ideological in intent and concerned with the feminist as *reader*. Happily, we have outgrown this necessary but theoretically unpromising approach. Today, the dominant mode of feminist criticism is "gynocritics," the study of woman as *writer*, of the "history, styles, themes, genres, and structures of writing by women; the psychodynamics of female creativity; the trajectory of the individual or collective female career; and the evolution and laws of a female literary tradition." The shift from "feminist critique" to "gynocritics"— from emphasis on woman as reader to emphasis on woman as writer—has put us in the position of developing a feminist criticism that is "genuinely woman-centered, independent, and intellectually coherent."

> To see women's writing as our primary subject forces us to make the leap to a new conceptual vantage point and to redefine the nature of the theoretical problem before us. It is no longer the ideological dilemma of reconciling revisionary pluralisms but the essential question of difference. How can we constitute women as a distinct literary group? What is the *difference* of women's writing?[9]

But why should the activity of the woman writer be more conducive to theory than the activity of the woman reader is? If it is possible to formulate a basic conceptual framework for disclosing the "difference" of women's writing, surely it is no less possible to do so for women's reading. The same difference, be it linguistic, biological, psychological, or cultural, should apply in either case. In addition, what Showalter calls "gynocritics" is in fact constituted by feminist *criticism*— that is, *readings*—of female texts. Thus, the relevant distinction is not between woman as reader and woman as writer, but between feminist readings of male texts and feminist readings of female texts, and there is no reason why the former could not be as theoretically coherent (or irreducibly pluralistic) as the latter.

On the other hand, there are good reasons for feminist criticism to engage reader-response criticism. Both dispute the fetishized art object, the "Verbal Icon," of New Criticism, and both seek to dispel the objectivist illusion that buttresses the authority of the dominant critical tradition. Feminist criticism can have considerable impact on reader-response criticism, since, as Culler has noticed, it is but a small step from the thesis that the reader is an active producer of meaning to the recognition that there are many different kinds of readers, and that women—because of their numbers if because of nothing else—constitute an essential class. Reader-response critics cannot take refuge in the objectivity of the text, or even in the idea that a gender-neutral criticism is possible. Today they can continue to ignore the implications of feminist criticism only at the cost of incoherence or intellectual dishonesty.

It is equally true that feminist critics need to question their allegiance to text- and author-centered paradigms of criticism. Feminist criticism, we should remember, is a mode of *praxis*. The point is not merely to interpret literature in various ways; the point is to *change the world*. We cannot afford to ignore the activity of reading, for it is here that literature is realized as *praxis*. Literature acts on the world by acting on its readers.

To return to our earlier question: What will happen to reader-response criticism if feminists enter the conversation? It is useful to recall the contrast between Booth's story and those of Malcolm X and Virginia Woolf. Like Booth's story, the "stories of reading" that currently make up reader-response theory are mythically abstract, and appear, from a different vantage point, to be by and about readers who are fantastically privileged. Booth's story had a happy ending; Malcolm's and Mary's did not. For Mary, reading meant encountering a tissue of lies and silence; for Malcolm it meant the verification of Elijah Muhammad's shocking doctrines.

Two factors—gender and politics—which are suppressed in the dominant models of reading gain prominence with the advent of a feminist perspective. The feminist story will have *at least* two chapters: one concerned with feminist readings of male texts, and another with feminist readings of female texts. In addition, in this story, gender will have a prominent role as the locus of political struggle. The story will speak of the difference between men and women, of the way the experience and perspective of women have been systematically and fallaciously assimilated into the generic masculine, and of the need to correct this error. Finally, it will identify literature—the activities of reading and writing—as an important arena of political struggle, a crucial component of the project of interpreting the world in order to change it.

Feminist criticism does not approach reader-response criticism without preconceptions. Actually, feminist criticism has always included substantial reader-centered interests. In the next two sections of this paper, I will review these interests, first with respect to male texts, then with respect to female texts. In the process, I will uncover some of the issues that might be addressed and clarified by a feminist theory of reading.

The Female Reader and the Literary Canon

Although reader-response critics propose different and often conflicting models, by and large the emphasis is on features of the process of reading that do not vary with the nature of the reading material. The feminist entry into the conversation brings the nature of the text back into the foreground. For feminists, the question of *how* we read is inextricably linked with the question of *what* we read. More specifically, the feminist inquiry into the activity of reading begins with the realization that the literary canon is androcentric, and that this has a profoundly damaging effect on women readers. The documentation of this realization was one of the earliest tasks undertaken by feminist critics. Elaine Showalter's 1971 critique of the literary curriculum is exemplary of this work.

> [In her freshman year a female student] . . . might be assigned an anthology of essays, perhaps such as *The Responsible Man* . . . or *Conditions of Man*, or *Man in Crisis*, or again, *Representative Man: Cult Heroes of Our Time*, in which thirty-three men represent such categories of heroism as the writer, the poet, the dramatist, the artist, and the guru, and the only two women included are the actress Elizabeth Taylor, and the existential Heroine Jacqueline Onassis.
>
> Perhaps the student would read a collection of stories like *The Young Man in American Literature: The Initiation Theme*, or sociological literature like *The Black Man and the Promise of America*. In a more orthodox literary program she might study eternally relevant classics, such as *Oedipus*; as a professor remarked in a recent issue of *College English*, all of us want to kill our fathers and marry our mothers. And whatever else she might read, she would inevitably arrive at the favorite book of all Freshman English courses, the classic of adolescent rebellion, *Portrait of the Artist as a Young Man*.
>
> By the end of her freshman year, a woman student would have learned something about intellectual neutrality; she would be learning, in fact, how to think like a man. And so she would go on, increasingly with male professors to guide her.[10]

The more personal accounts of other critics reinforce Showalter's critique.

> The first result of my reading was a feeling that male characters were at the very least more interesting than women to the authors who invented them. Thus if, reading their books as it seemed their authors intended them, I naively identified with a character, I repeatedly chose men; I would rather have been Hamlet than Ophelia, Tom Jones instead of Sophia Western, and, perhaps, despite Dostoevsky's intention, Raskolnikov not Sonia.
>
> More peculiar perhaps, but sadly unsurprising, were the assessments I accepted about fictional women. For example, I quickly learned that power was unfeminine and powerful women were, quite literally, monstrous. . . . Bitches all, they must be eliminated, reformed, or at the very least, condemned. . . . Those rare women who are shown in fiction as both powerful and, in some sense, admirable are such because their power is based, if not on beauty, then at least on sexuality.[11]

For a woman, then, books do not necessarily spell salvation. In fact, a literary education may very well cause her grave psychic damage: schizophrenia "is the bizarre but logical conclusion of our education. Imagining myself male, I attempted to create myself male. Although I knew the case was otherwise, it seemed I could do nothing to make this other critically real."[12]

To put the matter theoretically, androcentric literature structures the reading experience differently depending on the gender of the reader. For the male reader, the text serves as the meeting ground of the personal and the universal. Whether or not the text approximates the particularities of his own experience, he is invited to validate the equation of maleness with humanity. The male reader feels his affinity with the universal, with the paradigmatic human being, precisely because he is male. Consider the famous scene of Stephen's epiphany in *Portrait of the Artist as a Young Man*.

> A girl stood before him in midstream, alone and still, gazing out to sea. She seemed like one whom magic had changed into the likeness of a strange and beautiful seabird. Her long slender bare legs were delicate as a crane's and pure save where an emerald trail of seaweed had fashioned itself as a sign upon the flesh. Her thighs, fuller and softhued as ivory, were bared almost to the hips where the white fringes of her drawers were like featherings of soft white down. Her slateblue skirts were kilted boldly about her waist and dovetailed behind her. Her bosom was as a bird's soft and slight, slight and soft as the breast of some darkplumaged dove. But her long fair hair was girlish: and touched with the wonder of mortal beauty, her face.[13]

A man reading this passage is invited to identify with Stephen, to feel "the riot in his blood," and, thus, to ratify the alleged universality of the experience. Whether or not the sight of a girl on the beach has ever provoked similar emotions in him, the male reader in invited to feel his *difference* (concretely, *from the girl*) and to equate that with the universal. Relevant here is Lévi-Strauss's theory that woman functions as currency exchanged between men. The woman in the text converts the text into a woman, and the circulation of this text/woman becomes the central ritual that establishes the bond between the author and his male readers.[14]

The same text affects a woman reader differently. Judith Fetterley gives the most explicit theory to date about the dynamics of the woman reader's encounter with androcentric literature. According to Fetterley, notwithstanding the prevalence of the castrating bitch stereotype, "the cultural reality is not the emasculation of men by women, but the *immasculation* of women by men. As readers and teachers and scholars, women are taught to think as men, to identify with a male point of view, and to accept as normal and legitimate a male system of values, one of whose central principles is misogyny."[15]

The process of immasculation does not impart virile power to the woman reader. On the contrary, it doubles her oppression. She suffers "not simply the power-lessness which derives from not seeing one's experience articulated, clarified, and legitimized in art, but more significantly, the powerlessness which results from the endless division of self against self, the consequence of the invocation to identify as male while being reminded that to be male—to be universal—. . . is to be *not female.*"[16]

A woman reading Joyce's novel of artistic awakening, and in particular the passage quoted above, will, like her male counterpart, be invited to identify with Stephen and therefore to ratify the equation of maleness with the universal. Androcentric literature is all the more efficient as an instrument of sexual politics because it does not allow the woman reader to seek refuge in her difference. Instead, it draws her into a process that uses her against herself. It solicits her complicity in the elevation of male difference into universality and, accordingly, the denigration of female difference into otherness without reciprocity. To be sure, misogyny is abundant in the literary canon.[17] It is important, however, that Fetterley's argument can stand on a weaker premise. Androcentricity is a sufficient condition for the process of immasculation.

Feminist critics of male texts, from Kate Millett to Judith Fetterley, have worked under the sign of the "Resisting Reader." Their goal is to disrupt the process of immasculation by exposing it to consciousness, by disclosing the androcentricity of what has customarily passed for the universal. However, feminist criticism written under the aegis of the resisting reader leaves certain questions unanswered, questions that are becoming ripe for feminist analysis: Where does the text get its power to draw us into its designs? Why do some (not all) demonstrably sexist texts remain appealing even after they have been subjected to thorough feminist critique? The usual answer—that the power of male texts is the power of the false consciousness into which women as well as men have been socialized—oversimplifies the problem and prevents us from comprehending both the force of literature and the complexity of our responses to it.

Fredric Jameson advances a thesis that seems to me to be a good starting point for the feminist reconsideration of male texts: "The effectively ideological is also at the same time necessarily utopian."[18] This thesis implies that the male text draws its power over the female reader from authentic desires, which it rouses and then harnesses to the process of immasculation.

A concrete example is in order. Consider Lawrence's *Women in Love*, and for the sake of simplicity, concentrate on Birkin and Ursula. Simone de Beauvoir and Kate Millett have convinced me that this novel is sexist. Why does it remain appealing to me? Jameson's thesis prompts me to answer this question by examining how the text plays not only on my false consciousness but also on my authentic liberatory aspirations—that is to say, on the very impulses that drew me to the feminist movement.

The trick of role reversal comes in handy here. If we reverse the roles of Birkin and Ursula, the ideological components (or at least the most egregious of these, e.g., the analogy between women and horses) stand out as absurdities. Now, if we delete these absurd components while keeping the roles reversed, we have left the story of a woman struggling to combine her passionate desire for autonomous conscious being with an equally passionate desire for love and for other human bonds. This residual story is not far from one we would welcome as expressive of a feminist sensibility. Interestingly enough, it also intimates a novel Lawrence might have written, namely, the proper sequel to *The Rainbow*.

My affective response to the novel Lawrence did write is bifurcated. On the one hand, because I am a woman, I am implicated in the representation of Ursula and in the destiny Lawrence has prepared for her: man is the son of god, but woman is the daughter of man. Her vocation is to witness his transcendence in rapt silence. On the other hand, Fetterley is correct that I am also induced to identify with Birkin, and in so doing, I am drawn into complicity with the reduction of Ursula, and therefore of myself, to the role of the other.

However, the process of immasculation is more complicated than Fetterley allows. When I identify with Birkin, I unconsciously perform the two-stage rereading described above. I reverse the roles of Birkin and Ursula and I suppress the obviously ideological components that in the process show up as absurdities. The identification with Birkin is emotionally effective because, stripped of its patriarchal trappings, Birkin's struggle and his utopian vision conform to my own. To the extent that I perform this feminist rereading *unconsciously*, I am captivated by the text. The stronger my desire for autonomous selfhood and for love, the stronger my identification with Birkin, and the more intense the experience of bifurcation characteristic of the process of immasculation.

The full argument is beyond the scope of this essay. My point is that *certain* (not all) male texts merit a dual hermeneutic: a negative hermeneutic that discloses their complicity with patriarchal ideology, and a positive hermeneutic that recuperates the utopian moment—the authentic kernel—from which they draw a significant portion of their emotional power.[19]

Reading Women's Writing

Showalter is correct that feminist criticism has shifted emphasis in recent years from "critique" (primarily) of male texts to "gynocritics," or the study of women's writing. Of course, it is worth remembering that the latter has always been on the feminist agenda. *Sexual Politics*, for example, contains not only the critique of Lawrence, Miller, and Mailer that won Millett such notoriety, but also her memorable rereading of *Villette*.[20] It is equally true that interest in women's writing has not entirely supplanted the critical study of patriarchal texts. In a sense "critique" has provided the bridge from the study of male texts to the study of female texts. As feminist criticism shifted from the first to the second, "feminist critique" turned its attention from androcentric texts per se to the androcentric critical strategies that pushed women's writing to the margins of the literary canon. The earliest examples of this genre (for instance, Showalter's "The Double Critical Standard," and Carol Ohmann's "Emily Brontë in the Hands of Male Critics") were concerned primarily with describing and documenting the prejudice against women writers that clouded the judgment of well-placed readers, that is, reviewers and critics.[21] Today we have more sophisticated and more comprehensive analyses of the androcentric critical tradition.

One of the most cogent of these is Nina Baym's analysis of American literature.[22] Baym observes that, as late as 1977, the American canon of major writers did not include a single woman novelist. And yet, in terms of numbers and commercial success, women novelists have probably dominated American literature since the middle of the nineteenth century. How to explain this anomaly?

One explanation is simple bias of the sort documented by Showalter, Ohmann, and others. A second is that women writers lived and worked under social conditions that were not particularly conducive to the production of "excellent" literature: "There tended to be a sort of immediacy in the ambitions of literary women leading them to professionalism rather than artistry, by choice as well as by social pressure and opportunity."[23] Baym adduces a third, more subtle, and perhaps more important reason. There are, she argues, "gender-related restrictions that do not arise out of the cultural realities contemporary with the writing woman, but out of later critical theories . . . which impose their concerns anachronistically, after the fact, on an earlier period."[24] If one reads the critics most instrumental in forming the current theories about American literature (F.O. Matthiessen, Richard Chase, Charles Feidelson, Lionel Trilling, etc.), one finds that the theoretical model for the canonical American novel is the "melodrama of beset manhood." To accept this model is also to accept as a consequence the exclusion from the canon of "melodramas of beset womanhood," as well as virtually all fiction centering on the experience of women.[25]

The deep symbiotic relationship between the androcentric canon and androcentric modes of reading is well summarized by Annette Kolodny.

> *Insofar as we are taught to read, what we engage are not texts, but paradigms.* . . . Insofar as literature is itself a social institution, so, too, reading is a highly socialized—or learned—activity. . . . We read well, and with pleasure, what we already know how to read; and what we know how to read is to a large extent dependent on what we have already read [works from which we have developed our expectations and learned our interpretive strategies]. What we then choose to read—and, by extension, teach and thereby "canonize"—usually follows upon our previous reading.[26]

We are caught, in other words, in a rather vicious circle. An androcentric canon generates androcentric interpretive strategies, which in turn favor the canonization of androcentric texts and the marginalization of gynocentric ones. To break this circle, feminist critics must fight on two fronts: for the revision of the canon to include a significant body of works by women, and for the development of the reading strategies consonant with the concerns, experiences, and formal devices that constitute these texts. Of course, to succeed, we also need a community of women readers who are qualified by experience, commitment, and training, and who will enlist the personal and institutional resources at their disposal in the struggle.[27]

The critique of androcentric reading strategies is essential, for it opens up some ideological space for the recuperation of women's writing. Turning now to this project, we observe, first, that a large volume of work has been done, and, second, that this endeavor is coming to look even more complicated and more diverse than the criticism of male texts. Certainly, it is impossible in the space of a few pages to do justice to the wide range of concerns, strategies, and positions associated with feminist readings of female texts. Nevertheless, certain things can be said. For the remainder of this section, I focus on an exemplary essay: "Vesuvius at Home: The Power of Emily Dickinson," by Adrienne Rich.[28] My commentary anticipates the articulation of a paradigm that illuminates certain features of feminist readings of women's writing.

I am principally interested in the rhetoric of Rich's essay, for it represents an implicit commentary on the process of reading women's writing. Feminist readings of male texts are, as we have seen, primarily resisting. The reader assumes an adversarial or at least a detached attitude toward the material at hand. In the opening pages of her essay, Rich introduces three metaphors that proclaim a very different attitude toward her subject.

> The methods, the exclusions, of Emily Dickinson's existence could not have been my own; yet more and more, as a woman poet finding my own methods, I have come to understand her necessities, could have served as witness in her defense. (p. 158)

> I am traveling at the speed of time, along the Massachusetts Turnpike. . . . "Home is not where the heart is," she wrote in a letter, "but the house and adjacent buildings" . . . I am traveling at the speed of time, in the direction of the house and buildings. . . . For years, I have been not so much envisioning Emily Dickinson as trying to visit, to enter her mind through her poems and letters, and through my own intimations of what it could have meant to be one of the two mid-nineteenth century American geniuses, and a woman, living in Amherst, Massachusetts. (pp. 158–59)

> For months, for most of my life, I have been hovering like an insect against the screens of an existence which inhabited Amherst, Massachusetts between 1830 and 1886. (p. 158) . . . Here [in Dickinson's bedroom] I become again, an insect, vibrating at the frames of windows, clinging to the panes of glass, trying to connect. (p. 161)

A commentary on the process of reading is carried on silently and unobtrusively through the use of these metaphors. The first is a judicial metaphor: the feminist reader speaks as a witness in defense of the woman writer. Here we see clearly that gender is crucial. The feminist reader takes the part of the woman writer against patriarchal misreadings that trivialize or distort her work.[29] The second metaphor refers to a principal tenet of feminist criticism: a literary work cannot be understood apart from the social, historical, and cultural context within which it was written. As if to acquiesce to the condition Dickinson had imposed on her friends, Rich travels through space and time to visit the poet on her own *premises*. She goes to Amherst, to the house where Dickinson lived. She rings the bell, she goes in, then upstairs, then into the bedroom that had been "freedom" for the poet. Her destination, ultimately, is Dickinson's mind. But it is not enough to read the poet's poems and letters. To reach her heart and mind, one must take a detour through "the house and adjacent buildings."

Why did Dickinson go into seclusion? Why did she write poems she would not publish? What mean these poems about queens, volcanoes, deserts, eternity, passion, suicide, wild beasts, rape, power, madness, the daemon, the grave? For Rich, these are related questions. The revisionary re-reading of Dickinson's work is of a piece with the revisionary re-reading of her life. "I have a notion genius knows itself; that Dickinson chose her seclusion, knowing what she needed. . . . She carefully selected her society and controlled the disposal of her time. . . . Given her vocation, she was neither eccentric nor quaint; she was determined to survive, to use her powers, to practice necessary economics" (p. 160).

> To write [the poetry that she needed to write] she had to enter chambers of the self in which
>> Ourself, concealed—
>> Should startle most—
> and to relinquish control there, to take those risks, she had to create a relationship to the outer world where she could feel in control. (p. 175)

The metaphor of visiting points to another feature of feminist readings of women's writing, namely, the tendency to construe the text not as an object, but as the manifestation of the subjectivity of the absent author—the "voice" of another woman. Rich is not content to revel in the textuality of Dickinson's poems and letters. For her, these are doorways to the "mind" of a "woman of genius." Rich deploys her imagination and her considerable rhetorical skill to evoke "the figure of powerful will" who lives at the heart of the text. To read Dickinson, then, is to try to visit with her, to hear her voice, to make her live *in* oneself, and to feel her impressive "personal dimensions."[30]

At the same time, Rich is keenly aware that visiting with Dickinson is *only* a metaphor for reading her poetry, and an inaccurate one at that. She signals this awareness with the third metaphor. It is no longer possible to visit with Dickinson; one can only enter her mind through her poems and letters as one can enter her house—through the backdoor out of which her coffin was carried. In reading, one encounters only a text, the trail of an absent author. Upstairs, at last, in the very room where Dickinson exercised her astonishing craft, Rich finds herself again "an insect, vibrating at the frames of windows, clinging to panes of glass, trying to connect." But though "the scent is very powerful," Dickinson herself is absent.

Perhaps the most obvious rhetorical device employed by Rich in this essay, more obvious even than her striking metaphors, is her use of the personal voice.

Her approach to Dickinson is self-consciously and unabashedly subjective. She clearly describes her point of view—what she saw as she drove across the Connecticut Valley toward Amherst (ARCO stations, MacDonald's, shopping plazas, as well as "light-green spring softening the hills, dogwood and wild fruit trees blossoming in the hollows"), and what she thought about (the history of the valley, "scene of Indian uprisings, religious revivals, spiritual confrontations, the blazing-up of the lunatic fringe of the Puritan coal," and her memories of college weekends in Amherst). Some elements of her perspective—ARCO and MacDonald's—would have been alien to Dickinson; others—the sight of dogwood and wild fruit trees in the spring, and most of all, the experience of being a woman poet in a patriarchal culture—would establish their affinity.

Rich's metaphors together with her use of the personal voice indicate some key issues underlying feminist readings of female texts. On the one hand, reading is necessarily subjective. On the other hand, it must not be wholly so. One must respect the autonomy of the text. The reader is a visitor and, as such, must observe the necessary courtesies. She must avoid unwarranted intrusions—she must be careful not to appropriate what belongs to her host, not to impose herself on the other woman. Furthermore, reading is at once an intersubjective encounter and something less than that. In reading Dickinson, Rich seeks to enter her mind, to feel her presence. But the text is a screen, an inanimate object. Its subjectivity is only a projection of the subjectivity of the reader.

Rich suggests the central motivation, the regulative ideal, that shapes the feminist reader's approach to these issues. If feminist readings of male texts are motivated by the need to disrupt the process of immasculation, feminist readings of female texts are motivated by the need "to connect," to recuperate, or to formulate—they come to the same thing—the context, the tradition, that would link women writers to one another, to women readers and critics, and to the larger community of women. Of course, the recuperation of such a context is a necessary basis for the nonrepressive integration of women's point of view and culture into the study of a Humanities that is worthy of its name.[31]

Feminist Models of Reading: A Summary

As I noted in the second section, mainstream reader-response theory is preoccupied with two closely related questions: (1) Does the text manipulate the reader, or does the reader manipulate the text to produce the meaning that suits her own interests? and (2) What is "in" the text? How can we distinguish what it supplies from what the reader supplies? Both of these questions refer to the subject-object relation that is established between reader and text during the process of reading. A feminist theory of reading also elaborates this relationship, but for feminists, gender—the gender inscribed in the text as well as the gender of the reader—is crucial. Hence, the feminist story has two chapters, one concerned with male texts and the other with female texts.

The focus of the first chapter is the experience of the woman reader. What do male texts *do* to her? The feminist story takes the subject-object relation of reading through three moments. The phrasing of the basic question signals the first moment. Control is conferred on the text: the woman reader is immasculated by the text. The feminist story fits well at this point in Iser's framework. Feminists insist that the androcentricity of the text and its damaging effects on women readers are not figments of their imagination. These are implicit in the "schematized aspects" of the text. The second moment, which is similarly consonant with the plot of Iser's story, involves the recognition of the crucial role played by the subjectivity of the woman reader. Without her, the text is *no-thing*. The process of immasculation is latent in the text, but it finds its actualization only through the reader's activity. In effect, the woman reader is the agent of her own immasculation.[32]

Here we seem to have a corroboration of Culler's contention that dualistic models of reading inevitably disintegrate into one of two monisms. Either the text (and, by implication, the author) or the woman reader is responsible for the process of immasculation. The third moment of the subject-object relation—ushered in by the transfiguration of the heroine into a feminist—breaks through this dilemma. The woman reader, now a feminist, embarks on a critical analysis of the reading process, and she realizes that the text has power to structure her experience. Without androcentric texts she will not suffer immasculation. However, her recognition of the power of the text is matched by her awareness of her essential role in the process of reading. Without her, the text is nothing—it is inert and harmless. The advent of feminist consciousness and the accompanying commitment to emancipatory *praxis* reconstitutes the subject-object relationship within a dialectical rather than a dualistic framework, thus averting the impasse described by Culler between the "dualism of narrative" and the "monism of theory." In the feminist story, the breakdown of Iser's dualism does not indicate a mistake or an irreducible impasse, but the necessity of *choosing* between two modes of reading. The reader can submit to the power of the text, or she can take control of the reading experience. The recognition of the existence of a choice suddenly makes visible the normative dimension of the feminist story: She *should* choose the second alternative.

But what does it mean for a reader to take control of the reading experience? First of all, she must do so without forgetting the androcentricity of the text or its power to structure her experience. In addition, the reader taking control of the text is not, as in Iser's model, simply a matter of selecting among the concretizations allowed by the text. Recall that a crucial feature of the process of immasculation is the woman reader's bifurcated response. She reads the test both as a man and as a woman. But in either case, the result is the same: she confirms her position as other. Taking control of the reading experience means reading the text as it was *not* meant to be read, in fact, reading it against itself. Specifically, one must identify the nature of the choices proffered by the text and, equally important, what the text precludes—namely, the possibility of reading as a woman *without* putting one's self in the position of the other, of reading so as to affirm womanhood as another, equally valid, paradigm of human existence.

All this is easier said than done. It is important to realize that reading a male text, no matter how virulently misogynous, could do little damage if it were an isolated event. The problem is that within patriarchal culture, the experience of immasculation is paradigmatic of women's encounters with the dominant literary and critical traditions. A feminist cannot simply refuse to read patriarchal texts, for they are everywhere, and they condition her participation in the literary and critical enterprise. In fact, by the time she becomes a feminist critic, a woman has already read numerous male texts—in particular, the most authoritative texts of the literary and critical canons. She has introjected not only androcentric texts, but also androcentric reading strategies and values. By the time she becomes a feminist, the bifurcated response characteristic of immasculation has become second nature to her. The feminist story stresses that patriarchal constructs have objective as well as subjective reality; they are inside and outside the text, inside and outside the reader.

The pervasiveness of androcentricity drives feminist theory beyond the individualistic models of Iser and of most reader-response critics. The feminist reader agrees with Stanley Fish that the production of the meaning of a text is mediated by the interpretive community in which the activity of reading is situated: the meaning of the text depends on the interpretive strategy one applies to it, and the choice of strategy is regulated (explicitly or implicitly) by the canons of acceptability that govern the interpretive community.[33] However, unlike Fish, the feminist reader is also aware that the ruling interpretive communities are androcentric, and that this androcentricity is deeply etched in the strategies and modes of thought that have been introjected by all readers, women as well as men.

Because patriarchal constructs have psychological correlates, taking control of the reading process means taking control of one's reactions and inclinations. Thus, a feminist reading—actually a re-reading—is a kind of therapeutic analysis. The reader recalls and examines how she would "naturally" read a male text in order to understand and therefore undermine the subjective predispositions that had rendered her vulnerable to its designs. Beyond this, the pervasiveness of immasculation necessitates a collective remedy. The feminist reader hopes that other women will recognize themselves in her story, and join her in her struggle to transform the culture.[34]

"Feminism affirms women's point of view by revealing, criticizing and examining its impossibility."[35] Had we nothing but male texts, this sentence from Catherine MacKinnon's brilliant essay on jurisprudence could serve as the definition of the project of the feminist reader. The significant body of literature written by women presents feminist critics with another, more heartwarming, task: that of recovering, articulating, and elaborating positive expressions of women's point of view, of celebrating the survival of this point of view in spite of the formidable forces that have been ranged against it.

The shift to women's writing brings with it a shift in emphasis from the negative hermeneutic of ideological unmasking to a positive hermeneutic whose aim is the recovery and cultivation of women's culture. As Showalter has noted, feminist criticism of women's writing proposes to articulate woman's difference: What does it mean for a woman to express herself in writing? How does a woman write as a woman? It is a central contention of this essay that feminist criticism should also inquire into the correlative process of *reading:* What does it mean for a woman to read without condemning herself to the position of other? What does it mean for a woman, reading as a woman, to read literature written by a woman writing as a woman?[36]

The Adrienne Rich essay discussed in the preceding section illustrates a contrast between feminist readings of male texts and feminist readings of female texts. In the former, the object of the critique, whether it is regarded as an enemy or as symptom of a malignant condition, is the text itself, *not* the reputation or the character of the author.[37] This impersonal approach contrasts sharply with the strong personal interest in Dickinson exhibited by Rich. Furthermore, it is not merely a question of friendliness toward the text. Rich's reading aims beyond "the unfolding of the text as a living event," the goal of aesthetic reading set by Iser. Much of the rhetorical energy of Rich's essay is directed toward evoking the personality of Dickinson, toward making *her* live as the substantial, palpable presence animating her works.

Unlike the first chapter of the feminist story of reading, which is centered around a single heroine—the woman reader battling her way out of a maze of patriarchal constructs—the second chapter features two protagonists—the woman reader and the woman writer—in the context of two settings. The first setting is judicial: one woman is standing witness in defense of the other; the second is dialogic: the two women are engaged in intimate conversation. The judicial setting points to the larger political and cultural dimension of the project of the feminist reader. Feminist critics may well say with Harold Bloom that reading always involves the "art of defensive warfare."[38] What they mean by this, however, would not be Bloom's individualistic, agaonistic encounter between "strong poet" and "strong reader," but something more akin to "class struggle." Whether concerned with male or female texts, feminist criticism is situated in the larger struggle against patriarchy.

The importance of this battle cannot be overestimated. However, feminist readings of women's writing opens up space for another, equally important, critical project, namely, the articulation of a model of reading that is centered on a female paradigm. While it is still too early to present a full-blown theory, the dialogic aspect of the relationship between the feminist reader and the woman writer suggests the direction that such a theory might take. As in all stories of reading, the drama revolves around the subject-object relationship between texts and reader. The feminist story—exemplified by the Adrienne Rich essay discussed earlier—features an intersubjective construction of this relationship. The reader encounters not simply a text, but a "subjectified object": the "heart and mind" of another woman. She comes into close contact with an interiority—a power, a creativity, a suffering, a vision—that is not identical with her own. The feminist interest in construing reading as an intersubjective encounter suggests an affinity with Poulet's (rather than Iser's) theory, and, as in Poulet's model, the subject of the literary work is its author, *not* the reader: "A book is not only a book; it is a means by which an author actually preserves [her] ideas, [her] feelings, [her] modes of dreaming and living. It is a means of saving [her] identity from death. . . . To understand a literary work, then, is to let the individual who wrote it reveal [herself] to us *in* us."[39]

For all this initial agreement, however, the dialogic relationship the feminist reader established with the female subjectivity brought to life in the process of reading is finally at odds with Poulet's model. For the interiorized author is "alien" to Poulet's reader. When he reads, he delivers himself "bound hand and foot, to the omnipotence of fiction." He becomes the "prey" of what he reads. "There is no escaping this takeover." His consciousness is "invaded," "annexed," "usurped." He is "dispossessed" of his rightful place on the "center stage" of his own mind. In the final analysis, the process of reading leaves room for only one subjectivity. The work becomes "a sort of human being" at "the expense of the reader whose life it suspends."[40] It is significant that the metaphors of mastery and submission, of violation and control, so prominent in Poulet's essay, are entirely absent in Rich's essay on Dickinson. In the paradigm of reading implicit in her essay, the dialectic of control (which shapes feminist readings of male texts) gives way to the dialectic of communication. For Rich, reading is a matter of "trying to connect" with the existence behind the text.

This dialectic also has three moments. The first involves the recognition that genuine intersubjective communication demands the duality of reader and author (the subject of the work). Because reading removes the barrier between subject and object, the division takes place *within* the reader. Reading induces a doubling of the reader's subjectivity, so that one can be placed at the disposal of the text while the other remains with the reader. Now, this doubling presents a problem, for in fact there is only one subject present—the reader. The text—the words on the page—has been written by the writer, but meaning is always a matter of interpretation. The subjectivity roused to life by reading, while it may be attributed to the author, is nevertheless not a separate subjectivity but a projection of the subjectivity of the reader. How can the duality of subjects be maintained in the absence of the author? In an actual conversation, the presence of another person preserves the duality. Because each party must assimilate and interpret the utterances of the other, we still have the introjection of the subject-object division, as well as the possibility of hearing only what one wants to hear. But in a real conversation, the other person can interrupt, object to an erroneous interpretation, provide further explanations, change her mind, change the topic, or cut off conversation altogether. In reading, there are no comparable safeguards against the appropriation of the text by the reader. This is the second moment of the dialectic—the recognition that reading is necessarily subjective. The need to keep it from being *totally* subjective ushers in the third moment of the dialectic.

In the feminist story, the key to the problem is the awareness of the double context of reading and writing. Rich's essay is wonderfully illustrative. To avoid imposing an alien perspective on Dickinson's poetry, Rich informs her reading with the knowledge of the circumstances in which Dickinson lived and worked. She repeatedly reminds herself and her readers that Dickinson must be read in light of her *own* premises, that the "exclusions" and "necessities" she endured, and, therefore, her choices, were conditioned by her own world. At the same time, Rich's sensitivity to the context of writing is matched by her sensitivity to the context of reading. She makes it clear throughout the essay that her reading of Dickinson is necessarily shaped by her experience and interests as a feminist poet living in the twentieth-century United States. The reader also has her own premises. To forget these is to run the risk of imposing them surreptitiously on the author.

To recapitulate, the first moment of the dialectic of reading is marked by the recognition of the necessary duality of subjects; the second, by the realization that this duality is threatened by the author's absence. In the third moment, the duality of subjects is referred to the duality of contexts. Reading becomes a mediation between author and reader, between the context of writings and the context of reading.

Although feminists have always believed that objectivity is an illusion, Rich's essay is the only one, as far as I know, to exhibit through its rhetoric the necessary subjectivity of reading coupled with the equally necessary commitment to reading the text as it was meant to be read.[41] The third moment of the dialectic is apparent in Rich's weaving—not blending—of the context of writing and the context of reading, the perspective of the author and that of the reader. The central rhetorical device effecting this mediation is her use of the personal voice. As in most critical essays, Rich alternates quotes from the texts in question with her own commentary, but her use of the personal voice makes a difference. In her hands, this rhetorical strategy serves two purposes. First, it serves as a reminder that her interpretation is informed by her own perspective. Second, it signifies her tactful approach to Dickinson; the personal voice serves as a gesture warding off any inclination to appropriate the authority of the text as a warrant for the validity of the interpretation. Because the interpretation is presented as an *interpretation*, its claim to validity rests on the cogency of the supporting arguments, *not* on the authorization of the text.

Rich accomplishes even more than this. She reaches out to Dickinson not by identifying with her, but by establishing their affinity. Both are American, both are women poets in a patriarchal culture. By playing this affinity against the differences, she produces a context that incorporates both reader and writer. In turn, this common ground becomes the basis for drawing the connections that, in her view, constitute the proper goal of reading.

One might ask: Is there something distinctively female (rather than "merely feminist") in this dialogic model? While it is difficult to specify what "distinctively female" might mean, there are currently very interesting speculations about differences in the way males and females conceive of themselves and of their relations with others. The works of Jean Baker Miller, Nancy Chodorow, and Carol Gilligan suggest that men define themselves through individuation and separation from others, while women have more flexible ego boundaries and define and experience themselves in terms of their affiliations and relationships with others.[42] Men value autonomy, and they think of their interactions with others principally in terms of procedures for arbitrating conflicts between individual rights. Women, on the other hand, value relationships, and they are most concerned in their dealings with others to negotiate between opposing needs so that the relationship can be maintained. This difference is consistent with the difference between mainstream models of reading and the dialogic model I am proposing for feminist readings of women's writing. Mainstream reader-response theories are preoccupied with issues of control and partition—how to distinguish the contribution of the author/text from the contribution of the reader. In the dialectic of communication informing the relationship between the feminist reader and the female author/text, the central issue is not of control or partition, but of managing the contradictory implications of the desire for relationship (one must maintain a minimal distance for the other) and the desire for intimacy, up to and including a symbiotic merger with the other. The problematic is defined by the drive "to connect," rather than that which is implicit in the mainstream preoccupation with partition and control—namely, the drive to get it right. It could also be argued that Poulet's model represents reading as an intimate, intersubjective encounter. However, it is significant that in his model, the prospect of close rapport with another provokes both excitement and anxiety. Intimacy, while desired, is also viewed as a threat to one's integrity. For Rich, on the other hand, the prospect of merging with another is problematical, but not threatening.

Let me end with a word about endings. Dialectical stories look forward to optimistic endings. Mine is no exception. In the first chapter the woman reader becomes a feminist, and in the end she succeeds in extricating herself from the androcentric logic of the literary and critical canons. In the second chapter the feminist reader succeeds in effecting a mediation between her perspective and that of the writer. These "victories" are part of the project of producing women's culture and literary tradition, which in turn is part of the project of overcoming patriarchy. It is in the nature of people working for revolutionary change to be optimistic about the prospect of redirecting the future.

Culler observes that optimistic endings have been challenged (successfully, he thinks) by deconstruction, a method radically at odds with the dialectic. It is worth noting that there is a deconstructive moment in Rich's reading of Dickinson. Recall her third metaphor: the reader is an insect "vibrating the frames of windows, clinging to the panes of glass, trying to connect." The suggestion of futility is unmistakable. At best, Rich's interpretation of Dickinson might be considered as a "strong misreading" whose value is in its capacity to provoke other misreadings.

We might say this—but must we? To answer this question, we must ask another: What is at stake in the proposition that reading is impossible? For one thing, if reading is impossible, then there is no way of deciding the validity of an interpretation—the very notion of validity becomes problematical. Certainly it is useful to be reminded that the validity of an interpretation cannot be decided by appealing to what the author "intended," to what is "in" the text, or to what is "in" the experience of the reader. However, there is another approach to the problem of validation, one that is consonant with the dialogic model of reading described above. We can think of validity not as a property inherent in an interpretation, but rather as a *claim* implicit in the *act* of propounding an interpretation. An interpretation, then, is not valid or invalid in itself. Its validity is contingent on the agreement of others. In this view, Rich's interpretation of Dickinson, which is frankly acknowledged as conditioned by her own experience as a twentieth-century feminist poet, is not necessarily a misreading. In advancing her interpretation, Rich implicitly claims its validity. That is to say, to read a text and then to write about it is to seek to connect not only with the author of the original text, but also with a community of readers. To the extent that she succeeds and to the extent that the community is potentially all-embracing, her interpretation has that degree of validity.[43]

Feminist reading and writing alike are grounded in the interest of producing a community of feminist readers and writers, and in the hope that ultimately this community will expand to include everyone. Of course, this project may fail. The feminist story may yet end with the recognition of the impossibility of reading. But this remains to be seen. At this stage I think it behooves us to *choose* the dialectical over the deconstructive plot. It is dangerous for feminists to be overly enamored with the theme of impossibility. Instead, we should strive to redeem the claim that it is possible for a woman, reading as a woman, to read literature written by women, for this is essential if we are to make the literary enterprise into a means for building and maintaining connections among women.

Notes

I would like to acknowledge my debt to David Schweickart for the substantial editorial work he did on this chapter.

1. Wayne Booth, Presidential Address, "Arts and Scandals 1982," *PMLA* 98 (1983):313. Subsequent references to this essay are cited parenthetically in the text.

2. *The Autobiography of Malcolm X*, written with Alex Haley (New York: Grove Press, 1964), p. 173. Subsequent references are cited parenthetically in the text.

3. Virginia Woolf, *A Room of One's Own* (New York: Harcourt Brace Jovanovich, 1981). Subsequent references are cited parenthetically in the text.

4. Jonathan D. Culler, *On Deconstruction: Theory and Criticism after Structuralism* (Ithaca: Cornell University Press, 1982), p. 42. (Subsequent references are cited parenthetically in the text.) Wayne Booth's essay "Freedom of Interpretation: Bakhtin and the Challenge of Feminist Criticism," *Critical Inquiry* 9 (1982): 45–76, is another good omen of the impact of feminist thought on literary criticism.

5. David Bleich, *Subjective Criticism* (Baltimore: Johns Hopkins University Press, 1978), p. 112.

6. Georges Poulet, "Criticism and the Experience of Interiority," trans. Catherine and Richard Macksey, in *Reader-Response Criticism: From Formalism to Structuralism*, ed. Jane Tompkins (Baltimore: Johns Hopkins University Press, 1980), p. 43. Poulet's theory is not among those discussed by Culler. However, since he will be useful to us later, I mention him here.

7. This argument was advanced by Samuel Weber in "The Struggle for Control: Wolfgang Iser's Third Dimension," cited by Culler in *On Deconstruction*, p. 75.

8. Stanley E. Fish, "Why No One's Afraid of Wolfgang Iser," *Diacritics* 11 (1981): 7. Quoted by Culler in *On Deconstruction*, p. 75.

9. Elaine Showalter, "Feminist Criticism in the Wilderness," *Critical Inquiry* 8 (1981): 182–85. Showalter argues that if we see feminist critique (focused on the reader) as our primary critical project, we must be content with the "playful pluralism" proposed by Annette Kolodny: first because no single conceptual model can comprehend so eclectic and wide-ranging an enterprise, and second because "in the free play of the interpretive field, feminist critique can only compete with alternative readings, all of which have the built-in obsolescence of Buicks, cast away as newer readings take their place" (p. 182). Although Showalter does not support Wimsatt and Beardsley's proscription of the "affective fallacy," she nevertheless subscribes to the logic of their argument. Kolodny's "playful pluralism" is more benign than Wimsatt and Beardsley's dreaded "relativism," but no less fatal, in Showalter's view, to theoretical coherence.

10. Elaine Showalter, "Women and the Literary Curriculum," *College English* 32 (1971): 855. For an excellent example of recent work following in the spirit of Showalter's critique, see Paul Lauter, *Reconstructing American Literature* (Old Westbury, N.Y.: Feminist Press, 1983).

11. Lee Edwards, "Women, Energy, and *Middlemarch*," *Massachusetts Review* 13 (1972): 226.

12. Edwards, "Women, Energy, and *Middlemarch*," p. 226.

13. James Joyce, *Portrait of the Artist as a Young Man* (London: Jonathan Cape, 1916), p. 195.

14. See also Florence Howe's analysis of the same passage, "Feminism and Literature," in *Images of Women in Fiction: Feminist Perspectives*, ed. Susan Koppelman Cornillon (Bowling Green, Ohio: Bowling Green State University Press, 1972), pp. 262–63.

15. Judith Fetterley, *The Resisting Reader: A Feminist Approach to American Fiction* (Bloomington: Indiana University Press, 1978), p. xx. Although Fetterley's remarks refer specifically to American Literature, they apply generally to the entire traditional canon.

16. Fetterley, *Resisting Reader*, p. xiii.

17. See Katharine M. Rogers, *The Troublesome Helpmate: A History of Misogyny in Literature* (Seattle: University of Washington Press, 1966).

18. Fredric Jameson, *The Political Unconscious: Narrative as a Socially Symbolic Act* (Ithaca: Cornell University Press, 1981), p. 286.

19. In *Woman and the Demon: The Life of a Victorian Myth* (Cambridge: Harvard University Press, 1982), Nina Auerbach employs a similar—though not identical—positive hermeneutic. She reviews the myths and images of women (as angels, demons, victims, whores, etc.) that feminist critics have "gleefully" unmasked as reflections and instruments of sexist ideology, and discovers in them an "unexpectedly empowering" mythos. Auerbach argues that the "most powerful, if least acknowledged, creation [of the Victorian cultural imagination] is an explosively mobile, magic woman, who breaks the boundaries of family within which her society restricts her. The triumph of this overweening creature is a celebration of the corporate imagination that believed in her" (p. 1). See also Auerbach's "Magi and Maidens: The Romance of the Victorian Freud," *Critical Inquiry* 8 (1981): 281–300. The tension between the positive and negative feminist hermeneutics is perhaps most apparent when one is dealing with the "classics." See, for example, Carol Thomas Neely, "Feminist Modes of Shakespeare Criticism: Compensatory, Justificatory, Transformational," *Women's Studies* 9 (1981): 3–15.

20. Kate Millett, *Sexual Politics* (New York: Avon Books, 1970).

21. Elaine Showalter, "The Double Critical Standard and the Feminine Novel," chap. 3 in *A Literature of Their Own: British Women Novelists from Brontë to Lessing* (Princeton: Princeton University Press, 1977), pp. 73–99; Carol Ohmann, "Emily Brontë in the Hands of Male Critics," *College English* 32 (1971): 906–13.

22. Nina Baym, "Melodramas of Beset Manhood: How Theories of American Fiction Exclude Women Authors," *American Quarterly* 33 (1981): 123–39

23. Baym, "Melodramas of Beset Manhood," p. 125.

24. Baym, "Melodramas of Beset Manhood," p. 130. One of the founding works of American Literature is "The Legend of Sleepy Hollow," about which Leslie Fiedler writes: "It is fitting that our first successful homegrown legend would memorialize, however playfully, the flight of the dreamer from the shrew" (*Love and death in the American Novel* [New York: Criterion, 1960] p. xx).

25. Nina Baym's *Women's Fiction: A Guide to Novels by and about Women in America, 1820–1870* (Ithaca: Cornell University Press, 1978) provides a good survey of what has been excluded from the canon.

26. Annette Kolodny, "Dancing through the Minefield: Some Observations on the Theory, Practice, and Politics of a Feminist Literary Criticism," *Feminist Studies* 6 (1980): 10–12. Kolodny elaborates the same theme in "A Map for Rereading: Or, Gender and the Interpretation of Literary Texts," *New Literary History* 11 (1980): 451–67.

27. For an excellent account of the way in which the feminist "interpretive community" has changed literary and critical conventions, see Jean E. Kennard, "Convention Coverage, or How to Read Your Own Life," *New Literary History* 8 (1981): 69–88. The programs of the MLA Convention during the last twenty-five years offer more concrete evidence of the changes in the literary and critical canons, and of the ideological and political struggles effecting these changes.

28. In Adrienne Rich, *On Lies, Secrets, and Silence: Selected Prose, 1966–1978* (New York: W. W. Norton, 1979). Subsequent references are cited parenthetically in the text.

29. Susan Glaspell's story "A Jury of Her Peers" revolves around a variation of this judicial metaphor. The parable of reading implicit in this story has not been lost on feminist critics. Annette Kolodny, for example, discusses how it "explores the necessary gender marking which *must* constitute any definition of 'peers' in the complex process of unraveling

truth or meaning." Although the story does not exclude male readers, it alerts us to the fact that "symbolic representations depend on a fund of shared recognitions and potential references," and in general, "female meaning" is inaccessible to "male interpretation." "However inadvertently, [the male reader] is a *different kind* of reader and, . . . where women are concerned, he is often an inadequate reader" ("Map for Rereading," pp. 460–63).

30.   There is a strong counter-tendency, inspired by French poststructuralism, which privileges the appreciation of textuality over the imaginative recovery of the woman writer as subject of the work. See, for example, Mary Jacobus, "Is There a Woman in This Text?" *New Literary History* 14 (1982): 117–41, especially the concluding paragraph. The last sentence of the essay underscores the controversy: "Perhaps the question that feminist critics should be asking is not 'Is there a woman in this text?' but rather: 'Is there a text in this woman?' "

31.   I must stress that although Rich's essay presents a significant paradigm of feminist readings of women's writing, it is not the only such paradigm. An alternative is proposed by Caren Greenberg, "Reading Reading: Echo's Abduction of Language," in *Women and Language in Literature and Society*, ed. Sally McConnell-Ginet, Ruth Borker, and Nelly Furman (New York: Praeger, 1980), pp. 304–9.

Furthermore, there are many important issues that have been left out of my discussion. For example:

a.   The relationship of her career as reader to the artistic development of the woman writer. In *Madwoman in the Attic* (New Haven: Yale University Press, 1980) Sandra Gilbert and Susan Gubar show that women writers had to struggle to overcome the "anxiety of authorship" which they contracted from the "sentences" of their predecessors, male as well as female. They also argue that the relationship women writers form with their female predecessors does not fit the model of oedipal combat proposed by Bloom. Rich's attitude toward Dickinson (as someone who "has been there," as a "foremother" to be recovered) corroborates Gilbert and Gubar's claim.

b.   The relationship between women writers and their readers. We need actual reception studies as well as studies of the way women writers conceived of their readers and the way they inscribed them in their texts.

c.   The relationship between the positive and the negative hermeneutic in feminist readings of women's writing. Rich's reading of Dickinson emphasizes the positive hermeneutic. One might ask, however, if this approach is applicable to *all* women's writing. Specifically, is this appropriate to the popular fiction written by women, e.g., Harlequin Romances? To what extent is women's writing itself a bearer of patriarchal ideology? Janice Radway addresses these issues in "Utopian Impulse in Popular Literature: Gothic Romances and 'Feminist Protest,' " *American Quarterly* 33 (1981): 140–62, and "Women Read the Romance: The Interaction of Text and Context," *Feminist Studies* 9 (1983): 53–78. See also Tania Modleski, *Loving with a Vengeance: Mass-Produced Fantasies for Women* (New York: Methuen, 1982).

32.   Iser writes:

Text and reader no longer confront each other as object and subject, but instead the "division" takes place within the reader [herself]. . . . As we read, there occurs an artificial division of our personality, because we take as a theme for ourselves something we are not. Thus, in reading there are two levels—the alien "me" and the real, virtual "me"—which are never completely cut off from each other. Indeed, we can only make someone else's thoughts into an absorbing theme for ourselves provided the virtual background of our personality can adapt to it. ("The Reading Process: A Phenomenological Approach," in Tompkins, *Reader-Response Criticism*, p. 67)

Add the stipulation that the alien "me" is a male who has appropriated the universal into his maleness, and we have the process of immasculation described in the third section.

33.   Stanley E. Fish, *Is There a Text in This Class? The Authority of Interpretive Communities* (Cambridge: Harvard University Press, 1980), especially pt. 2.

34.   Although the woman reader is the "star" of the feminist story of reading, this does not mean that men are excluded from the audience. On the contrary, it is hoped that on hearing the feminist story they will be encouraged to revise their own stories to reflect the fact that they, too, are gendered beings, and that, ultimately, they will take control of their inclination to appropriate the universal at the expense of women.

35.   Catherine A. MacKinnon, "Feminism, Marxism, Method, and the State: Toward Feminist Jurisprudence," *Signs* 8 (1981): 637.

36.   There is lively debate among feminists about whether it is better to emphasize the essential similarity of women and men, or their difference. There is much to be said intellectually and politically for both sides. However, in one sense, the argument centers on a false issue. It assumes that concern about women's "difference" is incompatible with concern about the essential humanity shared by the sexes. Surely, "difference" may be interpreted to refer to what is distinctive in women's lives and works, *including* what makes them essentially human; unless, of course, we remain captivated by the notion that the standard model for humanity is male.

37.   Although opponents of feminist criticism often find it convenient to characterize such works as a personal attack on authors, for feminist critics themselves, the primary consideration is the function of the text as a carrier of patriarchal ideology, and its effect as such especially (but not exclusively) on women readers. The personal culpability of the author is a relatively minor issue.

38.   Harold Bloom, *Kabbalah and Criticism* (New York: Seabury, 1975), p. 126.

39.   Poulet, "Criticism and the Experience of Interiority," p. 46.

40.   Poulet, "Criticism and the Experience of Interiority," p. 47. As Culler has pointed out, the theme of control is prominent in mainstream reader-response criticism. Poulet's story is no exception. The issue of control is important in another way. Behind the question of whether the text controls the reader or vice versa is the question of how to regulate literary criticism. If the text is controlling, then there is no problem. The text itself will regulate the process of reading. But if the text is not necessarily controlling, then, how do we constrain the activities of readers and critics? How can we rule out "off-the-wall" interpretations? Fish's answer is of interest to feminist critics. The constraints, he says, are exercised not by the text, but by the institutions within which literary criticism is situated. It is but a small step from this idea to the realization of the necessarily political character of literature and criticism.

41.   The use of the personal conversational tone has been regarded as a hallmark of feminist criticism. However, as Jean E. Kennard has pointed out ("Personally Speaking: Feminist Critics and the Community of Readers," *College English* 43 [1981]: 140–45), this theoretical commitment is not apparent in the overwhelming majority of feminist critical essays. Kennard found only five articles in which the critic "overtly locates herself on the page." (To the five she found, I would add three works cited in this essay: "Women, Energy, and *Middlemarch*," by Lee Edwards; "Feminism and Literature," by Florence Howe; and "Vesuvius at Home," by Adrienne Rich.) Kennard observes further that, even in the handful of essays she found, the personal tone is confined to a few introductory paragraphs. She asks: "If feminist criticism has on the whole remained faithful to familiar methods and tone, why have the few articles with an overt personal voice loomed so large in our minds?" Kennard suggests that these personal introductions are invitations "to share a critical response which depends upon unstated, shared beliefs and, to a large extent, experience; that of being a female educated in a male tradition in which she is no longer comfortable." Thus,

these introductory paragraphs do not indicate a "transformed critical methodology; they are devices for transforming the reader. I read the later portions of these essays—and by extension other feminist criticism—in a different way because I have been invited to participate in the underground. . . . I am part of a community of feminist readers" (pp. 143–44).

I would offer another explanation, one that is not necessarily inconsistent with Kennard's. I think the use of a personal and conversational tone represents an overt gesture indicating the dialogic mode of discourse as the "regulative ideal" for all feminist discourse. The few essays—indeed, the few introductory paragraphs—that assert this regulative ideal are memorable because they strike a chord in a significant segment of the community of feminist critics. To the extent that we have been touched or transformed by this idea, it will be implicit in the way we read the works of others, in particular, the works of other women. Although the ideal must be overtly affirmed periodically, it is not necessary to do so in all of our essays. It remains potent as long as it is assumed by a significant portion of the community. I would argue with Kennard's distinction between indicators of a transformed critical methodology and devices for transforming the reader. To the extent that critical methodology is a function of the conventions implicitly or explicitly operating in an interpretive community—that is, of the way members of the community conceive of their work and of the way they read each other—devices for transforming readers are also devices for transforming critical methodology.

42. Jean Baker Miller, *Toward a New Psychology of Women* (Boston: Beacon Press, 1976); and Nancy Chodorow, *The Reproduction of Mothering: Psychoanalysis and the Sociology of Gender* (Berkeley and Los Ageles: University of California Press, 1978); and Carol Gilligan, *In a Different Voice: Psychological Theory and Women's Development* (Cambridge: Harvard University Press, 1982).

43. I am using here Jürgen Habermas's definition of truth or validity as a claim (implicit in the act of making assertions) that is redeemable through discourse—specifically, through the domination-free discourse of an "ideal speech situation." For Habermas, consensus attained through domination-free discourse is the warrant for truth. See "Wahrheitstheorien," in *Wirklichkeit und Reflexion: Walter Schulz zum 60. Geburtstag* (Pfullingen: Nesge, 1973), pp. 211–65. I am indebted to Alan Soble's unpublished translation of this essay.

3

Gender Theory and The Yale School

Barbara Johnson

As Harold Bloom puts it in the opening essay of the Yale School's non-manifesto, *Deconstruction and Criticism:* "Reading well is not necessarily a polite process. . . . Only the capacity to wound gives a healing capacity the chance to endure, and so to be heard."[1] I hope, therefore, that my hosts will understand the spirit in which I will use them as the starting point for the depiction of a much larger configuration, and that by the end of this paper I will not have bitten off more of the hand that feeds me than I can chew.

In January of this year, shortly after the death of Paul de Man, I received a call from Robert Con Davis inviting me to attempt the painful and obviously impossible task of replacing de Man in a conference in which Geoffrey Hartman, Hillis Miller, and Paul de Man had been asked to speak about genre theory in relation to their own work. I was invited to speak, however, not about *my* own work but about de Man's. The reasons for this are certainly understandable. I could easily sympathize with the conference organizers' impulse: there is nothing I could wish more than that de Man had not died. But the invitation to appear as de Man's *supplément—* supplemented in turn by a panel of my own choosing—gave me pause. For it falls all too neatly into patterns of female effacement already well established by the phenomenon of the Yale School—and indeed, with rare exceptions, by the phenomenon of the critical "school" as such. Like others of its type, the Yale School has always been a Male School.

Would it have been possible for there to have been a female presence in the Yale School? Interestingly, in Jonathan Culler's bibliography to *On Deconstruction* Shoshana Felman's book *La Folie et la chose littéraire* is described as "a wide-ranging collection of essays by a member of the 'école de Yale.' "[2] Felman, in other words, *was* a member of the Yale School, but only in French. This question of the foreignness of the female language will return, but for now, suffice it to say that there was no reason other than gender why Felman's work—certainly closer to de Man's and Derrida's than the work of Harold Bloom—should not have been seen as an integral part of the Yale School.

At the time of the publication of *Deconstruction and Criticism*, several of us— Shoshana Felman, Gayatri Spivak, Margaret Ferguson, and I—discussed the possibility of writing a companion volume inscribing female deconstructive protest and affirmation centering not on Shelley's "The Triumph of Life" (as the existing volume was originally slated to do) but on Mary Shelley's *Frankenstein*. That book might truly have illustrated the Girardian progression "from mimetic desire to the monstrous double." Unfortunately, this *Bride of Deconstruction and Criticism* never quite got off the ground, but it is surely no accident that the project was centered around monstrosity. As Derrida puts it in "The Law of Genre"—which is also, of course, a law of gender—"As soon as genre announces itself, one must respect a norm, one must not cross a line of demarcation, one must not risk impurity, anomaly, or monstrosity."[3] After all, Aristotle, the founder of the law of gender as well as of the law of genre, considered the female as the first distortion of the genus "man" en route to becoming a monster. But perhaps it was not *Frankenstein* but rather *The Last Man*, Mary Shelley's grim depiction of the gradual extinction of humanity altogether, that would have made a fit counterpart to "The Triumph of Life." Shelley is entombed in both, along with a certain male fantasy of Romantic universality. The only universality that remains in Mary Shelley's last novel is the plague.

It would be easy to accuse the male Yale School theorists of having avoided the issue of gender entirely. What I intend to do, however, is to demonstrate that they have had quite a lot to say about the issue, often without knowing it. Before moving on to a female version of the Yale School, therefore, I will begin by attempting to extract from the essays in *Deconstruction and Criticism* and related texts an implicit theory of the relations between gender and criticism. For the purposes of this paper, I will focus on the four members of the Yale School who actually teach full time at Yale. Since Derrida, the fifth participant in *Deconstruction and Criticism*, has in contrast consistently and explicitly foregrounded the question of gender, his work would demand far more extensive treatment than is possible here. I will confine myself to the more implicit treatments of the subject detectable in the writings of Bloom, Hartman, Miller, and de Man.

Geoffrey Hartman, ever the master of the throwaway line, has not failed to make some memorable remarks about the genderedness of the reading process. "Much reading," he writes in *The Fate of Reading*, "is indeed, like girl-watching, a simple expense of spirit."[4] And in *Beyond Formalism*, he claims: "Interpretation is like a football game. You spot a hole and you go through. But first you may have to induce that opening."[5]

In his essay in *Deconstruction and Criticism*, Hartman examines a poem in which Wordsworth, suddenly waylaid by a quotation, addresses his daughter Dora with a line from Milton's Samson that harks back to the figure of blind Oedipus being led by his daughter Antigone:

> A Little onward lend thy guiding hand
> To these dark steps, a little further on! (DC, p. 215)

This is certainly a promising start for an investigation of gender relations. Yet Wordsworth and Hartman combine to curb the step of this budding Delilah and to subsume the daughter under the Wordsworthian category of "child," who, as everyone knows, is *Father* of the man. While the poem works out a power reversal between blind father and guiding daughter, restoring the father to this role of natural leader, the commentary works out its patterns of reversibility between Wordsworth and Milton. "Let me, thy happy guide, now point thy way/And how precede thee. . . . " When Wordsworth leads his daughter to the edge of the abyss, it is the abyss of intertextuality.

While brooding on the abyss in *The Fate of Reading*, Hartman looks back at his own precursor self and says:

> In *The Unmediated Vision* the tyranny of sight in the domain of sensory organization is acknowledged, and symbol making is understood as a kind of "therapeutic alliance" between the eye and other senses through the medium of art. I remember how easy it was to put a woman in the landscape, into every eyescape rather; and it struck me that in works of art there were similar centers, depicted or inferred.

Yet the woman in Wordsworth's poemscape is precisely what Hartman does not see. And this may be just what Wordsworth intended. In the short paragraph in which Hartman acknowledges that there may be something Oedipal about this Oedipus figure, he describes the daughter as *barred* by the incest prohibition. The poem would then transmit a disguised desire for the daughter, repressed and deflected into literary structures. Yet might it not also be that Wordsworth so often used incest figures in his poetry as a way, precisely, of barring the reality of the woman as other, a way of keeping the woman in and *only* in the eyescape, making a nun out of a nymph? For the danger here is that the daughter will neither follow nor lead, but simply leave:

> the birds salute
> The cheerful dawn, brightening for me the east;
> For me, thy natural leader, once again
> Impatient to conduct thee, not as erst
> A tottering infant, with compliant stoop
> From flower to flower supported; but to curb
> Thy nymph-like step swift-bounding o'er the lawn,
> Along the loose rocks, or the slippery verge
> Of foaming torrents. . . .

The family romance takes a slightly different form in Hillis Miller's essay, "The Critic as Host." In that essay, Miller discusses Booth's and Abrams's image of deconstructive criticism as "parasitical" on the "obvious or univocal reading" of a text. Miller writes:

> "Parasitical"—the word suggests the image of "the obvious or univocal reading" as the mighty oak, rooted in the solid ground, endangered by the insidious twining around it of deconstructive ivy. That ivy is somehow feminine, secondary, defective, or dependent. It is a cling vine, able to live in no other

way but by drawing the life sap of its host, cutting off its light and air. I think of Hardy's *The Ivy-Wife*. . . .

Such sad love stories of a domestic affection which introduces the parasitical into the closed economy of the home no doubt describe well enough the way some people feel about the relation of a "deconstructive" interpretation to "the obvious or univocal reading." The parasite is destroying the host. The alien has invaded the house, perhaps to kill the father of the family in an act which does not look like parricide, but is. Is the "obvious" reading, though, so "obvious" or even so "univocal"? May it not itself be the uncanny alien which is so close that it cannot be seen as strange? (DC, p. 218)

It is interesting to note how effortlessly the vegetal metaphor is sexualized in Miller's elaboration of it. If the parasite is the feminine, then the feminine must be recognized as that uncanny alien always already in the house—and in the host. What turns out, in Miller's etymological analysis, to be uncanny about the relation between host and parasite—and by extension between male and female—is that each is already inhabited by the other as a difference from itself. Miller then goes on to describe the parasite as invading virus in the following terms:

The genetic pattern of the virus is so coded that it can enter a host cell and violently reprogram all the genetic material in that cell, turning the cell into a little factory for manufacturing copies of itself, so destroying it. This is *The Ivy-Wife* with a vengeance. (DC, p.222)

Miller then goes on to ask, "Is this an allegory, and if so, of what?" Perhaps of the gender codes of literature, or of criticism. But this image of cancerous femininity may be less a fear of takeover by women than an extreme version of the desire to deny difference. There is perhaps something reassuring about total annihilation as opposed to precarious survival. The desire to deny difference is in fact, in a euphoric rather than a nightmarish spirit, the central desire dramatized by the Shelley poems Miller analyzes. The obsessive cry for oneness, for sameness, always, however, meets the same fate: it cannot subsume and erase the trace of its own elaboration. The story told, again and again, by Shelley is the story of the failure of the attempt to abolish difference. As Miller points out, difference is rediscovered in the linguistic traces of that failure. But a failed erasure of difference is not the same as a recognition of difference. Unless, as Miller's analysis suggests, difference can only be recognized in the failure of its erasure.

If the parasite is both feminine and parricidal, then the parasite can only be a daughter. Miller does not follow up on the implications of a parricidal daughter, but Harold Bloom, whose critical system is itself a garden of parricidal delights, gives us a clue to what would be at stake for him in such an idea. In *The Map of Misreading* he writes:

Nor are there Muses, nymphs who *know*, still available to tell us the secrets of continuity, for the nymphs certainly are now departing. I prophesy though that the first true break with literary continuity will be brought about in generations to come, if the burgeoning religion of Liberated Woman spreads from it clusters of enthusiasts to dominate the West. Homer will cease to be the inevitable precursor, and the rhetoric and forms of our literature then may break at last from tradition.[6]

In Bloom's prophetic vision of the breaking of tradition through the liberation of woman, it is as though the Yale School were in danger of becoming a Jael School.[7]

The dependence of Bloom's revisionary ratios upon a linear patriarchal filiation has been pointed out often enough—particularly in the groundbreaking work of Sandra Gilbert and Susan Gubar—that there is no need to belabor it here. I will therefore, instead, analyze the opening lines of Bloom's essay "The Breaking of Form" as a strong misreading of the question of sexual difference. The essay begins:

> The word *meaning* goes back to a root that signifies "opinion" or "intention," and is closely related to the word *moaning*. A poem's meaning is a poem's complaint, its version of Keats' Belle Dame, who looked *as if* she loved, and made sweet moan. Poems instruct us in how they break form to bring about meaning, so as to utter a complaint, a moaning intended to be all their own.
>
> (*DC*, p. 1)

If the relation between the reader and the poem is analogous to the relation between the knight-at-arms and the Belle Dame, things are considerably more complicated than they appear. For the encounter between male and female in Keats's poem is a perfectly ambiguous disaster:

LA BELLE DAME SANS MERCI
A Ballad

I

O what can ail thee, knight-at-arms,
Alone and palely loitering?
The sedge has withered from the lake,
And no birds sing.

II

O what can ail thee, knight-at-arms,
So haggard and so woebegone?
The squirrel's granary is full,
And the harvest's done.

III

I see a lily on thy brow,
With anguish moist and fever dew,
And on thy cheeks a fading rose
Fast withereth too.

IV

I met a lady in the meads,
Full beautiful—a fairy's child,
Her hair was long, her foot was light,
And her eyes were wild.

V

I made a garland for her head,
And bracelets too, and fragrant zone;
She looked at me as she did love,
And made sweet moan.

VI

I set her on my pacing steed,
And nothing else saw all day long,
For sidelong would she bend, and sing
A fairy's song.

VII

She found me roots of relish sweet,
And honey wild, and manna dew,
And sure in language strange she said—
"I love thee true."

VIII

She took me to her elfin grot,
And there she wept, and sighed full sore,
And there I shut her wild wild eyes
With kisses four.

IX

And there she lullèd me asleep,
And there I dreamed—Ah! woe betide!
The latest dream I ever dreamed
On the cold hillside.

X

I saw pale kings and princes too,
Pale warriors, death-pale were they all;
They cried—"La Belle Dame sans Merci
Hath thee in thrall!"

XI

I saw their starved lips in the gloam,
With horrid warning gapèd wide,
And I awoke and found me here,
On the cold hill's side.

XII

And this is why I sojourn here,
Alone and palely loitering,
Though the sedge has withered from the lake,
And no birds sing.

Rather than a clear "as if," Keats writes: "She looked at me *as* she did love,/ And made sweet moan." Suspicion of the woman is not planted quite so clearly, nor quite so early. In changing "as" to "as if," Bloom has removed from the poem the possibility of reading this first mention of the woman's feelings as straight description. "As she did love" would still be the knight's own interpretation, but it would be an interpretation that does not recognize itself as such. Perhaps Bloom is here demonstrating what he says elsewhere about the study of poetry being "the study of what Stevens called 'the intricate evasions of as.' " By the end of the poem, it becomes impossible to know whether one has read a story of a knight enthralled by a witch or of a woman seduced and abandoned by a male hysteric. And the fine balance of that undecidability depends on the "as."

If the poem, like the woman, "makes sweet moan," then there is considerable doubt about the reader's capacity to read it. This becomes all the more explicit in the knight's second interpretive assessment of the woman's feelings: "And sure in language strange she said—/'I love thee true.' " The problem of understanding the woman is here a problem of translation. Even her name can only be expressed in another tongue. The sexes stand in relation to each other not as two distinct entities but as two foreign languages. The drama of male hysteria is a drama of premature assurance of understanding followed by premature panic at the intimation of otherness. Is she mine, asks the knight, or am I hers? If these are the only two possibilities, the foreignness of the languages cannot be respected. What Bloom demonstrates, perhaps without knowing it, is that if reading is the gendered activity he paints it as, the reading process is less a love story than a story of failed translation.

That the question of gender is a question of language becomes even more explicit in an essay by Paul de Man entitled "The Epistemology of Metaphor."[8] Translation is at issue in that essay as well, in the very derivation of the word "metaphor." "It is no mere play of words," writes de Man, "that 'translate' is translated in German as 'übersetzen' which itself translates the Greek *'meta phorein'* or metaphor." (p. 17) In all three words, what is described is a motion from one place to another. As we shall see, the question of the relation between gender and figure will have a great deal to do with this notion of *place*.

De Man's essay begins as follows:

Metaphors, tropes, and figural language in general have been a perennial problem and, at times, a recognized source of embarrassment for philosophical discourse and, by extension, for all discursive uses of language including historiography and literary analysis. It appears that philosophy either has to give up its own constitutive claim to rigor in order to come to terms with the figurality of its language or that it has to free itself from figuration altogether. And if the latter is considered impossible, philosophy could at least learn to control figuration by keeping it, so to speak, in its place, by delimiting the boundaries of its influence and thus restricting the epistemological damage that it may cause. (p. 13)

This opening paragraph echoes, in its own rhetoric, a passage which occurs later in the essay in which de Man is commenting on a long quotation from Locke. Locke concludes his discussion of the perils of figuration as follows:

Eloquence, like the fair sex, has too prevailing beauties in it to suffer itself ever to be spoken against. And it is in vain to find fault with those arts of deceiving wherein men find pleasure to be deceived. (p. 15)

De Man glosses the Locke passage as follows:

Nothing could be more eloquent than this denunciation of eloquence. It is clear that rhetoric is something one can decorously indulge in as long as one knows where it belongs. Like a woman, which it resembles ("like the fair sex"), it is a fine thing as long as it is kept in its proper place. Out of place, among the serious affairs of men ("if we would speak of things as they are"), it is a disruptive scandal—like the appearance of a real woman in a gentleman's club where it would only be tolerated as a picture, preferably naked (like the image of Truth), framed and hung on the wall. (pp. 15–16)

Following this succinct tongue-in-cheek description of the philosophical tradition as a men's club, de Man goes on to claim that there is "little epistemological risk in a flowery, witty passage about wit like this one," that things only begin to get serious when the plumber must be called in, but the epistemological damage may already have been done. For the question of language in Locke quickly comes to be centered on the question, "What essence is the proper of man?" This is no idle question, in fact, because what is at stake in the answer is what sort of monstrous births it is permissible to kill. Even in the discussion of Condillac and Kant, the question of sexual difference lurks, as when de Man describes Condillac's discussion of abstractions as bearing a close resemblance to a novel by Ann Radcliffe or Mary Shelley, or when Kant is said to think that rhetoric can be rehabilitated by some "tidy critical housekeeping." De Man's conclusion can be read as applying to the epistemological damage caused as much by gender as by figure:

In each case, it turns out to be impossible to maintain a clear line of distinction between rhetoric, abstraction, symbol, and all other forms of language. In each case, the resulting undecidability is due to the asymmetry of the binary model that opposes the figural to the proper meaning of the figure. (p. 28)

The philosopher's place is always within, not outside, the asymmetrical structures of language and of gender, but that place can never, in the final analysis, be proper. It may be impossible to know whether it is the gender question that is determined by rhetoric or rhetoric by gender difference, but it does seem as though these are the terms in which it might be fruitful to pursue the question.

In order to end with a meditation on a possible female version of the Yale School, I would like now to turn to the work of a Yale daughter. For this purpose I have chosen to focus on *The Critical Difference* by Barbara Johnson.[9] What happens when one raises Mary Jacobus's question—"Is there a woman in this text?" The answer is rather surprising. For no book produced by the Yale School seems to have excluded women as effectively as *The Critical Difference*. No women authors are studied. Almost no women critics are cited. And, what is even more surprising, there are almost no female characters in any of the stories analyzed. *Billy Budd*, however triangulated, is a tale of three *men* in a boat. Balzac's *Sarrasine* is the story of a woman who turns out to be a castrated man. And in Johnson's analysis of "The Purloined Letter," the story of Oedipal triangularity is transformed into an endlessly repeated chain of fraternal rivalries. In a book that announces itself as a study of difference, the place of the woman is constantly being erased.

This does not mean, however, that the question of sexual difference does not haunt the book from the beginning. In place of a dedication, *The Critical Difference* opens with a quotation from Paul de Man in which difference is dramatized as a scene of exasperated instruction between Archie Bunker and his wife:

> Asked by his wife whether he wants to have his bowling shoes laced over or laced under, Archie Bunker answers with a question: "What's the difference?" Being a reader of sublime simplicity, his wife replies by patiently explaining the difference between lacing over and lacing under, whatever this may be, but provokes only ire. "What's the difference?" did not ask for difference but means instead "I don't give a damn what the difference is." The same grammatical pattern engenders two meanings that are mutually exclusive: the literal meaning asks for the concept (difference) whose existence is denied by the figurative meaning. As long as we are talking about bowling shoes, the consequences are relatively trivial; Archie Bunker, who is a great believer in the authority of origins (as long, of course, as they are the right origins) muddles along in a world where literal and figurative meanings get in each other's way, though not without discomforts. But suppose that it is a *de*-bunker rather than a "Bunker," and a de-bunker of the arche (or origin), an archie Debunker such as Nietzsche or Jacques Derrida, for instance, who asks the question "What is the Difference?"—and we cannot even tell from his grammar whether he "really" wants to know "what" difference is or is just telling us that we shouldn't even try to find out. Confronted with the question of the difference between grammar and rhetoric, grammar allows us to ask the question, but the sentence by means of which we ask it may deny the very possibility of asking. For what is the use of asking, I ask, when we cannot even authoritatively decide whether a question asks or doesn't ask?

Whatever the rhetorical twists of this magnificent passage, the fact that it is framed as an intersexual dialogue is not irrelevant.

Another essay in *The Critical Difference*, a study of Mallarmé's prose poem "The White Waterlily," offers an even more promising depiction of the rhetoric of sexual difference. The essay begins:

> If human beings were not divided into two biological sexes, there would probably be no need for literature. And if literature could truly say what the relations between the sexes are, we would doubtless not need much of it then, either. Somehow, however, it is not simply a question of literature's ability to say or not to say the truth of sexuality. For from the moment literature begins to try to set things straight on that score, literature itself becomes inextricable from the sexuality it seeks to comprehend. It is not the life of sexuality that literature cannot capture; it is literature that inhabits the very heart of what makes sexuality problematic for us speaking animals. Literature is not only a thwarted investigator but also an incorrigible perpetrator of the problem of sexuality. (p. 13)

But the prose poem in question ends up dramatizing an inability to know whether the woman one is expecting to encounter has ever truly been present or not. It is as though *The Critical Difference* could describe only the escape of the difference it attempts to analyze. This is even more true of the essay subtitled "What the Gypsy Knew." With such a title, one would expect to encounter at last something about female knowledge. But the point of the analysis is precisely that the poem does not tell us what the gypsy knew. Her prophecy is lost in the ambiguities of Apollinaire's syntax.

There may, however, be something accurate about this repeated dramatization of woman as simulacrum, erasure, or silence. For it would not be easy to assert that the the existence and knowledge of the female subject could simply be produced, without difficulty or epistemological damage, within the existing patterns of culture and language. *The Critical Difference* may here be unwittingly pointing to "woman" as one of the things "we do not know we do not know." Johnson concludes her preface with some remarks about ignorance that apply ironically well to her book's own demonstration of an ignorance that pervades Western discourse as a whole:

> What literature often seems to tell us is the consequences of the way in which what is not known is not *seen* as unknown. It is not, in the final analysis, what you don't know that can or cannot hurt you. It is what you don't *know* you don't know that spins out and entangles "that perpetual error we call life." (p. xii)

It is not enough to be a woman writing in order to resist the naturalness of female effacement in the subtly male pseudo-genderlessness of language. It would be no easy task, however, to undertake the effort of re-inflection or translation required to retrieve the lost knowledge of the gypsy, or to learn to listen with re-trained ears to Edith Bunker's patient elaboration of an answer to the question, "What is the difference?"

Notes

1.   "The Breaking of Form," in *Deconstruction and Criticism*, Harold Bloom, ed., (New York: The Seabury Press, 1979), pp. 6, 5. Further references to this and other essays in the volume will be indicated in the text by the abbreviation *DC* followed by a page number.

2.   Jonathan Culler, *On Deconstruction* (Ithaca, NY: Cornell University Press, 1982), p. 289.

3.   Jacques Derrida, "The Law of Genre," *Glyph*, 7 (Baltimore: The Johns Hopkins Univesity Press, 1980), pp. 203–04.

4.   Geoffrey Hartman, *The Fate of Reading* (Chicago: University of Chicago Press, 1975), p. 248.

5.   Geoffrey Hartman, *Beyond Formalism* (New Haven: Yale University Press, 1970), p. 351.

6.   Harold Bloom, *A Map of Misreading* (New York: Oxford University Press, 1975), p. 33. I would like to thank Susan Suleiman for calling my attention to this quotation.

7.   The story of Jael is found in Judges 4. Jael invites Sisera, the commander of the Canaanite army, into her tent, gives him a drink of milk, and then, when he has fallen asleep, drives a tent peg through his head and kills him. (I would like to thank Sima Godfrey for this pun.)

8.   Paul de Man, "The Epistemology of Metaphor," *Critical Inquiry*, 5 (1978).

9.   Barbara Johnson, *The Critical Difference*, (Baltimore: The Johns Hopkins University Press, 1980).

4

Gender and Afro-Americanist Literary Theory and Criticism

Valerie Smith

This essay attempts to contribute to the ongoing process of writing black literary feminism by mapping the changing status of gender in Afro-Americanist discourse and suggesting future directions in which the study of representations of race and gender might move.[1] Such an effort to position issues of gender in relation to questions of race seems particularly necessary now that increasing numbers of "others"—black men, white women, and white men—are studying and theorizing about black women's literary and cultural productions.

If, as Hazel V. Carby has argued, the black feminist enterprise cannot be defined solely in terms of a shared experience between "black women as critics and black women as writers who represent black women's reality,"[2] then the time is right to ask ourselves what we mean when we talk about black feminism; to engage discrete instances of black feminist criticism in discussion with each other; and to consider black feminism in relation to the professional and institutional circumstances out of which it is produced and within which it is disseminated. Moreover, given that white men and women and black men have different investments in black feminism than black women do, those of us who consider questions of race and gender must develop a way of talking about the varying kinds of political and professional returns we receive from working on these sorts of issues.

The project of this essay is complicated by the fact that the narrative of the place of gender in Afro-Americanist theoretical and critical discourse is highly charged.[3] Indeed, at one level, rehearsing the history of omissions and misreadings seems almost beside the point, since recent black feminist work is more concerned with developing ways of reading and talking about figurations of race and gender than with focusing on absences in the work of others. Moreover, to criticize the work of black men within the context of a volume edited by a white feminist would suggest that I had chosen, at least for the time being, one set of allies at the expense of another. And yet, at another level it seems to me that if oppositional discourses—black feminist, Afro-Americanist, feminist, Marxist, and so on—are to keep their edge even as they move into the academic mainstream—then practitioners must develop a mode of self-evaluation, and sustain a dialogue with those involved in related enterprises. To fail to confront the contingencies that both enable and impede our theoretical work, is to risk replicating the exclusionary self-mystification, the pretense to objectivity, that characterizes phallocentric humanism.

Therefore in order to suggest how questions of gender might, in the future, expand the possibilities of Afro-Americanist discourse, I have identified ways in which the issue of gender has entered in the past. My hope is that if those of us working on the connections between race, class, and gender in cultural productions acknowledge the relation of our theoretical work to our personal circumstances, then we will be able to expand the radical possibilities of our scholarship. When we consider our relation to the institutions within which we work and by means of which our ideas are circulated, we will be able to resist the conditions that commodify and threaten to divide us.[4]

I

The conditions of oppression provide the subtext of all Afro-Americanist literary criticism and theory. Whether a critic/theorist explores representations of the experience of oppression or strategies by which that experience is transformed, he/she assumes the existence of an "other" against whom/which blacks struggle. In the classic tradition of Afro-Americanist criticism and theory, one dominated by male-authored and -edited texts, the oppressive "other" is a figure of white power, whether individual or institutional. Texts as diverse as Arthur P. Davis's thematic, integrationist, historical "Integration and Race Literature" and Robert B. Stepto's self-consciously de-historicized study, *From Behind the Veil: A Study of Afro-American Narrative*, thus assume the experience of racism, the economic, social, and political articulations of racial oppression.

The discourse of Afro-Americanist literary study is therefore, like Anglo-American feminist discourse, clearly oppositional in origin and impulse, arising out of a specific kind of exclusion from both mainstream culture and criticism and literary history. Yet despite the challenge they offer to the canon and its custodians, both disciplines in their early stages have replicated the totalizing impulses of the tradition they seek to undermine. Among white feminists, this impulse has taken the form of presuming that one may generalize and theorize about women's experience on the basis of the lives and works of white women from the middle class. Similarly, Afro-Americanists, mostly male, have assumed that one may theorize about the experience of blacks in a racist culture on the basis of the lives of black men alone. As the increasingly visible presence of black feminists in the academy has introduced the issue of race into feminist theory, so has it raised the subject of gender in Afro-Americanist discourse. Black feminists have interrogated and explored the ways in which the experience of race affects the experience of gender, even as they examine ways in which the culturally constructed experience of gender, specifically of womanhood, affects the experience of race.

My consideration of the changing status of gender in Afro-Americanist discourse proceeds from the assumption that gender has generally been treated as a woman's issue, something women worry about but that is beside the point for men: one that gets raised "when and where [black women] enter."[5] Although it is generally not an explicit subject in male-authored discourse, I argue that the non-sex-specific voice of the male critic may be read as male. I consider some of the ways in which contemporary black literary feminism has gendered Afro-Americanist discourse during the past decade. Finally, I suggest directions in which gender study might productively move this field of literary explorations. My argument concentrates on contributions that the issue of gender can make to Afro-Americanist discourse; however, it has implications for ways in which oppositional fields of literary study might conceive of and represent those whom it marginalizes.

II

Historically, Afro-Americanist criticism before the advent of feminism dealt with issues of gender in one of three ways: in a biographical framework permeated by sexual stereotypes of women; in assertions of male authority within the Black Arts movement; and in an ostensibly gender-blind literary history that did not give equal weight to women's texts.

Darwin Turner's *In a Minor Chord: Three Afro-American Writers and Their Search for Identity* (1971) represents a moment before feminist and other modes of literary theory had influenced Afro-Americanist criticism. In his book Turner seeks to explain the inconsistency in quality and output of three skilled writers of the Harlem Renaissance—Jean Toomer, Countee Cullen, and Zora Neale Hurston— by reading their work in relation to their lives. The difficulties of such a method have been foregrounded by developments of the past two decades, but those difficulties are complicated by the difference between the way in which he uses biography to explain Toomer's and Cullen's work on the one hand and Hurston's on the other.

A key to the differential status he accords Hurston may be found as early as his "Introduction," where he describes his writers in the following manner: "Jean Toomer, generally acknowledged to be the most artistic craftsman of those who wrote before 1950; Countee Cullen, the precocious poet laureate of the Renaissance; and Zora Neale Hurston, the most competent black female novelist before 1950."[6] By describing Hurston in terms of her gender identity, her male counterparts in terms of their craft, Turner reveals his assumption that womanhood, but not man-hood, has an impact on literary and artistic production.

Turner's Toomer and Cullen chapters are structured differently from his Hurston chapter. In the first two, he begins by establishing their literary power. He then reads the unevenness of their careers against the backdrop of changes in their biographical circumstances, but does not suggest ways in which either Cullen's or Toomer's relation to constructions of masculinity figure in their writing. One might ask today how Toomer's assumptions of male privilege could have prompted him to eschew his racial identity and constitute himself as a raceless American.

The Hurston chapter is set up quite differently from these first two. Instead of establishing her literary power, Turner opens the chapter with an extended examination of her personal eccentricities. Drawing from her autobiography and recollections of her foes and associates alike, he devotes the first third of this chapter to creating an image of Hurston as one who was indifferent to her own and other blacks' dignity, obsequious to whites, opportunistic, and politically retrograde. The bridge from the assessment of her character to the evaluation of her work is the following paragraph:

> The Zora Neale Hurston who takes shape from her autobiography and from the accounts of those who knew her is an imaginative, somewhat shallow, quick-tempered woman, desperate for recognition and reassurance to assuage her feelings of inferiority; a blind follower of that social code which approves arrogance toward one's assumed peers and inferiors but requires total psychological commitment to a subservient posture before one's supposed superiors. It is in reference to this image that one must examine her novels, her folklore, and her view of the Southern scene.(98)

The references in this passage to Hurston's intellectual insubstantiality and erratic temperament characterize her in terms of cliches about women's character and gifts. What is even more problematic about this analysis, however, is Turner's assertion that this information is necessary if one is to understand Hurston's work. His *caveat* thus confirms one's sense that in 1971, gender was an issue for women but not for men.

Turner's view of gender in terms of feminine identity affects his reading of the text for which Hurston is best known, *Their Eyes Were Watching God*. In a pivotal scene in the novel, the protagonist, Janie, speaks of her own sense of loss to her husband on his deathbed, a man who throughout their marriage has silenced her. Janie says:

> "Listen, Jody, you ain't de Jody ah run off down de road wid. You's whut's left after he died. Ah run off tuh keep house wid you in uh wonderful way. But you wasn't satisfied wid me de way Ah was. Naw! Mah own mind had tuh be squeezed and crowded out tuh make room for yours in me."
>
> "Shut up! Ah wish thunder and lightnin' would kill yuh!"
>
> "Ah know it. And now you got tuh die tuh find out dat you got tuh pacify somebody besides yo'self if you wants any love and sympathy in dis world. You ain't tried tuh pacify *nobody* but yo'self. Too busy listening tuh yo' own big voice."[7]

This exchange is read today within a feminist framework as a victory for a woman denied her right to speak for herself and in her own voice. In 1971, however, this scene of Janie's speaking out against the man who has verbally and physically abused her was read as a sign of the author's racial self-hatred. Thus Turner writes,

> Either personal insensitivity or an inability to recognize aesthetic inappro-
> priatenesses caused Miss Hurston to besmirch *Their Eyes Were Watching God*
> with one of the crudest scenes which she ever wrote . . . Never was [Jody's]
> conduct so cruel as to deserve the vindictive attack which Janie unleashes
> while he is dying. For Janie, the behavior seems grotesquely out of character.
> It is characteristic, however, of Miss Hurston's continual emphasis upon
> intraracial and intrafamilial hatred.[8]

The next phase of Afro-Americanist critical theory that emerged during the Black
Arts Movement of the late sixties and early seventies was much more overtly
masculinist. Generally understood to represent the aesthetic counterpart of the
Black Nationalist Movement, the discourse of this movement similarly enshrines
the possibilities of black male power, relegating black women to the position to
which Stokely Carmichael assigned them, "prone."

Black Aestheticians concur that black art ought to transform the lives and
consciousness of black people. Yet the supreme confidence their essays display
testifies more to male fantasies of authority than women's; hence, writing in one
of the first anthologies of the movement in 1972, Addison Gayle dismisses the
subtle achievements, the nuanced inscriptions of resistance found in the work of
a poet like Phillis Wheatley. He writes: "Oblivious of the lot of her fellow blacks,
she sang not of a separate nation, but of a Christian Eden."[9]

The sexual politics of the movement become clearer in those essays when the
black aesthetic enterprise gets articulated in terms of the recovery of black male
sexual power. As Julian Mayfield in the same anthology hints in his essay tellingly
entitled "You Touch My Black Aesthetic and I'll Touch Yours," Gayle elsewhere
links black male sexuality explicitly to the construction of an Afro-American literary
tradition, arguing that "The inability of [white liberals] to see the black man as
other than an impotent sexual force accounts for much of the negative criticism
by white writers about black literature."[10] While the celebration of black manhood
came from the political need to reclaim racial pride, like other radical movements
of the 1970s, the Black Arts movement marginalized feminist politics, as we see
in Don L. Lee's (Haki Madhubuti's) appraisal of the protagonist of one of Mari
Evans's poems:

> The woman herein recreated is not fragmented, hysterical, doesn't have sexual
> problems with her mate, doesn't feel caught up in a "liberated womanhood"
> complex/bag—which is to say she is not out to define herself (that is, from
> the position of weakness, as "the others" do) and thus will not be looked
> upon as an aberration of the twentieth-century white woman.[11]

In the pioneering work on Afro-American narrative carried out in the late 1970s,
critics did not denigrate women's texts, but often ignored them altogether, gen-
eralizing about black writing on the basis of strategies and themes found in writing
by black men. Mary Helen Washington has argued perceptively that this ostensibly
gender-blind discourse actually inscribes the masculine experience of oppression

and liberation.[12] When, for instance, Robert Stepto describes a "pregeneric myth," "the quest for freedom and literacy," that informs all black writing, he outlines a pattern more prevalent in male-authored than woman-authored texts.[13] Thus, Frederick Douglass may privilege the moment at which he acquired literacy in his *Narrative of the Life of an American Slave*, but Harriet Jacobs makes virtually no mention of how she came to learn to read and to write. Maya Angelou in *I Know Why The Caged Bird Sings* emphasizes the liberating power of her love of reading, but that gift tends to be celebrated more throughout the body of black men's narratives than in those by women.

A gender-specific analysis of black narrative might now consider the source of the male narrator/protagonist's investment in literacy, the relationship between literacy and the assertion of male power, or the specifically masculine legacy that Douglass and other male slave narrators bequeath to future Afro-American writers. Considerations of gender might also foreground the alternative legacy of a woman slave narrator such as Jacobs. A tradition set in motion by her *Incidents in the Life of a Slave Girl* would necessarily focus on more indirect, surreptitious assertions of power and suggest differences in the ways in which Afro-American men and women represent their relation to language.

III

Marginalized within Afro-Americanist literary discourse, and ignored in similar ways in Anglo-American feminist writing, the black feminist voice emerged in the late seventies with increasing insistence. In recent years, black feminists have introduced the issue of gender into the ostensibly gender-blind discourse of Afro-Americanist literary theory by responding to their own omission from the category "black."[14] Pivotal works such as Frederick Douglass's *Narrative of the Life of Frederick Douglass, an American Slave, Written by Himself*, Richard Wright's *Native Son*, and Ralph Ellison's *Invisible Man*, to name but a few, have traditionally been understood as representations of the struggles of black people under the conditions of race and class oppression. From their earliest essays, however—Barbara Smith's "Toward a Black Feminist Criticism," Deborah E. McDowell's "New Directions for Black Feminist Criticism," and Mary Helen Washington's "New Lives and New Letters: Black Women Writers at the End of the Seventies,"—black feminists have argued that classic critical and imaginative texts such as these that construct themselves and are constructed by readers as "black" might more precisely and productively be read as "black male": representations of the struggles of a black male subject against (a) white male other(s) within the context of a gender-specific ritual ground and symbolic landscape. As Washington has recently written,

> Women have worked assiduously in [the Afro-American literary] tradition as writers, as editors, sometimes, though rarely as critics, and yet every study

of Afro-American narrative, every anthology of *the* Afro-American literary tradition has set forth a model of literary paternity in which each male author vies with his predecessor for greater authenticity, greater control over *his* voice, thus fulfilling the mission his *forefathers* left unfinished.

Women in this model are sometimes granted a place as a stepdaughter who prefigures and directs us to the real heirs (like Ellison and Wright) but they do not influence and determine the direction and shape of the literary canon. [15]

The black feminist gendering of Afro-American literary discourse has taken several forms. As I have suggested, their sense of having been omitted from or marginalized within the tradition has prompted them to call attention to the masculinist assumptions of the canon and its custodians. Their bibliographical and editorial projects have expanded and diversified the body of texts taught by and written about by members of the scholarly community. [16] In critical books and essays they complicate received ideas about the contours of the Afro-American tradition by exploring suppressed rituals, conventions, and narrative strategies in the writings of black women. [17] In their most recent work they theorize the interconnections among cultural constructions of race, class, *and* gender in both the language and the ideological assumptions of black texts.

Black feminists have also gendered the discourse of Afro-Americanist theory by writing specifically as women. This self-inscription may take the form of articulating a tradition of black women writing. However self-critical, this process of tradition-building provides intellectual and political antecedents for contemporary black feminists. I have in mind here Hazel V. Carby's brilliant and subtly nuanced *Reconstructing Womanhood: The Emergence of the Black Woman Novelist*, which examines the ways in which early black women's writing shaped and was in turn shaped by contemporary ideological debates about race, womanhood, and imperialism. Her Neo-Marxist study helps to locate historically her own and her contemporaries' enterprise.

The strategies of attribution in Mary Helen Washington's critical writing (for instance, the "Introduction" to *Invented Lives*) inscribe Washington within a community of historical as well as contemporary black feminist voices. Moreover, she writes herself as a black woman by challenging the boundaries that traditionally have separated personal, political, and theoretical writing, boundaries that support a hierarchy that has always excluded black women's cultural productions. Thus she locates her project not only within the context of black women's critical and imaginative writing, but also within that of the experiences of her women relatives.

Although it currently enjoys an unprecedented florescence, black literary feminism is not only a contemporary phenomenon. In the introduction to *A Voice from the South by a Black Woman from the South* (1892), an early instance of black feminist theoretical writing, a chapter entitled "Un [sic] Raison d'Etre," Anna Julia Cooper locates the space from which she as a black woman writes. If the race problem is the central issue facing the United States after the Civil War, then as the nation seeks to work out "the colored man's inheritance and apportionment," all pertinent constituencies must speak for themselves. Yet by Cooper's estimation, the American South is, Sphinxlike, more spoken about than speaking in this debate. The black male voice is, in particular, a "muffled strain," a "jarring chord," a "vague and uncomprehended cadenza." And black women are most silent of all, "the one mute and voiceless note." She argues that whites may not speak for blacks, nor can black men, preoccupied with their own concerns, "reproduce the exact voice of the Black Woman." The essays that comprise the rest of the volume are concerned largely with defining the character—gendering—the voice of black women, to determine what they specifically may add to the ongoing analysis of American culture.

As Carby shows, Cooper, like other early black women intellectuals (including Harriet Jacobs, Frances Ellen Watkins Harper, Ida B. Wells, and others), participates in and transforms the contemporaneous debates about the status of women. Cooper begins from the prevailing assumption that men and women inhabit and dominate separate spheres. She identifies men, predictably, with the workplace outside the home, the political arena, and commerce, women with home, hearth, and the attendant responsibilities. However, that separation is for her the source of women's power. Precisely because women are the care-givers, childrearers, and teachers of manners, they occupy a more influential role in culture than do men. Black men of achievement may represent the possibility of individual accomplishment, Cooper writes, but they cannot stand for the race. Only black women, as the conduit through which the race renews itself, can say: "when and where I enter, in the quiet, undisputed dignity of my womanhood, without violence and without suing or special patronage, then and there the whole *Negro race enters with me*." Precisely because black women are for her the generative source, or "root" of the race (29), they must be nurtured and treated respectfully, for "the position of woman in society determines the vital elements of its regeneration and progress."

Cooper's analysis might at first seem retrograde, for she appears to appropriate for her own uses a cultural conception of womanhood that minimizes women's influence by relegating them to the domestic sphere. However, when read in the context of her remarks about the higher education of women, Cooper's enterprise seems rather more radical than conciliatory. If the contemporary discourse declared higher education incompatible with femininity, Cooper argues to the contrary that higher education is essential to women's fulfillment of their role. To her mind, given the centrality of black women to the future of the race, they must be educated "for the duties and responsibilities that await the intelligent wife, the Christian mother, the earnest, virtuous, helpful woman, at once the lever and the fulcrum for uplifting the race" (45).

Cooper clearly does not advocate a course specifically tailored for ladies. Rather, she believes that the standard curriculum itself might enable women to project their own talents into the world while itself undergoing a necessary transformation. She writes,

Now I claim that it is the prevalence of the Higher Education among women, the making it a common everyday affair for women to reason and think and express their thought, the training and stimulus which enable and encourage women to administer to the world the bread it needs as well as the sugar it cries for; in short it is the transmitting the potential forces of her soul into dynamic factors that has given symmetry and completeness to the world's agencies. . . .

Religion, science, art, economics, have all needed the feminine flavor; and literature, the expression of what is permanent and best in all of these may be guaged (sic) at any time to measure the strength of the feminine ingredient. You will not find theology consigning infants to lakes of unquenchable fire long after women have had a chance to grasp, master, and wield its dogmas. You will not find science annihilating personality from the government of the Universe . . . you will not find jurisprudence formulating as an axiom the absurdity that man and wife are one, and that one the man . . . in fine, you will not find the law of love shut out from the affairs of men after the feminine half of the world's truth is completed. (57–58)

As higher education is critical to the training of black women, so must the teaching of women transform black men. When women become more powerful and influential nurturers, then not only will girls become strong and self-reliant, but boys will "supplement their virility by tenderness and sensibility" as well (61). Men and women so trained will likewise have a salutary effect on culture; when black men and women alike participate in the process of analyzing and reconstructing society, true progress is possible. Only then, in an accumulative period (as Cooper designates the turn of the century) will ideologies of wealth, conquest, and leisure be counterbalanced by "the conservation of those deeper moral forces which make for the happiness of homes and the righteousness of the country" (133).

Cooper's reflections on black women's cultural position might be read as background to her chapter on literature, "The Negro as Presented in American Literature," arguably the earliest sample of black feminist literary criticism. Cooper does not here take black women writers, or even black male writers as her subject. Rather, she analyzes issues of representation as they suggest themselves in writing by white men (Albion Tourgée, George Washington Cable, and William Dean Howells, for instance) about black people. As she had earlier argued that no one group may represent another in the political sphere, in this essay she questions the ability of whites to represent blacks in literature.

The issue of gender does not figure explicitly in Cooper's analysis here the way it does in her other essays, nor does it figure as centrally as the issue of race does. However, her rhetoric and concern with representation derive from the perspective of black women as she had earlier constructed it. One might therefore say that her discourse here is gendered, that Cooper is writing as a black woman.

For contemporary readers, *A Voice from the South* is of particular importance because it anticipates many of the issues black feminists continue to engage: the elitism and racism of white feminists, the sexism of black men, the specificity of the black woman's cultural position. Its significance as a prototype is especially clear given that here Cooper defines in her own terms the status and meaning of womanhood and lays claim to that inheritance for black women.

The heightened visibility of black feminist scholarly and imaginative writers has made gender issues increasingly important to male Afro-Americanists as well. Controversial responses by Stanley Crouch, Mel Watkins, Darryl Pinckney, and others to the fiction of black women demonstrate that works which foreground women's experience of their culturally constructed gender roles in turn prompt men to write out of their own. That is to say that these woman-centered texts, installments in a largely male-centered tradition, have prompted increasing numbers of male reviewers to identify themselves with and respond from the perspective of men who consider themselves to be marginalized.

Stanley Crouch's October 1987 *New Republic* review of Toni Morrison's *Beloved* exhibits the assumptions of such writing. Crouch ostensibly takes issue with Morrison for adhering to a post-Baldwinian position which assumes the literary value of stories of martyrdom and for casting her fictions in a melodramatic prose style. To his mind, it was bad enough when black male writers based narratives on the experience of the atrocities of racism; black women only compound the problem by introducing sexism to the litany of abuses. The rhetoric of Crouch's review suggests, however, that he submerges an *ad feminam* argument beneath an apparently philosophical disagreement.

First, in his actual denunciation of the feminist content of Morrison's work, he focuses on its political incorrectness, not on the limits of transforming suffering into art. He argues that the concern with gender oppression derives from a white feminist agenda, and constitutes nothing more than a recapitulation of ideologically repressive, time-worn stereotypes of black male behavior. The problem with this position, one that recurs throughout similar pieces, is the way that it seeks to marginalize the gendered content of the work in question. He suggests all-too-eagerly that any response to sexism is derivative and diversionary, beside the point of some larger political (or in this case aesthetic) project. Because gender oppression is not his issue, it is therefore not a "real" issue. As if to substantiate this claim, he indicts Morrison for the ways in which a white feminist like Diane Johnson writes about (fetishizes?) her.

A second way in which his response here seems gendered is the fact that he uses this review as the occasion to take pot shots not only at Morrison, but also at any number of other black women writers, including Alice Walker. Of Walker he writes:

> Writers like Alice Walker revealed little more than their own inclination to melodrama, militant self-pity, guilt-mongering, and pretensions to mystic wisdom. What the Walkers really achieved was a position parallel to the one held by Uncle Remus in *Song of the South:* the ex-slave supplies the white children and the white adults with insights into human nature and the complexity of the world through the tales of Brer Rabbit. Better, these black

women writers took over the role played by the black maids in so many old films: when poor little white missy is at a loss, she is given guidance by an Aunt Jemima lookalike.[18]

Finally, the rhetoric of his conclusion reveals the place of gender in his literary hierarchy, for he writes that Morrison lacks the "passion" and the "courage" to render slavery in a way that confronts "the ambiguities of the human soul, which transcend race." Had she this "courage," this "passion," he writes, her work "might stand next to, or outdistance, Ernest Gaines's *The Autobiography of Miss Jane Pittman* and Charles Johnson's *Oxherding Tale*." This formulation clearly constructs the literary marketplace in the terms of a competition between the sexes for turf.[19]

IV

Thankfully, the scholarly discourse authored by male Afro-Americanists has begun to address the relationship between issues of race and gender more productively. Recent work by critic/theorists such as Melvin Dixon, Houston A. Baker, Henry Louis Gates, and Richard Yarborough exemplifies new directions that gender study in Afro-Americanist discourse might take.[20] For instance, in a *New York Times* review of Washington's *Invented Lives*, Gates posits compellingly the contours of a black feminist tradition. Governed by neither Bloom's anxiety of influence nor Gilbert and Gubar's feminist response to it, an anxiety of authorship, this tradition, Gates argues, reveals its own specific characteristics. First, he notes, it is unique in generating virulent attacks by other blacks. Second, it is not especially self-promoting. Third and most importantly, he writes:

> [Black] female authors claim other black women as their ancestors (such as Zora Neale Hurston and Ann Petry) whereas most older black male writers denied any black influence at all—or worse, eagerly claimed a white paternity. No, the writers in this movement have been intent upon bonding with other women. And the "patricide" that characterized Mr. Baldwin's and Mr. Ellison's declarations of independence from Richard Wright has no counterpart in matricide. Indeed, Toni Morrison's generous stewardship has served as the model for bonding and the creation of a literary sisterhood that seems to take for granted that good writing will find a publisher. Gone forever is the notion that only one black writer can emerge from the group, in splendid commercial isolation, as "the" black writer of the decade.[21]

As Gates so trenchantly describes the status of women's gender in the construction of literary tradition, Baker analyzes the place of male gender in the construction of Afro-American critical tradition. In his essay, "Discovering America: Generational Shifts, Afro-American Literary Criticism, and the Study of Expressive Culture,"[22] Baker analyzes changes in the assumptions of Afro-American literary critical and theoretical writing during the past four decades. The movement he charts, from Integrationist Poetics through Black Aesthetics to Reconstructionism, productively suggests ways in which each stage in the development of the theory refutes its predecessor and "[establishes] a new framework for intellectual inquiry" (67). What is of particular value, however, is the implicit narrative that links each stage to the next, and suggests that the dynamics of the male acquisition of power actually inform the critical position of each generation.

In the highly allusive extended epigraph to this essay, Baker casts the connection of black expressive culture to literary criticism and theory in terms of the perennial battle between fathers and sons. Anxiety about paternity, he writes, occasions integrationist attempts to assert themselves into a legitimating relation with the white male structure of power: "the players are always founding (white) fathers, or black men who believe there are only a few more chords to be unnot(ted) [sic] before Afro-American paternity is secure" (65).

Baker illustrates this premise first by showing that Integrationists such as Arthur P. Davis and Richard Wright believe in a notion of American pluralism and thus anticipate a time when Afro-American literature will lose its specificity and be subsumed into a larger, "classless, raceless" Western literature. He then argues that the Black Aestheticians of the late sixties and early seventies "[invert] the literary-critical optimism and axiology" of the previous generation (73). Amiri Baraka (LeRoi Jones), Larry Neal, Stephen Henderson, and others argue in contrast to the Integrationists that by imitating the strategies and techniques of mainstream white literature, Afro-American writers have diverted the genuine emotional referents and authentic experiential categories of Afro-American life. They therefore support the notion of a "sui generis tradition of Afro-American art and a unique 'standard of criticism' suitable for analyzing it" (74).

The late seventies and early eighties saw the rise of the Reconstructionists, scholars who sought to employ insights and analytical methods acquired from contemporary literary-theoretical discourse in the pedagogy and study of Afro-American literature. Baker argues that as the Aestheticians rewrote the Integrationists, the Reconstructionists refuted the Aestheticians, valorizing the idea of America—which he calls AMERICA—in a manner unlike the Integrationists' position. As he demonstrates, "[the Reconstructionists'] goal was not to help actualize AMERICA by conceding cultural identity. Instead, they assumed that cultural identity was not at issue, suggesting that an advanced, theoretical vocabulary for the study of human expression was both transcultural and constitutive" (89).

Baker's reading of Afro-American literary history is of particular value precisely because it problematizes that history in fresh ways. Black feminists have demythologized the tradition by calling attention to the kinds of assumptions that have excluded black women's writing; they argue by implication that the failure to comprehend women's experience has prevented male Afro-Americanists from recognizing the forms of women's oppression and expression. Baker de-mythologizes that tradition from a different, albeit gender-based direction; he suggests that the critics' experience of masculinity, as much as their response to social and political change, has affected the way they read the work of earlier critics. What is needed now, I would argue, is some discussion of how the male Afro-Americanists' experiences of their relation to power, and to the rise of feminism, has affected their responses, respectively, to each other and to black women in the profession.

V

As Afro-Americanist discourse has exposed the absences in the work of mainstream critics, questions of gender have forced the Afro-Americanist tradition to be increasingly self-evaluative and self-critical. Not at all diversionary, these explorations rather complicate the field, for they enable considerations of the various ways in which people of color, male and female alike, experience the conditions of oppression. Indeed, further elaborations upon the relationship between gender, race, and class, hold great promise for enriching the discipline. Textually grounded future work needs to be done, for instance, on the way constructions of masculinity affect the experience of race, and the way that connection is represented in literature. Afro-Americanists might also expand upon Baker's work and consider the relationship of gender to the dynamic among critics from which black literary history derives and out of which black intellectual history develops.

Insofar as considerations of gender, like those of race and class, are grounded simultaneously in personal and intellectual experience, further explorations of gender issues might prompt Afro-Americanists to reflect upon the politics of our position as black men and black women in the academy. At a time when being black and/or working on questions of race and gender have a certain marketability, it would be useful to consider the effect of our commodification on our work and on our relations to each other. Black male critics and theorists might explore the nature of the contradictions that arise when they undertake black feminist projects. And perhaps most importantly, black feminists ourselves must name openly the conflicts that inhere in our position as critics and theorists in an area of literary study traditionally dominated by males and whites.

Notes

1. The critics and theorists currently engaged in this project include Abena Busia, Hazel V. Carby, Barbara Christian, Frances Smith Foster, Mae Henderson, Gloria Hull, Deborah McDowell, Nellie Y. McKay, Hortense Spillers, Claudia Tate, Cheryl Wall, Mary Helen Washington, and Gloria Watkins (bell hooks).

2. Hazel V. Carby, *Reconstructing Womanhood: The Emergence of the Afro-American Woman Novelist* (New York: Oxford University Press, 1987), p. 9.

3. I wish to thank Marianne Hirsch, Victoria Kahn, Sally Shuttleworth, Elaine Showalter, and Robert Stepto for their suggestions and advice.

4.   My thoughts about the relation between what we write and our place within institutions have been influenced by the following texts: Elly Bulkin, Minnie Bruce Pratt, and Barbara Smith, *Yours in Struggle: Three Feminist Perspectives on Anti-Semitism and Racism* (Brooklyn, NY: Long Haul Press, 1984); Teresa de Lauretis, *Technologies of Gender: Essays on Theory, Film, and Fiction* (Bloomington: Indiana University Press, 1987); Biddy Martin and Chandra Talpade Mohanty, "Feminist Politics: What's Home Got to Do With It?" and Nancy K. Miller, "Changing the Subject: Authorship, Writing, and the Reader," in Teresa de Lauretis, ed., *Feminist Studies/Critical Studies* (Bloomington: Indiana University Press, 1986), pp. 191–212 and 102–120 respectively; and Adrienne Rich, *Blood, Bread, and Poetry: Selected Prose 1979–1985*.

5.   Anna Julia Cooper, *A Voice from the South by a Black Woman of the South* (Xenia, Ohio: The Aldine Printing House, 1892), p. 31.

6.   Darwin T. Turner, *In A Minor Chord: Three Afro-American Writers and Their Search for Identity* (Carbondale and Edwardsville: Southern Illinois University Press, 1971), p. xix.

7.   Zora Neale Hurston, *Their Eyes Were Watching God* (1937) (Urbana: University of Illinois Press, 1978), p. 133.

8.   Turner, *In A Minor Chord*, p. 108.

9.   Addison Gayle, Jr., "The Function of Black Literature at the Present Time," in Gayle, ed., *The Black Aesthetic* (Garden City, NY: Anchor Books, 1972), p. 384.

10.   See Gayle, "Introduction" to *The Black Aesthetic*, p. xx, and Julian Mayfield, "You Touch My Black Aesthetic and I'll Touch Yours," in *The Black Aesthetic*, p. 25.

11.   Don L. Lee (Haki Madhubuti), "Toward a Definition: Black Poetry of the Sixties (After Leroi Jones)," in *The Black Aesthetic*, p. 227.

12.   See her essay, " 'The Darkened Eye Restored': Notes Toward a Literary History of Black Women," in Mary Helen Washington, ed., *Invented Lives: Narratives of Black Women 1860–1960* (Garden City, NY: Doubleday, 1987), pp. xv–xxxi.

13.   See Robert B. Stepto, *From Behind the Veil: A Study of Afro-American Narrative* (Urbana: University of Illinois Press, 1979).

14.   Of course, black feminists have called attention to the racist and classist assumptions of white feminist discourse as well, but for my purposes here I wish to focus on their impact on Afro-Americanist theory.

15.   Mary Helen Washington, " 'The Darkened Eye Restored,' " pp. xviii–xix.

16.   See, for instance, the reprints series which McDowell edits for Beacon Press and her Rutgers University Press reprint of Nella Larsen's *Quicksand* and *Passing*; Washington's three anthologies, *Black-Eyed Susans*, *Midnight Birds*, and *Invented Lives* and her Feminist Press edition of Paule Marshall's *Brown Girl, Brownstones*; Nellie McKay's edition of Louise Meriwether's *Daddy Was a Number Runner*; and Gloria T. Hull's edition of Alice Dunbar-Nelson's letters, *Give Us Each Day*, to name but a few. Black women are not exclusively responsible for these kinds of editorial projects. See also, William Andrews, *Sisters of the Spirit: Three Black Women's Autobiographies of the Nineteenth Century*; Henry Louis Gates's edition of Harriet E. Wilson's *Our Nig* and his Oxford University Press reprints series; and Jean Fagan Yellin's edition of Harriet Jacobs's *Incidents in the Life of a Slave Girl*.

17.   See, for instance, Barbara Christian, *Black Women Novelists: The Development of a Tradition, 1892–1976* (Westport, CT: Greenwood, 1980); Gloria T. Hull, *Color, Sex, and Poetry: Three Women Writers of The Harlem Renaissance* (Bloomington: Indiana University Press, 1987); Deborah E. McDowell, " 'The Changing Same': Generational Connections and Black Women Novelists," *New Literary History*, 18 (Winter 1987), 281–302;

and Hortense Spillers, "A Hateful Passion, a Lost Love," *Feminist Studies*, 9 (1983), 293–323.

18.   Stanley Crouch, "Aunt Medea," a review of *Beloved* by Toni Morrison, *The New Republic*, October 19, 1987, p. 39.

19.   Deborah McDowell discusses the implications of this brand of black feminist-baiting thoroughly and subtly in her essay "Reading Family Matters" in the forthcoming collection *Changing Our Own Words*, ed. Cheryl Wall (New Brunswick, NJ: Rutgers University Press, 1989).

20.   In addition to the Baker and Gates cited below, I refer as well to Melvin Dixon, *Ride Out the Wilderness: Geography and Identity in Afro-American Literature* (Urbana: University of Illinois Press, 1987) and Richard Yarborough, *Ideology and Black Characterization in the Early Afro-American Novel* (New York: Columbia University Press, forthcoming).

21.   Henry Louis Gates, Jr., "Reclaiming Their Tradition," review of *Invented Lives*, ed. Mary Helen Washington, *The New York Times Book Review*, pp. 3, 34–35.

22.   Houston A. Baker, Jr., "Discovering America: Generational Shifts, Afro-American Literary Criticism, and the Study of Expressive Culture," in *Blues, Ideology, and Afro-American Literature: A Vernacular Theory* (Chicago: University of Chicago Press, 1984).

READING GENDER

5

Creativity and the Childbirth Metaphor: Gender Difference in Literary Discourse

Susan Stanford Friedman

> Thus, great with child to speak, and helpless in my throes,
> Biting my trewand pen, beating myself for spite,
> "Fool," said my muse to me, "look in thy heart and write."
> Philip Sidney (1591)

> The poet is in labor. She has been told that it will not hurt but it has
> hurt so much that pain and struggle seem, just now, the only reality.
> But at the very moment when she feels she will die, or that she is
> already in hell, she hears the doctor saying, "Those are the shoulders
> you are feeling now"—and she knows the head is out then, and the
> child is pushing and sliding out of her, insistent, a poem.
> Denise Levertov (1967)

The childbirth metaphor has yoked artistic creativity and human procreativity for centuries in writers as disparate as Philip Sidney and Erica Jong, William Shakespeare and Mary Shelley, Alexander Pope and Denise Levertov. Men as well as women have used the metaphor extensively, taking female anatomy as a model for human creativity in sharp contrast with the equally common phallic analogy, which uses male anatomy for its paradigm.[1] As Sandra Gilbert and Susan Gubar have shown, the association of the pen and paintbrush with the phallus in metaphors of creativity has resulted in an "anxiety of authorship" for aspiring women writers: to wield a pen is a masculine act that puts the woman writer at war with her body and her culture.[2] In contrast to the phallic analogy that implicitly excludes women from creativity, the childbirth metaphor validates women's artistic effort by unifying their mental and physical labor into (pro)creativity.

The childbirth metaphor is a controversial one that has been both celebrated and rejected by contemporary feminist theorists, critics, and writers. On the one hand, French theorists who promote the concept of *l'écriture féminine* insist on a poetic of the female body. As Hélène Cixous writes, "women must write through their bodies." Women, "never far from 'mother,' " write "in white ink." Using the birth metaphor itself, Cixous describes "the gestation drive" as "just like the desire to write: a desire to live self from within, a desire for a swollen belly, for language, for blood."[3] Similarly, American poet Stephanie Mines seeks "a language structured like my body," and Sharon Olds describes both the birth of her child and her poem as "this giving birth, this glistening verb" in a "language of blood."[4] On the other hand, many feminists oppose modes of thought they consider biologically deterministic, essentialist, and regressive. Mary Ellmann's witty critique of all analogical thinking based on the body, whether phallic or ovarian, anticipates the more recent concerns of others.[5] Simone de Beauvoir warns that this concept of writing from the body establishes a "counter-penis," and Elaine Showalter and Nina Auerbach fear that it represents the development of a regressive biologism. Showalter asks "if to write is metaphorically to give birth, from what organ can males generate texts?" "Anatomy is textuality" within a biological paradigm, Showalter argues. Biological analogies ultimately exclude one sex from the creative process, and in a patriarchal society it is women's creativity that is marginalized. Ann Rosalind Jones further suggests that the concept of *l'écriture féminine* posits an essential female sexuality that lies outside culture, an ahistorical assumption that particularly ignores the differences among women across cultures and through time. Poet Erica Jong states flatly that the comparison of "human gestation to human creativity" is "thoroughly inexact."[6]

Without attempting to resolve this debate, this essay will contribute to it by examining the ways in which women and men have encoded different concepts of creativity and procreativity into the metaphor itself. Highlighting how, in Elizabeth Abel's words, "gender informs and complicates both the writing and the reading of texts," the childbirth metaphor provides a concrete instance of genuine gender difference in literary discourse as constituted both by the readers and the writers of a given text.[7] I will explore three aspects of the childbirth metaphor: first, the cultural resonance of the childbirth metaphor; second, gender difference in the metaphor's meaning as constructed in the process of *reading;* and third, gender difference as reflected in the process of *writing*. Examination of these aspects will reveal that women writers have often risked the metaphor's dangerous biologism in order to challenge fundamental binary oppositions of patriarchal ideology between word and flesh, creativity and procreativity, mind and body. Cixous's utopian call for women's writing from the body may lament that "with a few rare exceptions, there has not yet been any writing that inscribes feminity."[8] But women's use of the childbirth metaphor demonstrates not only a "marked" discourse distinct from phallogocentric male use of the same metaphor but also a subversive inscription of women's (pro)creativity that has existed for centuries.

Cultural Resonance of the Childbirth Metaphor

Contextual reverberations of the childbirth metaphor ensure that it can never be "dead," merely what Max Black calls "an expression that no longer has a pregnant metaphorical use."[9] The childbirth metaphor has always been "pregnant" with resonance because childbirth itself is not neutral in literary discourse. Whether it appears as subject or vehicle of expression, childbirth has never achieved what Roland Barthes calls "writing degree zero," the language of "innocence," "freed from responsibility in relation to all possible context."[10] The context of the childbirth metaphor is the institution of motherhood in the culture at large. Consequently, the meaning of the childbirth metaphor is overdetermined by psychological and ideological resonances evoked by, but independent of, the text. No doubt, there is variation in the intensity and kind of conscious and unconscious charge that any reader or writer brings to the metaphor. But because it relies on an event fundamental to the organization of culture and psyche, the birth metaphor remains "pregnant" with significance.

The paradox of the childbirth metaphor is that its contextual resonance is fundamentally at odds with the very comparison it makes. While the metaphor draws together mind and body, word and womb, it also evokes the sexual division of labor upon which Western patriarchy is founded. The vehicle of the metaphor (procreation) acts in opposition to the tenor it serves (creation) because it inevitably reminds the reader of the historical realities that contradict the comparison being made. Facing constant challenges to their creativity, women writers often find their dilemma expressed in terms of the opposition between books and babies. Ellen Glasgow, for example, recalled the advice of a literary man: "The best advise I can give you is to stop writing and go back to the South and have some babies. The greatest woman is not the woman who has written the finest book, but the woman who has had the finest babies."[11] Male paternity of texts has not precluded their paternity of children. But for both material and ideological reasons, maternity and creativity have appeared to be mutually exclusive to women writers.[12]

The historical separation evoked by the childbirth metaphor is so entangled with the language of creation and procreation that the metaphor's very words establish their own linguistic reverberation. Words about the production of babies and books abound with puns, common etymologies, and echoing sounds that simultaneously yoke and separate creativity and procreativity. This wordplay reveals not only currents of unconscious thought as Sigmund Freud has described but also the structures of patriarchy that have divided *labor* into men's *production* and women's *reproduction*. Underlying these words is the familiar dualism of mind and body, a key component of Western patriarchal ideology. *Creation* is the act of the mind that brings something new into existence. *Procreation* is the act of the body that reproduces the species. A man *conceives* an idea in his brain, while a woman *conceives* a baby in her womb, a difference highlighted by the post-industrial designation of the public sphere as man's domain and the private sphere as woman's place. The *pregnant* body is necessarily female; the *pregnant* mind is the mental province of genius, most frequently understood to be inherently masculine.[13] *Confinement* of men suggests imprisonment—indignities to, not the fulfillment of manhood. *Delivery* from confinement suggests the restoration of men's autonomy, not its death. *Confinement* of women, in contrast, alludes to the final stages of pregnancy before *delivery* into the bonds of maternity, the very joy of which has suppressed their individuality in patriarchy.

These linguistically inscribed separations echo religious ones, which in turn resonate through the childbirth metaphor. God's punishment of Adam and Eve in Genesis has provided divine authority for the sexual division of labor. Adam's *labor* is to produce the goods of society by the "sweat of his brow," an idiom that collapses man's muscular and mental work. Eve's *labor* is to reproduce the species in pain and subservience to Adam. More importantly, the Christian tradition built on the masculine monotheism of Judaism by appropriating the power of the Word for a masculine deity and his son. In the worship of ancient near-Eastern goddesses such as Inanna, Isis, and Demeter, woman's physical capacity to give birth served as the paradigm of all origins. But where God the Father supplanted the Goddess as Mother, the mind became the symbolic womb of the universe. According to the gospel of John, "In the beginning was the Word, and the Word was with God, and the Word was God. The same was in the beginning with God. All things were made by Him; and without Him was not any thing made that was made." The power of the Word became the paradigm of male creativity, indeed the foundation of Western patriarchal ideology.[14]

This masculine appropriation of the creative Word attempts to reduce women to the processes of their body. As Friedrich Nietzche's Zarathustra pronounces: "Everything concerning woman is a puzzle, and everything concerning woman has one solution: it is named pregnancy."[15] This "solution" projects the concept of woman as a being without thought, without speech, in the creation of culture. Before the discovery of the ovum, woman's womb was represented as the mere material vessel into which man dropped his divine seed. But even after women's active part in conception became understood, cultural representations of woman based in the mind-body split continued to separate the creation of man's mind from the procreation of woman's body. According to patriarchal definition, de Beauvoir writes, woman "has ovaries, a uterus; these peculiarities imprison her in her subjectivity, circumscribe her within the limits of her own nature. It is often said that she thinks with her glands."[16] Julia Kristeva argues that phallogocentric hegemony makes woman "a specialist in the unconscious, a witch, a bacchanalian. . . . *A marginal speech*, with . . . regard to science, religion, and philosophy of the *polis* (witch, child, underdeveloped, not even a poet, at best a poet's accomplice). *A pregnancy*."[17]

The linguistic, religious, and historical resonance of the childbirth metaphor contradicts the fundamental comparison the metaphor makes. Although its basic analogy validates women's participation in literary creativity, its contextual reference calls that participation into question. Because contextual resonance comes alive in a given text through the agency of the reader, the reader has a key role to play in the constitution of the metaphor's meaning.

Gender Difference: Reading the Childbirth Metaphor

Reader response theories emphasize the role of the reader to the construction of meaning in any text.[18] Situated differently in relationship to the issue of motherhood, female and male readers are most likely to hear the contextual resonance of the childbirth metaphor from their gendered perspectives. But I would like to focus on the presence of "the reader in the text" as it is established by the specific nature of metaphor. Contradiction is inherent in metaphor, which presents "an insight into likeness" seen "in spite of, and through, the different."[19] The interaction of a metaphor's component parts—that is, the similar and the dissimilar—requires a reader to complete the process of reconciliation. Paradoxically, a literal falsehood becomes a figurative truth in the mind of the reader. The reader "conceives" the new truth by seeing the dynamic interaction between contradictory elements that move toward resolution. Karsten Harries identifies this interaction as a "semantic collision" that leads to "semantic collusion" as the reader becomes aware of the grounds of comparison.[20] Paul Ricoeur describes this process as a "transition from literal incongruence to metaphorical congruence," that nonetheless retains a "split reference." From this "semantic clash" a new meaning emerges, but it continues to evoke the "previous incompatibility and the new compatibility."[21] For Paul de Man, this clash represents the inherently subversive nature of metaphor, which disrupts the logical discourse of the rational mind.[22] Metaphor's dependence on the reader for an awareness of contradiction and resolution represents a linguistic "cultivation of intimacy," according to Ted Cohen. Like a joke, a metaphor presents a puzzle to the reader, one which results in a "sense of close community" and "shared awareness" once it has been resolved.[23]

Levertov's extended narrative metaphor (see epigraph), which invites the reader to feel the exultant pain of giving birth to a poem, provides a good example for the role of the reader in the creation of meaning. The tension that gives this metaphor its potency is built upon the reader's awareness of both "incompatibility" and "compatibility." The first collision that the reader must overcome is the metaphor's literal falsehood: the equation of poem and baby. The poet's extreme effort to birth the head, the momentary hesitation at the baby's shoulders, and the final insistence of delivery are details so precisely tied to the last moments of childbirth that they heighten the dissimilarity of creativities at the same time that they intensify the comparison. The second collision exists specifically in the reader's mind as a result of the metaphor's historical resonance. Levertov's metaphor defies the cultural separation of creation and procreation by joining the functions and feelings of mind and body. To move this collision toward collusion, the reader must follow Levertov's subversion of historical forces.

The reader's sex and perspective on childbirth no doubt affect the resolution of Levertov's metaphor, a variation that I will not address in this essay. Instead, the gender difference in the reading of the metaphor that I will explore is the alteration of meaning that results from the reader's awareness of the sex of the metaphor's author. We seldom read any text without knowledge of the author's sex. The title page itself initiates a series of expectations that influence our reading throughout, expectations intensified by the overdetermined childbirth metaphor. The reader's knowledge that Levertov is a woman, potentially a mother, "informs and compli- cates" the reading of her metaphor. This knowledge changes the interaction process of the metaphor—its incongruity, its movement toward congruity, and its implied "community" of author and reader. Change the pronoun to "he" and the reader's construction of meaning would alter profoundly: "The poet is in labor. He has been told that it will not hurt but it has hurt so much. . . . The child is pushing out of him, insistent, a poem." This change introduces a new collision, one present to some degree in *all* metaphors featuring a parturient father. Confined to "headbirths," men *cannot* literally conceive and birth babies.[24] The reader's awareness of this biological collision contributes to a perpetual tension in the metaphor, one that threatens to overwhelm the movement toward resolution.

Levertov herself appears to have been sensitive to the impact of gender on the reader's completion of the metaphor's meaning. Immediately following her metaphor of the mother-poet is a metaphor of a father-poet who must watch from a distance the birth of the poem he begat. Levertov deliberately avoids making the two metaphors precisely parallel: "The poet is a father. Into the air, into the fictional landscape of the delivery room, wholly man-made. . . . emerges . . . the remote consequence of a dream of his, acted out nine months before, the rhythm that became words."[25] Levertov's refusal to envision male creation of a poem in the concrete terms of female physiological delivery underlines the significance of the actor's biological capacity to the reading of the metaphor. Her evocative description of the impersonal, scrubbed delivery rooms of the fifties and sixties heightens the reader's awareness of historical context. The similar, yet dissimilar analogies further clarify the multilayered complexities of reading the birth metaphor. As a woman writer, Levertov has used the birth metaphor to describe both a female and a male act of creativity. In reading these metaphors, we are not only aware of her perspective as a woman, but also of how the shift in the actor's biological sex subtly alters the dynamics and meaning of the metaphor.

By focusing on the reader's awareness of the author's (or actor's) sex, we can pinpoint the gender difference in male- and female-authored metaphors. A male childbirth metaphor has three collisions for the reader to overcome: the literally false equation of books and babies, the biological impossibility of men birthing both books and babies, and the cultural separation of creation and procreation. These collisions do more than provide effective tension for the metaphor. The metaphor's incongruity overshadows congruity; collision drowns out collusion. The methaphor's tenor (creativity) and vehicle (procreativity) are kept perpetually dis- tinct. More than an interaction of sameness and difference, the male metaphor is an analogy at war with itself. History and biology combine to make it a form of literary *couvade*, male appropriation of procreative labor to which women have been confined. Man's womblike mind and phallic pen are undeniably contrasting images of creativity, but underlying both metaphors are resonating allusions to a brotherhood of artists. The "close community" to which Cohen refers is established through a "shared awareness" of male birthright and female confinement.

The impact on the reader of these heightened collisions in the male childbirth metaphor is evident in an eighteenth-century mock-heroic conceit about a self-indulgent poet: "He produced a couplet. When our friend is delivered of a couplet, with infinite labour, and pain, he takes to his bed, has straw laid down, the knocker tied up, and expects his friends to call and make inquiries."[26] The irony of this extended metaphor depends upon the reader's continuing awareness of the comparison's biological impossibility. The speaker, Reverend Sidney Smith, maintains the separation of tenor and vehicle in order to diminish the poet *manqué* for acting ridiculously like what he is not and could never be—a postpartum mother. Fusion of creation and procreation in the mind of the reader would destroy the metaphor's humor.

The way in which cultural as well as biological resonances intensify the contradictory core of the male birth metaphor is evident in James Joyce's more recent variations of the analogy in his letters and *Ulysses*. In a letter to his wife Nora on 21 August 1912, Joyce writes: "I went then into the backroom of the office and sitting at the table, thinking of the book I have written, the child which I have carried for years and years in the womb of the imagination as you carried in your womb the children you love, and of how I had fed it day after day out of my brain and my memory."[27] Joyce's metaphor compares his mental production with Nora's pregnancies, an analogy that draws together the labor of women and men. But at the same time, Joyce evokes the distinction between the mind and the body, between his wife's procreativity and his own creativity. His comparison replicates the sexual division of labor and reinforces the mind-body split permeating the patristic tradition that influenced his own Jesuit background. Joyce carried his childbirth metaphor to elaborate lengths in the planning and execution of "Oxen in the Sun," the episode in *Ulysses* in which Bloom visits the lying-in hospital where Mrs. Purefoy has been in labor for three days. As the tired woman labors to birth a baby, the exhausted narrator moves through the gestation of literary style from the earliest English alliterative poetics up to the "frightful jumble" of modern dialects. Mind and body, word and deed, man and woman, are simultaneously drawn together in analogy but separated irrevocably in function. Joyce's extensive plans for the chapter highlight this continuing separation. He charted the gestation of styles according to the nine months of pregnancy and assigned to each style images and motifs appropriate to the corresponding stages of fetal development. Like Nora, Mrs. Purefoy is delivered of a baby. Like Joyce himself, the narrator is delivered of the Word. The fact that Joyce partly envies the fecundity of female flesh and despairs at the sterility of male minds does not alter the fundamental sexual dualism of his complex birth metaphors: Joyce's women produce infants through the channel of flesh, while his men produce a brainchild through the agency of language.[28]

Paradoxically, the childbirth metaphor that reinforces the separation of creation and procreation in a male text becomes its own opposite in a female text. Instead of contributing to the reification of Western culture, the female metaphor expresses a fundamental rebellion against it. It represents a defiance of historical realities and a symbolic reunion of mind and body, creation and procreation. The female metaphor establishes a matrix of creativities based on woman's double-birthing potential. As Amy Lowell asks in "The Sisters," her poem about the female poetic tradition: "Why are we/ Already mother-creatures, double bearing/With matrices in body and brain?"[29] Within the matrices of body and brain, *both* creation and procreation become multifaceted events—physical and mental, rational and emotional, conscious and unconscious, public and private, personal and political.

The different meaning of the female childbirth metaphor results from the way the reader alters the interaction of incongruity and congruity in a woman's analogy. The metaphor's literal falsehood remains the same as it does in a male comparison. Babies are never books. But the reader's awareness that the metaphor features a woman changes how the biological and historical resonances work. First, the reader knows that the author has the biological capacity men lack to birth both books and babies. Second, the reader recognizes that the author's analogy defies the cultural prescription of separated creativities. The metaphor's historical resonance does not emphasize the division of creativity and procreativity, as it does in a male text. Rather, it makes the reader aware that the woman's reclamation of the pregnant Word is itself a transcendence of historical prescription, one that perfectly conjoins form and content. Consequently, the woman's authorship of the birth metaphor enhances the metaphor's movement toward a reconciliation of contradictory parts. The intensification of collusion and congruity in the female metaphor allows the tenor and vehicle to mingle and fuse, while the same elements in the male metaphor remain irrevocably distinct. This resolution, which relies on the reader's awareness of the author's sex, not only completes the metaphor but more fundamentally affirms woman's special access to creativity. In so doing, the woman's metaphor is genuinely subversive or "disruptive."[30] Rather than covertly excluding women from the community of artists as the male metaphor does, the woman's birth metaphor suggests that her procreative powers make her specially suited to her creative labors. God the Father is no longer the implicit model of creativity. Instead, the Goddess as Mother provides the paradigm for the (re)production of woman's speech.

A seventeenth-century poem by Katherine Philips, well-known in her day as "The Matchless Orinda," illustrates how the poet's double-birthing potential reduces the childbirth metaphor's collision and moves its contradiction swiftly toward resolution. The poem is an elegy for her infant who died just forty days after birth.

Tears are my Muse and sorrow all my art,
So piercing groans must be thy elegy.
. . . .
An off'ring too for thy sad tomb I have,
Too just a tribute to thy early hearse,
Receive these gasping numbers to thy grave,
The last of thy unhappy mother's verse.[31]

Elegies conventionally move from the poet's grief to a consolation based on immortality achieved through art. Orinda's "tribute" to her baby is no exception. What makes her elegy different is the presence of the childbirth metaphor to affirm this immortality. The "piercing groans" of grief that produce the elegy recall the pain of childbirth. The poet's "gasping" labor with her verse, motivated by a new mother's grief, echoes her own labor in delivery forty days ago. Both labors result in a poem that (re)births her son in the permanent domain of literature. Tenor and vehicle reverberate back and forth, each describing the experience of the other in a poem whose subject is simultaneously the pains of creativity and procreativity saddened by death. The reader's awareness of Orinda's biological and artistic motherhood makes this fusion of creation and procreation into (pro)creation possible.

Anne Bradstreet's poem, "The Author to Her Book," not only demonstrates the significance of biology, but it also illustrates how the reader's knowledge of female authorship changes the metaphor's historical resonance. Bradstreet's poem, found among her papers after her death, served as the preface to the posthumous second edition of her poems. Her brother-in-law had published the first edition without her knowledge. In a prefatory poem, he called the anonymous volume her "infant" and imagined how she would "complain 't is too unkind/ To force a woman's birth, provoke her pain,/ Expose her labors to the world's disdain."[32] Like Orinda's birth metaphor, his comparison depends heavily on Bradstreet's biological maternity. Bradstreet answers and extends this childbirth metaphor for the entire twenty-five lines of the poem, addressing her book as "Thou ill-formed offspring of my feeble brain,/ Who after birth didst by my side remain/ Till snatched from thence by friends, less wise than true."[33] The self-deprecation of her metaphor may reflect the insecurity of the woman writer in the public domain of letters. But it also exhibits an entirely conventional modesty characteristic of seventeenth-century male tropes which frequently beg mercy from the critics for their brainchilds.[34]

What makes Bradstreet's metaphor different from the birth metaphors of her time is the reader's awareness that her analogy defies the cultural prescription to procreativity. Like the male metaphor, her comparison of motherhood and authorship reminds the reader of their historical separation. But unlike the male metaphor, her analogy subverts that contextual resonance instead of reinforcing it. This defiance of history strengthens the comparison and promotes the resolution toward which all metaphors move. Where Joyce's tenor and vehicle remain distinct in "Oxen in the Sun," Bradstreet's metaphor unites motherhood and authorship into a new whole. Tenor and vehicle become indistinguishable as the poem becomes a definition of mothering children as well as books. Pride and modesty, joy and irritation, love and hate, represent the feelings she has as both mother and author toward the intertwined labors that fill her with ambivalence:

> At thy return my blushing was not small,
> My rambling brat (in print) should mother call,
> I cast thee by as one unfit for light,
> Thy visage was so irksome in my sight;
> Yet being mine own, at length affection would
> Thy blemishes amend, if so I could:
> I washed thy face, but more defects I saw,
> And rubbing off a spot still made a flaw.
> I stretched thy joints to make thee even feet,
> Yet still thou run'st more hobbling than is meet;
> In better dress to trim thee was my mind,
> But nought save homespun cloth i'th'house I find.
> In this array 'mongst vulgars may'st thou roam.
> In critic's hands beware thou dost not come . . .[35]

The role of the reader in completing the birth metaphors of Reverend Smith and Philips, Joyce and Bradstreet, is crucial, so important, in fact, that it suggests a possible methodology for the broader attempt to identify gender difference or a feminine aesthetic in literary discourse or the visual arts. Such attempts usually posit gendered qualities independent of the reader residing in a given text's words, images, style, or technique. Virginia Woolf, for example, describes a feminine sentence, and Judy Chicago identifies circular forms in the visual arts as female imagery.[36] However useful in identifying gender-related tendencies, this approach is often imprecise at best and implicitly prescriptive at worst. Attempts to identify the sex of a writer or an artist without external clues often fail. Exceptions for either sex are problematic. How, for example, should we describe a male painter who uses core imagery or a woman who favors pointed shapes? The terms "feminine" and "masculine" as descriptions of qualities inherent in the image suggest that the man who uses "feminine" imagery and the woman who uses "masculine" imagery are not painting "through the body."

The case of the childbirth metaphor highlights such theoretical and methodological problems and illustrates the usefulness of a reader response approach to the identification of gender difference.[37] The distinction between female and male discourse lies not in the metaphor itself but rather in the way its final meaning is constituted in the process of reading. Without external contexts, it is often impossible to identify the sex of an author using a childbirth metaphor, especially because male use has been at least as common as female use. Take, for example, the extended metaphor of nineteenth-century writer:

> To pass from conception to execution, to produce, to bring the idea to birth, to raise the child laboriously from infancy, to put it nightly to sleep surfeited,

to kiss it in the mornings with the hungry heart of a mother, to clean it, to clothe it fifty times over in new garments which it tears and casts away, and yet not revolt against the trials of this agitated life—this unwearying maternal love, this habit of creation—this execution and its toil.

This loving description of literary parentage is less ambivalent and more sentimental than Bradstreet's, but it presents a similar emphasis on birth leading to a lifetime of maternal nurturance. A theoretical approach that identifies male or female discourse as a quality solely in the text would have difficulty explaining that this metaphor is Honoré de Balzac's description of the creative process.[38] An approach that focuses on the *reader* in the identification of gendered discourse is better equipped to deal with the revelation of authorship. The meaning of Balzac's metaphor changes with the reader's awareness of its generator's sex. As a male metaphor, this nineteenth-century passage expresses a biologically impossible and historically unlikely embrace of motherhood. As a female metaphor, this passage would express a defiant reunion of what patriarchal culture has kept mutually exclusive—"this unwearying maternal love, this habit of creation." This difference of meaning in the very same words exists in the mind of the reader because of how gender generates alternative readings of the childbirth metaphor.

Gender Difference: Writing the Childbirth Metaphor

The significance of "the reader in the text" does not preclude a corresponding analysis of the writer in the text. Gender "informs and complicates" the *writing* as well as the *reading* of the childbirth metaphor. Any given birth metaphor exists within the artist's individual vision and specific formulation—the function it serves within the larger text and project of the artist. Sidney's metaphor (see epigraph), for example, serves the larger purpose of implicating poetic inspiration with desire and initiating the Renaissance love plot: Astrophel's love for Stella makes "great with child to speak." Balzac identifies with woman's lifetime labor and Joyce separates himself from it. Levertov's mother- and father-poets exist to make her point that the poet is "in the world," not separate from it. T.S. Eliot takes recourse to the metaphor to express the opposite, his theory of the text's autonomy: "he is oppressed by a burden which he must bring to birth in order to obtain relief . . . And then he can say to the poem: 'Go away! Find a place for yourself in a book— and don't expect *me* to take any further interest in you.' "[39] Jean Rhys uses the metaphor to decide when to let go of *Wide Sargasso Sea*. Her publisher reported that "she wrote to tell me that she had been having a recurring dream in which, to her dismay, she was pregnant. Then it came again, only this time the baby had been born and she was looking at it in its cradle—'such a puny weak thing. So the book must be finished, and that must be what I think about it really. I don't dream about it any more.' "[40] The pervasive use of the birth metaphor at Los Alamos to describe the creation of the first atomic bomb (known as "Oppenheimer's baby," christened informally as "Little Boy," and dropped from a plane named Enola Gay, after the pilot's mother) serves to obscure the bomb's destructiveness and implicate women in its birth.[41] At first glance, individual variation appears more significant than the author's sex to the full meaning of the childbirth metaphor.

Nonetheless, without denying exceptions to generalization, we can broadly cluster formulations of the birth metaphor along gender lines. These gender differences in the *writing* of the metaphor originate in the contrasting perspectives toward childbirth that women and men bring to their individual formulations. For biological and historical reasons, childbirth is an event whose meaning is constituted differently by women and men. This difference informs why they use it and what they use it for. Men's use of the metaphor begins in distance from and attraction to the Other. Karen Horney, for example, asks if men's "impulse to create" is "due to their feeling of playing a relatively small part in the creation of living beings, which constantly impels them to an overcompensation in achievement." Gershon Legman applies this theory specifically to the male birth metaphor, which he calls a "male motherhood of authorship," an archetypal fantasy of great power and persistence determined by largely unconscious fear and envy of woman's sexual and reproductive powers. Elizabeth Sacks expands on this "womb envy" to say that the male metaphor serves as "an essential outlet for unconscious or repressed feminine elements in the masculine psyche."[42] Its use reflects the attempt to reabsorb into consciousness those repressed elements in themselves that culture has projected onto woman. Because of these psychological determinants, then, the male metaphor might be a covert, indeed, largely unconscious, tribute to woman's special generative power, a vestige from the worship of the primal goddess as paradigm of (pro)creativity. This "tribute" is deceptive, however. The male comparison of creativity with woman's procreativity equates the two as if both were valued equally, whereas they are not. This elevation of procreativity seemingly idealizes woman and thereby obscures woman's real lack of authority to create art as well as babies. As an appropriation of women's (pro)creativity, the male metaphor subtly helps to perpetuate the confinement of women to procreation.

On the whole, the function of male birth metaphors within the context of the writer's larger vision tends to reflect the dominant cultural representations of woman's nature current in a given historical era. Throughout the evolution of Judeo-Christian patriarchy, women have served as the symbol for qualities men desire and reject, revere and fear, envy and hate. Defined and controlled within an androcentric system of representation, the ideological concepts of women's sexual and reproductive powers have been the backbone of these ambivalent perspectives. This general representation stands behind the evolution of meaning in the male birth metaphor described by Terry Castle. She notes, for example, that male birth metaphors were abundant both during the Enlightenment and the Romantic era— but with opposite meanings. Satirists like Pope and Dryden associated the human birth process with "deformed poetic productivity" and regularly deflected it onto the enemy poet. The bad poet was above all a "begetter" who breeds out of his own distempered fancy repulsive "offspring" because his lack of reason makes him like "the one who gives birth, who conceives and brings forth, [who] is nowhere in control, but rather is subject to a purely spontaneous animal function." Castle argues that the equally abundant, but overwhelmingly positive uses of the birth metaphor in the Romantic period resulted from a fundamental change in poetics. The Romantics repeatedly used the metaphor not to condemn their enemies but to define the production of art as "a spontaneous process independent of intention, precept, or even consciousness.[43] Women's lack of control over pregnancy attracted the Romantics, who affirmed the "organic nature of poetic genius" that produces a poem effortlessly, without the painful struggle of the intellect. As Percy Shelley wrote in his *Defense of Poetry*, "a great statue or picture grows under the power of the artist as a child in the mother's womb."[44]

What Castle did not note is that this shift from repulsion to idealization parallels a historical evolution in the representation of women. In both periods, the organic processes of the human body were symbolically associated with women, along with emotion and intuition. However, the Enlightenment celebration of Reason incorporated a definition of the body as the inferior, "animal" aspect of human nature. Although the eighteenth century saw the dramatic rise of writing by and for women, disgust for sheer physicality or emotionalism often represented by woman was common among the Augustan satirists.[45] Consequently, eighteenth-century male birth metaphors embodied this intertwined disgust for woman and the human body she represented. In his *Essay Concerning Human Understanding*, John Locke's attack on all metaphor as a mode of knowledge illustrates this matrix of meaning. He calls metaphor a "monstrous birth," a dangerous "changeling" of the rational mind, and further denounces it by likening it to woman, whose seductive power enslaves the masculine mind. As woman seduces man, so metaphor traps reason, and procreativity inhibits creativity.[46] Within such a gynophobic ethos, the childbirth metaphor becomes the ultimate insult to a male artist's creativity.

The Romantic period's embrace of intuition, emotion, and organicism—all qualities associated with the feminine—transformed the birth metaphor into something positive. But whether rejected as repulsive or celebrated as creative, woman's procreativity in both the Enlightenment and the Romantic periods was perceived through an androcentric lens as a mindless, unconscious, uncontrolled act of the body. Both the positive and negative manifestations of the male metaphor perpetuate the mind-body split it attempts to transcend through analogy. Both therefore reaffirm creativity as the province of men and procreativity as the primary destiny of women.

For women, as for men, use of the childbirth metaphor is psychologically charged and overdetermined. But while men's use of the metaphor begins in a fascination for the Other, women's use originates in conflict with themselves as Other. Unlike men, women using the metaphor necessarily confront the patriarchally imposed, essential dilemma of their artistic identity: the binary system that conceives woman and writer, motherhood and authorship, babies and books, as mutually exclusive.

Women writers have faced childbirth with an ambivalence born of its association with their status in society. Consequently, their birth metaphors variously encode the very issues of their authorship as women and their womanhood as authors.

The childbirth metaphors of women and men differ not only in their psychological charge but also in their function within the larger work. While men's metaphors often reflect the ethos of their times, women's metaphors tend to be deeply personal statements about how they try to resolve their conflict with cultural prescription. Because of its affirmation of a unified (pro)creation, Levertov's birth metaphor is more like the birth metaphors of Bradstreet and Philips than it is like the ambivalent birth metaphors of some contemporary women writers. Not so predictably in tune with the times as male metaphors, female metaphors are often figurative expressions of the strategies by which their authors confront the double bind of the woman writer: how to be a woman and a writer within a discourse that has steadfastly separated the two. Consequently, where men's metaphors tend to perpetuate the separation of creativities, women's metaphors tend to deconstruct it.

In general, women's birth metaphors cover a wide spectrum of personal statement, reproducing the central debates over the relationship between poetics and the body. At one end of the continuum, women's birth metaphors express a fundamental acceptance of a masculinist aesthetic that separates creativity and procreativity. At the other end of the continuum is a defiant celebration of (pro)creation, a gynocentric aesthetic based on the body. At points along the spectrum are expressions of fear, ambivalence, and a dialectical search for transcendence of the binary system of creativity. Although any one of these metaphoric expressions might be found at different historical periods, the more widespread feminism has been at any given point in time, the more likely it has been for birth metaphors to cluster at the subversive end of the spectrum. In the twentieth century, the spread of feminism has combined with the greater freedom for discourses on sexuality to break the relative silence about childbirth in literary discourse. Although childbirth has been central to women's experience, it has been at the periphery of literary representation until the last fifty years. As Muriel Rukeyser notes, "one is on the edge of the absurd the minute one tries to relate the experience of birth to the silence about it in poetry."[47] For a long time women have indirectly addressed this largely ignored, trivialized, distorted, or taboo subject by introducing their versions of the birth metaphor into literary discourse. Concurrent with the second wave of feminism from about 1965 to the present, there has been an explosion of women's writing about pregnancy, childbirth, nursing, and motherhood. Birth imagery to describe the self-creation of both woman and artist permeates contemporary women's writing. Nonetheless, women's birth metaphors still retain an individual stamp encoding each woman's negotiation of the conflict between creation and procreation. An exploration of women's writing at different points along the continuum will illustrate representative resolutions of this conflict, as well as the basic contrast with male birth metaphors.

The first point on the continuum of women's birth metaphors is the use of the metaphor to confirm the patriarchal separation of creativities. Fanny Appleton Longfellow, for example, relies on the metaphor to explain her resignation from creative work to engage in procreative labor. She stopped writing her journal after the birth of her first baby and notes in her final entry: "With this day my journal ends, for I have now a living one to keep faithfully, more faithfully than this." Less Victorian than Mrs. Longfellow, Elinor Wylie nonetheless uses the metaphor to express her sense of failure as a woman after repeated miscarriages. She thinks of her poems as substitute children, born of a mother *manqué*. Margaret Mead, a writer, mother, and feminist, projects her anxiety about this rebellious combination onto her statement that "something very special happens to women when they know that they will not have a child—or any more children. . . . Suddenly, their whole creativity is released—they paint or write as never before."[48] These women from different historical periods nonetheless write into their analogies a belief that procreation and creation are mutually exclusive.

The next point along the continuum is birth metaphors encoding a fear of combining creation and procreation. Given that the underside of fear is often desire, such metaphors contain a matrix of forbidden wish and guilt for trespass. Mary Shelley, daughter of feminist Mary Wollstonecraft, did not have her mother's intrepid belief that women could fulfill the desire for both writing and mothering.[49] In *Frankenstein*, she relies on an elaborate narrative of the birth metaphor to express her essential fear that the patriarchal separation of creativities is necessary. The novel is a macabre reversal of the male Romantic metaphors of organic creativity. Shelley uses the metaphor negatively in both the narrative and her 1831 preface to a later edition. She refers to her book as "my hideous progeny," an "offspring" about a scientist who seeks to discover "the deepest mysteries of creation" by procreating life. Frankenstein's quest takes the form of doing with his brain what women do with their bodies, a point Shelley emphasizes with her pervasive analogies between his work and the stages of woman's "confinement" throughout the preface and the narrative.[50] The life he creates from the womb of his brain, however, is not the beautiful child of woman's production, but a hideous-looking monster who terrifies his "father" and "creator." Frankenstein rejects his creation, denies the monster's repeated requests for love, and thereby sets in motion the monster's revengeful destruction of Frankenstein's family. One approach to this multifaceted tale is to read it as an exploration of creativity ridden with anxiety and anger about gender, motherhood, and artistic creation. Look at what happens, Shelley seems to say, when men try to procreate. And what will happen when I try to create like a man?[51]

Mary Shelley's encoded ambivalence is not far on the spectrum from women's use of the metaphor to explore more directly their desire for and fear of possible fusion of literary and literal motherhood. Sylvia Plath's fascination for pregnancy and childbirth is evident in a number of pathbreaking poems about women's ambivalence toward the changes in their bodies and identity that pregnancy brings, works such as "Three Women: A Poem for Three Voices," "Metaphors," "Morning Song," "You're," "Heavy Women," and "Nick and the Candlestick." "I'm a riddle in nine syllables/ . . . /I've eaten a bag of green apples,/Boarded the train there's no getting off," she writes in "Metaphors."[52] Delighted with her experience of natural childbirth, what Adrienne Rich has called unalienated labor, Plath could write playfully about procreation as well.[53] But first as a "riddle in nine syllables" and later, a mother-poet who, in the last year of her life, had to write at four A.M. before her babies awoke, Plath's childbirth metaphors for creativity are ridden with self-loathing and fear of motherhood as biological entrapment. The "childless woman" in "Childless Woman" is a poet whose "womb/ Rattles its pod/ . . . / Uttering nothing but blood." After the birth of her second child, she wrote a terrifying poem called "Barren Woman," in which her womb's emptiness is a metaphor for the emptiness of her creative mind.[54] In "Stillborn," the union of creation and procreation presages the silence of death.

> These poems do not live: it's a sad diagnosis.
> They grew their toes and fingers well enough
>
> . . . .
>
> They sit so nicely in the pickling fluid!
> They smile and smile and smile and smile at me.
>
> . . . .
>
> But they are dead, and their mother near dead with distraction,
> And they stupidly stare, and do not speak of her.[55]

In contrast to Plath, Erica Jong lives in a time and place where feminism has made the combination of motherhood and authorhood more acceptable. Reflecting this historical change, her birth metaphors are less fearful than Plath's. Nonetheless, Jong's ambivalence leads her to embrace and then reject the metaphor, a wavering that suggests her awareness of the metaphor's double potential for regression and liberation. Poetry written before her own pregnancy repeatedly uses metaphors of menstruation, pregnancy, and birth to test out the relationship between her body and her art. In "Dear Marys, Dear Mother, Dear Daughter," she recognizes that "Doctor Frankenstein/ was punished/ for his pride:/ the hubris of a man/ creating life."[56] In "Menstruation in May," Jong attempts to unite mind and body, creation and procreation.

> I squeeze my breast
> for the invisible ink of milk.
> I bear down hard—
> no baby's head appears.
> The poems keep flowing monthly
> like my blood.
> The word is flesh, I say
> still unconvinced.

> The Flesh is flesh.
> The word is on its own.[57]

Jesus was the incarnate God, the Word made flesh. Can woman, Jong asks, unite her word with her flesh? She tries out the same metaphoric equation of milk and ink that Cixous uses, but her attempt to posit a single (pro)creative process leaves her "still unconvinced." In "Playing with the Boys," Jong expresses more confidence in a body-based aesthetic as she links her pen, menstruation, and potential to birth babies in the definition of her art.

> I am not part of their game.
> I have no penis.
> I have a pen, two eyes
> & I bleed monthly.
>
> When the moon shines on the sea
> I see the babies
> riding on moonwaves
> asking to be born.[58]

When Jong became pregnant, however, this wavering turned into outright hostility to the birth metaphor in her essay "Creativity vs. Generativity." "Only a man (or a woman who had never been pregnant)," she writes, "would compare creativity to maternity, pregnancy to the creation of a poem or novel."[59] Underlying her resistance to the metaphor is both anger and fear. She quotes Joyce's letter to his wife and hears a territorial hostility to women writers in the male metaphor: "Men have the feeling that women can create life in their bodies, therefore, how dare they create art?"[60] Even more deeply, she fears that pregnancy will sabotage her creative drive: "I have dreaded pregnancy as a loss of control over my destiny, my body and my life. I had fantasies of death in childbirth, the death of my creativity during pregnancy, the alteration of my body into something monstrous, the loss of my intelligence through mysterious hormonal sabotage."[61]

While Jong oscillates between inviting, then banishing, the association of creation and procreation, H.D. uses the birth metaphor to explore the process of moving from ambivalence toward motherhood to a celebration of its connection to authorship. She represents a further point on the continuum, the move to use the metaphor as a poetic for women's writing. In her *roman à clef, Asphodel*, for example, H.D. expresses the fear she felt during her first pregnancy that the attempt to combine speech and childbirth was a form of madness:

> When her flaming mind beat up and she found she was caught, her mind not taking her as usual like a wild bird but her mind-wings beating, beating and her feet caught, her feet caught, glued like a wildbird in a bird lime. . . . No one had known this. No one would ever know it for there were no words

> to tell it in. . . . Women can't speak and clever women don't have children.
> So if a clever woman does speak, she must be mad. She is mad. She wouldn't
> have had a baby, if she hadn't been.[62]

The image of a wild bird caught in bird lime is a metaphor for the tie between
creation and procreation against which the poet struggles in fear. This pregnancy
ends traumatically in stillbirth. But later in the novel, H.D. transforms that bondage
into a powerful bond. With the flight of a wild swallow as omen, she decides not
to abort her second pregnancy but to take the birth of her child as a symbol of a
regenerated poetic identity. The experience of pregnancy itself doesn't hinder, but
rather releases, her creative drive.[63] H.D. later encodes this resolution into the
mythos of her complex epics of the forties and fifties. Incarnating the birth metaphor,
the Lady in *Trilogy* and Isis in *Hermetic Definition* are goddesses whose procreative
power can regenerate human life and inspire the poet. The Lady is the pregnant
Word, but she appears to the poet without the Child, bearing instead the empty
book of life which the poet must complete. Isis inspires the aging poet who feels
silenced by men, either in their capacity as lovers or as fellow poets. The lover's
double rejection of her writing and womanhood has been particularly devastating.
The poet frees herself from his negative influence by writing a poem about him,
a poem whose progress she charts as the trimesters of pregnancy. Her poem is the
child; its birth signals her freedom from obsession. The poet-as-procreator fuses
with the mother-as-poet in the metaphoric world of the poem.[64] H.D.'s Isis and
Lady serve as Mother-Muses whose (pro)creative message implies an aesthetic
based on the female body.

Like H.D., the experience of childbirth itself altered Muriel Rukeyser's poetics
and led her to use the childbirth metaphor in "The Poem as Mask" to articulate
her new sense of poetic identity and direction. Recalling the dismemberment of
the archetypal poet Orpheus, the poet regards her earlier Orpheus poems as false
masks that testify to her alienation. They were "myself, split open, unable to speak,
in exile from myself." Childbirth, however, functions as her literal "dismemberment," one which allows her poet-self to incarnate the real Orpheus: "There is
memory/ of my torn life, myself split open in sleep, the rescued child/ beside me
among the doctors." No more are her poems "masks": "Now, for the first time,
the god lifts his hand,/ the fragments join in me with their own music."[65] Attesting
to the inspirational power of her new (pro)creative aesthetic, "Nine Poems for the
Unborn Child" and *Body of Waking* weave meditations on pregnancy and art that
insistently relate authorship and motherhood.

"Split open" in the stillbirth of her premature baby, Anaïs Nin similarly experiences a transformation, one that leads her to embrace (pro)creation as a self-
conscious, prescriptive aesthetic. As the next point on the continuum, Nin uses
the birth metaphor to advocate a feminine form of writing, one that proceeds from
the body. Otto Rank, her analyst, sharply posed the tradition of separated creativities for her: "Perhaps," he told her, "you may discover now what you want—

to be a woman or an artist." Later, he added that "to create it is necessary to destroy. Woman cannot destroy . . . that may be why she has rarely been a great artist."[66] While pregnant, Nin struggled to finish *Winter of Artifice* and repeatedly used the birth metaphor in her diary to describe her labor: "Writing now shows the pains of childbearing. . . . I yearn to be delivered of this book. It is devouring me."[67] Writing about the stillbirth in her diary and the short story "Birth" led Nin to counter Rank's phallic aesthetic with a body-based aesthetic of her own. "The art of woman," she writes, "must be torn in the womb-cells of the mind. . . . woman's creation far from being like man's must be exactly like her creation of children, that is it must come out of her own blood, englobed by her womb, nourished with her own milk."[68] As she pursues the meaning of a womb-based art, however, Nin becomes entangled in the regressive biologisms that concern Showalter, Auerbach, and de Beauvoir. "Woman does not forget she needs the fecundator," Nin muses, "she does not forget that everything that is born of her is planted in her. If she forgets this she is lost . . . a woman alone creating is not a beautiful spectacle. . . . The woman was born mother, mistress, wife, sister, she was born to represent union, communion, communication. . . . Woman was born to *be* the connecting link between man and his human self. . . . Woman's role in creation should be parallel to her role in life."[69] Nin's difficulty in separating the womb from woman's traditional role as man's support led her to create a birth metaphor that was itself a trap. Its determinism prescribed what women should write and how they must direct their creative energies toward the support of men, who are the necessary fecundators of women's writing.

Not all self-consciously formulated poetics of the female body have led women into prescriptive or deterministic entrapment, however. Representing the next point along the spectrum, Ntozake Shange uses the birth metaphor to chart the evolution of her poetics from the "universality" of male discourse to the specificity of female discourse. In "wow . . . yr just like a man," she tells of how she sought the approval of male poets by suppressing "alla this foolishness bout . . . bodies & blood & kids & what's really goin on at home/ well & that ain't poetry/ that's goo-ey gaw/ female stuff/ & she wasn't like that/ this woman they callt a poet." The birth metaphor is sign and symptom of her transformation:

> as a woman & a poet/ i've decided to wear my ovaries on my sleeve/ raise my poems on milk/ & count my days by the flow of my mensis/ the men who were poets were aghast/ they fled the scene in fear of becoming unclean . . . and she waz left with an arena of her own . . . where music & mensis/are considered very personal/ & language a tool for exploring space.[70]

Shange's recent volume of poetry celebrates this female poetic in an uproarious poem entitled "Oh, I'm 10 Months Pregnant," in which a weary, pregnant poet complains to her doctor about how "the baby was confused/ the baby doesn't know/ she's not another poem":

>this baby wants to jump out of my mouth
>at a reading someplace/
>the baby's refusing to come out/down
>she wants to come out a spoken word
>& i have no way to reach her/she is
>no mere choice of words/how can i convince her
>to drop her head & take on the world like the
>rest of us[71]

Shange's new female poetic, fed by her own disruptively "unclean" body, is written in black English, a linguistic act that implicitly characterizes her aesthetic not only as female but also as Afro-American. In her essay "One Child of One's Own," Alice Walker uses the childbirth metaphor to define even more directly the fusion of her womanhood and blackness in her writing. She makes black women's double-birthing powers the foundation of a (pro)creativity that defies both sexism and racism. White feminists, she writes, have ignored black women's motherhood of both books and babies—by leaving black women's writing out of their anthologies and critical books; by keeping black women's sexuality and mothering invisible, as in the nonvaginal design of the Sojourner Truth plate in Judy Chicago's *Dinner Party*. Walker's completion of her first novel three days before her daughter's birth reconstitutes the (pro)creativity that racism and sexism have suppressed: "I had changed forever. From a woman whose 'womb' had been in a sense, her head— that is to say, certain small seeds had gone in, rather different if not larger or better 'creations' had come out—to a woman who . . . had two wombs! No. To a woman who had written books, conceived in her head, and who had also engendered at least one human being in her body."[72]

Lesbian writers have faced an even more severe cultural denial of their procreative womanhood in the homophobic belief that lesbianism and motherhood are mutually exclusive categories. Lesbians, many of whom are themselves mothers, use the childbirth metaphor to define a poetic of the body and affirm a vision of regenerated womanhood and world. In "Metamorphosis," Pat Parker describes how her love for a woman impregnated her with the vision central to her poetry: "fill me with you/ & I become/ pregnant with love/ give birth/ to revolution."[73] Like Paula Gunn Allen's celebration of the Spider Creatrix of Southwest Indian religion in "Prologue" and in "Grandmother," Judy Grahn's hymn "She Who" envisions a multidimensioned birth that reenacts the primal power of woman's (pro)creativity.

>the labor of She Who carries and bears is the first
>labor all over the world
>the waters are breaking everywhere
>everywhere the waters are breaking
>the labor of She Who carries and bears
>and raises and rears is the first labor,
>there is no other first labor.[74]

Lucille Clifton's sequence of Kali poems serves as a fitting conclusion to the wide spectrum of uses to which women writers of all periods have put the birth metaphor. In brilliantly condensed form, Clifton fuses literary and biological childbirth in a way that incorporates experience and aesthetic, terror and joy, ambivalence and celebration, separation and transcendence, body and spirit, animal and divine, pain and exultation. "She Understands Me" is a central poem in the sequence about her muse, the terrifying force of creativity she names after the black Hindu Goddess Kali:

> it is all blood and breaking
> blood and breaking.the thing
> drops out of its box squalling
> into the light.they are both squalling,
> animal and cage.her bars lie wet, open
> and empty and she has made herself again
> out of flesh out of dictionaries,
> she is always emptying and it is all
> the same wound the same blood the same breaking.[75]

The line "out of flesh out of dictionaries" is key, invoking the familiar birth metaphor linking babies and words. But where the male poet's conceit necessarily reinforces the division of mind and body, Clifton creates an ambiguity of subject highlighted by the absence of space between sentences and the lack of capitalization. The poem is simultaneously about the birth of a child and a poem. It is a visceral, raw view of childbirth, one that stresses the animal-like power of a transrational force but not in the negative mode of the Enlightenment metaphors. Clifton forthrightly names the process of (pro)creativity: the pregnant mind-body empties herself, squalling and bloody. The title, which suggests that the muse and mother understand each other, unifies the two subjects of the poem so that creativity and procreativity are inseparably joined. Indeed, the poem suggests ultimately that the poet's pregnancy produces multiple births. "She has made herself again": she is her own mother as well as mother to squalling babies and poems. She is both word and flesh, by divine and poetic authority.

Conclusion

The childbirth metaphor for creativity illustrates how gender "informs and complicates the reading and writing of texts." The basic analogy of creation and procreation remains the same for both women and men. However, female and male metaphors mean differently and mean something different, indeed something opposite. Male metaphors intensify difference and collision, while female metaphors enhance sameness and collusion. In spite of individual variation, male metaphors often covertly affirm the traditional separation of creativity and procreativity. Female metaphors, in contrast, tend to defy those divisions and reconstitute woman's fragmented self into a (pro)creative whole uniting word and flesh, body and mind.

These gender differences in childbirth metaphors project contrasting concepts of creativity. The male childbirth metaphor paradoxically beckons woman toward the community of creative artists by focusing on what she alone can create, but then subtly excludes her as the historically resonant associations of the metaphor reinforce the separation of creativities into mind and body, man and woman. The female childbirth metaphor challenges this covert concept of creativity by proposing a genuine bond between creation and procreation and by suggesting a subversive community of artists who can literally and literarily (pro)create. This biologic poetic does indeed run the risk of biological determinism, as de Beauvoir and others have feared. It theoretically privileges motherhood as the basis of all creativity, a position that symbolically excludes women without children and all men. It also tends toward a prescriptive poetic that potentially narrows the range of language and experience open to women writers. But women's childbirth metaphors have also served for centuries as a linguistic reunion of what culture has sundered, a linguistic defense against confinement. Long before Cixous's utopian essay about the *future* inscription of femininity, women have subverted the regressive birth metaphor and transformed it into a sign representing their own delivery into speech through (pro)creativity. Emerging like women themselves from the confinement of patriarchal literary tradition, birth metaphors have celebrated women's birthright to creativity. Women's oppression begins with the control of the body, the fruits of labor. Consequently, many women writers have gone directly to the source of powerlessness to reclaim that control through the labor of the mind pregnant with the word.

Notes

An earlier version of this essay was delivered at the Symposium on Childbirth at the University of Wisconsin in Madison in May 1981. I am greatly indebted to Elizabeth Black, whose bibliographic work for me was supported by a grant from the Women's Studies Research Center at the University of Wisconsin at Madison. For their criticisms and encouragements, I would also like to thank Judith Walzer Leavitt, Nellie McKay, Cyrena N. Pondrom, Alicia Ostriker, Phillip Herring, Eric Rothstein, and Jocelyn Moody. For permission to quote from H.D.'s manuscript, I am grateful to Perdita Schaffner and the Beinecke Rare Book and Manuscript Library, Yale University. Quotations are from Philip Sidney, *Astrophel and Stella* (1591, 1598), in *The Renaissance in England*, ed. Hyder E. Rollins and Herschel Baker (Boston: Heath, 1954), 323; and Denise Levertov, *The Poet in the World* (New York: New Directions, 1973), 107.

1. For discussions of male childbirth metaphors, see Terry J. Castle, "La'bring Bards: Birth *Topoi* and English Poetics," *Journal of English and Germanic Philology* 78 (April 1979): 193–208; Mary Ellmann, *Thinking about Women* (New York: Harcourt Brace Jovanovich, 1968), 2–27; Elizabeth Sacks, *Shakespeare's Images of Preganancy* (New York: St. Martin's Press, 1980); Ernst Robert Curtius, *European Literature and the Latin Middle Ages*, trans. Willard R. Trask (New York: Putnam, 1953), 131–34; Gershon Legman, *Rationale of the Dirty Joke: An Analysis of Sexual Humor* (New York: Grove Press, 1968), 592–96; John H. Smith's "Dialogic Midwifery in Kleist's *Marquise von O* and the Hermeneutics of Telling the Untold in Kant and Plato," PMLA 100 (March 1985): 203–18;

and Patricia Yaeger's letter to Smith in *PMLA* 100 (October 1985): 812–13. For discussions of female birth metaphors, see Susan Gubar, "The Birth of the Artist as Heroine: (Re)production, the *Kunstlerroman* Tradition, and the Fiction of Katherine Mansfield," in *The Representation of Women in Fiction*, ed. Carolyn G. Heilbrun and Margaret R. Higonnet (Baltimore: Johns Hopkins University Press, 1983), 19–59; Susan Gubar, " 'The Blank Page' and the Issues of Female Creativity," *Critical Inquiry* 8 (Winter 1981): 243–64; and Sandra M. Gilbert, *Mother-Rites: Studies in Literature and Maternity*, a work in progress.

2. See Sandra M. Gilbert and Susan Gubar, *The Madwoman in the Attic: The Woman Writer and the Nineteenth-Century Literary Imagination* (New Haven: Yale University Press), 2–106, esp. 2–16; see also Ellmann, 2–27.

3. Hélène Cixous, "The Laugh of the Medusa," trans. Keith Cohen and Paula Cohen, in *New French Feminisms: An Anthology*, ed. Elaine Marks and Isabelle de Courtivron (Amherst: University of Massachusetts Press, 1980), 256, 251, 261. See also Luce Irigaray, *This Sex Which Is Not One*, trans. Catherine Porter (Ithaca: Cornell University Press, 1985), 23–33, 205–18; Carolyn Greenstein Burke, "Report from Paris: Women's Writing and the Women's Movement," *Signs* 3 (Summer 1978): 843–55; Ann Rosalind Jones, "Writing the Body: Toward an Understanding of *l'Écriture féminine*," *Feminist Studies* 7 (Summer 1981): 247–63; and Susan Rubin Suleiman, "(Re)Writing the Body: The Politics and Poetics of Female Eroticism," in *The Female Body in Western Culture: Contemporary Perspectives*, ed. Susan Rubin Suleiman (Cambridge: Harvard University Press, 1986): 7–29.

4. Stephanie Mines, "My Own Impression," in *Networks: An Anthology of San Francisco Bay Area Women Poets*, ed. Carol A. Simone (Palo Alto: Vortext, 1979), 118; Sharon Olds, "The Language of the Brag," *Ms. Magazine* (August 1980): 38.

5. Ellmann, *Thinking about Women*, 2–27.

6. Simone de Beauvoir, "Interview with Alice Schwarzer," *Der Spiegel* (April 1976): quoted in Silvia Bovenschen, "Is There a Feminine Aesthetic?" *New German Critique* 10 (Winter 1977): 122; Elaine Showalter, "Feminist Criticism in the Wilderness," *Critical Inquiry* 8 (Winter 1981): 187–88; Nina Auerbach, "Artists and Mothers: A False Alliance," *Women and Literature* 9 (Spring 1978): 3–5, and her review of *Madwoman in the Attic*, by Gilbert and Gubar, *Victorian Studies* 23 (Summer 1980): 506; Jones, 61–63; Erica Jong, "Creativity vs. Generativity: The Unexamined Lie," *The New Republic* 180 (13 Jan. 1979): 27.

7. Elizabeth Abel, Editor's Introduction, *Critical Inquiry* 8 (Winter 1981): 173.

8. Cixous, 248. This view may do more to dismiss and trivialize the subversive achievement and survival of women writers against a hostile culture than the patriarchal canon itself. See Alicia Ostriker, Comment on Margaret Homans's "Her Very Own Howl": The Ambiguities of Representation in Recent Women's Fiction," *Signs* 10 (Spring 1985): 597–600.

9. Max Black, "More about Metaphor," in *Metaphor and Thought*, ed. Andrew Ortony (New York: Cambridge University Press, 1979), 26.

10. Roland Barthes, *Writing Degree Zero*, trans. Annette Lavers and Colin Smith (New York: Hill & Wang, 1976), 75–77. See also Catharine R. Stimpson's discussion of Barthes in "Zero Degree Deviancy: The Lesbian Novel in English," *Critical Inquiry* 8 (Winter 1981): 363–80. For discussions of contextual analysis of metaphors, see George Whalley, "Metaphor," in *Princeton Encyclopedia of Poetry and Poetics* (Princeton: Princeton University Press, 1974), 494; and Wayne C. Booth, "Ten Literal 'Theses,' " in *On Metaphor*, ed. Sheldon Sacks (Chicago: University of Chicago Press, 1978), 173–74.

11. Quoted in Tillie Olsen, *Silences* (New York: Delta, 1972), 199–200.

12. For discussions of the incompatibility of motherhood and authorship, see, for example, Virginia Woolf, *A Room of One's Own* (1929; reprint, New York: Harcourt Brace & World, 1957), 20–24, 69–70; Olsen, 6–21; Lola Ridge, "Woman and the Creative Will" (1919), in *Michigan Occasional Papers* 18 (Spring 1981): 1–23; Catharine R. Stimpson, "Power, Presentations, and the Presentable," in *Issues in Feminism: A First Course in Women's Studies*, ed. Sheila Ruth (Boston: Houghton Mifflin, 1980), 426–40; Adrienne Rich, *Of Woman Born: Motherhood as Experience and Institution* (New York: Norton, 1976), 156–62; and the sharp exchange between George Sand and a male writer in Bovenschen, 114–15.

13. See, for example, the theories of female inferiority of intellect and creative genius by men such as Aristotle, Aquinas, Rousseau, Kant, Darwin, and Schopenhauer, excerpted in *History of Ideas on Women: A Source Book*, ed. Rosemary Agonito (New York: Putnam, 1977). See also critiques of scientific theories of female inferiority in Ruth Bleier, *Science and Gender: A Critique of Biology and Its Theories on Women* (New York: Pergamon Press, 1984); and James Hillman, *The Myth of Analysis: Three Essays in Archetypal Psychology* (Evanston: Northwestern University Press, 1972), 215–99.

14. Gen. 3: 16–19; John, 1: 1–4. See also Mary Daly, *Beyond God the Father: Toward a Philosophy of Women's Liberation* (Boston: Beacon, 1973); Gilbert; Diane Wolkstein and Samuel Noah Kramer, *Inanna: Queen of Heaven and Earth, Her Stories and Hymns for Sumer* (New York: Harper, 1983); J.A. Phillips, *Eve: The History of an Idea* (New York: Harper & Row, 1984); Merlin Stone, *When God Was a Woman* (New York: Harcourt Brace Jovanovich, 1978).

15. Friedrich Nietzche, *Thus Spake Zarathustra* (1883), trans. and selected by Agonito in her *History of Ideas on Women*, 268.

16. Simone de Beauvoir, *The Second Sex*, trans. H.M. Parshley (1949: reprint, New York: Bantam, 1968), xv.

17. Julia Kristeva, *About Chinese Women*, trans. Anita Barrows (New York: Urizen Books, 1974), 35–36.

18. See, for example, Susan R. Suleiman and Inge Crossman, eds., *The Reader in the Text: Essays on Audience and Interpretation* (Princeton: Princeton University Press, 1980).

19. Paul Ricoeur, "The Metaphorical Process as Cognition, Imagination, and Feeling," in *On Metaphor*, 146. For recent theoretical debates on metaphor, see, in addition to *On Metaphor*, Whalley; Ortony; and *Philosophical Perspectives on Metaphor*, ed. Mark Johnson (Minneapolis: University of Minnesota Press, 1981). For a discussion of metaphor and speech act theory, see Ted Cohen, "Figurative Speech and Figurative Acts," in *Philsosphical Perspectives on Metaphor*, 182–99.

20. Karsten Harries, "Metaphor and Transcendence," in *On Metaphor*, 71.

21. Ricoeur, in *On Metaphor*, 145–47, 151–54.

22. Paul de Man, "The Epistemology of Metaphor," in *On Metaphor*, 11–14, 28.

23. Ted Cohen, "Metaphor and the Cultivation of Intimacy," in *On Metaphor*, 6, 7.

24. The term "headbirths," a variation on the more common "brainchild," is featured in Günter Grass's novel *Headbirths, or the Germans Are Dying Out*, trans. Ralph Mannheim (New York: Harcourt Brace Jovanovich, 1982). Advertisements for the novel show an embryo emerging from a male head, still attached to the brain by a twisting umbilical cord, a visual form that highlights the biological incongruity of the male birth metaphor.

25. Levertov, 107.

26.   Lady Holland, *Memoir,* quoted in Legman, 593. Like Levertov's father-poet, this metaphor features a female author and male actor, a dissonance that contributes to the metaphor's wit as much as the actor's biological incapacity to give birth.

27.   Richard Ellmann, ed. *Selected Letters of James Joyce* (New York: Viking, 1975), 202–3. See also his *James Joyce: A Biography* (London: Oxford University Press, 1959), 306–9.

28.   James Joyce, *Ulysses* (1922; rev. ed., New York: Random House, 1961), 383–428. See also Ellmann, ed., *Selected Letters,* 230, 251–52; and the discussion of "Oxen in the Sun" in Phillip F. Herring, *Joyce's Ulysses Notesheets in the British Museum* (Charlottesville: University of Virginia Press, 1972), 30–37, 162–264. Joyce's envy of female procreation is evident in Bloom's hallucination of giving birth in the "Circe" episode of *Ulysses* (429–609) and in the irony that perpetually undercuts the products of men's minds in his works (such as the narrator's increasingly jumbled words in "Oxen in the Sun" and Stephen's sterility in both *Ulysses* and *Portrait of the Artist as a Young Man.*

29.   Amy Lowell, "The Sisters," in *No More Masks! An Anthology of Poems by Women,* ed. Florence Howe and Ellen Bass (New York: Anchor, 1973), 40.

30.   Paul de Man describes all metaphors in *On Metaphor,* 11–14, 28.

31.   Katherine Philips, "Upon the Death of Hector Philips," in *The World Split Open: Four Centuries of Women Poets,* ed. Louise Bernikow (New York: Random House, 1974), 59–60. For a discussion of women poets' re-vision of conventional elegy, see Celeste M. Schenck, "Feminism and Deconstruction: Re-Constructing the Elegy," *Tulsa Studies in Women's Literature* 5 (Spring 1986): 13–28.

32.   John Woodbridge, "To My Dear Sister, The Author of These Poems," in *The Poems of Mrs. Anne Bradstreet,* with Introduction by Charles Eliot Norton (New York: The Duodecimos, 1897), 8.

33.   Jeannine Hensley, ed., *The Works of Anne Bradstreet* (Cambridge: Harvard University Press, 1967), 221.

34.   See, for example, James Smith, "Epistle Dedicatory, to the Reader" (1658), in which he writes: "Curteous Reader, I had not gone my full time when by a sudden fright, occasioned by the Beare and Wheel-barrow on the Bank-side, I fell in travaile, and therefore cannot call this a timely issue, but a Mischance, which I must put out to the world to nurse; hoping it will be fostered with the greater care, because of its own innocency," quoted in Sacks, *Shakespeare's Images of Pregnancy,* 6–7.

35.   See *Works of Anne Bradstreet,* 221.

36.   Woolf, 156–62. Judy Chicago, *Through the Flower: My Struggle As a Woman Artist* (1975; rev. ed. New York: Anchor Books, 1982), 141–44. See also Judy Chicago and Miriam Schapiro, "Female Imagery," *Womanspace Journal* 1 (Summer 1973): 11–14; Lucy R. Lippard, *From the Center: Feminist Essays on Women's Art* (New York: Dutton, 1978), 80–95; and Bovenschen.

37.   Although beyond the scope of this essay, it would be fruitful to extend a reader response approach beyond the issue of the reader's awareness of the author's sex to the sex and perspective of the reader. A female reader, for example, might be more likely to hear the collisions in the male metaphor than a male reader. A woman who has experienced chilbirth may be more likely to feel the reunion of creation and procreation in a female metaphor than a woman who cannot have or chooses not to have children. Women who resent the privilege that mothers in patriarchy have in relationship to women without children may find the childbirth metaphor oppressive rather than subversive. Any discourse charged

with gender issues will be differently understood by women and men and by individuals whose perspectives on those issues differ.

38. Quoted in Olsen, 12.

39. T.S. Eliot, *The Three Voices of Poetry* (New York: Cambridge University Press, 1954), 29–30.

40. Diana Athill, *Smile Please: An Unfinished Biography* (New York: Harper & Row, 1979), 8–9.

41. I am indebted to Evelyn Fox Keller for sending her "Exposing Secrets," a Paper delivered at the conference "Feminist Studies: Reconstituting Knowledge," Milwaukee, April 1985, in which she quotes selected birth metaphors for the bomb collected by Brian Easlea in *Fathering the Unthinkable: Masculinity, Scientists, and the Nuclear Arms Race* (London: Pluto Press, 1983). Karen Horney, *Feminine Psychology* (New York: Norton, 1967), 61; Legman, 592–96.

42. Elizabeth Sacks, *Shakespeare's Images of Pregnancy*, 5.

43. Castle, 201–2, 205.

44. Percy Shelley, *Defence of Poetry*, in *Critical Theory Since Plato*, ed. Hazard Adams (New York: Harcourt Brace Jovanovich, 1971), 511. See Brewster Ghiselin's discussion of this organicism and the birth metaphor in his Introduction to *The Creative Process: A Symposium* (New York: Mentor, 1952), 21, and the examples of the birth metaphor in his selections from Thomas Wolfe, Allen Tate, Stephen Spender, Paul Valery, A.E. Houseman, and Amy Lowell. See also the repeated organic birth metaphors in Cary Nelson, *The Incarnate Word: Literature as Verbal Space* (Urbana: University of Illinois Press. 1973), 6, 22–23, 50–51, 126–27, 129–43, 161, 182–83, 196–97, 242.

45. See, for example, Susan Gubar, "The Female Monster in Augustan Satire," *Signs* 3 (Winter 1977): 380–94.

46. John Locke, *An Essay Concerning Human Understanding*, ed. John W. Yolton (New York, 1961), 2: 105–6, 115, 175. See de Man's discussion of Locke's fear of metaphor's disruptive discourse in *On Metaphor*, 11–28. See also Arthur O. Lovejoy, *The Great Chain of Being* (Cambridge: Harvard University Press, 1957).

47. Muriel Rukeyser, "A Simple Theme," *Poetry* 74 (July 1949): 237. For a similar complaint, see E.M. Forster, *Aspects of the Novel* (1927; reprint, New York: Harcourt Brace & World, 1974), 75. Women's private writings before the twentieth century are a much richer source for women's perspectives on childbirth than public discourse. See Judith Walzer Leavitt and Whitney Walton, " 'Down to Death's Door': Women's Perceptions of Childbirth," in *Women and Health in America: Historical Essays*, ed. Judith Walzer Leavitt (Madison: University of Wisconsin Press, 1984), 155–65. For criticism on representations of childbirth in literature, see Gubar, "The Birch"; Rich, 164–67; Carol H. Poston, "Childbirth in Literature," *Feminist Studies* 4 (June 1978): 18–31; Madeleine Riley, *Brought to Bed* (New York: A.S. Barnes, 1968); Loralee MacPike, "The Social Values of Childbirth in the Nineteenth-Century Novel," *International Journal of Women's Studies* 3 (March–April 1980): 117–30; John Hawkins Miller, " 'Temple and Sewer': Childbirth, Prudery, and Victoria Regina," in *The Victorian Family: Structure and Stresses*, ed. Anthony S. Wohl (New York: St. Martin's Press, 1978); Irene Dash, "The Literature of Birth Abortion," *Regionalism and the Female Imagination* 3 (Spring 1977): 8–13; Rachel Blau DuPlessis, "Washing Blood," *Feminist Studies* 4 (June 1978): 1–12; Alicia Ostriker, "Body Language: Imagery of the Body in Women's Poetry," in *The State of Language*, ed. Leonard Michaels and Christopher Ricks (Berkeley: University of California Press, 1980), 247–63.

48. Fanny Appleton Longfellow, *Mrs. Longfellow*, ed. Edward Wagenknecht (New York: Longmans, Green, 1956); Cheryl Walker, "The Experienced Woman Poet" (Paper delivered at the Modern Language Association Convention, December 1981); Margaret Mead, *Blackberry Winter: My Earlier Years* (New York: William Morrow, 1972), 246–47.

49. See Mary Poovey, " 'My Hideous Progeny': Mary Shelley and the Feminization of Romanticism," PMLA 95 (May 1980): 332–47.

50. Mary Shelley, *Frankenstein; or The Modern Prometheus* (1818; reprint, London: Oxford University Press, 1969), 10, 41, 48, 51–57, 99–109, 160, 222.

51. For different readings of Shelley's anxiety about motherhood, see Ellen Moers, *Literary Women: The Great Writers* (New York: Anchor, 1977), 138–51; Gilbert and Gubar, 213–47; Poovey; and Paul Sherwin, *"Frankenstein"*: Creation or Catastrophe," PMLA 96 (October 1981): 883–903.

52. Sylvia Plath, *The Collected Poems*, ed. Ted Hughes (New York: Harper & Row, 1981), 116. For Plath's poems on pregnancy and birth as experience and/or metaphor, see 141–42, 157–58, 176–87, 240–42, 259, 272–73.

53. See, for example, "Metaphors," "You're," and "Heavy Women" in *Collected Poems*, 116, 141, 158. According to Ted Hughes, the birth of her first child was an exhilarating experience that contributed to the beginning of Plath's genuine poetic voice. See "Notes on the Chronological Order of Sylvia Plath's Poems," in *The Art of Sylvia Plath: A Symposium*, ed. Charles Newman (Bloomington: University of Indiana Press, 1970), 193. For a discussion of the alienated and unalienated labors of childbirth, see Rich, 157–85.

54. Plath's *Collected Poems* 259, 157. See also Ostriker's discussion of Plath's negative body imagery in "Baby Language," 250–52.

55. Plath's *Collected Poems*, 142. Plath's friend Anne Sexton also used the metaphor of aborted birth to describe her feeling of artistic failure in "The Silence," in which "the words from from my pen . . . leak out of it like a miscarriage." See *The Book of folly* (Boston: Houghton Mifflin, 1972), 32–33.

56. Erica Jong, *Loveroot* (New York: Holt, Rinehart, & Winston, 1975), 16–18.

57. Jong, *Loveroot*, 72–73.

58. Jong, *Loveroot*, 58–59.

59. Jong, "Creativity vs. Generativity," 27.

60. Jong, "Creativity vs. Generativity," 27, and Erica Jong, *Here Comes and Other Poems* (New York: Signet, 1975), 9.

61. Jong, "Creativity vs. Generativity," 28. See also "Penis Envy" in *Loveroot*, 81–82, and "Mother," in *Tangled Vines: A Collection of Mother & Daughter Poems*, ed. Lyn Lifson (Boston: Beacon Press, 1978), 52. Since the birth of her child, Jong once again relates procreation and creation. See her letter in the *New York Times Book Review* (18 Dec. 1983): 30, which lists recent women's writing about childbirth, including her most recent volumes. *At the Edge of the Body*, published about the time of her child's birth, includes birth metaphors (New York: Holt, Rinehart, & Winston, 1979), 7–9, 24, 63.

62. H.D. (Hilda Doolittle) *Asphodel* (1921–22), 12. The unpublished manuscript is at Beinecke Rare Book and Manuscript Library, Yale University. I am indebted to Beinecke Library and Perdita Schaffner (H.D.'s daughter and literary executor) for permission to quote from the manuscript.

63. For H.D.'s discussion of the creative "womb-brain," see her *Notes on Thought and Vision*, an essay on poetics written in 1919 shortly after the birth of her daughter (San Francisco: City Lights Books, 1982), 19–22. For other accounts of childbirth reinforcing

artistic creativity for women in the visual arts, see Tania Mourand in Lucy Lippard, "The Pains and Pleasures of Rebirth: Women's Body Art," *Art in America* 64 (May/June 1976): 79; Sandra Donaldson, " 'Suddenly you've become somebody else': A Study of Pregnancy and the Creative Woman" an unpublished paper; Joelynn Synder-Ott, *Women and Creativity* (Millbrace, Calif.: Les Femmes, 1978).

64.   H.D., *Trilogy* (New York: New Directions, 1973), 89–105. H.D., *Hermetic Definition* (New York: New Directions, 1972). For related discussions of H.D., see Susan Stanford Friedman, *Psyche Reborn: The Emergence of H.D.* (Bloomington: Indiana University Press, 1981), 45–55; Deborah Kelley Kloepfer, "Flesh Made Word: Maternal Inscription in H.D.," *Sagetrieb* 3 (Spring 1984): 27–48; Vincent Quinn, "H.D.'s 'Hermetic Definition': The Poet as Archetypal Mother," *Contemporary Literature* 18 (Winter 1977): 51–61.

65.   Muriel Rukeyser, "The Poem as Mask," *The Collected Poems* (New York: McGraw-Hill, 1978), 435. See also 283–91, 303–10, 397–434, 404, 411, 415, 148.

66.   Anaïs Nin, *The Diary, Volume One, 1931–1934*, ed. Gunther Stuhlmann (New York: Harcourt Brace Jovanovich, 1966), 309. See also 280–83, 290–94. Anaïs Nin, *The Diary, Volume Two, 1934–1939*, ed. Gunther Stuhlmann (New York: Harcourt Brace Jovanovich, 1967), 31. For a defense of Rank's treatment of Nin, see Sharon Spencer, "Delivering the Woman Artist from the Silence of the Womb: Otto Rank's Influence on Anaïs Nin," *The Psychoanalytic Review* 69 (Spring 1982): 111–29.

67.   Nin, *Diary, Volume One*, 314–15.

68.   Nin, *Diary, Volume Two*, 234, 233. Anaïs Nin, "Birth," in *Under a Glass Bell* (Chicago: Swallow Press, 1948), 96–101.

69.   Nin, *Diary, Volume Two*, 233–34.

70.   Ntozake Shange, *Nappy Edges* (New York: Bantam, 1978), 17.

71.   Ntozake Shange, *A Daughter's Geography* (New York: St. Martin's Press, 1983), 31. See also "We Need a God Who Bleeds Now," 51.

72.   Alice Walker, *In Search of Our Mothers' Gardens: Womanist Prose* (New York: Harcourt Brace Jovanovich, 1983), 368, 361–83. Birth metaphors in the work of women of color and other minorities are especially common among contemporary writers. See also Audre Lorde, "Paperweight" and "Now That I Am Forever with Child" in *Coal* (New York: Norton, 1976), 21, 49; Sylvia Gonzales, "Chicana Evolution," in *Networks*, 112–17; Sonia Sanchez, "Rebirth," in *A Blues Book for Blue Black Magical Women* (Detroit: Broadside Press, 1974), 47; E.M. Broner, *Her Mothers* (Berkeley: Berkeley Medallion, 1975).

73.   Pat Parker, *Movement in Black* (Oakland, Calif.: Diana Press, 1978), 132.

74.   Paula Gunn Allen, "Prologue," in *The Woman Who Owned the Shadows* (San Francisco: Spinsters, Ink, 1983), 1–2, and "Grandmother," in *The Third Woman: Minority Women Writers of the United States*, ed. Dexter Fisher (Boston: Houghton Mifflin, 1982), 126. See "She Who," in *The Work of a Common Woman: The Collected Poetry of Judy Grahn*, 1964–77 (Trumansburg, N.Y.: Crossing Press, 1978), 85, 76–109. See also Radclyffe Hall's central birth metaphor at the end of *The Well of Loneliness* (1928; reprint, New York: Pocket Books, 1950), 437.

75.   Lucille Clifton, *An Ordinary Woman* (New York: Random House, 1974), 50. For the Kali sequence, see 47–62. Clifton writes extensively about motherhood in this volume and in her *Two-Headed Woman* (Amherst: University of Massachusetts Press, 1980).

6

The Masculine Mode

Peter Schwenger

"If we insist on discovering something we can clearly label as a 'feminine mode,' then we are honor-bound, also, to delineate its counterpart, the 'masculine mode.' " This statement by Annette Kolodny does not affirm that such a counterpart exists;[1] Kolodny instead is making a point about the difficulty of determining common traits of writing by women. To suggest a similar assessment of writing by men is to remind us that the rich variety of writing by either sex resists any attempt at limiting its nature by sexual characteristics alone. Yet in the remainder of her essay, Kolodny investigates certain traits of perception and style which, if not definitive of writing by women, are recurrently found in it; and she argues convincingly for the value of such investigations.

Why, then, shouldn't there be a similar value in investigating the possible nature of a masculine mode? With us already is the social context out of which such an investigation would naturally arise; and it is similar to that which saw the rise of women's studies about ten years ago. As a men's movement begins to evolve, an increasing number of books are being published which analyze the nature of masculinity; magazines and newsletters proliferate; conferences are organized.[2] Like the women's movement, which provided both its model and its initial impetus, the men's movement is prone to dissension from within, misunderstanding and ridicule from without. Its course, however, is not likely to parallel that of the women's movement simply because the masculine role which it scrutinizes has configurations which are peculiar to itself. The most obvious point of difference is that the men's movement lacks the concrete rallying point of economic discrimination; it must necessarily address itself to the subtler psychological dynamics of the male role. It is here that literature, for several reasons, is liable to be called upon: literature provided experiences which, though artificial, may be the common property of millions; it contains insights which, though unsystematized, are still valid; it provides words for perceptions which, until named, may not even be recognized.

The danger here is that books may be viewed merely as case books, a happy hunting ground for Men We Disapprove Of and Good Guys. It cannot be stressed too often that if these studies accept the literary nature of the works with which they deal, they must concern themselves with the relation between perceptions (sexual, perhaps, in ways that may not be generally recognized) and words. Yet even if this is the most fruitful approach to the study of a masculine mode in literature, it is not fruitful for the work of every male author. A writer's sexuality may underlie his work, but it may underlie it at such a basic level as to illuminate nothing about the work's uniqueness and special richness. Using sexual generalities to link one writer with another reduces each to a low common denominator indeed. Again, with writers of both sexes, we should take into account their tendencies to work against the sexual grain. We know that an author may neutralize himself so that he becomes, in Joyce's words, "invisible, refined out of existence, indifferent, paring his fingernails." Or the author may be protean, adopting masculine and feminine modes according to the characters whose vision he adopts. Such an author gives free play to what both Virginia Woolf and Coleridge called the "androgynous mind."

If there is a masculine mode, then, it is clear that it is not simply made up of all male writers. It is better to limit the mode to writers who, rather than neutralize, contradict, or simply ignore their male sexuality, take it as their explicit subject. In this way we may consider with more certainty and subtlety the relation of this conscious preoccupation and the words used to describe it.

Is there really such a thing as a masculine style of writing? What are its characteristics and why just these characteristics? Can we distinguish the masculine style from the explicit masculine content? The writers I will examine in this context are necessarily a selection from the number of those who might be included. They are all twentieth-century authors. Perhaps, as Woolf suggests in *A Room of One's Own*, it is because of the beginnings of the women's movement in the preceding century that "virility has now become self-conscious."[3] At any rate there seems to be little explicit questioning of the male role, in literature or outside of it, until our own century. I do not mean to suggest, however, that these writers only question the received images of maleness; often they set out to validate those images or, through such images, to validate themselves. Their explorations of maleness are not abstract but intensely individual. They are not straightforward but riddled with contradictions and paradoxes. As a result, it is difficult to extract didactic points from their works. Always knowledge is rooted in experience and inseparable from it. The masculine mode is above all an attempt to render a certain *maleness of experience*.

This maleness of experience, at a primary level, must mean the infusion of a particular sense of the body into the attitudes and encounters of a life. I am not saying biology is destiny but rather, in James Dickey's words, that "the body is nothing less or more than the sense of being of a particular creature at a particular time and place. Everything he perceives and thinks depends upon his bodily state."[4] More than obesity, emaciation, sickliness, or robustness, or any of the infinite variations of physical type, the underlying fact of one's sexuality must affect the perception not only of oneself but of the world. Yet, as with most other aspects of the body, the effect of this underlying fact may be rendered transparent, as it were, by simple habituation. If this is true in life, it is even more true in literature, as Woolf asserts in her essay "On Being Ill." Illness, for Woolf, is an instance of the body intensely asserting its power over human perception—a power which is always there but largely disregarded by writers. In English literature the body is either a transparent vessel for conversations and thoughts or is viewed from the outside, as an object. Seldom has a writer attempted to render the unique relations we really have with our own bodies. To oneself, as the phenomenologists have pointed out, one's own body is wholly neither object nor subject. True, one's body may be objectified: I may inspect my hand in the same disinterested way that I observe the grain of the table on which it lies. But this perception is only partial and momentary. Still more difficult is the attempt to view the body as completely subjective, to deny its vulnerability as an object in the world. Ultimately all the paradoxes and complexities of being-in-the-world center on the body; but such complexities have generally been sidestepped by writers. They prefer instead to render the complexities of the soul, which, as Descartes once remarked, is easier to know than the body. In the masculine mode, though, the body's paradoxes operate with unusual force. Some social or psychological expectation in the male seems to push him, insofar as he accedes to it, toward the idea of his body as *en-soi*, partaking of the solidity and confidence of pure object. Yet the will to become such an object is itself an act of the *pour-soi*, the force that is conscious of itself and strives for itself.

An extreme illustration of this paradox is found in Yukio Mishima's works. In *Confessions of a Mask* Mishima tells us of his intense attraction, as a schoolboy, to the body of Omi, an older boy. He resists at that time every indication that Omi is other than pure object. The express desire to be Omi—that is, to be an object—is at the source of both his life's complexities and his death. Mishima's strenuous training of his body toward perfect physical development is really a pursuit of something abstract, something which he hopes to realize in himself. "If the body could achieve perfect, non-individual harmony," Mishima tells us in *Sun and Steel*, "then it would be possible to shut individuality up for ever in close confinement."[5] In all his years of physical training, Mishima attained a precious few moments of release from that self-awareness which was antithetical to his idea of the male. But of course the very moment at which he knew himself to be released was also a moment of self-awareness. Such Gordian complexities, in the end, could only be resolved by the point of a dagger; and on 25 November 1970, Mishima committed hara-kiri. The moment of sudden death baffles all expectation before the event and allows no reflection after it. That moment was for Mishima the union of subject and object, of the knower and the known, in an ultimate gesture of virility.

Mishima's statement that he sought "a language of the body" indicates the close relationship between his pursuit of virility and his art as a writer.[6] At first, it is true, Mishima considered that the function of muscles was precisely opposite to that of words; and he was attracted by muscularity to the same degree that he was repulsed by the words which he saw as white ants, eating away at reality. The more "literary" these words, the more they encouraged and glorified the individual perceptions which Mishima sought to escape in the pursuit of his great abstraction. Yet as Mishima's body freed itself from words and gained its own power, he was increasingly able to turn that power back upon words in order to change their nature. He speaks of learning "how to pursue words with the body (and not merely pursue the body with words)." That is to say, the body is no longer merely a subject described by the writer's words; it "pursues" those words with the demand that the writer's style conform to the body's own qualities. Mishima describes his style as "something appropriate to my muscles."[7] All excess ornament is stripped away; the pace of his writing is imperturbable, with no variations in speed; it has "the tension of the all-night watch," a watch that guards against imagination and sensibility. Mishima's style, he says, "was on the verge of non-communication; it was a style that did not accept but rejected." Nothing less can be expected when the body, whose nature is fundamentally wordless, becomes the model for words.

Mishima's description of his ideal style is in accordance with a common notion of "strong and silent" masculinity. Also in accordance with this notion is the style of Ernest Hemingway, a conspicuously masculine writer. His writing, too, is "on the verge of non-communication" by virtue of a deliberate distancing from the sense of self-awareness. A first-person narrator like Jake Barnes of *The Sun Also Rises* observes the changes in his own emotions with as much detachment as he observes the weather or the lay of the land, and with somewhat less detail. This spareness has its own power, of course, in that it encourages the reader to flesh out the emotions using as clues the relatively minute variations in an otherwise noncommittal surface. Hemingway's discovery was that "you could omit anything if you knew that you omitted . . . and make people feel something more than they understood."[8] This discovery was a refinement after the fact, though: even in his high school days Hemingway was writing a hard-bitten prose. The origin of his style may be his early concern with masculine reserve, in life as well as in art. Nowhere does this concern emerge more fully than in the strongly autobiographical Nick Adams stories, which are in so many ways about growing up male. The central theme of masculine reserve is established in "Indian Camp," the first in order of composition as well as the first in the chronology of Nick Adams. Hemingway omitted, in the published version of this story, an introductory section which places the young Nick on a hunting trip with his father and uncle and which contrasts their expectations that "you don't want to ever be frightened in the woods" with Nick's newly discovered fear of death. In "Indian Camp" Nick accompanies his father, a doctor, when he is taken to an Indian woman who has been in labor for two days. With perfect efficiency, the doctor does what must be done—we are only informed later that this was a caesarean operation performed with a penknife and no anesthetic. "Her screams are not important," his father says to Nick. "I don't hear them because they are not important." At this the woman's husband, in the bunk above, rolls over against the wall and is later discovered to have slit his throat in despair. Nick's loyalty to his father is unshaken. The equation then is clear: those who feel emotion die; those who reject it are practical men. Thus when the story concludes with Nick feeling "quite sure that he would never die," this comes not from some redeeming epiphany nor from childish faith—for that faith has already been broken. Rather it is in the nature of a willed assertion, a choice. The young Nick guards against his emotions as he would guard against death. Tied up and threatened in "The Killers," for instance, he first tries to "swagger it off." Faced by the spectacle of Ole Andreson impassively waiting for death, Nick confesses his feelings to George:

"I can't stand to think about him waiting in the room and knowing he's going to get it. It's too damned awful."
"Well," said George, "you better not think about it."

This practical advice ends the story, slamming the door on any further flow of feeling. In "A Way You'll Never Be" Nick recalls the moment he learned that he *can* die, when he finds himself observed with the same unfeeling practicality by "the man with the beard who looked at him over the sights of the rifle, quite calmly before squeezing off." Now, although he "noticed everything in such detail to keep it all straight so he would know just where he was," feeling pours forth regardless in a monologue that is a mad parody of dispassionate observation and practicality. Reserve is reinstated, uneasily, in "Big Two-Hearted River," the best-known example of Hemingway's ability to convey feeling by omitting it. Hemingway called this a story "about coming back from the war but there was no mention of the war in it."[9] We nevertheless sense the thing left out, partly through passing hints and half-buried symbolical elements. The effect of the war on Nick is primarily conveyed by the varying rhythms in which Hemingway renders the masculine rituals of practicality. Serene, luminous, almost liturgical at one moment, sentences become staccato, nervous, and obsessive the next. These changes represent the shifting front of continuing battle against the death that is implicit in feeling. Nick Adams must fight his battle in this way if he is to survive. Hemingway, however, can afford to be somewhat more ambivalent toward the practicality that cleanses—or merely empties—a man of his own feelings. "The Three-Day Blow" satirically attacks the male fetish for practicality by anatomizing a conversation between two men consciously devoid of emotion. Such an instance makes us aware that Hemingway's habit of dispassionate observation could extend far enough to include itself as object.

If Mishima and Hemingway are reserved in style, they are less reserved in subject matter as they freely incorporate into their works many of the most intimate elements of their lives. This is going to be the case in many works of the masculine mode, since a man's relation to his own masculinity is always an intimate matter. A confessional element then must be considered and accounted for in an investigation of masculine style. A comment by Michel Leiris indicates one way of taking it into account. Following his *Manhood*—a work similar in nature to Mishima's *Sun and Steel*—Leiris writes an afterword on "The Autobiographer as Torero."

There he claims that a writing style must show its greatest brilliance at exactly the point at which the writer is most threatened; and no confessional writing can afford to be without this element of danger, even death, which he calls "the bull's horn." To write about certain aspects of one's life is to change that life. The writing becomes not a passive reflection but an act in itself, full of risk and consequence. As with the sculptural flourishes of the matador's cape, the writer's cape of words coaxes a kind of death—conceals it—and at the moment of truth reveals it.

A similar consciousness of confession is expressed by Peter Tarnopol, the purported author of the works presented in Philip Roth's *My Life as a Man*, Tarnopol's biographical statement reads in part:

> Presently Mr. Tarnopol is preparing to forsake the art of fiction for a while and embark upon an autobiographical narrative, an endeavor which he approaches warily, uncertain as to both its advisability and usefulness. Not only would the publication of such a personal document raise serious legal and ethical problems, but there is no reason to believe that by keeping his imagination at bay and rigorously adhering to the facts, Mr. Tarnopol will have exorcised his obsession once and for all.[10]

This dry prose explicates the nature of a "bull's horn" over which, elsewhere in the book, words glide with nervous urgency. The dangers indicated—legal, ethical, and most of all psychological—may also explain the book's structure, which is intricately refracted and reflexive. Two short stories by Tarnopol are followed by the autobiographical narrative which reveals the "sources" of these fictionalizations and is parodically entitled "My True Story." However, the truth of his story—that of his conflict-ridden marriage—is almost impossible to find. At every turn we are presented with different versions: in the two "Useful Fictions," in the comments of various characters in those fictions, in a psychoanalytic interpretation, in Tarnopol's own shifting attitudes and his shifts in style. And of course we speculate throughout on Tarnopol's relation to Roth. *My Life as a Man*, though, is not only about how difficult it is to render in words the truth about a past experience; it is also about how words and the expectations they set up may affect an experience before and while it happens. And at the center of all this is a question of male identity: the desire to "get to be what is described in the literature as *a man*."[11] No *Bildungsroman*, though, *My Life as a Man* is ultimately the chronicle of how the writer, entangled in the multiple relationships between life and literature, "squandered [his] manhood."[12]

The theme of squandered manhood has been treated by Roth before this, comically, in *Portnoy's Complaint*. Though in this book there is nothing of the complexity of *My Life as a Man*, we may still sense an influence of the "bull's horn" on language. In *Portnoy's Complaint* the tang of spoken American expands hyperbolically to match the enormities Portnoy discloses on the psychiatrist's couch. So far is the brilliance stretched that it becomes burlesque, rebounding upon itself to imply clearly a theatrical Jewish self-laceration.

Portnoy's Complaint is also interesting because of its treatment of a subject peculiar to the masculine mode, the penis. *Sine qua non* of maleness, instrument of the adolescent's awakening virility, center and symbol of his manhood to the adult—the penis has enormous importance in the life of the male and very little in literature. When not sublimated entirely, the penis is portrayed only as an object viewed in a general erotic context. Lawrence's rendering of "John Thomas" is in the end not a whit more satisfactory than the flowery similes of the pornography he so loathed. Neither reveals anything of the psychological relationship between a man and his own penis. Phenomenologists, too, who have explored the perception of one's own hand and foot and eye have been oddly demure where this part is concerned. *Portnoy's Complaint* at least makes a modest beginning—though not a demure one—at rendering the male's relationship to a part which, especially at puberty, seems more obsessively virile than the whole. "Ven der putz shteht, ligt der sechel in drerd," says Portnoy's Yiddish wisdom; the part has a propensity to conflict with the whole and to domineer over it. An apt emblem of this state is provided by Alberto Moravia in the closing lines of *Io et Lui* (which has been translated as *The Two of Us*). The weary Federico, at the end of a fruitless campaign to sublimate the dominance of his penis, returns to his patient wife, penis swollen with pride and triumph:

> Fausta's hand undid the chain, the door opened, and she appeared on the threshold in her dressing-gown. She looked at me, looked down, saw "him" and then, without saying a word, put out her hand to take hold of "him," as one might take hold of a donkey's halter to make it move. Then she turned her back to me, pulling "him" in behind her, and, with "him," me. She went into the flat: "he" went behind her; I followed them both.[13]

Much more than Gogol's nose, the penis has a quality of independence from the body: it has movements and moods, it sulks, it overbears, it overpowers. So it seems natural to find Federico having conversations and arguments with "him" just as Portnoy does with "his." It seems the literary version of a normal psychological experience. It is then a shock and a challenge for the reader to find, halfway through the novel, that the narrator, with whom the reader has been identifying, is *not* normal. In an interview with a psychologist friend, Federico admits that he literally does hear a voice from his penis and that both the animation of this part and his hostility toward it stem from an ambivalent sexual experience with his mother. Of course Federico resents this forced admission, resists it, and ultimately ignores it. Curiously enough, the reader ignores it too and continues to identify with the narrator as before. Only an undercurrent of strangeness remains as implied comment on the normal male's relationship to his sexual organ.

What words, then, for the penis? What style is adequate to its nature? As Federico's penis points out to him, in a memorable monologue, the phallus is a god of dark and mysterious force. Yet the tone adopted when speaking of it is as often as not a comic one, whether in popular slang terms or, for example, in works like Robert Graves's arch poem, "Down, Wanton, Down!" Undeniably, there must be a comic aspect to something which—as Molly Bloom observes—looks at one moment like a turkey neck and gizzards and at the next like a hat rack. This comic aspect is not necessarily at odds with the idea of the penis as a dark and awesome power. Comic and terrible meet in the style, of all styles, appropriate to the penis: that of the grotesque. The grotesque, of course, is not to be summed up in a single definition any more than is the penis. But in listing some of the grotesque's possible characteristics, we note how appropriate they are to this subject. The grotesque, for all its comic element, implies an underlying terror arising from the sense that things are out of control. There is a force behind the grotesque that is inhuman, both stupid and vital at the same time. It is a force strongly bound up with the physical; it is a force that goes to extremes. By virtue of its excesses, it deforms proportion and classical contours. In this respect, it is allied to caricature. But whereas caricature exaggerates features which express individual character, the grotesque absorbs individuality entirely into the inhuman. The part which in caricature reveals the nature of the whole, in the grotesque actually usurps the position of the whole: de Gaulle's nose is no longer just an identifying mark in David Levine's later drawings of him; it is an enormous, vigorous force which the general follows dazedly. Similarly, Beardsley's illustrations to *Lysistrata* and certain of Picasso's erotic engravings present us with a male grotesque. They express, in another medium, the same kind of extreme state rendered by Roth and Moravia.

Such writers demonstrate that there is room within the masculine mode for styles entirely different from the reservedly "masculine" ones of a Mishima or a Hemingway. A style is, to a considerable degree, a strategy: thus, there are strategic reasons for some writers to approach the subject of maleness in a style apparently at complete odds with masculinity. Such a style is Alfred Jarry's in *The Supermale*.[14] The title character, Marcueil, conceals his remarkable gifts beneath the life of an idle socialite with an unprepossessingly average exterior. Only the young daughter of an American magnate suspects his true nature; and to win her love, Marcueil, incognito, displays his physical prowess in a fantastical bicycle race and a record-breaking sexual marathon with the lady herself as partner. These exploits are recounted in a style which is wholly that of the dandy: it has his polished, over-civilized diction, his penchant for absurdity and ludicrous exaggeration, his moments of languor. *The Supermale's* style is thus one which most people would call effeminate. More attention to the dandy as a type, however, might dispel or at least modify this notion. Recalling only Beau Brummel's fastidious concern with dress, we tend to pass over the style of that dress. Its elegance was the product of a new restraint which still dominates our notions of male clothing. A corresponding restraint of emotion may well have been the invention of the Regency dandies. Far from condemning a man's display of emotion, the eighteenth century made it fashionable to be a man of feeling. But the dandy is now deliberately impassive and without emotional depth. He offers only his coruscatingly brilliant surface; and, in the purest versions of the dandy, there is nothing beneath that surface. In the creation of his facade, the dandy creates his entire life as a work of art built over a void. Baudelaire, who projected a work on literary dandyism, called dandyism a *"culte de soi-même"*; it has its affinities with such male types as the Don Juan and, yes, the bodybuilder, in a version as sophisticated as Mishima's. The dandy is above all a man striking an existential posture, a species of Camus's rebel. He disengages himself from all that is not of his own designing. He scorns even the society which is his milieu and which he manipulates with consummate skill. For that society's adulation he returns only an arrogant disdain, itself the mark of his eminence. The dandified style of *The Supermale* accordingly hurls a kind of challenge in the teeth of society, in language that is a heightened version of its own. It is language not opposed to the characteristics of the supermale but parallel to them. For Marcueil's virility is also a heightened version of characteristics which society favors. But carried to such an extreme, these characteristics rebound with almost apocalyptic force on the society which encouraged them. At the novel's close, Jarry's hero is destroyed by society, which takes advantage of the supermale's momentary lapse into the emotion of sentimental love. But the ironies with which Jarry recounts this defeat establish beyond it the triumph of style.

For all its ostentatiously civilized quality, then, the "effeminate" style of *The Supermale* is masculine in its suppressed capacity for destruction. No more effeminate than the style of *Ubu Roi* is childlike, it operates as a kind of ferocious negation of itself. As a strategy of style this self-negation is complex but not unique in the masculine mode. Lincoln Kirstein does a similar thing in his *Rhymes and More Rhymes of a Pfc*, which uses experiences of World War II to bring out the underlying mechanisms of masculinity.[15] Kirstein has little sympathy for the masculine patterns which are his subject but still does justice to their subtlety. For the work's style, though, he chooses the most unsubtle of possible models: the "rhymes" of Rudyard Kipling and Robert W. Service. The effect of this choice is surprisingly intricate. Viewing World War II through the lenses of earlier wars results in a disquieting awareness of disparities. Jog-trot cadences and hearty personae evoke nostalgia but also a sense of ludicrous naiveté. The style which once expressed a bluff confidence in the manly virtues is now made to communicate the questioning of those virtues. The irony of the situation turns the style upon itself.

An added irony is the fact that Kirstein is a homosexual and makes no bones about it; so is Mishima, for that matter. Homosexuals, of course, are by no means to be excluded from the masculine mode, any more than lesbians are to be ignored by feminist criticism. As a male who is himself fascinated and attracted by the nature of masculinity, the homosexual is fully capable of insight into that masculine nature. He may tend to see men in isolation from women and to define men's sexuality exclusively in its own terms. But in that he is no different from heterosexual writers. Women, when they do appear in ostentatiously male works, are reflectors of masculine sexuality; or they threaten it; or they only stand and wait, excluded from the male redemption in Hemingway's fishing excursions and Dickey's canoeing trips. Generally the male gauges his own masculinity not by women but by other men. Masculinity becomes reflexive, both perceiver and perceived.

It is perhaps for this reason that one so often feels, in the works I have been discussing, a despairing sense of sterility beneath the richness and the vigor. This is the frequent accompaniment of a life that turns in upon itself instead of opening outwards to the world and must to some degree be the familiar of every man who pursues his own nature. Within the masculine mode, though, the despair that shadows a reflexive life becomes peculiarly intensified by its subject matter. To think about masculinity is to become less masculine oneself. For one of the most powerful archetypes of manhood is the idea that the real man is the one who acts, rather than the one who contemplates. The real man thinks of practical matters rather than abstract ones and certainly does not brood upon himself or the nature of his sexuality. To think about himself would be to split and turn inward the confident wholeness which is the badge of masculinity. And to consider his own sexuality at any length would be to admit that his maleness can be questioned, can be revised, and, to a large degree, has been created rather than existing naturally and irresistibly as real virility is supposed to. Like MacLeish's perfect poem, the perfect male "must not mean but be." Self-consciousness is a crack in the wholeness of his nature.

Literature itself, of course, is a species of self-consciousness. The words for an action are something other than the action itself and reflect upon it as a thing past. They create an equivalent for a certain shape or form of real experience—an equivalent so insidiously powerful that it tends to usurp the place of reality. Thus when Mishima bursts out with "Oh, the fierce longing simply to see, without words!"[16] it is an expression of his equally fierce longing simply to *be* in a state of male wholeness, without the corrosion of wholeness that is his self-consciousness. Mishima's battle against words is parallel to his battle against self-consciousness. To win against self-consciousness he had to become one who "sacrifices existence for the sake of seeing"; to win against words his style also had to sacrifice, almost to the point of noncommunication. This mistrust of words is perhaps characteristic of the masculine mode. The works examined here are written in styles that to various degrees annihilate themselves; they are self-consuming artifacts. We see this in the stripped-down, noncommittal styles of Mishima and Hemingway more readily than we do in the stylistic extremes of Jarry and Kirstein. Yet both the art that conceals art and the art that flaunts itself arise out of the same mistrust of words. By going to an extreme, the style of writers like Jarry and Kirstein calls attention to itself as a style, implies its own artifice and falsity. The reader feels a sense of disparity with the subject—a sense which, upon further analysis, is seen to be itself the subject of such works.

I have been speaking of self-annihilation in regard to style, but it may go beyond that. Mishima's suicide was to a large degree the inevitable outcome of his lifelong pursuit of masculinity. Having cast himself in the role of warrior, he found his muscular body merely decorative, and therefore effeminate, unless it lived up to its implicit purpose, to confront death. Likewise in fiction, when masculinity is intensely pursued this is often done at the risk of self-annihilation. The masculine rite of passage described in Dickey's *Deliverance* results in the death of one member of the canoeing party; and those who survive are humanized to the degree that they are haunted by the specter of physical destruction. Even the purely mental sport of Robert Coover's *The Universal Baseball Association* results in self-annihilation. Following the classic pattern noted by Warren Farrell, a man with a dull job, in this case an accountant, fulfills his masculinity by identification with the heroism and drama of the game. Henry Waugh's game is entirely self-created and consists of statistics, history, picturesque lore—common counters in masculine conversation. So absorbed does he become by the game that he is ultimately destroyed by it, though the game itself continues on a mythological plane.

The game (to pick up that metaphor) is seen as continuing in all the works I have dealt with here. After the male dynamic has worked through to its own destruction, there remains a stable social context. A patient psychiatrist or wife takes in hand the sexually tormented. A tender memento and a placid marriage replace the crucified Supermale. Deep waters cover the deep terrors of Dickey's canoeing trip and offer choice new lakeside lots to a new generation. And Nick Adams, in "Fathers and Sons," sees his child eager to continue the life pattern of his father and grandfather. The very stability of the social context, which seems so opposed to the male destructive element, ensures its continuation; for it is in social expectations that the male mythology has its origin. Like war, masculinity may be nourished by society until it has grown to a point where it turns to destroy that which brought it into being.

General observations like this last are encouraged by the very nature of studying a masculine mode in literature. Yet each of these works finds its own terms to express the dynamics of manhood; and it is on its own terms that it must be approached. Literary analysis should not fall into the error, common in social revolutions, of overthrowing old patterns only to establish new and equally rigid patterns. It would be unfortunate if general observations on the relations between masculinity and literature were used in a way that hindered perception rather than aiding it. Such observations are properly used as a ground from which figures detach themselves, and against which they may be more clearly perceived. In literature and in the masculine mode especially, the individual vision is as important as the social mythology, the variations as important as the theme.

Notes

1. Annette Kolodny, "Some Notes on Defining a 'Feminist Literary Criticism.' " *Critical Inquiry* 2 (Autumn 1975): 78.

2. Recently published books on the subject include the following: *The Forty-nine Percent Majority*, ed. Deborah S. David and Robert Brannon (Reading, Mass.: Addison-Wesley,

1976); Warren Farrell, *The Liberated Man* (New York: Random House, 1974); Marc Fasteau, *The Male Machine* (New York: McGraw Hill, 1974); *A Book of Men*, ed. Ross Firestone (New York, 1976); and *Men and Masculinity*, ed. Joseph Pleck and Jack Sawyer (Englewood Cliffs, N.J.: Prentice-Hall, 1974). The leading magazine of the movement is *Brother*, published in Berkeley.

3. Virginia Woolf, *A Room of One's Own* (1928: New York: Harcourt, 1963), p. 105.

4. James Dickey, *Sorties* (New York: Doubleday, 1971), p. 59.

5. Yukio Mishima, *Sun and Steel*, trans. John Bester (New York: Grove Press, 1970), p. 17.

6. Mishima, *Sun and Steel*, p. 70.

7. Mishima, *Sun and Steel*, pp. 49, 46.

8. Ernest Hemingway, *A Moveable Feast* (New York: Scribner, 1964), p. 75.

9. Hemingway, *A Moveable Feast*, p. 760.

10. Philip Roth, *My Life as a Man* (New York: Holt, Rinehart, and Winston, 1974), p. 100.

11. Roth, *My Life as a Man*, p. 299.

12. Roth, *My Life as a Man*, p. 95.

13. Alberto Motavia, *The Two of Us*, trans. Augus Davidson (London, 1972), p. 353.

14. Alfred Jarry, *The Supermale* (1902), trans. Ralph Gladstone and Barbara Wright (New York, 1977).

15. Lincoln Kirstein, *Rhymes and More Rhymes of a Pfc* (New York: New Directions, 1966).

16. Mishima, *Sun and Steel*, p. 66.

7

Androgyny, Mimesis, and the Marriage of the Boy Heroine on the English Renaissance Stage

Phyllis Rackin

Recent literary historians have pointed out that the English Renaissance theater was an important site of cultural transformation—a place where cultural change was not simply reflected but also rehearsed and enacted (Greenblatt; Moretti; Montrose). Thus it is instructive to examine theatrical representations of gender during that period, for the theater provided an arena where changing gender definitions could be displayed, deplored, or enforced and where anxieties about them could be expressed by playwrights and incited or repressed among their audiences.

The English Renaissance stage is an especially interesting subject for gender studies because women's parts were played by boys. As the term *gender roles* indicates, there is an important sense in which gender is a kind of act for all women, not only for actresses and not only for boys pretending to be women. Sandra Gilbert, for instance, points out that among modern writers, the women, in contrast to the men, perceive the fundamental sexual self as a kind of costume rather than as the naked bedrock reality it seems to their male contemporaries. On a stage where female characters were always played by male actors, feminine gender was inevitably a matter of costume; and in plays where the heroines dressed as boys, gender became doubly problematic, the unstable product of role-playing and costume, not only in the theatrical representation but also within the fiction presented on stage.[1]

For a Renaissance audience, the sexual ambiguity of the boy heroine in masculine attire was likely to invoke a widespread and ambivalent mythological tradition centering on the figure of the androgyne (Slights; Hayles, "Ambivalent"). The androgyne could be an image of transcendence—of surpassing the bounds that limit the human condition in a fallen world, of breaking through the constraints that material existence imposes on spiritual aspiration or the personal restrictions that define our roles in society. But the androgyne could also be an object of ridicule or an image of monstrous deformity, of social and physical abnormality. Both these images of the androgyne appear in the plays of Shakespeare and his contemporaries, expressing radically different conceptions of human life and society and of dramatic imitation as well.

The idealized image of the androgyne—supported by Neoplatonic, alchemical, and biblical traditions—appeared frequently in the literature of the sixteenth century (Keach 191). Increasingly, however, the high Renaissance image of the androgyne as a symbol of prelapsarian or mystical perfection was replaced by the satirical portrait of the hermaphrodite, a medical monstrosity or social misfit, an image of perversion or abnormality.[2] The spiritualized conception of the *super*natural androgyne gave way to a more limited vision, confined within the social and natural worlds of ordinary life, which produced the image of the *un*natural hermaphrodite. At the same time, literary theory increasingly subordinated art to nature: nature became the object of artistic imitation and the standard by which art was to be judged.[3]

I

These changing conceptions of gender, androgyny, and theatrical mimesis can be seen in the representations of transvestite heroines in five English Renaissance comedies: John Lyly's *Gallathea* (c. 1587); William Shakespeare's *Merchant of Venice* (c. 1596), *As You Like It* (1599), and *Twelfth Night* (c. 1601); and Ben Jonson's *Epicoene* (1609). Although the five plays cover a span of only twenty-two years, they are well qualified to exhibit a changing theatrical tradition. Lyly, writing in the 1580s for Queen Elizabeth's court, was the most influential comic playwright of his age (Bradbrook 75–76; Thorp 49); and of all his plays, *Gallathea* seems to have exerted the greatest influence on Shakespeare (Scragg). He is also the only comic dramatist mentioned in Jonson's tribute to Shakespeare in the First Folio. Jonson, in turn, did more than any other Elizabethan playwright to influence the drama of his successors. John Dryden considered him "the most learned and judicious writer which any theatre ever had" and singled out *Epicoene* as a model for the writers of his own age (247–49).

The five plays are also well qualified to display changing conceptions of gender. In each of them, the plot centers on marriage, the paradigm that governed the lives and defined the identities of Renaissance women (Maclean 18–20, 57, 75, 85). As *The Lawes Resolutions of Women's Rights* (1632) proclaimed, "all women are understood either married, or to be married" (qtd. in Maclean 75). But the institution of marriage was changing profoundly, and the Renaissance "redefinition of marriage" necessarily entailed "a redefinition of the feminine" (Belsey 179). The archetypal relationship between men and women, marriage is also an archetypal symbol for the relations between contrasted sets of gender attributes. Thus what the marriages express is not only their authors' and audiences' changing visions of what is desirable and undesirable in relationships between persons of different sex but also—and perhaps more important—their changing gender definitions and changing visions of the relations between masculine and feminine gender attributes within an individual human psyche and within the culture that shapes it. Various conceptions of these relations can be seen in the changing figure of the boy heroine, who occupies a central position in all five plays. In each one, the bride-to-be wears a transvestite disguise, and in each the disguise plays a crucial role in the plot, impeding, enabling, or even motivating the marriage.

In *Gallathea*, the earliest of the plays, the two heroines, disguised as boys, fall in love with each other. When their true sex is revealed, the possibility of their marriage seems to be precluded; but at the end of the play the gods intervene, and we learn that the problem will be resolved by a kind of celestial sex-change operation (at the time of the marriage, one of the girls will be changed into a boy; we are not told—and the girls do not care—which one). By contrast, in *Epicoene*, the latest of the five plays, there are no gods, there is no heroine, and marriage represents not the object of the desired resolution but the chief obstacle to its achievement. Epicoene is a boy disguised as a girl and married to Morose. The play ends happily with the *dissolution* of the marriage when Epicoene is revealed as a boy. The hero, Dauphine, has arranged the deception so that he can secure his rightful inheritance by thwarting Morose's plan to marry and beget another heir.

Gallathea and *Epicoene* represent opposite extremes. Although money is a central issue in *Epicoene*, in *Gallathea* it is important only in the realistic, comic subplot, where Rafe, Robin, and Dick, three impoverished boys, seek their fortunes in various dubious trades. Mercenary concerns have no impact on the marriage of Lyly's heroines. One girl's father states that he wishes to keep his daughter a girl in order to preserve his son's inheritance intact, but no one pays any attention to his wishes. In *Epicoene* the claims of inheritance are opposed throughout to a character's wish to marry, and here it is Dauphine's desire to secure his inheritance (a desire the audience is made to share) that prevails.

There is a close connection in these plays between the value assigned to androgyny and the value assigned to marriage.[4] *Gallathea* ends in a validation of both, *Epicoene* in a repudiation of both. Sexual identity is an obstacle to marriage in both plays; but in *Gallathea* it proves infinitely malleable in the hands of the gods and irrelevant in the eyes of the audience (since we neither know nor care which girl will become a boy), while in *Epicoene* it becomes the decisive factor in determining the outcome of the plot. No androgyne and no heroine, Epicoene, the "silent woman" of Jonson's subtitle, is simply a pretty boy in female disguise, a pawn in Dauphine's economic game with no stake in the outcome of the plot and no will or character of his own. The androgynous characters who do appear in the play—the mannish "collegiate ladies" and their effeminate male consorts—are minor characters conceived in purely satiric terms, present only to be mocked and abhorred by their fellow characters, their playwright, and their audience.

In their differing treatments of androgyny, Lyly and Jonson make strikingly different statements not only about gender but also about the relation between the play world and the real world. Gender is, above all, a social construct, arbitrary and varying from one society to another, related to sex but not identical with it; and gender roles vary from one culture to another just as the words we use to signify our meanings vary from one language community to another. Moreover, the relations between gender and sex are as various and problematic as those between signifying words and signified meanings or between poetic fictions and the elusive "realities" they imitate.[5] Just as different cultures and even different individuals within a single culture can construe all those relations differently, so too the relation between gender and sex can be construed in a variety of ways. Thus in *Epicoene*, where reality is social, gender is an ineluctable reality; instead of celebrating androgyny, the play indulges in homophobic satire, and sex roles are rigidly enforced. In contrast to Jonson's realistic social satire, set in a recognizable contemporary London, Lyly's fantasy, set in a never-never land where Greek gods can appear on the banks of the Humber, uses liberal doses of myth and magic and celebrates androgyny. For the girls and the gods in *Gallathea*, gender is arbitrary, unreal, and reversible because the vantage point transcends the social to include the realm of fantastic imagination and spirit where androgyny is an image of human self-completion rather than an aberrant social category.

The three Shakespearean plays, written after Lyly's and before Jonson's, are more ambivalent in their treatment of monetary considerations, the value of romantic love, and the significance of gender identity. Shakespeare celebrates romantic love, but he also satirizes it (in Silvius and Phebe, in Orsino, in Olivia, and even in Orlando and Rosalind); and although money and status are never the primary issues for his protagonists, they are never wholly discounted.[6] Portia, like a princess in a fairy tale, will be won only by the suitor who can answer the fantastic riddle of the caskets, but the first thing we hear about her is that she is a "lady richly left"; and if Bassanio ends like a romantic hero, he begins very much like a fortune hunter. Orlando and Rosalind fall in love at first sight, but their wedding is crowned not only by the miraculous appearance of Hymen but also by the revelation that Rosalind's father has recovered his dukedom. Olivia is beautiful and she inspires Orsino's romantic love, but she is also a rich heiress, the object of Malvolio's dreams of social and economic advancement.[7]

Most important for my purposes, unlike either Lyly or Jonson, Shakespeare refuses to dissolve the difference between the sex of the boy actor and that of the heroine he plays; and he uses his boy heroines' sexual ambiguity not only to complicate his plots but also to resolve them. Portia's masculine disguise enables her to save Antonio, but her female reality, which enables her to love and marry Bassanio, is what motivates her to do it in the first place. By playing the boy's part of Ganymede, Rosalind enables Silvius to marry Phebe. By playing the girl's part of Rosalind, she enables Orlando to marry herself. These heroines' transvestite disguises are neither fully repudiated (as in *Epicoene*) nor fully authenticated (as in *Gallathea*). Instead, they become provisionally real, as, for instance, in *Twelfth Night*, Viola's disguise as the boy Cesario is both repudiated when she marries Orsino and authenticated when her twin brother, Sebastian, marries Olivia. Like Lyly, Shakespeare ends these comedies in the marriages of his boy heroines, but his conclusions vindicate the reality principle as well as the power of love and illusion. If Lyly and Jonson represent opposite extremes, Shakespeare occupies an ambiguous middle ground between them.

II

Even after such a cursory description of these five plays, an obvious question arises: what are we to make of the differences in their treatments of androgynous figures? Perhaps still more pressing for those of us who are primarily interested in Shakespeare's representations of women is the curious fact that his festive comedies celebrate heroines who are clearly the dominant figures in their worlds,[8] while his later plays depict heroines who are either weaker or less sympathetic and, although still played by boy actors, almost never dressed in boys' clothing.[9] Moreover, it is in Jonson's play, the latest of the five, that women are most powerless and most subject to misogynist satire.

Various explanations suggest themselves. Perhaps the passing of the English throne from a powerful and beloved queen to a misogynist king influenced the entire climate of English opinion regarding women (or at least the tastes of London's theater-going public). Perhaps the shift from public to private theaters was responsible: as Alfred Harbage points out, the misogynist picture of women and the debased view of marriage that emerge from plays written for the private theaters differ markedly from the more enlightened view that prevails in the public-theater play (*Rival Traditions* 222–58). Still, even Harbage's distinction between the two audiences has been questioned (Cook). Moreover, Lyly was writing for Queen Elizabeth's court, and the misogyny of a writer like Jonson seems to persist whether he is writing for the public or the private theater—indeed, it is evident even in his private conversation (*Conversations*, Jonson 1: 141–42).

The issue of the changing positions of women in Renaissance England has been much debated in recent years. Was humanist education a force for women's liberation (Dusinberre 2), or did it inculcate "docility and obedience" (Jardine 53)? Was the presence of a powerful female ruler "a spur to feminism" (Dusinberre 303), or was Elizabeth the proverbial "token" woman who reinforces patriarchal restraints on the rest of her sex (Jardine 195)? Does the *hic-mulier* controversy of the early seventeenth century point to a widespread female practice of transvestism and a growing assertiveness among women (Woodbridge 156–57, 265–66); does it betoken an intensified enforcement of patriarchal restrictions; or is it simply an expression of a general uneasiness about increased social mobility and disorder (Jardine 158–62)? Did the rising middle class elevate the status of women (Dusinberre 7), or did feminism do better in an aristocratic society with "a solid royalist regime" (Woodbridge 328; cf. Kelly)? Did Protestantism and Puritanism, with their new conceptions of marriage, undermine "the old Pauline orthodoxies about women" and provide for a significant advance in women's status during the late sixteenth and early seventeenth centuries (Dusinberre 5; Stone, *Crisis* 269–302)? Or did

"the Reformation actually [remove] some of the possibilities for women's independent thought and action" (Jardine 49) and the Puritan conception of marriage
actually lead to "greater patriarchy in husband-wife relations," a "decline" in the
status and legal rights of wives, and the increased subordination of women within
an increasingly sanctified and nuclear family structure (Stone, *Family* 136–37)?

Although different writers, examining similar evidence, come to opposite conclusions (Neely 20–21), the preponderance of evidence suggests that in most ways
the position of women declined during the Renaissance. The reasons for that decline
are complicated and still somewhat obscure, its course is uneven and difficult to
chart (Prior), but a variety of indicators suggest a loss of status and opportunity
for women in virtually every area of English life. By the end of Elizabeth's reign,
the humanist tradition of female learning was already fading, the learned woman
a subject for ridicule (Plowden 168). During the late sixteenth and the seventeenth
centuries, English women were increasingly excluded from work they had earlier
performed; removed from participation in economic, political, and cultural life;
relegated to a marginal and dependent economic status; excluded from the public
arenas of political power and cultural authority; and confined within the rising
barriers that marked off the home as a separate, private sphere (Clark; Kelly).

The plays I have chosen to discuss delineate a similar pattern of decline. It
would, of course, be a mistake to attempt to make simple equations between the
boy heroines in these five plays and the real women who watched them in Renaissance audiences. All five heroines are the creations of men: not only the playwrights who wrote their parts but also the actors who played them were male.
Moreover, the relation between actual life and theatrical representation is inherently
complicated and problematic, a dialectical process that inevitably involves anxiety,
compensation, and wish fulfillment rather than simple, mimetic reproduction. Male
writers in every period have managed to celebrate feminine projections of their
own ideals while maintaining misogynist attitudes and practices in their responses
to actual women. In this case, the relation between reality and representation is
particularly complicated because, as I hope to show, the issue of gender is intimately
connected in the drama of the English Renaissance to the issue of theatrical
representation itself.

III

The theater of a world in transition, the English Renaissance stage offered a field
of contention for competing ideologies. The changing conceptions of gender and
theatrical mimesis it displayed were intimately related to the changing conceptions
of language, nature, and human society produced by the emergent discursive field
that was to shape the age to come.[10] The ascendancy of a literalist copy theory of
language that sought to tighten the relation between word and "thing" had obvious
affinities with the tightening of the sex-gender relation. Moreover, feminist historians of science have shown how the new science, rejecting the ancient ideal of

Nature as a nurturing mother and the traditional alchemical metaphors of erotic union and androgynous perfection, played an important part in the reification and polarization of gender definitions and the devaluation of the feminine at the beginning of the modern age (Merchant; Keller). An analogous process can be traced in the English drama of the late sixteenth and early seventeenth centuries, where changing conceptions of the dramatists' art are related to increasingly rigid and degraded conceptions of gender and femininity. In delineating a variety of relations between the sex of the actor and that of the character he plays, these playwrights express varying assumptions about the relation between art and life, which is analogous in all these plays to relations between gender and sex. The androgyne, in fact, becomes the fullest expression of both relations.

Thus, in Jonson's play, which subscribes to the neoclassical ideal of art as an imitation of life, gender also imitates life—both in a limited, literal sense, since the sex of Epicoene is finally revealed as male (the sex of the actor who played the part), and in a broader sense, since women in the play are subjected to the same calumny, stereotyping, and social restrictions that real women suffered in Jonson's world. For Lyly and for Shakespeare, the relation between art and life is complementary as well as reflective: that is, it resembles the relation between two complementary angles, one growing as the other decreases. What is real in one world becomes unreal in the other, what is impossible in one world becomes possible in the other, and the work of the world of art is not only to imitate the defects of the real world but also to supply what is wanting. Thus, in these plays, the true gender of the transvestite figure turns out to be feminine, the opposite of the real sex of the boy who played her part. Similarly, the dynamics of the plots make femininity a desideratum rather than the liability it was in actual life, and within the represented action female characters exercise power, even though the boy actors who played them were either apprentices, the lowliest members of an adult company, or subjected to the miserable conditions of a children's company.[11]

The best example of the relation I am calling complementary is the characterization of Portia in *Merchant of Venice*. The chief inhabitant of the fantastic world of Belmont, Portia is introduced to the audience as a kind of mythical fairy-tale princess:

> In Belmont is a lady richly left,
> And she is fair and, fairer than that word,
> Of wondrous virtues. . . .
> Nor is the wide world ignorant of her worth,
> For the four winds blow in from every coast
> Renowned suitors, and her sunny locks
> Hang on her temples like a golden fleece,
> Which makes her seat of Belmont Colchis' strond,
> And many Jasons come in quest of her. (1.1.161–72)

And one of the first things we hear Portia say is the curious disclaimer she makes when she tells her waiting woman, "you will come into the court and swear that

I have a poor pennyworth in the English" (1.2.70–72). She speaks the lines, of course, in English on an English stage, but they seem calculated not only to indicate that Portia is an Italian lady, the inhabitant of a remote and exotic country, but also to remind the audience that their world and their language are different from hers. Shakespeare's allusion to the tacit stage convention that allows almost all his characters, even his ancient Romans, to speak beautiful English invokes and insists on the difference between the world represented on stage and the world inhabited by the audience, between the rich and powerful Italian lady and the poor and powerless English boy who played her part.

The same difference is invoked when Portia leaves her fantastic realm of Belmont to enter the more prosaic and contemporary world of Venice (which, although Italian, is still part of the literal geography of the sixteenth century), a world where trials take place in law courts rather than in the form of a fairy-tale contest in which suitors from many countries attempt to win a rich and beautiful wife by solving the riddles of the caskets. When Portia moves from Belmont to Venice, she takes on the disguise of a boy, dressing in garments of the same gender that the real boy who played her part would have worn when he stepped outside the theater. What is important, I think, is that this is a false appearance. The reality within the play—the reality that Portia is a woman—can be seen only in the fantastic world of Belmont, a world that is not a reflection but a reversal of the world the play's audience actually inhabited. In Belmont the boy actor takes on a false gender that belies his true sex to depict the truth about the character he plays. The Elizabethan platitude about poets and playwrights holding mirrors up to nature is more complicated and problematic than it seems: a mirror image always reverses the reality it reflects.

The complementary relation to nature and society that I have ascribed to dramatic fantasy can be figured by the yin-yang diagram that symbolizes the relation of male and female, the fantastic dramatic complement playing the part of the female principle, the "reality" it complements playing the part of the male. The association is most apparent in fantastic plays because they flaunt their artificiality, but it can be said to characterize dramatic representation per se. In an androcentric culture, the female principle is negative, like the blank space that defines a positive pictorial image or like the concept of feminine gender that allows the male to define itself as masculine; it is also supplementary, like the artistic imitation that represents natural life.[12] Fantastic drama reverses this equation, locating the reality principle within the world of art rather than outside it, creating an antiworld where object becomes subject and the feminine can be characterized as real. Realistic art, by contrast, strives to replicate within itself the hierarchal relations that its society has defined as natural. Thus it is not surprising that Jonson's realistic dramatic technique is often praised for its virility or that his play ends by banishing the feminine principle, or that Lyly's fantasy can make a marriage between two characters who started out as girls.

Close analogies can be drawn between changing conceptions of gender and androgyny and changes in mimetic theory and practice. Neoplatonic tradition idealized the androgyne and exalted the feminine, stressing "the spirituality of woman and her close link with the mysteries" (Maclean 55, 90). It also provided the basis for the Renaissance literary theory that described poetic fictions as idealized visions of supernatural perfection transcending the limitations of ordinary life and nature. This conception of poetry can be found in Sir Philip Sidney's description of the poet making "things either better than nature bringeth forth, or, quite anew, forms such as never were in nature. . . . Nature never set forth the earth in so rich tapestry as divers poets have done. . . . Her world is brazen, the poets only deliver a golden" (157).

The golden world is a focus for nostalgia. Sidney associates it with prelapsarian nature, and Shakespeare associates it with a romanticized version of the feudal past. Portia's Belmont, Duke Senior's forest court, and Illyria are places where wealth comes by inheritance and social status through kinship (a system that some feminist historians would argue was in fact more hospitable to women than the one that was replacing it in Shakespeare's time). By contrast, Venice is a world of "commodity" and "trade" (3.1.27–30), and the bonds of kinship are disrupted in both households in act 1 of *As You Like It*. The same contrast can be seen in *Gallathea*, where the comic subplot anticipates Jonson's contemporary characters and settings, his satiric treatment of alchemy, and his emphasis on the harsh economic realities of a changing world. Rafe, Robin, and Dick search for masters and go hungry in a recognizable sixteenth-century Lincolnshire where the woods are being cut down to make ships (1.4.70–71), while Gallathea and Phyllida exist on another plane entirely—idealized, mythological, and ahistorical.

The inhabitants of the golden world are not realistic contemporary portraits; instead, they are images of ideal types. Sidney's Neoplatonic poet "painteth not Lucretia whom he never saw, but painteth the outward beauty of such a virtue." In creating characters, the poet does not imitate "what hath been, or shall be" but considers "what may be or should be." Nature never "brought forth so true a lover as Theagenes, so constant a friend as Pylades, so valiant a man as Orlando, so right a prince as Xenephon's Cyrus, so excellent a man every way as Virgil's Aeneas." The poet, inspired "with the force of a divine breath . . . bringeth things forth far surpassing [Nature's] doings" to depict images of the perfection that disappeared from the world with "that first accursed fall of Adam" (157–58). The androgyne, also associated in Neoplatonic tradition with an ideal perfection lost at the time of the Fall, is exactly the sort of subject Sidney envisions here.

The association of the androgyne with magic, prevalent in primitive cultures as well as in Renaissance tradition, is echoed by Lyly's magical transformations and also by the hint of magic associated with Shakespeare's Rosalind, who claims to have conversed with a magician from the age of three (5.1.60) and who comes on stage to her marriage accompanied by the god Hymen. The association of androgyny with alchemy and of both with dramatic fantasy is not directly expressed in these plays, but Lyly's subplot, which anticipates Jonson's satire on alchemy as a hoax, also anticipates his rejection of androgyny and his realistic subject matter. The boys in Lyly's subplot, contemporary English types, never lose their social or sexual identities, and at the end of the play their problems are resolved when they are invited to sing at Gallathea and Phyllida's wedding—invited, that is, to become the boy choristers their actors really were. His fantastic main plot, by contrast, celebrates androgyny and relies for its resolution on the power of magic transformation.

Sidney distinguishes poetry from every other form of discourse by its maker's refusal to be bound by the limitations of nature: "Only the poet, disdaining to be tied to any such subjection, lifted up with the vigor of his own invention, doth grow in effect another nature." For Jonson, by contrast, although poets may "invent, faine, and devise many things," they must "accommodate all they invent to the use and service of nature"; "[t]he true Artificer will not run away from nature, as hee were afraid of her, or depart from life and the likenesse of Truth" (*Timber*, Jonson 8: 609–10, 587). Rejecting the extravagant fantasies of his predecessors and contemporaries and anticipating the taste of the age to come, Jonson's prefatory letter to *The Alchemist* warns his readers, "thou wert never more fair in the way to be cos'ned (then in this Age) in Poetry, especially in Playes: wherin . . . to runne away from Nature, and be afraid of her, is the onely point of art that tickles the Spectators" (5: 291).

Jonson's *Alchemist* can, in fact, be read as an extended metaphor condemning fantastic playwrights who transgress the rule of nature and the hierarchical order of human society. Poets who attempt to improve on nature are no better than the cozening alchemists who pretend to transmute base metals into gold and poor persons into rich. Sir Epicure Mammon sounds, in Subtle's description, very much like Sidney's poet of the golden world:

> He will make Nature asham'd, of her long sleepe: when art, Who's but a step-dame, shall doe more, then shee, In her best love to man-kind, ever could. If his dreame last, hee'll turne the age, to gold.
>
> (5: 1.4.25–29)

With the philosopher's stone and the wealth it will bring, Mammon plans to "make an old man, of fourescore, a childe" (2.1.53) and transform his cook into a knight (2.2.87). Reminded that the fulfillment of his extravagant desires will not be tolerated in a monarchy, "being a wealth unfit for any private subject," he proposes to move to a free state (4.1.147–56). Jonson's satire in *The Alchemist* associates the subversive power of alchemy with the power of new money to undermine the established social and political order, and his letter "To the Reader" points up an additional association with the subversive power of theatrical representation. The actor, no less that the alchemist, transgresses the social and ontological categories that keep the world an orderly place. Taking on a variety of roles, an actor belies his own identity. Theatrical impersonation transforms the poor into the rich, the commoner into the king, the old into the young, the male into the female (Barish).

In his analogy between fantastic playwrights and cozening alchemists, Jonson attempts to deal with the antisocial aspects of theatrical representation by relegating them to the rejected category of dramatic fantasy. Renaissance writers took various positions on fantasy and on the theater itself. Some praised the actors for their protean ability to assume disparate shapes, while others condemned them as hypocrites who belied the natures and roles that God had seen fit to give them, but admirers and detractors alike understood that the player was a dangerous anomaly in a hierarchical society, a creator of "anti-structures" that, like the inversions of carnival, could undermine as well as reinforce existing social hierarchies (Montrose, "Purpose" 55–65). In his condemnation of false artificers who run away from nature and in his satire of mannish women who transgress their gender roles, Jonson attempts to contain this subversive potential by drawing sharp distinctions between legitimate and illegitimate uses of dramatic representation and subjects his art to the laws of nature and society. True art, for Jonson, is conservative, offering a "rule and Patterne of living well . . . and disposing us to all Civill offices of Society" (*Timber* 636).

The issue of gender-role transgression is intimately related, not only in Jonson but in other Elizabethan discussions of the theater, to the issue of theatrical representation. The negative association that I am suggesting, the pejorative analogy between the boy actor's sexual ambiguity and the ambiguity of dramatic mirroring, is a familiar feature of Puritan diatribes against the stage. Typically, the argument begins by echoing the Platonic charge that poets misrepresent the world they imitate, but it almost invariably ends by citing the scriptural injunctions against transvestism (Deut. 22.5). As Rabbi Zeal-of-the-Land Busy tells the puppets in Jonson's *Bartholomew Fair*, "my maine argument against you, is, that you are an *abomination:* for the Male, among you, putteth on the apparell of the *Female*, and the *Female* of the *Male*" (6: 5.5.98–100).[13]

The proscription, of course, involved sexual as well as social and political anxieties. As Lisa Jardine points out, the incitement to homosexual lust with which the Puritans charged the pretty boy actresses wearing female clothes may have been more than a matter of overheated Puritan imagination (9–36). In his homophobic satire in *Epicoene* Jonson foregrounds the social dimension of the prohibition: he characterizes the mannish "collegiates" as unnatural, but chiefly because they violate the hierarchical divisions between the sexes that should prevail in society. But the sexual dimension is also present, for instance, in Truewit's scornful description of Clerimont melting away his time "betweene his mistris abroad, and his engle at home" (5: 1.1.23–25). Shakespeare, by contrast, emphasizes the attractiveness of his transvestite heroines, to other women as well as to the men they love, and Lyly's transvestite heroines are depicted as more beautiful and more worthy than Hebe—a character named for Jove's female cupbearer, who was replaced, after she fell and exposed her private parts, by Ganymede, the archetypal catamite whose name Shakespeare's Rosalind will take to go with her transvestite disguise.

In *Epicoene*, Jonson attempts to deal with the dangers of social and sexual transgression by upholding the socially sanctioned gender division and by resolving his play in the abolition of sexual ambiguity: the transvestite figure is finally revealed as the boy the actor who played him really was. In *Bartholomew Fair* Jonson uses another strategy. There, the puppet Dionisius (named for the androgynous god in whose festivals the Greek drama originated) confutes the Puritan by lifting up its garment to show that the puppets (like souls redeemed in Christ), "have neither male nor female amongst us" (6: 5.5.105). Human actors have sexual bodies, but the characters they play are "whatever sex . . . the playwright asserts" (Kimbrough, "Androgyny" 17). By making his actor a sexless puppet, Jonson avoids the dangerous duplicity between sex and gender embodied in the figure of the boy actress. Shakespeare, by contrast, insists on this duplicity, most notably in *As You Like It*, where he uses a complicated layering on of disguise to render Rosalind's sexual identity thoroughly ambivalent (Hayles, "Disguise" 65–66). Played by a boy actor, Rosalind is a female character who disguises herself as a boy and then, wearing that masculine disguise, playacts the part of her own female self. And the ambiguities of the conclusion to that play involve not only gender but sex itself, and not only the character Rosalind but also the boy actor who played her part. In the epilogue, that ambivalent figure refuses to choose between actor and character or between male and female but instead insists on the ambiguities: within the same short speech, she is both the lady Rosalind (when she says, "it is not the fashion to see the lady the epilogue") and the boy who played Rosalind's part (when he promises, "If I were a woman I would kiss as many of you as had beards that pleas'd me, complexions that lik'd me, and breaths that I defied not . . .").[14]

IV

The epilogue to *As You Like It* associates Rosalind's sexual ambiguity with the complicated relations between the male actor and the female character he portrays, the dramatic representation and the reality it imitates, the play and the audience that watches it. Rosalind (or the boy who plays her part) insists that the audience must cooperate if the play is to work:

> I charge you, O women, for the love you bear to men, to like as much of this play as please you; and I charge you, O men, for the love you bear to women (as I perceive by your simp'ring, none of you hates them), that between you and the women the play may please.

The epilogue's suggestive reference to a sexual transaction between the men and women in Shakespeare's audience echoes the multiple marriages that have just been depicted on stage and also implies that the relation between the play and its audience is a kind of sexual transaction or marriage.[15] To be successful, the play must win both sexes with a playful androgynous appeal that is most appropriately expressed by the ambiguous figure who no longer has a single name or sexual identity, combining in one nature Rosalind, Ganymede, and the boy who played their parts.

The relationship Rosalind proposes between Shakespeare's play and its audience is significantly different from the relationships between play and audience contemplated in *Gallathea* and in *Epicoene*. Written for boys to perform at Queen Elizabeth's court, *Gallathea* addressed an audience for whom, as for the gods within the play, all things were possible and for whom life, like the play itself, was a kind of elaborate, artificial spectacle.[16] *Epicoene* was written for boys to perform in a private theater before an audience for whom the very act of attending the play was an assertion of social status.[17] In both cases, the actors and the audience constituted two homogeneous groups, the boys performing on stage clearly inferior to the adults who watched them. Shakespeare's plays, by contrast, were written for an adult company to perform for a mixed audience. The leading actors were shareholders in the company—entrepreneurs rather than unpaid workers for a master—and their heterogeneous audience would include people whose social rank and economic power were less than their own.

In the first two situations, the reality of the audience dominates that of the actors.[18] One of Lyly's girls becomes a man in order to marry the other, and Jonson's boy is revealed as a boy so that a marriage can be annulled and an inheritance ensured. But despite these differences, there are important similarities. Both plays resolve the tensions between real sex and illusory gender, and both resolutions privilege the sex that wielded authority in the plays' audience. Designed to please a female monarch who wielded patriarchal authority, *Gallathea* looks beyond the end of the play for its resolution—a resolution in which one of the girls will become a boy in order to please the other. In Jonson's play, all the important characters are male, and at the end the revelation that the boy is a boy satisfies a man's desire for money, restores to the actor the sex he has offstage, and gratifies a status-hungry audience. In Shakespeare's transvestite comedies, the relation between sex and gender and the relation between play world and audience world, like the relation between adult actors and their heterogeneous audience, remain dialectical, with neither reality obliterating the other.[19]

That neither we nor the characters know or care which of Lyly's girls will be transformed demonstrates the arbitrary quality of sexual difference in *Gallathea*. Like the terms in a Euphuistic paradox, sexual difference is endlessly reversible. In the artificial world of Lyly's fantasy, deceptive gender can become a model for true sex, costume for body, name for thing, disguise for reality. The result, however, is paradoxically similar to Jonson's, for although Lyly transforms a sexual disguise into truth to permit a marriage and Jonson removes a sexual disguise to annul a marriage, both plays end in the abolition of sexual ambiguity. Jonson strips away Epicoene's deceptive gender identity to reveal his true sex, rejecting artifice and grounding his resolution in nature. Lyly invokes the supernatural to dissolve that ground and celebrate the power of artifice. Jonson comes to rest in the masculine reality principle. Lyly contains it within the comic subplot. In the main plot, he wishes it away. But Lyly, no less than Jonson, resolves the marriage plot by rejecting the troublesome discrepancy between sex and gender embodied in the figure of the boy heroine.

Shakespeare's transvestite comedies, unlike Lyly's and Jonson's, sustain that ambiguity to the end. Rejecting both Lyly's abolition of sexual difference and Jonson's denial of the inevitable gap that separates physical sex from social gender, Shakespeare marries his unlike lovers, joining male and female characters on his stage just as he joins masculine and feminine qualities in the androgynous figures of his boy heroines. Refusing to collapse the artistic representation into a simple replica of the world outside the theater or to abandon that world for a flight into escapist fantasy, he insists on the necessary ambivalence of his play as a kind of marriage, a mediation between opposites, which can be brought together only by the power of love and imagination.

V

That marriage, however, becomes increasingly difficult to sustain. It seems perfect at the end of *As You Like It*, when the saucy Epilogue, like Jonson's saucy puppet lifting its garment in *Bartholomew Fair*, seems to dissolve in sophisticated laughter the problematic questions of gender and of the status of dramatic representations. In *Twelfth Night*, however, Shakespeare returns to those problems, and this time he insists on their seriousness. Viola, like Lyly's disguised girls and unlike Portia and Rosalind, is unhappy in her transvestite disguise; and, almost as Rabbi Busy might do, she refers to her disguised self as a "monster" and characterizes her disguise as "a wickedness wherein the pregnant enemy does much" (2.2.27–34).

This is not to say that Shakespeare abandons fantasy in *Twelfth Night*. The entire play is set in the fantastic world of Illyria, where sanity looks like madness and madness like sanity, and Viola's true sex is the opposite of that of the actor who played her part. Here as in *The Merchant of Venice* the truth in the play is an illusion from the point of view of the literal world, and the disguise in the play corresponds to the truth in the literal world. Here, however, as in *As You Like It*, the disguise is associated with the fantasy world within the play,[20] and the scheme is complicated by the presence of Viola's twin brother, Sebastian. He provides a kind of reality principle, and his presence, no less than Viola's, is necessary before the marriages that resolve the plot can take place.

In assuming her masculine disguise, Viola "imitates" Sebastian's reality (3.3.383), just as art was said in Renaissance literary theory to imitate natural life. Olivia falls in love with the imitation, thus providing for a wonderfully complicated plot in which the disguised Viola adores Orsino, who is hopelessly in love with Olivia, who, in turn, dotes on Viola, whom she takes for the boy Cesario. Helpless in the face of this muddle, Viola comments, "Poor lady, she were better love a dream"

(2.2.26); and later, when she first suspects that her brother has miraculously appeared in Illyria, she prays, "Prove true, imagination, O, prove true, /That I, dear brother, be now ta'en for you" (3.4.375–76).[21] Finally, of course, the dream and the imagination do "prove true" when Sebastian materializes on stage to marry Olivia and untangle the love triangle. Thus the conclusion of the play vindicates both the imagination that proves true and the truth that proves it. Without the illusion (Viola's disguise as a boy), the right characters would not have fallen in love; without the reality, they could not have married. In the figure of Sebastian, gender and sex correspond, both within the play world and between the play world and the world of the audience. *Twelfth Night* incorporates the reality principle in its conclusion by splitting the unitary figure of the androgyne into the marvelously identical boy-girl twins who are needed to make the resolution possible.[22]

At the end of the recognition scene, Orsino says to Viola-Cesario, "Give me thy hand / And let me see thee in thy woman's weeds" (5.1.272–73), a curious statement, which seems to make their marriage contingent on her change of costume. Orsino's demand serves to bring Malvolio back on stage for the attempted resolution of the gulling plot, for Viola is apparently unable to obtain a set of women's clothes without his intercession. Her women's clothes are being held by the captain who brought her ashore—a figure from the presumably real world outside Illyria—but he has been imprisoned on a lawsuit initiated by the puritanical, literal-minded Malvolio, the refuser of Illyrian madness and fantasy, who wants to marry Olivia for the same reasons Jonson's Dauphine does not want Morose to marry anyone— out of concern for his own social and economic status. Without the cooperation of the reality principle that Malvolio and the captain represent, the boy actor cannot put on Viola's clothes, and the play ends on an equivocal note, with Malvolio stalking off the stage crying "I'll be reveng'd on the whole pack of you" (5.1.378) and the clown singing a melancholy song that contrasts the ease and pleasing wish fulfillment of the festival world with conditions in the outside world, where "the rain it raineth every day." As C. L. Barker remarks, "in the 1640's, Malvolio *was* revenged on the whole pack of them" (257), and even within Shakespeare's career, this is the last play where an androgynous heroine can put on her femininity with a theatrical costume.

The Puritans closed the theaters, and a multitude of causes, which we are only beginning to understand, closed off many of the opportunities and possibilities that had been open to women at the beginning of the modern age (Keller 62–63; Clark; Kelly). Changing portrayals of transvestite heroines on the Renaissance stage help to illuminate the early phase of the process, and they also give us a glimpse of a liminal moment when gender definitions were open to play. At the time these plays were written, gender was still defined according to the old, medieval associations of masculinity with spirit and femininity with body (Montrose, "Shaping" 73; Keller 48; Merchant 1–40). But on the stage, the boy actress's body was male, while the character he portrayed was female. Thus inverting the offstage associations, stage illusion radically subverted the gender divisions of the Elizabethan world. The

increasingly masculinist thinking of the seventeenth and eighteenth centuries—
expressed in forms as diverse as the persecution of witches, the suppression of
women, and the rise of Baconian science—also expressed itself in new theories
of mimesis that drew sharp distinctions between the reality of the world and the
illusions of art and betrayed a deepening antitheatrical prejudice, even among
writers for the stage (Barish 337). If, as the new historians of Renaissance literature
are now arguing, the Elizabethan theater was a creator as well as a creation of its
culture, "shap[ing] the fantasies by which it [was] shaped, beget[ting] that by which
it [was] begotten" (Montrose, "Shaping" 86), then it is perhaps worth remembering
that the masculinist ideology that shaped the modern world established its hegemony
in the same period when the theaters were closed.[23]

Notes

1. For examples of transvestite heroines, see the chapter entitled "The Female Page"
in Freeburg (61–99).

2. The first recorded English use of *hermaphrodite* occurred in 1594, closely following
a cluster of other words of similar meaning and similar pejorative connotations (Brown).
Jackson argues brilliantly that the fantasy of sexual self-sufficiency was a widespread and
powerful expression of the Renaissance ideal of transcendence, that it was associated with
the figure of the androgyne, that this ideal was increasingly rejected, and that Jonson in
particular was criticizing it.

3. Sidney's *Apology* manages to advocate both views, without any apparent awareness
of contradiction (Rackin 206). For an account of the debate between the Renaissance
advocates of icastic and fantastic imitation, see Hathaway. For an example, see the selections
from Torquato Tasso and Jacopo Mazzoni in Allen Gilbert.

4. As Kimbrough points out, "marriage is often presented as a symbol of androgyny—
the sign of human fulfillment, the mark of wholeness, the token of primordial unity and
apocalyptic reunion . . . " ("Macbeth" 190). Shakespeare invokes this ideal in *Antony and
Cleopatra*, where Cleopatra renounces her sex ("I have nothing of woman in me") just before
she claims Antony as her husband in the life to come (5.2.239, 287). He also invokes it
when he describes the mysterious union of the Phoenix and the Turtle: "Single nature's
double name / Neither two nor one was called."

5. As Barbara Johnson argues, "Literature . . . inhabits the very heart of what makes
sexuality problematic for us speaking animals" (qtd. in Abel 1), and, as Abel goes on to
remark, "sexuality and textuality both depend on difference." Cf. Belsey 177–78.

6. Montrose, in fact, discusses *As You Like It* as a representation of male anxieties
about money and status (" 'Place . . .' ").

7. Williamson shows how Queen Elizabeth's practice of eroticizing her relationships
with men at court, together with her power to bestow the largest rewards in society, provides
a revealing social context for the characterization of the heroines in Shakespeare's romantic
comedies, who fulfill the heroes' social and economic ambitions as well as their romantic
desires (ch.1).

8. These three Shakespearean plays all belong to what Barber calls his "festive comedies," but Barber sees the heroines' transvestite disguises as a reassertion of male power
in the real world: "Just as a saturnalian reversal of social roles need not threaten the social

structure, but can serve instead to consolidate it, so a temporary, playful reversal of sexual roles can renew the meaning of the normal relation" (245). Cf. Linda Woodbridge's argument that "transvestite disguise in Shakespeare does not blur the distinction between the sexes but heightens it" (154). Davis, however, argues that the comic and festive sexual inversion that was "a widespread form of cultural play" in preindustrial Europe "could *undermine* as well as reinforce patriarchal authority" (129–31).

9.   Imogen and Cleopatra are notable exceptions, but Cleopatra never wears masculine attire on stage, and Imogen, who adopts the disguise in obedience to a man's suggestion (3.4.151–72), becomes a completely passive figure in her boy's clothes. As Bono explains, "In the later plays, although boys still play the woman's part, the extradramatic referents of their play have become an imagined woman, not an excluded middle term" (202n). For an argument that the change in Shakespeare's treatment of his female characters results from differences in dramatic genre, see Bamber.

10.   See, e.g., Foucault's argument:

> At the beginning of the seventeenth century . . . thought ceases to move in the element of resemblance. Similitude is no longer the form of knowledge but rather the occasion of error, the danger to which one exposes oneself when one does not examine the obscure region of confusions. . . . The age of resemblance is drawing to a close.   (51)

Such a change would emphasize gender distinctions and reject androgyny as a misleading chimera ("the chimeras of similitude loom up on all sides, but they are recognized as chimeras" [51]), just as Jonson does in *Epicoene,* a play written at the very time Foucault describes.

11.   For the point about the apprentices I am indebted to Carolyn Heilbrunk who made it at a panel discussion on women in Shakespeare at Columbia University on 12 November 1983. As for the actor in the children's company, Harbage writes that he "was little more than a chattel," "divorced from his parents, huddled up in lodgings, . . . worked to what must often have been the limit of physical endurance," and provided only with his subsistence (*Shakespeare's Audience* 32–33).

12.   On art as supplement, see Derrida 144–45. On the association between the artistic imitation and the feminine, see Zeitlin, who points out that "the ambiguities of the feminine and those of art [are] linked together in various ways in Greek notions of poetics from their earliest formulations" (133).

13.   I am indebted to Maureen Quilligan for the reference to Rabbi Busy and the puppets.

14.   The epilogue exemplifies what Erickson calls "heterosexual androgyny"—a gender-role exchange that does not "dissolve the boundary between 'male' and 'female' " but instead crosses "back and forth over a boundary no longer seen as a rigid barrier dividing the two sexes into two absolutely separate groups" (133). Erickson, of course, would dispute my use of his term here, since he uses it in his description of *Antony and Cleopatra* to distinguish that play from *As You Like It,* which he sees as a play that uses androgyny in the service of male bonds.

15.   On the presence of women in Shakespeare's audience, see Harbage, *Shakespeare's Audience* 74–78. On their presence in Jacobean theaters, see Woodbridge 250–52.

16.   See Powell. See also Saccio: "the conventional allegorization of the Iphis-Ianthe story told in Ovid" (Lyly's source for the sex-change plot) was "*that men should despaire of nothing: since althings were in the power of the Gods to give . . .* " (146).

17.   See, e.g., Shapiro (*Children* 66–71), where he observes:

> In the private theaters, opportunities for self-dramatization probably attracted members of the upper classes who felt their social status to be precarious: either old-line aristocrats struggling to maintain

their standing; or gentry, *nouveaux riches*, and young men from the inns of court striving for higher status. Whatever its actual size, this group of spectators set the tone for private-theater audiences. . . .

He also points out that "in *Epicoene*, Jonson provides his audience with a pleasing image of itself while directing its mockery to a gallery of deviants from its aristocratic ethos" (82). Even if, as most recent scholarship concludes, there was much more overlap between public and private theater audiences than we formerly assumed, I believe the distinction remains valid; for, although many of the same people may have gone to both kinds of theater, they are very likely to have gone for different kinds of entertainment and to have assumed different roles once they got there. I might go to the opera one night and to a baseball game the next, but my motives, expectations, dress, and behavior would be very different on the two occasions. Moreover, as Shapiro argues, "the efforts at Paul's and Blackfriars to recreate the conditions and atmosphere of court performance would probably have produced a more aristocratic ambiance in those playhouses than what prevailed in public theatres like the Globe" ("Boying" 2n).

18. As Lancashire points out, *Gallathea* is "essentially a court entertainment . . . designed to be a part of court social life" (Lyly xix). And Shapiro argues that unlike adult plays, where even passages of metadramatic self-reference "can sometimes strengthen the illusion created by the dramatic action," plays written for the children's troupes were generally designed "to make the dramatic action seem artificial in comparison with the audience's world" (*Children* 108–09).

19. A similar pattern can be seen in the three authors' treatments of their androgynous characters: in each case the degree of autonomy accorded the character corresponds to the degree of power available to the actors who performed the play. Although Shakespeare's transvestite heroines, like Lyly's and Jonson's, were played by boys, they exhibit the same autonomy that distinguished the adult actors who constituted Shakespeare's company from the powerless boys who acted in *Gallathea* and *Epicoene*. Epicoene is Dauphine's creation and acts at his command. Although Lyly's disguised girls have wills of their own, they do not choose their male disguises but are compelled to wear them by their fathers, and their problems are solved at the end by the intervention of the gods. By contrast, Shakespeare's Portia, Rosalind, and Viola choose and act for themselves, and all three are central characters in their respective plays—the ones with whom the audience identifies, the ones who see the most, the ones who, by virtue of their transvestite disguises, make possible the marriages that bring joy and well-being to the other characters. Just as Jonson's satirical treatment of androgyny expresses his uneasiness about the dangers of theatrical impersonation, Shakespeare's celebration of androgynous heroines implies a celebration of the actor's freedom.

20. I am indebted to Marianne Novy for this important observation. The difference is important because it shows a progression from the simple chiasmic relation between reality and fantasy in *The Merchant of Venice* to their more complicated intermingling in *As You Like It*, where the green world of the forest is subject to winter and rough weather, where Rosalind and Celia must buy their sheep farm for money, and where a fantasy shepherd like Silvius keeps company with a real one like Corin.

21. On the association between dreams and poetic fantasy, see Mazzoni: "the phantasy is the common power of the mind for dreams and for poetic verisimilitude. . . . the phantasy is the power on which dreams depend . . . poetic verisimilitude is also founded on the same power of the mind" (*On the Defense of the Comedy of Dante* 1.67, in A. Gilbert 386–87).

22. For a perceptive discussion of the "identical" opposite-sex-twins symbol, including a reminder that Shakespeare himself was the father of opposite-sex twins, see Heibrun 34–45.

23.   Earlier versions of this paper were presented in 1984 at the Ohio Shakespeare Conference, the Berkshire Conference on Women's History, and a conference entitled After *The Second Sex* at the University of Pennsylvania. In revising and expanding my discussion I have profited greatly from the stimulating discussions at the Ohio Shakespeare Conference and from the commentaries of Maureen Quilligan and Carolyn Heibrun, the respondents at the Berkshire and Pennsylvania conferences.

Works Cited

Abel, Elizabeth, ed. *Writing and Sexual Difference*. Chicago: U of Chicago P, 1982.

Adams, Hazard, ed. *Critical Theory since Plato*. New York: Harcourt, 1971.

Bamber, Linda. *Comic Women, Tragic Men: A Study of Gender and Genre in Shakespeare*. Stanford: Stanford UP, 1982.

Barber, C.L. *Shakespeare's Festive Comedy*. Princeton: Princeton UP, 1959.

Barish, Jonas A. "The Antitheatrical Prejudice." *Critical Quarterly* 8 (1966): 329–48.

Belsey, Catherine. "Disrupting Sexual Difference: Meaning and Gender in the Comedies." *Alternative Shakespeares*. Ed. John Drakakis. London: Methuen, 1985. 166–90.

Bono, Barbara J. "Mixed Gender, Mixed Genre in Shakespeare's *As You Like It*." *Renaissance Literary Genres: Essays in Theory, History, and Interpretation*. Ed. Brabara K. Lewalski. Harvard English Studies 14. Cambridge: Harvard UP, 1986. 189–212.

Bradbrook, Muriel C. *The Growth and Structure of Elizabethan Comedy*. 1955. Baltimore: Penguin, 1963.

Brown, Steve. " '. . . and his ingle at home': Notes on Gender in Jonson's *Epicoene*." Renaissance Society of America. Philadelphia, 21 Mar. 1986.

Clark, Alice. *Working Life of Women in the Seventeenth Century*. London: Cass, 1919.

Cook, Ann Jennalie. *The Privileged Playgoers of Shakespeare's London*. Princeton: Princeton UP, 1981.

Davis, Natalie Z. "Women on Top." *Society and Culture in Early Modern France*. Stanford: Stanford UP, 1975. 124–51.

Derrida, Jacques. *Of Grammatology*. Trans. Gayatri Chakravorty Spivak. Baltimore: Johns Hopkins UP, 1974.

Dryden, John. "An Essay of Dramatic Poesy." 1668. Adams 228–57.

Dusinberre, Juliet. *Shakespeare and the Nature of Women*. New York: Macmillan, 1975.

Erickson, Peter. *Patriarchal Structures in Shakespeare's Drama*. Berkeley: U of California P, 1985.

Foucault, Michel. *The Order of Things: An Archaeology of the Human Sciences*. New York: Vintage, 1973.

Freeburg, Victor Oscar. *Disguise Plots in Elizabethan Drama: A Study in Stage Tradition*. New York: Blom, 1965.

Gilbert, Allen, ed. *Literary Criticism: Plato to Dryden*. New York: American, 1940.

Gilbert, Sandra. "Costumes of the Mind: Transvestism as Metaphor in Modern Literature." Abel 193–219.

Greenblatt, Stephen, ed. *The Power of Forms in the English Renaissance*. Norman: Pilgrim, 1982.

———. *Renaissance Self-Fashioning: From More to Shakespeare*. Chicago: U of Chicago P, 1980.

Harbage, Alfred. *Shakespeare and the Rival Traditions*. Bloomington: Indiana UP, 1952.

———. *Shakespeare's Audience*. New York: Columbia UP, 1941. Hathaway, Baxter. *Marvels and Commonplaces: Renaissance Literary Criticism*. New York: Random, 1968.

Hayles, Nancy. "The Ambivalent Ideal: The Concept of Androgyny in English Renaissance Literature." Diss. U of Rochester, 1976.

———. "Disguise in *As You Like It* and *Twelfth Night*." *Shakespeare Survey* 32 (1979): 63–72.

Heilbrun, Carolyn. *Toward a Recognition of Androgyny*. New York: Knopf, 1973.

Jackson, Gabriele Bernhard. "Structural Interplay in Ben Jonson's Drama." *Two Renaissance Mythmakers: Christopher Marlowe and Ben Jonson. Selected Papers from the English Institute, 1975–76*. Ed. Alvin Kernan. Baltimore: Johns Hopkins UP, 1977. 113–45.

Jardine, Lisa. *Still Harping on Daughters: Women and Drama in the Age of Shakespeare*. Brighton: Harvester, 1983.

Jonson, Ben. *Ben Jonson*. Ed. C.H. Herford, Percy Simpson, and Evelyn Simpson. 11 vols. Oxford: Clarendon, 1925–52.

Keach, William. *Elizabethan Erotic Narratives: Irony and Pathos in the Ovidian Poetry of Shakespeare, Marlowe, and Their Contemporaries*. New Brunswick: Rutgers UP, 1977.

Keller, Evelyn Fox. *Reflections on Gender and Science*. New Haven: Yale UP, 1985.

Kelly, Joan. "Did Women Have a Renaissance?" *Becoming Visible: Women in European History*. Ed. Renate Bridenthal and Claudia Koonz. Boston: Houghton, 1977. 137–63.

Kimbrough, Robert. "Androgyny Seen through Shakespeare's Disguise." *Shakespeare Quarterly* 33 (1982): 17–33.

———. "Macbeth: The Prisoner of Gender." *Shakespeare Studies* 16 (1983): 175–90.

Lyly, John. *Gallathea and Midas*. Ed. Anne Begor Lancashire. Regents Renaissance Drama Series. Lincoln: U of Nebraska P, 1969.

Maclean, Ian. *The Renaissance Notion of Woman: A Study in the Fortunes of Scholasticism and Medical Science in European Intellectual Life*. Cambridge: Cambridge UP, 1980.

Merchant, Carolyn. *The Death of Nature: Women, Ecology, and the Scientific Revolution*. San Francisco: Harper, 1980.

Montrose, Louis Adrian. " 'The Place of a Brother' in *As You Like It:* Social Process and Comic Form." *Shakespeare Quarterly* 32 (1981): 28–54.

———. "The Purpose of Playing: Reflections on a Shakespearean Anthropology." *Helios* ns 7.2 (1980): 51–74.

———. " 'Shaping Fantasies': Figurations of Gender and Power in Elizabethan Culture." *Representations* 1 (1983): 61–94.

Moretti, Franco, " 'A Huge Eclipse': Tragic Form and the Deconsecration of Sovereignty." *Genre 15 (1982): 7–40*.

Neely, Carol Thomas. *Broken Nuptials in Shakespeare's Plays*. New Haven: Yale UP, 1985.

Plowden, Alison. *Tudor Women: Queens and Commoners*. New York: Atheneum, 1979.

Powell, Jocelyn. "John Lyly and the Language of Play." *Elizabethan Theatre*. Stratford-upon-Avon Studies 9. New York: St. Martin's, 1967. 147–67.

Prior, Mary, ed. *Women in English Society: 1500–1800*. London: Methuen, 1985.

Rackin, Phyllis, "Shakespeare's Boy Cleopatra, the Decorum of Nature, and the Golden World of Poetry." *PMLA* 87 (1972): 201–12.

Saccio, Peter. *The Court Comedies of John Lyly: A Study in Allegorical Dramaturgy*. Princeton: Princeton UP, 1969.

Scragg, Leah. *The Metamorphosis of Gallathea: A Study in Creative Adaptation*. Washington: UP of America, 1982.

Shakespeare, William. *The Riverside Shakespeare*. Ed. G. Blakemore Evans. Boston: Houghton, 1974.

Shapiro, Michael. "Boying Her Greatness: Shakespeare's Use of Coterie Drama in *Antony and Cleopatra*." *Modern Language Review* 77 (1982): 1–15.

———. *Children of the Revels: The Boy Companies of Shakespeare's Time and Their Plays*. New York: Columbia UP, 1977.

Sidney, Sir Philip. *An Apology for Poetry*. 1595. Adams 154–77.

Slights, William W. E. " 'Maid and Man' in *Twelfth Night*." *Journal of English and Germanic Philogy* 80 (1981): 327–48.

Stone, Lawrence. *The Crisis of the Aristocracy, 1558–1641*. Oxford: Clarendon, 1965.

———. *The Family, Sex and Marriage: In England 1500–1800*. New York: Harper, 1977.

Thorp, Willard. *The Triumph of Realism in Elizabethan Drama: 1558–1612*. New York: Gordian, 1970.

Williamson, Marilyn. *The Patriarchy of Shakespeare's Comedies: The Plays in History*. Detroit: Wayne State UP, 1986.

Woodbridge, Linda. *Women and the English Renaissance: Literature and the Nature of Womankind, 1540–1620*. Urbana: U of Illinois P, 1984.

Zeitlin, Froma I. "Travesties of Gender and Genre in Aristophanes' *Thesmaphoriazousae*." Abel 131–57.

8

The Politics of Emerson's Man-Making Words

David Leverenz

Several years ago I heard of a scholar who got tenure at one of our best universities primarily because of a brilliant book he had written about Emerson. The work had been accepted, by Oxford University Press, with glowing reader reports and suggestions for only a few minor revisions. But in the course of revising, the writer changed his mind. So he withdrew his book and completely rewrote it. Again he submitted the manuscript, again it was accepted with great enthusiasm, and again he changed his mind. The years have been passing, and there is still no sign of his Emerson book.

Anyone who has tried to write about Emerson hears that story with a mixture of delight and terror. Apocryphal or not, it shows the ferocious difficulties inherent in trying to make sense of his prose. One of Emerson's most subtle readers, Jonathan Bishop, announces at the outset of his study that "There is something at the heart of Emerson's message profoundly recalcitrant to the formulations of the discursive intelligence" (6). James Russell Lowell called him "a chaos full of shooting-stars" (45). Emerson himself read his words with bemusement. "Here I sit & read & write with very little system," he wrote to Carlyle in 1838, "& as far as regards composition with the most fragmentary result: paragraphs incompressible each sentence an infinitely repellent particle" (*Correspondence* 185). The confusion does not seem to bother him at all; he seems quite nonchalant about it. He goes on to talk about his garden.

Emerson is intrinsically baffling. Yet Emerson's critical stock has never been higher. He has become the avatar of the strong mind heroically overcoming personal and social limitations to liberate its genius. That perception is especially odd because Emerson has never had an interpretive community. Eric Cheyfitz is among the most candid about the problem: "Putting Emerson aside, we cannot remember what we have read or if we have read anything . . ." (10).[1] From the beginning of Emerson's lecturing career his eloquence was received by most of his audience with floundering incomprehension. His Western listeners wanted something "burlier and more definite." Artemus Ward drew belly laughs across the country—and taught Mark Twain how to give a comic lecture—by doing a grave burlesque of Emerson's abstracted hesitations and disjointed juxtapositions.[2]

From the 1840s to the 1980s, however, Emerson's cultural centrality has been ensured, not by general assent but by the advocacy of two very different pressure groups: intellectuals and businessmen. In political terms, we could call them his interpretive constituencies. Emerson's prose begins to make sense not in and of itself or in relation to intellectual and literary traditions but as an implicitly political response to contemporary American expectations for becoming a man.[3] His contradictions speak to his contradictory constituencies.

In recent years two prominent national figures have been traveling the country to preach Emerson's greatness: Harold Bloom and Woody Hayes. These two infinitely repellent particles have more than a little in common. Both men are strenuously embattled champions of combat. Like the former Ohio State football coach, the Yale professor is self-confessedly preoccupied with being "strong." Both men graphically evoke the anxieties of competition with other strong men, and both delight in the will that perseveres despite recurrent defeat. Bloom and Hayes have different Emersons, of course. Hayes affirms the country's dominant gospel of competitive success, while Bloom delights in the mind's revelatory gnostic leaps beyond social convention. One speaks to postindustrial businessmen and the athletes who entertain them, while the other speaks to an alienated elite who seek to repair what Bloom calls, in *The Anxiety of Influence*, the "disease of self-consciousness" (29).[4] But both speakers love Emerson because Emerson inspires feelings of access to manly power.

Emerson's voice gains its own access to power as he becomes what he calls for, a man speaking to men, in a country where "The young men were born with knives in their brain" (*Works* 10: 311).[5] Transforming the desperate competitiveness that he saw around him and within him, Emerson developed a style of imperious nonchalance, a manliness beyond any competition. "I never argue," he once said to a questioner. For him power means an inward experience of spontaneous metamorphosis, not a public rivalry for dominance. Paradoxically, his calls for self-reliance rest on his faith in self-decentering. To be incessantly reborn from a disembodied, cosmic womb-mind becomes his alternative to the conventional arts of manly disputation and animates his hopes for a new kind of manly language. As Emerson confidently demands of the universe in his 1841 journal, "Give me initiative, spermatic, prophesying man-making words" (271).[6]

Emerson's language of man making launches some wonderfully destabilizing flights. He unsettles the vocabularies of businessmen, merchants, and landed gentry who are imprisoned in their rivalries for money, dominance, property, and status. He senses the vacuum of self-confidence filled by those social codes. In particular, Emerson calls for men like himself and his brothers to abandon their father's patrician conformity and create a new elite. But while his most forceful rhetoric unmans the manly types, his contradictory affirmations of individual will and intellectual infinitude blur the conflicts that give vitality to his prose. His "man-making words" hold his own rivalries and resentments in suspension, while his presentation of power absorbs, without acknowledging, the class conflicts that intensified the ideology of manhood from 1825 to 1850.

As one crucial consequence, the women's world of relations and feelings becomes irrelevant. Though Emerson challenges the social definitions of manhood and power, he does not question the more fundamental code that binds manhood and power together at the expense of intimacy. Emerson's ideal of manly self-empowering reduces womanhood to spiritual nurturance while erasing female subjectivity. "Self-Reliance" takes for granted the presence of faceless mothering in the mind, an ideal state of mental health that he sums up in a memorable image: "The non-chalance of boys who are sure of a dinner" (2: 29).

Emerson's various paradoxes reflect contradictions in the emerging ideology of individualism, which erected an ideal of free, forceful, and resourceful white men on the presumption of depersonalized servitude from several subordinated groups. Such solitary male freedom, as Emerson slowly discovers, depersonalizes him as well. To empower his voice, Emerson's rhetoric requires as its speaker a free-floating self whose nonchalance deliberately rides above emotional commitment and social groupings. In taking his female support system for granted and in reducing intimacy to faceless nurturing, Emerson cuts himself off from experiencing feelings except through rivalry and detachment. Although he may have triumphed over his father, he has ceased to recognize himself.

In "Experience" he cannot even mourn for himself, projected through the death of his son—he can mourn only for the loss of access to power. The essay's seemingly brutal candor about being unable to feel masks an uglier and more evasive note of depressive accusation, directed at the women who take care of him. If "Experience" shows his intellectual tenacity, it also reveals the self-cauterization exacted by the American ideology of manhood, an ideology that Emerson ambivalently resists and intensifies.

I

Emerson's early essays proclaim an explicit rhetoric of man making. "The American Scholar," "The Divinity School Address," and "Self-Reliance" in particular insist on manly power as the essence of mental energy and rail against what society does to manhood. Men have lost the "fountain of power," he says in "The American Scholar." "Yes, we are the cowed,—we the trustless." "The state of society is one in which the members have suffered amputation from the trunk, and strut about so many walking monsters—a good finger, a neck, a stomach, an elbow, but never a man." "The main enterprise of the world for splendor, for extent, is the upbuilding of a man" (1: 53, 64, 53, 65). "Society everywhere is in conspiracy against the manhood of every one of its members," he declares in "Self-Reliance." "We are parlor soldiers," "city dolls," "a mob." A true man should be a "firm column" who as soon as he realizes his inborn power "throws himself unhesitatingly on his thought, instantly rights himself, stands in the erect position," and "works miracles" (2: 29, 43, 41, 50). "The Divinity School Address" makes similar claims. "Once man was all; now he is an appendage, a nuisance." "Now man is ashamed of himself; he skulks and sneaks through the world . . . " (1: 80, 88). The quotations could be tripled. Emerson seeks man-making words; he wants "the institution of preaching" to become once again "the speech of man to men" (1: 92).

John Jay Chapman was the first to call attention to Emerson's obsession with being a man. Emerson has nothing essential to do with philosophy, Chapman says in his still compelling 1898 essay "Emerson": "We must regard him and deal with him simply as a man." Emerson's manhood comes into being through an agonized struggle with the "atmospheric pressure" of his country's intellectual timidity. "He felt he was a cabined, cribbed, confined creature, although every man about him was celebrating Liberty and Democracy, and every day was Fourth of July. He taxes language to its limits in order to express his revolt. . . . If a soul be taken and crushed by democracy till it utter a cry, that cry will be Emerson" (166, 201–02; rpt. in Konvitz 110, 116–17). Harold Bloom, in *Agon*, translates Chapman's manly Emerson into a modernist mode that emphasizes the subversive play of Emerson's voice more than the desperate cry. Eric Cheyfitz, challenging and retroping Bloom, says that Emerson's manly eloquence really transforms his sense of his female defects, especially his sense of powerlessness and his inability to make up his mind (see also Poirier, "Writing").

That fantasy of transformation may seem—and indeed is—bizarre and sexist. Yet other male readers have noted something similar in the relation of Emerson's manhood to femaleness. The elder Henry James, whose letters to Emerson have the needy and exuberant tone of Melville's letters to Hawthorne, finally decided "that Emerson himself was an unsexed woman, a veritable fruit of almighty power in our *nature*." He came to that conclusion, he says, after repeatedly locking himself up with Emerson in the bedroom (Grattan 43–44).

The elder James often complained to his friend about his intense love and his intense frustration. Both feelings came from the same source: Emerson's serene refusal to meet James's need for manly leadership. Where James wanted forceful arguments that he could follow and contend with, Emerson seemed already else-where, attending another inspiration. His "difficult staccato," as John Morley called it (Konvitz 77), fascinated and infuriated James, who expostulated in an 1843 letter, "Oh you man without a handle! . . . [S]hall one never be able to help himself out of you, according to his needs, and be dependent only upon your fitful tippings-up?" (Perry 1: 51). Jonathan Bishop sympathizes with James's frustrated response, and he also casts it in masculine-feminine terms. "It is possible to feel that Emerson does not step forward enough, does not play a proper 'masculine' role," he says. Elsewhere Bishop comes close to calling Emerson a flirt (153–54, 44–45).[7]

I suspect that the temptation to call Emerson a woman, one that Bishop and James momentarily indulge and that Cheyfitz ambiguously expands into a book, is a conventional male response to frustrated possessiveness. Feeling vaguely uneasy with the kind of manliness Emerson is interested in and given so little to advocate or to argue with, these three male readers try to account for their bafflement by labeling his power "female." Emerson himself would do that trick in a more demeaning way when he got back at his dead father's awesome severity by recurrently accusing the genteel clergy, his father's profession, of being effeminate. The label "woman" indirectly acknowledges how insinuating and comprehensive Emerson feels to these readers and how dangerous William Emerson seemed to his son. But it also suggests that Emerson's power proves more frustrating than liberating to the manliness of some of his most candid devotees.

As Cheyfitz says, Emerson implicitly or explicitly rejected not just one but three vocations that could have channeled his powers of eloquence into conventional manly roles: the pulpit, the press, and politics. All three would have required organized modes of persuasion (103).[8] For the young minister, however, intellectual instability began as a self-confessed defect, then grew to be the signal of his receptivity to spontaneous power. To be a real man, for Emerson, meant exactly what the elder James attributed to him: being free of handles. In a society that defined manhood competitively by possessiveness and possessions, Emerson would define manhood paradoxically by abandonment and self-dispossession. His nonchalance often makes grasping men look foolish.

Barbara Packer finds the right note when she speaks of Emerson's insouciance, his air of unself-consciousness, the "curiously evasive action" of his mind in effacing himself from his own prose powers. Those characteristics, she says, typically provoke critics to assert that Emerson was unconscious of something absolutely essential to his text (19–20, 122).[9] He seeks the shock of unconscious or transconscious power through his voice without mediation or control. "Man-making words" knock down the social walls by which we protect ourselves from being perceivers instead of possessors. Perceivers of what? "Gleams," he says; intuitions, spontaneities, fluidity, infinitude—he is not sure what. But he is utterly confident that such perception is the only real power, that it flows through the mind, and that he can best express it when he abandons argumentation for an imperious nonchalance.

"I wish to be a true & free man, & therefore would not be a woman, or a king, or a clergyman, each of which classes in the present order of things is a slave" (July 1834; *Emerson in His Journals* 125–26). But manhood at present is in bondage. Men conform to the market as surely as women conform to the home. "In America out of doors all seems a market; indoors, an air tight stove of conventionalism. Every body who comes into the house savors of these precious habits, the men, of the market; the women, of the custom" (May 1843; 306). Becoming a man, Emerson came to feel, meant escaping conformity either to the rivalries of the marketplace, where men became things, or to the suffocations of domestic gentility, where men become women.[10]

To be a real man, as every foreign observer remarked of Americans at this time, meant having strong opinions on a narrow range of subjects while bending one's life and liberty to the pursuit of money and property. But American men were not nearly so practical as they claimed to be. Their fanciful speculations reminded Harriet Martineau of the Irish. Barbara Packer picks up on that insight to emphasize that American money making had much less to do with greed than with proving one's worth. As she says, Americans "did not really want money, but the sense of self-esteem its possession would confer" (96). She and Joel Porte connect Emerson's reliance on spiritual capital and mental mobility to the boom-and-bust cycles of American capitalism at takeoff point (Porte, *Representative* 257–66, 292).[11]

This was an America, as the younger Henry James would later say, with only three kinds of people, and by people he meant men: the busy, the tipsy, and Daniel Webster. Emerson chose to be a Webster of the spirit. He reconceived eloquence as the free flight of the mind through the mind, "dispossessed" from what he calls in an 1845 journal entry the "adhesive self." The entry builds its eloquence by self-consciously naming and revising the conventions of manly social action:

> It is the largest part of a man that is not inventoried. He has many enumerable parts: he is social, professional, political, sectarian, literary, & of this or that set & corporation. But after the most exhausting census has been made, there remains as much more which no tongue can tell. And this remainder is that which interests. This is that which the preacher & the poet & the musician speak to. This is that which the strong genius works upon; the region of destiny, of aspiration, of the unknown. Ah they have a secret persuasion that as little as they pass for in the world, they are immensely rich in expectancy & power. Nobody has every yet dispossessed this adhesive self to arrive at any glimpse or guess of the awful Life that lurks under it.
>
> For the best part, I repeat, of every mind is not that which he knows, but that which hovers in gleams, suggestions, tantalizing unpossessed before him. His firm recorded knowledge soon loses all interest for him. But this dancing chorus of thoughts & hopes is the quarry of his future, is his possibility, & teaches him that his man's life is of a ridiculous brevity & meanness, but that it is his first age & trial only of his young wings, but that vast revolutions, migrations, & gyres on gyres in the celestial societies invite him.
>
> (Nov. 1845–Mar. 1846; 350)[12]

The power of the passage depends not simply on an opposition between mind and society but on the ability of Emerson's voice to transform the usual manly preoccupations: "interest," "rich," "expectancy & power," "interest" again, "quarry," possession and dispossession. Like a good businessman he takes inventory; like a good citizen his takes a census; he adds up every item of "firm recorded knowledge" but finds his interest and profit in the "remainder" "which no tongue can tell," "tell" meaning "reckon" as well as "say." We should be hunters or miners of a different kind of quarry, the quarry of the mind, where a "dancing chorus of thoughts and hopes" unpossesses our possessiveness.

The nonchalance here comes largely through the puns, which mine and undermine the common meanings of manly words to illuminate the spiritual possibilities.

Emerson's manliness is a state of transformation, in which Emerson springs loose the play of meanings from the "properties" of words that have become fixed by their social uses. "The one thing which we seek with insatiable desire, is to forget ourselves, to be surprised out of our propriety," he says at the end of "Circles." "The way of life is wonderful: it is by abandonment" (2: 190).

Emerson frequently involves a Neoplatonic sense of ultimate form and generative harmony that joins birth, passivity, and power in a cosmic vagueness. But his more pungent descriptions of power often connect thinking to abandonment in every sense. His epigrams pop up like loons from a vast fluidity. While the great lines make him the patron saint of overachievers, the explicit self-decentering liberates jaunty aggression against strong social men.

"God offers to every mind its choice between truth and repose," he writes in "Intellect." "Between these, as a pendulum, man oscillates." The man who chooses repose "will accept the first creed, the first philosophy, the first political party he meets,—most likely, his father's." But the man of truth "will keep himself aloof from all moorings and afloat. He will abstain from dogmatism, and recognize all the opposite negations between which, as walls, his being is swung" (2: 202; cf. *Journals* 5: 112). The mind's passive pendulum oscillates between, not beyond, the strong walls of the father's. Thinking exposes the father's dogmatic negations by abandoning their fixity.

In one of his most astonishing destabilizations of manhood, a passage near the start of "The Transcendentalist," Emerson's flight of scientific fancy transforms solidity into motion, earth into space, nouns into verbs and then into still more indeterminate participles. As mass converts to pure energy, sturdy self-reliance becomes a dazzling imaginative openness, as pliable as language itself. Yet throughout, as we finally discover, the passage's power floats on a startling emptiness:

> The materialist, secure in the certainty of sensation, mocks at fine-spun theories, at star-gazers and dreamers, and believes that his life is solid, that he at least takes nothing for granted, but knows where he stands, and what he does. Yet how easy it is to show him, that he also is a phantom walking and working amid phantoms, and that he need only ask a question or two beyond his daily questions, to find his solid universe growing dim and impalpable before his sense. The sturdy capitalist, no matter how deep and square on blocks of Quincy granite he lays the foundations of his banking-house or Exchange, must set it, at last, not on a cube corresponding to the angles of his structure, but on a mass of unknown materials and solidity, red-hot or white-hot, perhaps at the core, which rounds off to an almost perfect sphericity, and lies floating in soft air, and goes spinning away, dragging bank and banker with it at a rate of thousands of miles the hour, he knows not whither,—a bit of bullet, now glimmering, now darkling through a small cubic space on the edge of an unimaginable pit of emptiness. And this wild balloon, in which his whole venture is embarked, is a just symbol of his whole state and faculty.
> (1: 202)

This wonderful send-up of old Boston bankers and new "venture" capitalists launches them on a "wild balloon" of intellectual speculation, as panic-inducing as the economic speculations that launched the Panic of 1837 five years before.[13] First Emerson presents the materialist in language that mimics the man's voice as well as his worldview. Pithy phrases and reductive verbs evoke a rather truculent fellow who aggressively sports his certainties, almost to excess. His hard-sounding words and choppy phrases mock the stargazers and dreamers. For him knowledge means simply opinions and work, in the good old American way: "where he stands, and what he does." This is a man who holds tight to what he knows: "he at least takes nothing for granted."

The passage then introduces him to the "nothing" that he *should* take for granted. As soon as he "ventures" into questions beyond his knowledge, he discovers uncertainties whose powers he can ride but never own. While the pleasures of discovery are "easy to show" with simple astronomy, it is the easy showmanship of Emerson's voice that conveys his real argument: to relish dislocation. He turns the materialist's hard-edged language into a receptive softness, lightening the *s*'s and loosening the rhythms to a more extended flow. If the assertions seem bizarre at first, the voice seems oddly assured and inviting, much more expansive than the skeptical materialist seems to be. Casual and informal ("he need only ask a question or two"), welcoming and even chummy ("he also is a phantom . . . amid phantoms"), the speaker can leap from fact to imagination in a phrase. Emerson intimates that real security rests not in "the uncertainty of sensation" but in the uncertainty of what lies "before his sense."

Then the long, magnificent transformational sentence flings the materialist toward everything he has mocked. Finespun theories take him "spinning away" from foundations; dreamers find him part of their "wild balloon." His deep, square, cubic blocks turn out to be "no matter" at all, at best "a small cubic space" on the edge of a boundless space. Motion becomes everything that matters. The materialist discovers himself first self-possessed, as a sturdy capitalist, then unpossessed, as a whirl of mind. Since he is also a characterized reader, we too experience a giddy displacement from a sturdy world to "a bit of bullet" hurtling through a universe that offers no place to take a stand. At the apex of receptive perception, the "whole" darts along the edge of an immeasurable hole. We gain power only by acknowledging our perpetual motion through "an unimaginable pit of emptiness."

The passage is self-consciously dazzling. It is a bravura showpiece of finespun rhetorical effects. Yet it is also self-consciously scary, especially in its precipitous ascent or plunge—we cannot tell which—from womblike security to abandonment. We stand on a world "which rounds off to an almost perfect sphericity, and lies floating in soft air." Yet that world transforms to "a bit of bullet, now glimmering, now darkling" in a void. Are we lying in the lap of immense intelligence, as he says in "Self-Reliance," or are we riding a gunshot to nowhere?

In the next paragraph Emerson explicitly demands that we relocate power in the mind, not in society, government, property, and "sensible masses." Yet like the materialist, we have to accept dislocation as the price of our access to the mind. And if we perceive ourselves rightly, we see that "mental fabric is built up on just as strange and quaking foundations as his proud edifice of stone."

II

Why is Emerson so at ease with this kind of eloquence? How can he announce his imperatives in such a nonchalant tone, while manly power draws on female fullness and emptiness in his themes? Close readings would take us further and further toward deconstruction for its own sake. Instead of deconstructing his prose I want to reconstruct its politics. We have to shift our focus from his contradictory language of mental process to the social manhood that his rhetoric addresses. What does he want his power of eloquence to do?

The usual thing to say about Emerson's politics is that while he sometimes seems elitist, he actually has a radically egalitarian vision of what people can be. I propose the reverse. Emerson calls for a new cultural elite, whose ideal of manly conversion to intellectual activity both dramatizes and transcends class conflicts. Emerson's claims for the potential convertibility of every man to intellectual power veil a politics that divides people into a new elite and the mob. He dreams of an intelligentsia that could preserve the patrician valuing of culture over business and politics, while he also dreams of empowering culture with the capital of American manhood. For Emerson the mind is the richest liquid asset.

The ideal of a manly intellectual elite allows Emerson to reject alliance with the new middle class of entrepreneurial managers and professionals, whose aggressiveness and competitive strife disturb and offend him. Emerson also rejects alliance with his own "cultivated classes," which as he says in "Self-Reliance" seem "timid," with at best a "feminine rage" (2: 33). Disengaging from those two groups and from the ministry and the Whig Party that straddle the line, he incorporates their contrary modes of social power in the self-abandoning mind, which he equates with the flow of the cosmos.

From that extraterrestrial base Emerson addresses his politics of man making to all the potential constituencies that might enable his cultural elite to thrive. Emerson's business and intellectual constituencies, however, have used him from the start to fortify their separate turfs. This rivalry reflects the nascent condition of capitalist dominance and elite alienation that Emerson strives to transcend and transform.

As "The American Scholar" proclaims, "Man Thinking" has to be rescued from a fading gentility for whom manly power means patriarchy, property, and social status and from the rising class of businessmen for whom manly power means entrepreneurial competition and money-making. Emerson especially reaches out to his real cultural constituency, the feminized clergy in the middle:

The so-called "practical men" sneer at speculative men, as if, because they speculate or *see*, they could do nothing. I have heard it said that the clergy,— who are always more universally than any other class, the scholars of their day,—are addressed as women: that the rough, spontaneous conversation of men they do not hear, but only a mincing and diluted speech. (1: 59)

Emerson's attempt to rescue the clergy from the contemptible status of women partly confronts and partly evades his lifelong resentment of his minister father, who died when Emerson was seven. Until Gay Wilson Allen's recent biography of Emerson, various psychological and social critics followed Quentin Anderson's lead in locating Emerson's sense of selfhood within the broader American context of the search for the absent or failed father. But Allen's biography and Joel Porte's *Representative Man* make Emerson's resentment clear and abundant.[14] Allen begins his book with an account of the writer's profound and enduring hostility to William Emerson, who not only plunged Ralph in the ocean for curative baths when he was six but expected him to be reading before the age of three. Young Emerson grew up among incessantly competitive brothers, presided over in the early years by a father who makes Joseph Kennedy look like Mr. Rogers.

From the beginning Ralph was a relative failure, unable or unwilling to measure up. "Ralph does not read very well yet," his father complained to a friend, a week before his son's third birthday. The boy continued to disappoint his father, who supervised all the boy's education with a stern and demanding hand. Three of Ralph's brothers—a fourth was retarded and a fifth died very young—seemed to thrive in this atmosphere of high expectations. William, Charles, and Edward always excelled, while Ralph always lagged behind. The family felt that all the Emerson boys were "born to greatness," and Ralph became keenly conscious of being the "ugly duckling," as Allen calls him. While the other three boys graduated from Harvard at or near the top of their classes, Ralph graduated thirtieth in a class of fifty-nine. He became class poet only because the first six choices turned the title down (4, 10, viii).

All three brothers then went out into the wide world and fell apart. William, the oldest, had great difficulty establishing himself as a lawyer and frequently became sick, starving himself for a time. Edward went violently crazy in 1828, thrashing about in a manic-depressive frenzy that lasted at least a week. He needed two men with him every minute, to hold him down. Ralph, now Waldo, writes to William with a graphic description of the derangement and finishes, "But whats the need of relating this—there he lay—Edward the admired learned eloquent thriving boy—a maniac." This was the brother to whom Waldo felt closest. Seven years later, in 1835, Edward died. As Allen says, "Edward's devouring ambition to excel would destroy his health; and Charles, no less ambitious than Edward, was torn by self-destructive anxiety." Charles died a year after Edward. Only then, looking over Charles's journals, did Waldo discover the depth of his brother's self-doubts, "melancholy, penitential, self-accusing" (117, 73, 264, 266; see *Emerson in His Journals* 153).

How did Emerson escape? The early years of his journal teem with similar self-flagellations for not being great. He too periodically became sick, especially with eye disease and diarrhea, often when facing tasks about which he felt anxious or ambivalent.[15] From this man-breaking family, how did he find his man-making words?

At least three strategies helped Emerson resist and transform his family's expectations. First, he developed what Allen calls his "self-protecting frivolous streak" (22). Second, he slowly became able to see his father as a member of a class losing power. Third, he discovered that he could disengage from his anxious, competitive self by splitting mind from feelings. All three strategies led him to reconceive power as thinking.

In his July 1828 journal Emerson ruminates about "the constitutional calamity of my family," especially the "towering hopes" that had been buried with brother Edward's fall. He concludes by thanking Providence for his defects. "I have so much mixture of *silliness* in my intellectual frame," he says. Edward "lived & acted & spoke with preternatural energy," but "my actions (if I may say so) are of a passive kind. Edward had always great power of face. I have none." Yet "all this imperfection . . . is a ballast—as things go—is a defence" (67). When William wrote home from his garret in New York to say he had been ill, Waldo wrote back to remind William "that all the Emersons overdo themselves." He urged William to try out the laziness that he himself had been enjoying.

But Waldo's brothers, as Allen says, were "career-haunted" (114; see also 39). In mulling over Charles's death, Emerson is baffled at first by the shocking disparity between his brother's strong character and the self-hatred revealed in Charles's journal (May 1836; 147–48). Finally, six months later, he concludes that "Like my brother Edward, Charles had a certain severity of Character which did not permit him to be silly—no not for moments, but always self possessed & elegant whether morose or playful; no funning for him or for Edward" (Nov. 1836; 153). This "self-possessed & elegant" character mirrored the father's "power of face." Father had always dismissed playfulness as "levity." But inward playfulness gave Emerson a habit of mind that Allen calls "intellectual strolling." Silliness also encouraged a more benign self-inspection. "It was a kind of gift for humor, an ability to look at himself from the point of view of a detached bystander, to see his shortcomings not with the tragic regret of his Aunt Mary but as the comic failures of a limited person" (118–19, 22).

His Aunt Mary, William's sister, had become the dominant force in the Emerson family after his father's death, and Emerson was always much more devoted to her than to his self-effacing mother. He liked to call her "Father Mum." His aunt's quasi-Calvinist intensity of faith made her sharply critical of her brother's worldly gentility, even while William lived. Aunt Mary's critiques gave the boy some measure of freedom to think of his father's power as worldly rather than spiritual. But she too expected young Ralph to be a minister, preaching her own faith. Emerson's gift for detachment protected him from the ways by which both his strong-minded instructors tried to induce accommodation and guilt. He was able to fend off his father's demands that he push himself harder academically and his aunt's demands that he share her evangelical self-denial (Cheyfitz 161–63).[16]

Emerson's lifelong gratitude to his aunt, despite his disengagement from nearly everything she wanted him to do, suggests that she helped him get free of his father, whose death must have complicated and arrested his ambivalent feelings. Mary helped the boy begin to see William Emerson not as the originator of awesome power but as the product of a Boston gentility that was already starting to lose social dominance. Emerson's father had dined with the governor on the day Ralph was born. He had the governor over for a party in his home the day after, presumably while his wife was upstairs with the baby. He was personable, fairly tall, immaculately dressed, and always the consummately polished gentleman. Urbane to the core, he became "the confidant and companion of the social and political elite of the city, who in religion might be Unitarian, Congregationalist, or Episcopalian, but in politics were rigid Federalists." As the pastor of the First Church of Boston, he "was at ease in this mercantile society," for whom he performed every Sunday, reading his unmemorable sermons in "a charming baritone voice" with "perfect enunciation" (Allen 4–6). He was at the center of social power, and he knew it. He would make sure that his sons got there too.

But social power was changing. Emerson's conscious politics remained relatively Whig, the party that inherited the Federalist mantle of wealth while straining for a broader evangelical appeal. His deeper politics developed from a love-hate relation with his class. "All conservatives . . . have been effeminated by position or nature," he declares in "Fate," "born halt and blind, through luxury of their parents, and can only, like invalids, act on the defensive" (Whicher, *Selections* 335). His insistent taunting of the elite "fathers" was as much a rescue fantasy as a wish for generational parricide. This class should be the source of magnificent souls, he writes in his September 1832 journal. But the Everetts and Cannings seem self-degraded to the level of "ordinary persons." They "seek only huzzas & champagne" (85–86). Throughout the 1840s he peppers his journals with scornful remarks about various new parties of the rabble. As he says in early 1845:

> A despair has crept over the Whig party in this country. They the active, enterprizing, intelligent, well meaning, & wealthy part of the people, the real bone & strength of the American people, find themselves paralysed & defeated everywhere by the hordes of ignorant & deceivable natives & the armies of foreign voters . . . and by those unscrupulous editors & orators who have assumed to lead these masses. The creators of wealth and conscientious, rational, & responsible persons . . . find themselves degraded into observers, & violently turned out of all share in the action & counsels of the nation.
>
> (333).

If Emerson's class made him a Whig, his dream of power brought him partially beyond his class to search for a more forceful elite. From the beginning of his adulthood he had hoped for fame as a writer or orator. Gradually, throughout the

1820s and early 1830s, his recurrent journal entries on that theme reflect not only a greater self-confidence but a growing willingness to quarrel with his class. Disengaging from his accommodation to the conventional ministry, he sought a more confrontational social preaching, in which words might roll back "the cloud of ceremony & decency" over "smooth plausible people" and convert them to spiritual force. Like Luther's, he wrote in 1832, such words should be "half battles" (87). "The whole secret of the teacher's force lies in the conviction that men are convertible," he writes in 1834. "Get the soul out of bed . . . and your vulgar man, your prosy selfish sensualist awakes a God & is conscious of force to shake the world" (123).

An evangelical political fantasy spurs Emerson's hopes. It emerges as early as 1823, when a lengthy journal entry discusses the dangerous marginality of respectable men on the frontier, where "the off-scouring of civilized society" threatens to engulf the nation. In considering the problem, Emerson couples the country's need for moral oracles with his own need for greatness. There is danger, he says, "that the Oracles of Moral law and Intellectual wisdom in the midst of an ignorant & licentious people will speak faintly & indistinctly." If that were to happen, "Human foresight can set no bounds to the ill consequences of such a calamity . . . " But if the oracles of the elite could regain social power,

> if the senates that shall meet hereafter in those wilds shall be made to speak a voice of wisdom & virtue, the reformation of the world would be to be expected from America. How to effect the check proposed is an object of momentous importance. And in view of an object of such magnitude, I know not who he is that can complain that motive is lacking in this latter age, whereby men should become great. (29)

Here is the "egg, embryo, and seminal principle" (69) of Emerson's political vision. His personal greatness will come as he emboldens other respectable speakers. His task is to increase their impact in the senates of his frontier country. If they "shall be made to speak a voice of wisdom & virtue," America can bring about "the reformation of the world." Emerson's political motive and calling, in every sense, are therefore to reform their voices. He will bring a marginal elite from timidity to power.

This is a conventional upper-class fantasy of the time, shared by Whig leaders and John Calhoun alike. For Emerson to empower his own voice requires one further quarrel with his class, a quarrel that gives public legitimacy to his conflicts with his father. He reconceives the lower orders of people as a source of energy as well as a frightening barbarism to be "checked" by respectable speech. He discovers how to tap Jacksonian energies by developing a rhetoric that simultaneously accuses dead patriarchs while imagining the cowed self's potential to convert the mob. Here Emerson finds his most forceful language of power by shifting from a narrow ideology of class to a broader ideology of manhood. Presenting the manly self as a seemingly dialectical process that synthesizes contemporary class tensions, Emerson incorporates Jacksonian rebelliousness and entrepreneurial resourcefulness into his vision of an intellectual elite in the making.[17]

In 1833 Wordsworth told Emerson that America had no culture because it lacked a leisure class (*Emerson in His Journals* 113–14). A year later Emerson writes in his journal that perhaps Jacksonian democracy may be a symptom of the cure as well as of the disease. "I suppose the evil may be cured by this rank rabble party, the Jacksonism of the country, heedless of English & of all literature—a stone cut out of the ground without hands—they may root out the hollow dilettantism of our cultivation in the coarsest way & the new-born may begin again to frame their own world . . . " (125; see also 128). Here he takes up not only Jacksonian energy but also the language of birth. He comes close to the theme, though not to the imperious, irreverent voice, that opens "Nature." There he says that his age "builds the sepulchres of the fathers" only to rob their graves. "Why should we grope among the dry bones of the past?" Emerson wants birth, not cemetery grubbing, for his father's bones. We should be "Embosomed" in nature, "whose floods of life stream around and through us" and invite us to natural energies of our own (1: 7).

Rarely, however, does Emerson find manhood in the dignity of labor. He seeks a natural nobility of genius.[18] As early as 1827 he muses that "those writings which indicate valuable genius treat of common things. Those minds which God has formed for any powerful influence over men, have never effeminately shrunk from intercourse with unnurtured minds. . . . They have taken hold with manly hand on its vulgar wants" (*Emerson in His Journals* 62). But the manliness is in the hand of "genius," not in the minds of the vulgar. Emerson's attitude toward workers has something of Thoreau's contempt for the Irish, though without *Walden*'s puckish mockery. Emerson takes them more seriously, with a more profound contempt. They are the herd, the mob, the mass, "bugs and spawn," at best a kind of larva. In the two broad groupings into which Emerson usually divides society, the workers will forever be inert, unless a few self-reliant men bring them to intellectual vitality. "The life of labor does not make men, but drudges," he writes in May 1843. "The German and Irish millions, like the Negro," he says in "Fate," "have a great deal of guano in their destiny" (Whicher, *Selections* 220, 337). Toward the end of "Nature" Emerson goes so far as to say, "you cannot freely admire a noble landscape, if laborers are digging in the field hard by" (1: 39).

The language of man making takes Emerson temporarily beyond his class to challenge his father's demands for genteel success. He struggles out of recurrent and often fierce depressions in which he caustically takes inventory of his inability to meet his own perfectionist standards, really his father's expectations. He wins that struggle by reconceiving his father's demands in broader social terms, as crippled conformity to patrician norms that were thwarting a great variety of entrepreneurial sons. His most pugnacious essays, especially "The American Scholar" and "The Divinity School Address," have young versions of his father, his brothers, and himself as his actual and characterized audience. Emerson wants to save their souls. He prophesies a new mode of manhood that will shatter genteel controls to incarnate a truly revolutionary elite.

In "History," which Emerson chose to begin his first volume of selected essays, he all but directly attacks his father, ostensibly by describing the evils of "priest-craft." The passage condenses and universalizes Emerson's own childhood struggle.

> The priestcraft of the East and West . . . is expounded in the individual's private life. The cramping influence of a hard formalist on a young child in repressing his spirits and courage, paralyzing the understanding, and that without producing indignation, but only fear and obedience, and even much sympathy with the tyranny,—is a familiar fact explained to the child when he becomes a man, only by seeing that the oppressor of his youth is himself a child tyrannized over by those names and words and forms, of whose influence he was merely the organ to the youth. (2: 16)

In one long, highly charged sentence Emerson sums up his liberation. First comes the hard tyranny of his formalist father, so "paralyzing" as to produce only "fear and obedience, and even much sympathy with the tyranny." Then, after the dash's deep breath, comes a sudden ease of perception: the tyrant is himself a child, merely an "organ" for society's forms. When the child "becomes a man," his mind can see, accuse, and transform his social bonds.

"The American Scholar" is his finest public drama of accusation and transformation. Emerson begins and ends that address by speaking of the "indestructible instinct" that has miraculously survived "amongst a people too busy to give to letters any more" (1: 52). His peroration makes the opposition more pungent. Poignantly if indirectly invoking the fates of his two brothers, he declares that the world of business is killing the young. "There is no work for any but the decorous and the complaisant. Young men of the fairest promise . . . are hindered from action by the disgust which the principles on which business is managed inspire, and turn drudges, or die of disgust—some of them suicides" (1: 69).

The "remedy" begins "if the single man plant himself indomitably on his instincts." Then comes a swift sequence of brilliant transformational turns. The single man's "planting" will be the axis on which "the huge world will come round to him." That turning will bring about "the conversion of the world" (1: 69). As Emerson does so often, he builds his prophetic confidence from converting accusation into a demand for metamorphosis, of selves, words, and social meanings. Change itself will bring the experience of power. The 1848 revolutions, he later says disparagingly, will probably lead to the same old thing, "a scramble for money. . . . When I see changed men, I shall look for a changed world" (Whicher, *Selections* 316).[19]

Emerson's man-making words proved personally liberating and socially galvanic. But his contempt for laborers and his tendency to see society as divided into a few real men and the masses ultimately crippled his rhetoric as well as his hopes. It was not simply his refusal to get organized that left his dream stranded in himself.

It was also a failure of social vision. Emerson's attentiveness to the play of his mind liberates his tussle with contemporary definitions of power and manhood. But his faith in the infinitude of the private man evades his own ambivalence about rivalry. Moreover, his call for the conversion of individual men to self-reliant thinking blocks awareness of how his rhetoric builds on several power struggles in the Northeast: between fathers and sons, between ministers and gentry, and between the gentry, the new middle class, and the new working class being created by industrialization.

Recent social histories by Paul Johnson, Anthony Wallace, Mary P. Ryan, Joseph Kett, Nancy Cott, and Daniel Walker Howe broadly agree that a drastic change in social conditions came about from 1825 to 1850, especially for men. The dominance of small patriarchal shops and a patrician class yielded to the rise of entrepreneurial managers and professionals in conflict with wage laborers. Scholars disagree about whether the complementary rise of evangelical fervor functioned primarily to teach workers self-discipline or to give mothers an intensified domestic role and some measure of influence in their communities.[20] But it is clear that expectations for young men were in a confused transition from patriarchal and agrarian or mercantile norms. After 1840, Joseph Kett says, the isolated, ambitious male self was expected to rise beyond his father in a world where everyone felt "marginal and insecure" (107–08). Emerson's emphasis on mental fluidity, while serenely transposing what Mary Ryan calls "the open and anxious question" of male identity at this time, finally denies the conflicts to which his rhetoric implicitly responds (153).[21]

In his later essays, less able to find power surging through his voice, he more explicitly refuses to take sides. "Politics," for instance, says of Democrats and Whigs what had become conventional, that "one has the best cause, and the other contains the best men." Yet Emerson adopts a plague-on-both-your-houses tone. "The spirit of our American radicalism is destructive and aimless," he asserts; it grows from "hatred and selfishness." "On the other side, the conservative party, composed of the most moderate, able, and cultivated part of the population, is timid, and merely defensive of property" (3: 122–23). His solution retreats to detachment and conventional character building, a tepid reduction of his earlier self-abandoning metamorphoses.

The rather sniffy and querulous tone of "Politics" shows his disillusionment with any prospects for social man making by 1843. But his cause had been lost from the start, because his rhetoric of man making aimed to bring an elite to cultural dominance at just the moment that the elite class was being displaced from social leadership. In fact his cause was really the old Federalist cause for the leadership of reasonable patricians, with the difference that Emerson emphasized spontaneity rather than reasoning as the road to intellectual power. Yet that approach too could be seen as an old Federalist dodge: to appropriate the language of one's opponents for a politics that maximized the presence of "representative men" while minimizing the opposing interests of different groups.

That was how the Federalists, in passing the Constitution, had preserved the power of the propertied gentry against the "new men," Gordon Wood concludes.

> The result was the beginning of a hiatus in American politics between ideology and motives that was never again closed. By using the most popular and democratic rhetoric available to explain and justify their aristocratic system, the Federalists helped to foreclose the development of an American intellectual tradition in which differing ideas of politics would be intimately and genuinely related to differing social interests. . . . [An] encompassing liberal tradition . . . often obscured the real social antagonisms of American politics.
>
> (562)[22]

Emerson's politics of man making, by any measure, helped that tradition to thrive long after the Whigs went the way of the Federalists. Emerson was more his father's son than he knew.

III

Emerson's championing of a manly cultural elite reinforced his most personal form of self-protective transformation: a disengagement from anxious rivalry by separating his mind from his feelings. He depoliticizes power by imagining a self that watches the mind's powers flow into his voice. If his father is the covert target for his most polemical public addresses—the man who is accused for his own good—Emerson himself becomes the ideal implied reader: the spectator and midwife for our common self in the making. To be that kind of reader conceals the inescapable connection between power and social conflict and deliberately disconnects power from personal feeling.

"One cannot think at all, Emerson is prepared to say, as long as one is the victim of feeling." That summation by Jonathan Bishop is the other side of Bishop's praise for Emerson's "quasi-physical agility of the free mind" (48, 85).[23] Feeling for Emerson meant pain, powerlessness, resentment, and the perils of the body, all of which he dumped on the laboring masses. His grand disdain for those whose sense of self comes from their daily tasks, needs, and relations reflects his discomfort with his own body and his fear of intimacy. As he says in "The Poet," "the centrifugal tendency of a man" seeks "passage out into free space . . . to escape the custody of that body in which he is pent up, and of that jail-yard of individual relations in which he is enclosed" (3: 16). Relations bring on a sense of being trapped; the passage into intellectual space brings nonchalance. There he can yield to aggressiveness with tranquility and voice its thunder charges as a natural flow of self-discoveries.[24]

The numbed, truculent return of depressiveness in Emerson's later essays, however, especially in "Experience," shows that without power he has only abandoned, empty feelings. The only relation he has allowed himself to value is the bond between power and manhood. When that self-abstracting greatness breaks down, Emerson experiences himself too as faceless. He blames that facelessness on the women who care for him at the margins of power, while he relegates them to the margins of his text.

Toward the beginning of "Self-Reliance," Emerson speaks of "The nonchalance of boys who are sure of a dinner" as "the healthy attitude of human nature." An adult man, by contrast, "is, as it were, clapped into jail by his consciousness. . . . Ah, that he could pass again into his neutrality!" Then his opinions "would sink like darts into the ear of men, and put them in fear." A true nonchalance will bring fear to other men, because it strips men of their social conciliations. "A boy is in the parlour what the pit is in the playhouse; independent, irresponsible . . . he tries and sentences [people and facts] on their merits, in the swift summary way of boys," with no troubling over interests or consequences. Here is one of Emerson's most direct amalgamations of "parlour" and "pit," as he asserts the power of the free mind to make men like his father cringe (2: 29).

Once again we have a passage that seeks to unfix parlour men and plunge them into panic—or awe. The centerpiece of aspiration is that fine introductory phrase "The nonchalance of boys who are sure of a dinner." The line itself has a nonchalant and boyish lift. It lopes along with an iambic swing and strong, steady, wide-open vowels, then springs into a dactylic sprint with the word *boys*. Yet the boys' breezy freedom, like the line's jaunty stride, depends on being "sure of a dinner," not sure of themselves. And what about the girls? One can picture them in the kitchen with the angels of the house, getting more faceless and sexless by the minute while they put out the meals for their surefooted brothers. To achieve a bold male self-reliance presumes a depersonalized female support system. What dinnertime is to a boy, the cosmos will be to the mature soul. This source sustains the private infinitude that buoys up self-confidence and restores the wondering little boy to the dispirited man.

Emerson's presumption raises questions about his mother, about whom we know almost nothing. Quiet, patient, dutiful, not very pretty but with "kindly dark eyes," she bore eight children, lost three, and "never complained, regarding affliction and hardship as the will of Providence." Much more devout than her husband, Ruth Haskins Emerson took as her one personal prerogative an hour of privacy every morning for religious meditation. Always reserved, she never raised her voice. Gay Wilson Allen concludes that "her reserve and habitual restraint of emotion in speech" not only "created an intangible atmosphere of remoteness" but more specifically gave young Ralph "an inhibited emotional life" (8; "Psychologically, and perhaps subconsciously, Emerson was striving for emotional invulnerability," Allen says later [226–27]).

Allen, Jonathan Bishop, and John Jay Chapman all finally blame Emerson's inhibited mother for the restricted range of feeling in Emerson's prose.[25] I think his ambivalence about male rivalry was more basic. These three knowledgeable and loving readers unwittingly mimic Emerson's own depressive strategy of displacing resentment. Blaming mother is the other side of taking mother's nourishment for granted. It is comparatively safe. Both responses evade the primary arena for Emerson's resentment: the struggle for a feeling of power. Symptomatically, his responses to mothering recast intimacy as a power relation, in which dependence or isolation are the only options. The reduction of woman's subjectivity to a mothering role legitimates male uses of rage, disdain, and dependency to restore feelings of power, in ways that have become typically American.[26]

One could argue that since Emerson's family provided so many reasons for emotional withdrawal, his mother became his first model for disengaging from competition. But the main point is that, like everyone else, Emerson seems to have taken Ruth for granted, though she lived in his house for over twenty years, from 1830 until her death. Did she share the resentments that Aunt Mary voiced, that Lidian would sometimes release in her many years of "black moods," and that evangelical piety explicitly submerged in women, as Susan Warner's 1850 best-seller, *The Wide, Wide World*, makes abundantly clear?[27] We will probably never know. She was just there, like the dinners. She coped, she endlessly dealt with the family's money problems after her husband's death, she probably disagreed with Aunt Mary about how to raise baby Caroline, and she kept her feelings to herself and her God. Her death in November 1853 goes unremarked in Allen's massive biography, except in the chronology.

The death that mattered to Emerson, of course, was the death in 1842 of his five-year-old son, named for himself. He felt, as he wrote to Carlyle, as if an eye had been plucked out (*Correspondence* 320). Yet his poem "Threnody" makes it clear that his feelings about his son's death are really thoughts about his own inability to be born. Waldo seemed to him the divine mind, now blocked from fruition in the world. The boy's nonchalance, which so delighted Emerson, will never again embody the father's man-making dreams.

"Experience" ruthlessly explores Emerson's sudden, permanent aging. He no longer experiences himself as universal or representative. Instead, he finds his life defined mostly by its surfaces. If, as Clark Kerr once said, a college president's fate is to be nibbled to death by ducks, Emerson discovers that he has been nibbled to near-death by a fate more boring than ducks: marriage, family, conversations, social routine, and his own temperament. The essay amounts to a private prospective wake for himself. He sits by the bier of his hopes, alternately crabby, depressed, hopeful, baffled, dyspeptic, philosophical, wistful, resolute, and resigned, remembering the good times and puzzled, too, by his inability to mourn.

Beneath the prevailing mood of depressive acquiescence, Emerson harbors what Joel Porte calls "an undercurrent of bitterness at life's forcing him to sing *vive la bagatelle* so bravely" (*Representative* 195). Almost every critic finds "Experience" deeply moving, in part because of Emerson's candor about himself. For Stephen Whicher, the essay shows Emerson openly struggling with his skepticism about transcendent dreams (*Freedom* 111–22). For Barbara Packer, the essay exposes the mature self's "secret cruelty" (150). Yet how candid is he? Where Packer hears Emerson admitting that he cannot find his feelings, Porte detects an oblique anger at the Being that has robbed him of his son. "Anger, however, is not Emerson's strong suit" (185). Instead, he retaliates by robbing Being of reality.

For me the essay has an uglier evasiveness. While Emerson disowns his feelings by denying reality to anyone else's, he partially vents his unacknowledged resentment as a glancing snideness about the dull lives of his wife and his mother, the women who care for him. The essay is "disturbing" and "shocking," as various critics have rightly said, but it is also deliberately insulting to those readers for whom grief and intimacy have meant something. For Emerson such feelings are only the bitter unrealities of Mother Nature. Oscillating between a puzzled calm and a crusty petulance, he accepts and indicts the female surfaces that have blocked his access to creative energy.

The opening poem sets the scene: "Little man, least of all," walks aimlessly among the legs of his masked guardians, the Lords of Life. Mother Nature, seeing his "puzzled look," takes little man by the hand and whispers, " 'Darling, never mind!/ . . . / The founder thou! these are thy race!' " (3: 25). The poem evokes its own puzzle, which the essay expands on. Do the Lords of Life emanate from man's littleness of mind, blocking his access to divinity and power with idle dreams, faces, and games? Or do the surfaces emanate from Mother Nature, who indulgently comforts and praises man for fathering her fraudulent creations? "Darling, never mind!" becomes her ominous message as well as her comfort. Mother has nothing to do with mind. In fact mother rather likes it when man feels so belittled. Then her powers can come into view.

That might be an unfair extrapolation from a gnomic epigraph, except that the essay recurrently returns to a mood of passive blaming. The urgency about manhood that suffuses the earlier essays has vanished. The word *man* itself rarely appears. Instead, in circling about the surfaces of ordinary life, Emerson keeps rediscovering the omnipresence of mother and the frustrations of a child. "The child asks, 'Mamma, why don't I like the story as well as when you told it me yesterday?' " The response: because stories, like any lasting relations, become monotonous. We were "born to a whole"; now we endure particulars. The "plaint of tragedy" here has a touch of accusation. Our most intimate relations, whether to art or to people, have an "absence of elasticity" and give "no power of expansion." Power may go to the muscles, but culture "ends in headache." Those who think about the problem can feel "quite powerless and melancholy. . . . Unspeakably sad and barren" (3: 33–34). Better not to think about it, mother implies.

For a time at least, Emerson seems to speak in Mother Nature's realistic voice. "The whole frame of things preaches indifferency," he concludes a few lines later. "Life is not intellectual or critical, but sturdy." If things are in the saddle and ride the mind, nonetheless life's sturdy frame rewards "well-mixed people" who enjoy without questioning. Why? Because the world belongs to Nature, and, like a good mother, "Nature hates peeping." Now Emerson attributes a little more oppressiveness to mother's alliance with Nature: "our mothers speak her very sense when they say, 'Children, eat your victuals, and say no more of it' " (35). Good mothering tells little man to shut up, in effect, and adjust himself to littleness.

Emerson has learned to be both accommodating and hidden. "A man is like a bit of Labrador spar" at best, deep and beautiful in just one place, while "the Power which abides in no man and in no woman" hops like a bird from spar to spar and "for a moment speaks from this one, and for another moment from that one" (33–34). Better to "awake, and find the old world, wife, babes, and mother," with "the dear old devil not far off."[28] Better to seek the "mid-world," where Nature "comes eating and drinking and sinning" and where "Her darlings" have no interest in divinity. "If we will be strong with her strength," we have to live in the present and show ourselves as Nature's creatures (36–37).

That voice of resigned acceptance is a mask. By the end of his paragraph on the "darlings" of the midworld Emerson is pleading with himself to dismiss the illusory surfaces of life. "But thou, God's darling! heed thy private dream: thou wilt not be missed in the scorning and skepticism: there are enough of them: stay there in thy closet, and toil, until the rest are agreed what to do about it." These are not man-making words. Let Nature's people treat you as a stubborn child, he says; let them prescribe remedies for "thy puny habit." While big people pound on the closet door to force recalcitrant little dreamers into the world, the child-man knows that life itself is a dream. If energy flows to the midworld, at least "dig away in your garden, and spend your earnings as a waif or godsend to all serene and beautiful purposes" (38).

The puzzle of the opening poem has taken a larger turn. Does the midworld emanate from a dream, or does Nature create the hapless dreamer? The answer depends on Emerson's shifts of mood, from detached hope to dependent blame and back again. Yet blame keeps returning. Why, he asks, have scholars been such traitors to the mind? Because "nature causes each man's peculiarity to superabound. . . . Irresistible nature made men such" (38). "Fate" makes the accusation more directly. "Men are what their mothers made them" (Whicher, *Selections* 334). Ultimately the failure of power to be intellectual rather than worldly comes from how mothers bear and raise us. The passages that critics put forward to celebrate the mature vitality of "Experience" show Emerson conjuring up his old ecstasies of rebirth and metamorphic surprise.[29] But the discovery of power has yielded to "infantine joy and amazement" for its own sake, as man-making words have yielded to mother-made selves (41).

No longer "man talking to men," Emerson ends up talking to himself, explicitly about failure and implicitly about women. "A man is a golden impossibility," he now concludes, no matter how plain it is "[i]n the street and in the newspapers. . . . that manly resolution and adherence to the multiplication-table through all weathers, will insure success" (38–39). Besieged by frivolous conversations, the man of thought has to take refuge in a "preoccupied attention" and a higher aim, an aim whose "other politics," he knows, is irreconcilable with worldly impact.

Once he had imagined otherwise. "But I have not found that much was gained by manipular attempts to realize the world of thought." The "eager persons" who try to experiment with visionary dreams on earth "acquire democratic manners, they foam at the mouth, they hate and deny." So Emerson disowns both his anger and his hopes. The best we can do, he says, is "dress our garden, eat our dinners, discuss the household with our wives," and then forget those trivial surfaces "in the solitude to which every man is always returning" (47–49).

Emerson's numbed and prickly mood does have a larger social dimension, though in a mode opposite from the prophetic rhetoric of the earlier essays. His brief experience editing the *Dial* had already indicated that oracular intellectuality had little potential for man-making impact. Baffled by the possibility that the American future might demand a self-narrowing specialization and a divergence between intellectuals and businessmen, not a protean self-expansion, Emerson was thrown back on the isolation of his temperament. He had lost confidence in equating himself with the embryonic possibilities of a new social elite.

"We are like millers on the lower levels of a stream, when the factories above them have exhausted the water," he ends the first paragraph of "Experience." "We too fancy that the upper people must have raised their dams." As striking as his sad, passive, powerless tone is the uncertainty of self-location. Emerson shifts the source of blame for his state of confused deprivation from "factories" to "the upper people," as if stranded midway between a genteel disdain for the emergence of heavy industry and an older peasant consciousness of arbitrary, self-serving Lords. All he can be sure of is that he feels shut off from water and clear vision. His confusion slips into metaphors that indirectly expose mother's control of our birth. The "Genius" who stood by the door poisoned our drink with lethargy as we entered, and now we have lost our way on the stairs of life and consciousness. Or was it that she withheld something? "Did our birth fall in some fit of indigence and frugality in nature, that she was so sparing of her fire and so liberal of her earth, that . . . we have no superfluity of spirit for new creation?" "Ah that our Genius were a little more of a genius!" (3: 27). In either case, mindless mother has shut off little man's creativity.

A language that reduces both power and love to property gives Emerson some momentary if ironic solace. The death of little Waldo now seems no more than the loss of "a beautiful estate," a "great inconvenience," like "the bankruptcy of my principal debtors" (29). But from beginning to end Emerson still yearns for creative power, for what he at last invokes as the "great and crescive self, rooted in absolute nature," which "supplants all relative existence, and ruins the kingdom of mortal friendship and love." If this "magazine of substance" were to rise again to its full phallic yet receptive explosiveness—the closest he gets to rage—it would expose the impossibility of every relation, even marriage, the "gulf between every me and thee" (44).

This widening gulf is what Emerson thinks experience teaches. Throughout, however, a vindictive, patronizing subtext drives the voice that claims to have no emotions. "Two human beings are like gloves, which can touch only in a point," he concludes; "the longer a particular union lasts the more energy of appetency the parts not in union acquire" (44). Emerson's impersonal geometry disconnects desire from intimacy as well as from marriage. His brutal self-abstraction balances his wife's thirty years of depressions. Whenever I read that passage, I want to write in the margin, "Poor Lidian."

My deflationary reading of "Experience" opposes almost every recent critical assessment. Though Emerson's business constituency shies away from the essay's depressive complexities, intellectuals have found more and more to praise. At the December 1983 MLA convention, in welcoming deconstructionist approaches, Lawrence Buell noted that "Experience" is "the hottest text these days." It self-destructs its own meanings; it exposes Emerson's resistance to his own will to power; it presents him as *bricoleur* of his own text, at odds with what the essay calls the "rapaciousness" of a self whose senses have fallen into the world. As an ironic yet yearning exposure of the will to power, the essay may be a deconstructive masterpiece. In its approach to feeling, however, the essay seems to me annoying, petulant, and evasive at almost every turn.

"Experience" has little to do with Emerson's real experience, which springs and recoils from male rivalry. His dream of manly power gains its broader appeal from its implicit rebellions. The wild fizzing energy of his early prose throws off his father's yoke with a great deal of anger as well as play. His imperious nonchalance liberates him from fear and addresses the fear he sees in the cowed men all around him. Emerson was able to empower his voice in a world he found disempowering. As a student once said, he writes sentences that you want to tack on the wall or send to a depressed friend. Now he has lost touch with those energies. What seems to be a crusty self-encounter is really self-avoidance. Its most inhumane by-product is his displacement of anxiety about manhood into passive indictments of mothering.

Those critics who praise the ethical and social mission of Emerson's allegedly representative self minimize or miss the political and personal mystifications that protect him from conflict. The social connections I have proposed encourage a different sense of his major texts. We can see how the earlier essays transform conflicts in himself and his audience by provoking, dramatizing, and prophesying an elite manhood of the mind. We can also see how "Experience" retreats from his hopes for manly transformation to a private depressiveness that implicitly accuses the women he takes for granted. Emerson's obsession with power reflects the fears of failure, the desperate rivalries for success, and the fluidity of a social frame in which power itself was uncertainly shifting from one group of men and one mode of manhood to another. In disengaging the mind from personal and political struggle, however, his major essays inaugurate the tradition of alienated liberalism that is still the dominant ideology in American literary criticism.

Reading Emerson at his best is like bodysurfing the cosmos, a cosmos inside the mind. To float too long on the suspensions of close reading, however, can lead to a more precious alienation, the modernist pleasures of the text detached from social history. To focus critical attention on the politics of Emerson's voice—whom does he address and why? with what fears and hopes?—can reconnect his literary language to the realities of American lives, including his own life. As a contemporary journalist said, his voice had shoulders that he himself lacked. His prose is as close to the speeches of Eugene V. Debs as to the poems of Walt Whitman. He plays some of the first variations on a pervasive American theme, the "melodramas of beset manhood" (to use Nina Baym's term) that shape so much of what is currently canonized in our literature and criticism.[30]

In this essay I have tried to lower Emerson's critical stock to the level of his assets. I share a baffled fascination with his free flights of language, and I deeply admire his efforts to rescue his mind from depressive turmoil. The anxious competitiveness that pressed on him can still seem more natural than the air we breathe. Nevertheless, Emerson's partial liberation from male rivalry leads to a politics of man making that trivializes women and feelings, while his passion for the mind's abstracted buoyancy strips power of conflict, as if power were a river in air.

At times when I think I have cut through Emerson's fog of self, it is hard to disengage from his disengagements without wanting to dismiss him entirely. In other moods, the free play of his unself-conscious self-consciousness can seem endlessly absorbing. The way beyond the perpetually circling problem of Emerson's appeal is not to take a stand within that paradoxical either-or but to see how his language resonates with the unresolved tensions of his life and time. If his limitations then seem at least equal to his achievements, his resisting response to history gains a surprising intimacy, whose power increases as his struggles become more visible.[31]

Notes

1.   See also Paul Berman's fine review of the Library of America edition of Emerson.

2.   See Edgar Branch, esp. 968–70. On Western responses, see Bishop 154–55.

3.   Bishop observes that Emerson's special audience consisted of young men in search of an identity at variance with social expectations (146–50). For general histories of manhood, see David Pugh and Peter Stearns.

4.   Cheyfitz 83–96. Larzer Ziff discusses writers and marketplace dynamics (56–59).

5.   I am indebted to Evelyn Barish for this reference and to her essay "Moonless Night."

6.   Joel Porte explores Emerson's "spermatic" eloquence in *Representative Man*, esp. 215–17, 233–47, 276–79. Unless otherwise noted, all quotations of the journals are from Emerson, *Emerson in His Journals*. All quotations of his essays are from *Collected Works*.

7.   McAleer cites a Jan. 1850 entry in Bronson Alcott's diary: "The best of Emerson's intellect comes out of its feminine traits, and were he not as stimulating to me as a woman and as racy, I should not care to see him and to know him intimately nor often" (21–22).

It is striking that women such as Annie Fields and Virginia Woolf, while experiencing extraordinarily strong responses to Emerson's voice and mind, do not indicate any associations to conventional femininity. Field's response can be found in Bode 78, 86; Woolf reviewed Emerson in the *Times Literary Supplement*. I am indebted for this last reference to Celeste Goodridge.

8. Cheyfitz is citing James Elliot Cabot's observation that Emerson's public speaking made his audiences uncomfortable because "People like a preacher who has made up his mind. . . . " James McIntosh notes that Emerson's model of the mind resembles a New England town meeting (238). Emerson did have a brief quasi-political career, serving on the Concord school board in the mid-1830s.

9. See also Bishop on Emerson's modesty and self-annihilation in the discovery of common powers (151–57) and on the aggressive-yielding doubleness in his tone (130–42). In *A World Elsewhere*, Richard Poirier makes similar observations about the tensions between relinquishment and possession in Emerson's voice (68–69).

10. Carolyn Porter discusses Emerson extensively from a Marxist point of view, in the context of reification. Her sense of his resistance to and replication of bourgeois ideology has many parallels with my argument (see 38–39, 58–61, 91–118). It seems to me, however, that class and gender relations are more fundamental than man-thing relations.

11. Unlike Packer, Porte tends to shift his discussion to sexual issues. See also Ziff 15–30.

12. Stephen Whicher, in his influential textbook *Selections from Ralph Waldo Emerson*, rightly uses this entry as a coda for Emerson's prose (406).

13. I am indebted to Kathleen O'Connell for calling this passage to my attention. See Michael Gilmore's account of Emerson's ambivalent and changing responses to the new capitalist market; see also Carolyn Porter 58–61.

14. Porte suggests that "The Divinity School Address" uses antinomian language to overthrow a book that Emerson's father had written on Anne Hutchinson, while the first paragraph of "Nature" uses hidden biblical allusions to accuse murderous fathers. The paragraph "is laced with more anger than we are normally willing to hear" (76). Later Porte highlights Emerson's account of the severity of his father in forcing the boy into the ocean. "Fear, shame, and anger are thoroughly mixed in this account," Porte concludes, and those feelings abet "a crippling habit of self-consciousness and self-questioning that threatens to paralyze the will" in Emerson's early adult years (156).

15. On Emerson's diseases, see Cheyfitz 49, 113 and Allen 189–90 for discussions of diarrhea; see also Barish, "Moonless Night."

16. Allen is exceptionally hard on Mary Moody Emerson, with a tone of patronizing mockery completely absent from his discussion of William's equally crazy demands. He says that she had "an overcharged ego" full of resentment (18) and that masochism may be the real secret of her "pathological" asceticism. For him "this frustrated anchorite" hated her body and launched herself into all manner of harsh, unpredictable, and eccentric behavior (20–24). Barish has unearthed a strange and revealing early fantasy of Emerson's concerning a witch figure who has some of her aunt's attributes; see Barish's "Emerson and 'The Magician' " and her expanded discussion in "Emerson and the Angel of Midnight," which presents the aunt as more of a muse. See also Phyllis Cole.

17. Here I differ from John Peacock's sense that Emerson's dialectic is more genuine than mystifying. On the conventional upper-class fantasy of the elite's conversion to power see Howe 25–32. Alfred Kazin emphasizes Emerson's concern with power (e.g., 47) but does not probe the issue. Michael Lopez explores romantic ideas of power.

18. Emerson's extravagant admiration for the "genius" of Whig senator Daniel Webster led him to feel bitterly betrayed after Webster endorsed the Fugitive Slave Law in 1850.

His anger at the perversion of manly oratory took Emerson toward polemics and anarchy, to the dismay of friends like Longfellow. See McAleer 509–13, 521–28 and Chapman 177.

19.   David Porter has a fine close reading of the transformation in "The American Scholar" (210–14).

20.   See, e.g., Ryan's critique of Johnson and Wallace (103–04). Also see Karen Halttunen for a cultural study of the impact of economic change at this time. Sean Wilentz's *Chants Democratic*, the best study of class formation in the United States, came to my attention after this essay was accepted.

21.   Kett discusses character as "an internal gyroscope" (107–08). Ryan sees the new stereotype of the self-made entrepreneur as the "privatizing" counterpart to the domesticity of the female (147–55). Nancy Cott (20–25, 70–74) sketches the conditions within which "women's self-renunciation was called upon to remedy men's self-alienation" (71). Halttunen emphasizes what she calls the "liminal fluidity" of America's transition from rural to urban experience.

22.   See also Richard Hofstadter, esp. chs. 1–4. Bishop notes that "the pleasures of the Emersonian tone are at their best when the speaker fronts the enemy and borrows one or another of his idioms to make his point . . . taking over some part of the businessman's or farmer's world to make a metaphor of it" (134).

23.   James McIntosh discusses isolation and self-decreation as the other side of "those moods when we think of ourselves as unmoored, abstracted, in a condition of potency" (239).

24.   See Whicher, *Selections* 81, for an Oct. 1837 journal entry that starkly sketches Emerson's struggle to disengage from himself and join "the All" (also in Emerson, *Journals* 391). In *The American Narcissus*, which appeared after this essay had been accepted, Joyce Warren forcefully critiques Emerson's disdain for social relations (23–54). Warren's feminist approach too simply allies Emerson with American individualism and misses the passionate, conflicted intensities in his struggle with manhood. But her analysis of Emerson's relation with Lidian is very perceptive, and her conclusions parallel mine in many respects.

25.   Bishop sensitively connects Emerson's "teasing" of women to a latent aggressiveness (44–45, 181–87). Chapman connects Emerson's dread of emotion to "the lack of maternal tenderness characteristic of the New England nature" (189–90). McAleer emphasizes but does not explore Emerson's affection for his mother (19–27, 536–37).

26.   It has by now become a convention, embedded in psychoanalysis and surfacing in movies like *Shoot the Moon*, that rage against mother deprivation voices authentic male feeling. The convention perpetuates male manipulations of anger to keep women in a mothering role that soothes men's self-hatred and supports solitary ambition. Both depressive and ambitious postures evade interpersonal feelings while nurturing a self born of rivalry and detachment. Nancy Chodorow examines the historical roots and the psychological effects of socializing women toward intimacy and men toward autonomous achievement.

27.   Ellen Tucker Emerson speaks of the "dungeon" of her mother's resentful thoughts, "in which she suffered for so many years." Despite a "hot & fiery" temperament, Lidian seems to have been a near-invalid from the early 1840s until the 1870s, with recurrently disabling depressions that may have been augmented by Emerson's detached self-preoccupation (128–29, 146, 155). Barbara Leslie Epstein emphasizes the connection of resentment to religiosity, though other historians, like Nancy Cott and Mary Ryan, stress the usefulness of evangelical religion in bringing women beyond private domesticity to active social roles.

28.   A May 1843 journal entry gives more bite to the association of woman with devil: "In every woman's conversation & total influence mild or acid lurks the *conventional devil*.

They look at your carpet, they look at your cap, at your saltcellar, at your cook & waiting maid, conventionally—to see how close they square with the customary cut in Boston & Salem & New Bedford" (306).

29. See esp. Porte, *Representative* 198–99, on the passage about the "born-again" traveler. As Porte says, "The reader who does not respond well to this passage will probably never be an Emersonian, because the excited shift of mood and the spontaneous exfoliation of joy out of literally nothing are among the best surprises Emerson has to offer" (198).

30. The journalists is N. P. Willis, qtd. in Chapman 185. Nick Salvatore's prize-winning biography, *Eugene V. Debs*, shows that Debs's appeal to industrial workers lay in his ability to invoke American traditions of manliness, not European traditions of socialism. Debs's calls to manhood both transcended and blurred the social perceptions of his working-class audiences, much as Emerson's did for the new middle class and the children of old gentility. Also see Baym on several decades of male criticism.

31. Of the readers who helped me with this essay, I am especially indebted to Frederick Crews, Tanya Gregory, T. Walter Herbert, Jr., and Cecil Jones.

Works Cited

Allen, Gay Wilson. *Waldo Emerson: A Biography*. New York: Viking, 1981.

Anderson, Quentin. *The Imperial Self: An Essay in American Literary and Cultural History*. New York: Knopf, 1971.

Barish, Evelyn. "Emerson and the Angel of Midnight: The Legacy of Mary Moody Emerson." *Mothering the Mind: Twelve Studies of Writers and Their Silent Partners*. Ed. Ruth Perry and Martine Watson Brownley. New York: Holmes, 1984. 218–37.

———. "Emerson and 'The Magician': An Early Prose Fantasy." *American Transcendental Quarterly* 31 (1976): 13–18.

———. "Moonless Night: Emerson's Crisis of Health, 1825–1827." Myerson 1–16.

Baym, Nina. "Melodramas of Beset Manhood: How Theories of American Fiction Exclude Women Authors." *American Quarterly* 33 (1981): 123–39.

Berman, Paul. "The ABC of Emerson." *Nation* (19 Nov. 1983): 513, 515.

Bishop, Jonathan. *Emerson on the Soul*. Cambridge: Harvard UP, 1964.

Bloom, Harold. *Agon: Towards a Theory of Revisionism*. New York: Oxford UP, 1982.

———. *The Anxiety of Influence: A Theory of Poetry*. New York: Oxford UP. 1973.

Bode, Carl, ed. *Ralph Waldo Emerson: A Profile*. New York: Hill, 1968.

Branch, Edgar M. " 'The Babes in the Wood': Artemus Ward's 'Double Health' to Mark Twain." *PMLA* 93 (1978): 955–72.

Buell, Lawrence. "Emerson's Conception of His Text." MLA Convention. New York, 29 Dec. 1983.

Chapman, John Jay. *The Selected Writings of John Jay Chapman*. Ed. Jacques Barzun. New York: Farrar, 1957.

Cheyfitz, Eric. *The Trans-Parent: Sexual Politics in the Language of Emerson*. Baltimore: Johns Hopkins UP, 1981.

Chodorow, Nancy. *The Reproduction of Mothering: Psychoanalysis and the Sociology of Gender*. Berkeley: U of California P, 1978.

Cole, Phyllis. "The Advantage of Loneliness: Mary Moody Emerson's Almanacks, 1802–1855." Porte, *Emerson* 1–32.

Cott, Nancy. *The Bonds of Womanhood: 'Woman's Sphere' in New England, 1780–1835*. New Haven: Yale UP, 1977.

Emerson, Ellen Tucker. *The Life of Lidian Jackson Emerson*. Ed. Delores Bird Carpenter. Boston: Twayne, 1980.

Emerson, Ralph Waldo. *The Collected Works of Ralph Waldo Emerson*. Ed. Robert E. Spiller et al. 3 vols. Cambridge: Belknap-Harvard UP, 1971–.

———. *The Correspondence of Emerson and Carlyle*. Ed. Joseph Slater. New York: Columbia UP, 1964.

———. *Emerson in His Journals*. Ed. Joel Porte. Cambridge: Belknap-Harvard UP, 1982.

———. *The Journals and Miscellaneous Notebooks of Ralph Waldo Emerson*. Ed. William Gillman et al. 15 vols. Cambridge: Belknap-Harvard UP, 1960–.

———. *Works*. Ed. Edward W. Emerson. 11 vols. Cambridge: Riverside, 1883.

Epstein, Barbara Leslie. *The Politics of Domesticity: Women, Evangelism and Temperance in Nineteenth-Century America*. Middletown: Wesleyan UP, 1981.

Gilmore, Michael T. "Emerson and the Persistence of the Commodity." Porte, *Emerson* 65–84.

Grattan, C. Hartley. *The Three Jameses: A Family of Minds*. New York: New York UP, 1963.

Halttunen, Karen. *Confidence Men and Painted Women: A Study of Middle-Class Culture in America, 1830–1870*. New Haven: Yale UP, 1982.

Hofstadter, Richard. *The American Political Tradition and the Men Who Made It*. New York: Knopf, 1948.

Howe, Daniel Walker. *The Political Culture of the American Whigs*. Chicago: U of Chicago P, 1979.

Johnson, Paul E. *A Shopkeeper's Millennium: Society and Revivals in Rochester, New York, 1815–1837*. New York: Hill, 1978.

Kazin, Alfred. *An American Procession*. New York: Knopf, 1984.

Kett, Joseph F. *Rites of Passage: Adolescence in America 1790 to the Present*. New York: Basic, 1977.

Konvitz, Milton R., ed. *The Recognition of Ralph Waldo Emerson: Selected Criticism since 1837*. Ann Arbor: U of Michigan P, 1972.

Lopez, Michael. "Transcendental Failure: 'The Palace of Spiritual Power.' " Porte, *Emerson* 121–53.

Lowell, James Russell. "Emerson the Lecturer." 1871. Konvitz 43–49.

McAleer, John. *Ralph Waldo Emerson: Days of Encounter*. Boston: Little, 1984.

McIntosh, James. "Emerson's Unmoored Self." *Yale Review* 65 (1976): 232–40.

Myerson, Joel, ed. *Emerson Centenary Essays*. Carbondale: Southern Illinois UP, 1982.

Packer, Barbara L. *Emerson's Fall: A New Interpretation of the Major Essays*. New York: Continuum, 1982.

Peacock, John. "Self-Reliance and Corporate Destiny: Emerson's Dialectic of Culture." *ESQ* 29 (1983): 59–72.

Perry, Ralph Barton. *The Thought and Character of William James*. 2 vols. Boston: Little, 1935.

Poirier, Richard. *A World Elsewhere: The Place of Style in American Literature*, New York: Oxford UP, 1966.

———. "Writing Off the Self." *Raritan* 1.1 (1981): 106–33.

Porte, Joel, ed. *Emerson, Prospect and Retrospect*. Cambridge: Harvard UP, 1982.

———. *Representative Man: Ralph Waldo Emerson in His Time*. New York: Oxford UP, 1979.

Porter, Carolyn. *Seeing and Being: The Plight of the Participant-Observer in Emerson, James, Adams, Faulkner*. Middletown: Wesleyan UP, 1981.

Porter, David. *Emerson and Literary Change*. Cambridge: Harvard UP, 1978.

Pugh, David G. *Sons of Liberty: The Masculine Mind in Nineteenth-Century America*. Westport: Greenwood, 1983.

Ryan, Mary P. *Cradle of the Middle Class: The Family in Oneida County, New York, 1790–1865*. Cambridge: Cambridge UP, 1981.

Salvatore, Nick. *Eugene V. Debs: Citizen and Socialist*. Urbana: U of Illinois P, 1982.

Stearns, Peter N. *Be a Man! Males in Modern Society*. New York: Holmes, 1979.

Wallace, Anthony F. C. *Rockdale: The Growth of an American Village in the Early Industrial Revolution*. New York: Norton, 1978.

Warner, Susan. *The Wide, Wide World*. By Elizabeth Wetherell (pseud.). 1850. New York: Putnam, 1851.

Warren, Joyce W. *The American Narcissus: Individualism and Women in Nineteenth-Century American Fiction*. New Brunswick: Rutgers UP, 1984.

Whicher, Stephen E. *Freedom and Fate: An Inner Life of Ralph Waldo Emerson*. Philadelphia: U of Pennsylvania P, 1953.

———. ed. *Selections from Ralph Waldo Emerson: An Organic Anthology*. Boston: Houghton, 1957.

Wilentz, Sean. *Chants Democratic: New York City and the Rise of the American Working Class, 1788–1850*. New York: Oxford UP, 1984.

Wood, Gordon. *The Creation of the American Republic 1776–1787*. New York: Norton, 1972.

Woolf, Virginia. "Emerson's Journals." *Times Literary Supplement* (3 Mar. 1910): 69–70.

Ziff, Larzer. *Literary Democracy: The Declaration of Cultural Independence in America*. New York: Viking, 1981.

9

The Female King:
Tennyson's Arthurian Apocalypse

Elliot L. Gilbert

> Yet in the long years liker must they grow
> The man be more of woman, she of man.
> Tennyson, *The Princess*

> Dr. Schreber believed that he had a mission to redeem the world and
> to restore it to its lost state of bliss. This, however, he could only bring
> about if he were first transformed from a man into a woman.
> Freud, "A Case of Paranoia"

> The happiest women, like the happiest nations, have no history.
> George Eliot, *The Mill on the Floss*

> Queen Victoria, there's a woman . . . when one encounters a toothed
> vagina of such exceptional size . . . .
> Lacan, "Seminar, 11 February 1975"

> La femme est naturelle, c'est-à-dire abominable.
> Baudelaire, *Mon Cœur mis à nu*

I

Sooner or later, most readers of the *Idylls of the King* find themselves wondering
by what remarkable transformative process the traditionally virile and manly King
Arthur of legend and romance evolved, during the nineteenth century, into the
restrained, almost maidenly Victorian monarch of Alfred Lord Tennyson's most
ambitious work. Many of the earliest of these readers of the *Idylls* deplored the
change, noting in it disquieting evidence of the growing domestication and even
feminization of the age.[1] And more recent critics, though they may have moderated
the emotionalism of that first response, continue to see in Arthur's striking metamorphosis a key element in any analysis of the poem. I will argue here, however,
that such a metamorphosis was inevitable, given the nineteenth-century confluence
of what Michel Foucault has called "the history of sexuality" with what we may
call the history of history, and that Tennyson's Arthurian retelling, far from being

weakened by its revisionary premise, is in fact all the stronger and more resonant for depicting its hero as a species of female king.

Tennyson was attracted to the legend of King Arthur as a prospective subject for literary treatment almost from the beginning of his career; "the vision of Arthur had come upon me," Hallam Tennyson quotes his father in the *Memoir*, "when, little more than a boy, I first lighted upon Malory" (2:128). *Poems, Chiefly Lyrical*, published in 1830, when Tennyson was just twenty-one, contains the picturesque fragment "Sir Lancelot and Queen Guinevere," and by 1833, when his next volume appeared, the poet had already written, or was in the process of writing, two of his best-known Arthurian works, "The Lady of Shalott" (1832) and the ambitious rendering of King Arthur's death that, at its first publication ten years later, he called "Morte d'Arthur."

By this time, however, Tennyson had come to question the propriety of a nineteenth-century artist devoting his energies to the reworking of medieval materials. That is, he came to feel that only some contemporary significance in the Arthurian retellings, only "some modern touches here and there" (as he puts it in "The Epic"), could redeem his poetry "from the charge of nothingness," from Thomas Carlyle's characterization of it as "a refuge from life . . . a medieval arras" behind which the poet was hiding "from the horrors of the Industrial Revolution" (quoted in Priestley 35) or from John Sterling's judgment that "the miraculous legend of 'Excalibur'. . . reproduced by any modern writer must be a mere ingenious exercise of fancy" (119).[2]

The idea that nineteenth-century artists ought to concern themselves with nineteenth-century subjects was a pervasive one (see Gent). When, for example, Matthew Arnold omitted *Empedocles on Etna* from a collection of his poetic works, he found it necessary to explain that he had not done so "because the subject of it was a Sicilian Greek born between two and three thousand years ago, *although many persons would think this a sufficient reason*" (italics mine). In the Preface to *Poems* (1853), Arnold goes on to quote "an intelligent critic" as stating that "the poet who would really fix the public attention must leave the exhausted past, and draw his subjects from matters of present import, and therefore both of interest and novelty" (1, 3). Four years later, in a long discourse on poetics in *Aurora Leigh*, Elizabeth Barrett Browning takes a similar position. "If there's room for poets in this world," Barrett Browning declares in book 5 of her blank-verse novel,

> Their sole work is to represent the age,
> Their age, not Charlemagne's
>
> . . . .
>
> To flinch from modern varnish, coat or flounce,
> Cry out for togas and the picturesque,
> Is fatal—foolish too. King Arthur's self
> Was commonplace to Lady Guenevere:
> And Camelot to minstrels seemed as flat
> As Fleet Street to our poets.   (200–13)

That Tennyson himself was influenced by such attitudes is plain from the fact that when he published "Morte d'Arthur" in 1842, he set his medieval story in a modern framing poem, "The Epic," whose only partly ironic theme is the irrelevance of such a historical subject to contemporary world. Edward Fitzgerald asserts that Tennyson invented this setting "to give a reason for telling an old-world tale" (quoted in H. Tennyson 1:194). Otherwise, as poet Everard Hall remarks in "The Epic," explaining why he has burned his own long Arthurian poem,

> "Why take the style of those heroic times:
> For nature brings not back the mastodon,
> Nor we those times; and why should any man
> Remodel models?"

The lapse of fifty-five years between the writing of the "Morte d'Arthur" in 1833 and the publication of the complete *Idylls of the King* in 1888 suggest how difficult a time Tennyson had finding the contemporary significance he was looking for in his medieval amterial. Nevertheless, nearly all readers agree with the poet that "there is an allegorical or perhaps rather a parabolic drift in the poem" that permits the work to be read as "a discussion of problems which are both contemporary and perennial" (H. Tennyson 2:126–27).

The exact nature of that discussion remains an open question, though a few facts about the allegory do seem clear. The book, proceeding seasonally as it does from spring in "The Coming of Arthur" to winter in "The Passing of Arthur," is certainly about the decline of a community from an original ideal state, about the corruption and nihilism that overtake a once whole and healthy social order. Just as surely, an important agency of this decline is identified by the story as human sexuality and, in particular, female passion. The four idylls published by Tennyson in 1859—"Vivien," "Guinevere," "Enid," and "Elaine"—under the general title *The True and the False* focus on the polar extremes of feminine purity and carnality, and however the author may have altered his plans for the book in the following years, his emphasis on the corrosiveness of female sexuality never changed. "Thou has spoilt the purpose of my life," Arthur declares grimly in "Guinevere," about to part forever from the queen and plainly placing the whole blame for the decay of the Round Table and the fall of Camelot on his wife's unfaithfulness.

The association of marital fidelity with the health of the state did not please all the first readers of the *Idylls*. Swinburne, for one, condemned what he felt was the reduction of Sir Thomas Malory's virile tales of chivalry to a sordid domestic quarrel. To him, Victorian King Arthur was a "wittol," or willing cuckold, Guinevere "a woman of intrigue," Lancelot "a co-respondent," and the whole story "rather a case for the divorce court than for poetry" (57). In the same essay, Swinburne refers to the *Idylls* as "the Morte d'Albert" (56), alluding to Tennyson's 1862 dedication of his poem to the recently deceased prince consort but, even more than that, to the royal family's celebrated bourgeois domesticity.

Swinburne was right to see that Tennyson's idylls turn on the issue of domestic relations and specifically on the willingness or unwillingness of men and women to play their traditional social and sexual roles in these relations. He was wrong, however, to think such a subject contemptible. Indeed, his sardonic reference to "the Morte d'Albert" inadvertently calls attention to a major theme in the poem as well as to one of the central problems of Victorian society: the growing assertion of female authority.

In his Dedication of the *Idylls of the King* to Prince Albert, Tennyson describes a relationship between husband and wife that on the surface is entirely conventional. Albert is presented as an active force in national life, as "laborious" for England's poor, as a "summoner of War and Waste to rivalries of peace," as "modest, kindly, all-accomplished, wise," and, most important, as the ultimate pater familias, "noble father" of the country's "kings to be." Victoria, by contrast, appears in the Dedication principally in the role of bereaved and passive wife, whose "woman's heart" is exhorted to "break not but endure" and who is to be "comforted," "encompassed," and "o'ershadowed" by love until God chooses to restore her to her husband's side.

What lies behind this traditional domestic relationship is, of course, a very different reality. In that reality, Victoria is the true holder and wielder of power, the repository of enormous inherited authority, while Albert possesses what influence and significance he does almost solely through his marriage. This reversal of the usual male-female roles, superimposed on the more conventional relationship depicted in Tennyson's Dedication, produces a curious dissonance, much like one that came to sound more and more insistently in the culture as a whole as the nineteenth century progressed and that received powerful expression in the *Idylls of the King*. Indeed, Tennyson's very contemporary poem can be read as an elaborate examination of the advantages and dangers of sexual role reversal, with King Arthur himself playing, in a number of significant ways, the part usually assigned by culture to the woman.

II

Such revision of the female role in the nineteenth century is closely associated with the period's ambivalent attitude toward history. It was during the nineteenth century that the modern discipline of history first came fully into its own as a truly rigorous inquiry into the past, demanding, as Frederic Harrison puts it, "belief in contemporary documents, exact testing of authorities, scrupulous verification of citations, minute attention to chronology, geography, paleography, and inscriptions" (121). Defined in this new way, history had a distinctly male bias. This was true for a number of reasons. To begin with, its "disavowal of impressionism" (Douglas 174) in favor of a preoccupation with hard facts permitted it for the first time to rival the natural sciences as a "respectable" career for intellectual young men. Francis Parkman, American student of the Indian Wars, "defiantly chose history," one commentator tells us, "as a protest against what he considered the effeminacy of the liberal church" (Douglas 173). In addition, as a record of great public events, history had always tended to dwell almost exclusively on the activities of men. "It should not be forgotten," writes Arthur Schlesinger, "that all of our great historians have been men and were likely therefore to be influenced by a sex interpretation of history all the more potent because unconscious" (126). In *Northanger Abbey*, Jane Austen alludes sardonically to this fact when her heroine dismisses history books for being full of "the quarrels of popes and kings, with wars and pestilences in every page; the men also good for nothing, and hardly any women at all" (108).

But nineteenth-century history was male-oriented in an even deeper and more all-pervasive sense than this; for to the extent that historians were principally concerned with recording the passage of power and authority through the generations, their work necessarily preserved the patrilineal forms and structures of the societies they investigated. "The centuries too are all lineal children of one another," writes Carlyle in *Past and Present*, emphasizing the intimate connection that has always existed between history and genealogy (45). In *The Elementary Structures of Kinship*, Lévi-Strauss argues that culture, and by extension history, can only come into existence after the concept of kinship has been established. But this means that in those societies where family structure is patrilineal, women must inevitably play a secondary role in history, since they do not have names of their own and therefore do not visibly participate in the passing on of authority from one generation to the next. The rise of "scientific" history in the nineteenth century, then, might have been expected to confirm, among other things, the validity of the traditional male-dominant and female-subordinate roles.

But in fact, those roles came more and more frequently to be questioned during the period, as did the new history itself. Ironically, it was the very success of scientific history at reconstituting the past that provoked this resistance. For what soon became clear was that, seen in too much detail and known too well, the past was growing burdensome and intimidating, was revealing—in Tennyson's metaphor—all the models that could not be remodeled. John Stuart Mill's celebrated dismay, reported in his *Autobiography*, that all the best combinations of musical notes "must already have been discovered" was one contemporary example of this anxiety. Another was George Eliot's declaration, in *Middlemarch*, that "a new Theresa will hardly have the opportunity of reforming a conventual life . . . the medium in which [her] ardent deeds took shape is for ever gone." For a nineteenth-century woman like Dorothea Brooke, George Eliot tells us, it is often better that life be obscure since "the growing good of the world is partly dependent on *un*historic acts" (612; italics mine).[3] Such a conclusion follows inevitably from the idea that history, simply by existing, exhausts possibilities, leaving its readers with a despairing sense of their own belatedness and impotence. And this despair in turn leads to anxious quests for novelty, to a hectic avant-gardism, and in the end to an inescapable fin de siècle ennui. "The world is weary of the past, / Oh, might it die or rest at last," Shelley declares in *Hellas*, expressing a desire for oblivion, a longing for the end of history. Only through such an apocalypse, the poet suggests, can life be made new and vital again.

The great apocalyptic event for the nineteenth century was the French Revolution, at its most authentic a massive and very deliberate assault on history. To be sure, regicide is the ultimate attack on the authority of the past, but if it is dealt with merely on a political level, its deeper significance is likely to be missed. To be fully understood, it must, rather, be placed in the context of the many other revolutionary acts whose collective intent was to overthrow not only the old historical regime but history itself. Among these acts were laws that abolished the right to make wills and that declared natural children absolutely equal with legitimate offspring. Both struck directly at the power of the past to control the present and, just as important, at the right of patrilineal authority to extend itself indefinitely into the future. Revolutionary calendar reforms were an even more literal attack on history. By decree, official chronology, for example, began at the autumn equinox of 1792; the first day of the new republic thus became the first day of the new world. Even the names of the months were changed in the revolutionary calendar, with the seasons replacing the Caesars—nature replacing history—as the source of the new nomenclature.

From these revolutionary activities two important principles emerged. The first is that wherever intolerable social abuses are the consequence of history, reform is only possible outside of history.[4] The French Revolution sought to incorporate this idea, at least symbolically, into an actual working community, a community for which not history but nature would provide the model. In that new dispensation, each person would be self-authorized, independent of genealogy, and each day would have the freshness of the first day or, rather, of the only day, of *illo tempore*, a moment in the eternal present unqualified and undiminished by an "exhausted past." Such an ambition has never been entirely fanciful. Mircea Eliade, for one, reminds us of "the very considerable period" during which

> humanity opposed history by all possible means . . . The primitive desired to have no "memory," not to record time, to content himself with tolerating it simply as a dimension of his existence, but without interiorizing it, without transforming it into consciousness. . . . That desire felt by the man of traditional societies to refuse history, and to confine himself to an indefinite repetition of archetypes, testifies to his thirst for the real and his terror of losing himself by letting himself be overwhelmed by the meaninglessness of profane existence. (*Cosmos* 90–91)

The Revolution's famous exchange of "fraternity" for "paternity" makes the same point. The father-son relationship is generational and thus principally a product of history. Brothers, on the other hand, are by their nature contemporaries, and their relationships are therefore more "spatial" than temporal. In *Parsifal*, Wagner describes the realm of the Grail knight brotherhood in just these terms. "Zum Raum," Gurnemanz explains to the at-first uncomprehending Parsifal, "wird hier die Zeit": "Time changes here to space." Significantly, James R. Kincaid finds this same idea built into the very structure of Tennyson's *Idylls*. "The overlaid seasonal progress in the [poem]," he writes, "suggests not so much objective, physical time as the spatial representations of time in medieval tapestry or triptychs. This emphasis on space seems to imply the absence of time, the conquest of time" (151–52). It is a conquest that Ann Douglas believes was, for the nineteenth century, inescapably gender-identified; distinguishing between "scientific" historians and feminine and clerical historians, she remarks that the latter, "in their well-founded fear of historicity . . . substituted space for time as the fundamental dimension of human experience" (199).

As the Douglas comment shows, the second principle established by the Revolution is closely related to the first, asserting that the apocalyptic end of history signals the end of a system in which women are instruments of, and subordinate to, patrilineal continuity. In particular, the revolutionary law making natural children the absolute equals of so-called legitimate offspring had the effect of taking from men their familiar right to direct and subdue female sexuality. In the saturnalia of sexual "misrule" that followed, with its release of aboriginal energy and its invitation to self-discovery and self-assertion, traditional gender roles were radically reexamined. Eliade's study of ceremonial transvestism describes this symbolic sex role reversal as

> a coming out of one's self, a transcending of one's own historically controlled situation, a recovering of an original situation . . . which it is important to reconstitute periodically in order to restore, if only for a brief moment, the initial completeness, the intact source of holiness and power . . . that preceded the creation. ("Mephistopheles" 113)

Interestingly, 1792, the first year of the new French Republic, was also the year in which Mary Wollstonecraft published her *Vindication of the Rights of Woman*, inaugurating the modern era of feminism. Wollstonecraft would later include in her own study of the French Revolution descriptions of the part women played in overturning the monarchy. "Early . . . on the fifth of October," she reports, "a multitude of women by some impulse were collected together; and hastening to the *hôtel de ville*, obliged every female they met to accompany them, even entering many houses to force others to follow in their train." The women are only temporarily delayed by national guardsmen with bayonets. "Uttering a loud and general cry, they hurled a volley of stones at the soldiers, who, unwilling, or ashamed, to fire on women, *though with the appearance of furies*, retreated into the hall and left the passage free" (133; italics mine).[5]

One can perhaps find in these latter-day Eumenides the originals of Dickens's Madame Defarge and her ferocious female companions of the guillotine. The same image seems to have occurred independently to Edmund Burke, who equated the insurrection on the continent with the dismemberment of King Peleas of Thessaly by his daughters, an act contrived by the vengeful Medea (109).[6] Clearly, the

nineteenth century perceived the French Revolution as juxtaposing two key contemporary themes, the attack on history and the assertion of female authority. The
reading of Tennyson's *Idylls of the King* proposed here focuses precisely on this
juxtaposition: on the rich potential for a new society that emerges from the original
association of these two themes and on the disaster Tennyson says overtakes such
a society once all the implications of the Arthurian apocalypse are revealed.

III

The coming of Arthur at the beginning of the *Idylls* is plainly an apocalyptic event,
recognized as such by the whole society.[7] The advent of a king who proposes to
reign without the authorization of patrilineal descent is an extraordinary and threatening phenomenon. "Who is he / That he should rule us?" the great lords and
barons of the realm demand. "Who hath proven him King Uther's son?" The
community first attempts to see if the situation can be regularized, to see, that is,
if some evidence can be found that Arthur is, after all, the legitimate heir of an
established line of kings. Leodogran, the king of Cameliard, is particularly anxious
for such confirmation since Arthur has asked to marry his daughter, Guinevere.
"How should I that am a king," Leodogran asks, "Give my one daughter saving
to a king, / And king's son?" In seeking evidence of Arthur's legitimacy, Leodogran,
parodying the methodical inquiries of a historian, tracks down one source of
information after another: an ancient chamberlain, some of Arthur's own closest
friends, a putative step-sister. None can supply the absolute assurance the king
wants, and over against their only partly convincing stories stands the undoubted
truth that, while Arthur's supposed parents, Uther and Ygerne, were dark-haired
and dark-eyed, the new monarch is himself "fair / Beyond the race of Britons and
of men."

What emerges from all this investigation is the fact that Arthur represents not
a continuation and fulfillment of history but rather a decisive break with it. Indeed,
the failure of Leodogran's conventional historical research to establish some connection with the past suggests that in Arthur's new dispensation even the traditional
methods for acquiring knowledge have become ineffectual. "Sir and my Liege,"
cries a favorite warrior after one of Arthur's victories, "the fire of God / Descends
upon thee in the battle-field. / I know thee for my King!" Here is a way of recognizing
authority very different from one requiring the confirmation of genealogy. Arthur's
fair coloring also confounds genealogy. Not only does it set him apart from the
people most likely to have been his parents, it isolates him as well from all other
Britons and even, we are told, from all other men. Radically discontinuous with
the past in every one of its aspects, Arthur is like some dramatic mutation in
nature, threatening the integrity of the genetic line as the only means of infusing
new life into it.

In fact, nature does replace history as the sponsor of the new king. Tennyson
affirms this idea both in what he chooses to drop from the traditional account of

the coming of Arthur and in what he invents to replace the omission. Perhaps the best known of all legends associated with the identification of Arthur as England's rightful king is the story of the sword in the stone. In Malory, for example, young Arthur wins acceptance as lawful ruler because he is the only person in England capable of removing a magic sword from a marble block on which have been inscribed the words "Whoso pulleth out this sword of his stone and anvil is rightwise king born of all England."

In nearly every retelling of the Arthurian stories down to our own time, this dramatic incident plays a prominent part. Tennyson's omission of the anecdote from his own rendering of the Arthurian material, then, is at least noteworthy and may even be a significant clue to one of the poet's principal intentions in the *Idylls*. For what the phallic incident of the sword in the stone emphasizes is that Arthur, though not as incontrovertibly a descendant of the previous king as the people of England might like, is nevertheless the inheritor of some kind of lawful authority, the recipient of legitimate power legitimately transferred. And the participation in this ritual of the church, with its traditional stake in an orderly, apostolic succession, further ensures that such a transfer is, at least symbolically, patrilineal. Tennyson's rejection of this famous story, therefore, may well suggest that the poet was trying to direct attention away from conventional continuity in the passing of power to Arthur and toward some alternative source of authority for the new king.

What that alternative source of authority might be is hinted at in "Guinevere," the eleventh of the twelve idylls, an unusual work in that, as Jerome Buckley points out in his edition of the poetry, it draws on little "apart from Tennyson's own imagination" (536). This "self-authorized" and so-to-speak "unhistorical" idyll contains a striking description of the early days of Arthur's reign—the account of a magical initiatory journey, invented by Tennyson, we may conjecture, as a substitute for the omitted episode of the sword in the stone. We hear this story from a young novice, who repeats the tale her father had told her of his first trip to Camelot to serve the newly installed king. "The land was full of signs / And wonders," the girl quotes her father's narrative of that trip. By the light of the many beacon fires on the headlands along the coast

> the white mermaiden swam,
> And strong man-breasted things stood from the sea,
> And sent a deep sea-voice thro' all the land,
> To which the little elves of chasm and cleft
> Made answer, sounding like a distant horn.
> So said my father—yea, and furthermore,
> Next morning, while he past the dim-lit woods
> Himself beheld three spirits mad with joy
>
> . . . .
>
> And still at evenings on before his horse
> The flickering fairy-circle wheel'd and broke
> Flying, and link'd again, and wheel'd and broke

> Flying, for all the land was full of life.
> And when at last he came to Camelot,
> A wreath of airy dancers hand-in-hand
> Swung round the lighted lantern of the hall;
> And in the hall itself was such a feast
> As never man had dream'd; for every knight
> Had whatsoever meat he long'd for served
> By hands unseen; and even as he said
> Down in the cellars merry bloated things
> Shoulder'd the spigot, straddling on the butts
> While the wine ran.

This visionary scene both celebrates and ratifies the coming of Arthur, affirming that the young king's authority over the land proceeds directly from the land itself, from the deepest resources of nature, and that "all genealogies founder," as J.M. Gray puts it, "in that 'great deep' " (11). Metaphors of depth and interiority are everywhere: seas, woods, chasms, clefts, cellars. All the spirits of nature rejoice in Arthur, seeing in him their rightful heir, the repository of their power. In Tennyson's remarkable vision, radically departing as it does from historical sources, Arthur's coming fulfills that revolutionary law of the French National Convention which declared "natural children absolutely equal with legitimate."

This Romantic idea that the true source of kingly power is natural and internal rather than historical and external is more fully developed in the first of the idylls. There, Arthur's legitimacy is shown to derive from two sources: an inner strength, of which his successful military adventures are symbols, and the depths of nature, themselves metaphors for the young king's potent inwardness. When we first meet Arthur in the *Idylls*, he is a newly fledged warrior, driving the patriarchal Roman Caesars from his land as determinedly as the French would later drive them from the calendar.[8] Later, we see the young monarch receiving the sword Excalibur from the Lady of the Lake, a mystic wielder of subtle magic who "dwells down in a deep" and from whose hand, rising "out of the bosom of the lake," the new king takes the emblem of his authority.

To the extent that such derivation of power from the deep symbolizes access to one's own interior energy, Arthur's kingly mission is ultimately self-authorized; and in particular, it is authorized by that part of himself which, associated with creative, ahistorical nature, is most distinctly female. Tennyson emphasizes this idea not only by assigning the Lady of the Lake a prominent role in the establishment of Arthur's legitimacy but also by introducing the mysterious muselike figures of the "three fair queens" who attend the young king at his coronation: "the friends / Of Arthur, gazing on him, tall, with bright / Sweet faces, who will help him at his need."[9] In his Preface to *The Great Mother*, Erich Neumann declares that the "problem of the Feminine [is important] for the psychologist of culture, who realizes that the peril of present-day mankind springs in large part from the one-sidedly patriarchal development of the male intellectual consciousness, which is no longer kept in balance by the matriarchal world of the psyche" (xlii). Clearly, the new dispensation promised by the coming of Tennyson's nineteenth-century Arthur will involve, as an important part of its program, the freeing of that matriarchal psyche, of feminine energy, from its long subservience to male authority and consciousness. Everything we know about the new king makes this certain. The very manner of his accession directly challenges such authority and consciousness, and his establishment of the community of the Round Table can best be understood as an attempt to assert the wholeness of the human spirit in the face of that sexual fragmentation described by Neumann.

What the dominance of male consciousness over female psyche can lead to in society is made plain in the *Idylls* through Tennyson's description of the all-male community of King Pellam in "Balin and Balan," the last of the books to be written. Pellam, a rival of King Arthur's, determines to outdo the court of Camelot in piety, and as a first step he pushes "aside his faithful wife, nor lets / Or dame or damsel enter at his gates / Lest he should be polluted." As a manifestation of abstract male reason and will, such suppression of the feminine renders the society moribund. The aging Pellam, described by Tennyson as "this gray king," has "quite foregone / All matters of this world" and spends his listless days in a hall "bushed about . . . with gloom," where "cankered boughs . . . whine in the wood." Nature here, rejected as a source of energy and replenishment, takes suitable revenge on its sullen oppressor.

King Pellam is the guardian of a most appropriate relic. The old monarch, who "finds himself descended from the Saint / Arimathaean Joseph," is the proud possessor of "that same spear / Wherewith the Roman pierced the side of Christ" as he hung on the cross. Death-dealing, Roman, phallic, linear, the spear—its ghostly shadow haunting the countryside—symbolizes the dessicated male society of Pellam's court; indeed, it is very literally the male "line" through which Pellam— who, unlike Arthur, is deeply interested in genealogy—traces the source of his authority back to Joseph of Arimathaea. Significantly, as a symbol of the linear and the historical, the spear belies the cyclical promise of the resurrection represented by the Grail, the companion relic from which, in the sexually fragmented culture described both by Neumann and by Tennyson, it has long been separated.[10]

As the country of King Pellam is the land of the spear, so Arthur's Camelot is the court of the Grail. At least, it is from Camelot that the knights of the Round Table, tutored in Arthur's values,[11] set out on their quest for the sacred cup, familiar symbol both of nature and of the female, a womblike emblem of fecundity associated with what, in pagan legend, is the Cauldron of Plenty, an attribute of the Goddess of Fertility.[12] Such female energy is, in traditional mythography, ahistorical, a fact to which the Grail also testifies. The vessel's circular form, like that of the Round Table itself and like the "flickering fairy circles" and "wreaths of airy dancers" associated with the coming of Arthur, mimics the timeless cycles of nature, a timelessness in which the Round Table knights themselves participate. As we noted earlier, fraternal relationships are necessarily contemporaneous ones, expressing themselves in space rather than in time. The whole of Camelot partakes of this anachronistic quality. The young knight Gareth, catching his first glimpse of the sculptured gates of the city, marvels at how intermingled—how contiguous rather than continuous—all the events depicted there seem to be: "New things and old co-twisted, as if Time / Were nothing." His intuition of the ahistorical character of Camelot is confirmed by the "old seer" at the gate, who speaks of the city as a place "never built at all, / And therefore built forever." Significantly, the principal subject of "Gareth and Lynette" is young Gareth's commitment "to fight the brotherhood of Day and Night" in "the war of Time against the soul of man," a war in which, in this early idyll, the soul signally triumphs.[13]

IV

The optimism expressed in the early idylls about the joyous and lively new society that would result from an apocalyptic release of natural and, by extension, female energy into a world heretofore dominated by history and male authority was largely a product of one form of nineteenth-century Romantic ideology. Traditionally, nature has been seen as the enemy of rational and historical human culture. Indeed, it has been argued that culture functions to permit human beings to assert their independence of—and superiority to—nature. In examining the origins of kinship, for example, Lévi-Strauss suggests that the whole elaborate and extended structure of the family can best be understood as a means by which "culture must, under pain of not existing, firmly declare 'Me first,' and tell nature, 'You go no further' " (31).[14] In this view, nature is dangerous, anarchic, indifferent to human concerns. Its frightening power may have to be placated or invoked on special occasions, but it must always be treated warily, must be controlled and even suppressed.

The Romanticism of the early nineteenth century, as one of its most striking innovations, managed momentarily to suspend the traditional enmity between nature and culture. In the benign natural world of the Wordsworthian vision, for example, breezes are "blessings," vales are "harbors," clouds are "guides," groves are "homes." Where human culture is a burden, it wearies the poet precisely because it is "unnatural." Under such circumstances, Wordsworth attempts to reconcile these traditionally polar opposites, submitting his cultivated sensibility to a sustaining and unthreatening nature in order to receive a new infusion of energy. It is nature in this ameliorative sense that underlies the scene in the *Idylls* in which the coming of Arthur is celebrated by all the mermaidens, elves, fairies, spirits, and merry bloated things we would naturally expect to find inhabiting a land that is "full of life."

The same Romantic optimism that permitted nature to be so readily domesticated in many early nineteenth-century works of art, that allowed nature's powers to be courted so fearlessly, also made possible the hopeful invocation of female energy that is such a striking feature of the *Idylls*. Historically, this benignant view of female power is unusual. Both in history and in myth women have for the most part been associated with the irrational and destructive forces of nature that threaten orderly male culture. As maenads, bacchantes, witches, they express in their frenzied dances and murderous violence an unbridled sexuality analogous to the frightening and sometimes even ruinous fecundity of nature. Indeed, the control of female sexuality is among the commonest metaphors in art for the control of nature (just as the control of nature is a metaphor for the control of women; see, e.g., Smith and Kolodny). And as Lévi-Strauss points out, the earliest evidences of culture are nearly always those rules of exchange devised by men to facilitate the ownership and sexual repression of women.

Tennyson's departure, in the early idylls, from this traditional fear of female sexuality coincides with a dramatic development in modern cultural history. "Between the seventeenth and the nineteenth centuries," Nancy F. Cott remarks about this change, "the dominant Anglo-American definition of women as especially sexual was reversed and transformed into the view that women were less carnal and lustful than men" (221). Or as Havelock Ellis put it more succinctly in his *Studies in the Psychology of Sex,* one of the most striking creations of the nineteenth century was "woman's sexual anesthesia" (3:193–94). Cott substitutes for Ellis's "anesthesia" her own term "passionlessness," linking it with Evangelical Protestantism, which "constantly reiterated the theme that Christianity had elevated women above the weakness of animal nature for the sake of purity for men, the tacit condition for that elevation being the suppression of female sexuality" (227). Plainly, Tennyson's nineteenth-century recreation of Camelot depends to a considerable extent on this contemporary theory of female passionlessness—what another critic calls woman's "more than mortal purity" (Christ 146)—and its ameliorative influence on male sensuality.[15] Unlike the society of King Pellam, which preserves the earlier view of women as sexually insatiable and which adopts a grim monasticism as the only defense against feminine corrosiveness, Arthur's court welcomes women for their ennobling and now safely denatured regenerative powers. In this respect, Camelot seems to resemble the many nineteenth-century utopian communities that attempted to experiment with a new and higher order of relationship between the sexes and that Tennyson himself had already commented on obliquely in *The Princess.*[16]

It is in his own "passionlessness" that Arthur most clearly embodies the nineteenth-century feminine ideal on which he seeks to build his new society.[17] "Arthur the blameless, pure as any maid," he is called, sardonically but accurately, in "Balin and Balan," and it is in these terms that he becomes a model for all his knights, urging them

> To lead sweet lives in purest chastity,
> To love one maiden only, cleave to her,
> And worship her by years of noble deeds.

Such sexual restraint will, according to Arthur, win for the Round Table knights the moral authority to purify a land "Wherein the beast was ever more and more,

/ But man was less and less." These lines perfectly express the Evangelical Protestant belief, just noted, that "Christianity had elevated women above the weakness of animal nature for the sake of purity for men," and they confirm that it is on the female ideal of passionlessness that Arthur means to found his new community. Tennyson even goes so far as to alter his sources in order to make this point, rejecting Malory's designation of Modred as Arthur's illegitimate son and instead having the king refer to the usurper as "my sister's son—no kin of mine."

V

The scene would now appear to be set for the triumph of the Round Table experiment. With the apocalyptic overturning of history and male authority and the substitution for them of a benign nature and a safely contained female energy, Arthur's new society ought certainly to flourish. How, then, are we to account for the famous decline of this ideal community into corruption and nihilism, how explain the fall of Camelot? Tennyson's revision of the story of Modred's origins may offer one answer to these questions. As I have suggested, the point of the poet's departure from Malory is to maintain unblemished the record of Arthur's sexual purity. But the textual change has unexpected ramifications that reveal a serious flaw in the Arthurian vision. For if Modred is not Arthur's son, illegitimate or otherwise, then in the story as we receive it, Arthur has no children at all. He and Guinevere produce no offspring, and even the foundling he brings to his wife to rear as her own dies.

Such sterility, appropriate symbol of a denatured sexuality, means the end of Arthur's dream of a new society; the rejection of history and patriarchy that is the source of the young king's first strength here returns to haunt the older monarch, who now perceives that without the continuity provided by legitimate descent through the male line, his vision cannot survive him.[18] This point has already been made obliquely in the passage from "Guinevere" describing the natural magic that filled the land when Arthur first began to rule. The story, we know, is recounted by a young novice who explains that she is repeating a tale her father had told her. Thus, even this early in Arthur's reign, the dependence of the king's authority on the preservation of a historical record is recognized, a preservation that in turn—the passage reminds us—requires men capable of begetting children through whom to transmit that record.[19]

It is precisely Arthur's incapacity to propagate his line that renders his new society so vulnerable. In "The Last Tournament," for example, the Red Knight calls tauntingly from the top of a brutally phallic tower:

> Lo! art thou not that eunuch-hearted king
> Who fain had clipt free manhood from the world—
> The woman-worshipper?

The Red Knight's equation of Arthur's sterility with a worship of woman suggests how enfeebling the king's sentimentalizing of nature has become. The female ideal worshiped by Arthur (and scorned by the Red Knight) is tame, disembodied, passionless, itself the product of an abstract male rationalism and no real alternative source of strength. Lancelot, describing to Guinevere, in "Balin and Balan," a dream he has had of "a maiden saint" who carries lilies in her hand, speaks of the flowers as "perfect-pure" and continues:

> As light a flush
> As hardly tints the blossom of the quince
> Would mar their charm of stainless womanhood.

To which Guinevere replies, resenting such an imposition of the ideal on the natural,

> Sweeter to me . . . this garden rose
> Deep-hued and many-folded! sweeter still
> The wild-wood hyacinth and the bloom of May!

In the end, Guinevere's reality triumphs over Arthur's and Lancelot's abstraction in the *Idylls of the King*, just as her irresistible sexual energy at last defeats her husband's passionlessness.

Given the subject and the theme of the *Idylls*, this outcome is inevitable. Indeed, Tennyson's profoundest insight in the poem may be that nature cannot be courted casually, that the id-like energy of the deep must not be invoked without a full knowledge of how devastating and ultimately uncontrollable that energy can be. Again, for the nineteenth century it was the French Revolution that most dramatically embodied this insight. We have already seen how that event, for all its celebration of myth over history, nature over culture, female over male, itself began by trying to contain the outburst of insurrectionary energy it had released within a number of easily manipulated abstractions: new laws governing the inheritance of property, new names for the months of the year. Even regicide was intended as a kind of abstract statement, the removal of a symbol as much as of a man.

But unaccountably, the blood would not stop flowing from the murdered king's decapitated body. It poured into the streets of Paris from the foot of the guillotine and ran there for years, as if newly released from some source deep in the earth. From the first, the bloodstained Terror was associated with female sexuality. The key symbol of the Revolution was the figure Liberty, later memorably depicted by Eugène Delacroix as a bare-breasted bacchante striding triumphantly over the bodies of half-naked dead men. The Dionysian guillotine haunted the imagination of Europe; a mechanical *vagina dentata*, it produced, with its endless emasculations, an unstoppable blood flow, the unhealing menstrual wound curiously like the one suffered by the maimed king in the story of the Grail. In primitive societies, such menstrual bleeding is the ultimate symbol of a polluting female nature, an unbridled sexual destructiveness that the power of patriarchal authority must at all costs contain. In nineteenth-century England, the bloody denouement of the French Revolution produced a similar reaction, a suppression of sex and a repression of women that to this day we disapprovingly call Victorian.

From the beginning of his career, Tennyson had been preoccupied with these issues—with what Gerhard Joseph has called the poet's "notion of woman as cosmic destructive principle" (127)—and in particular with the point at which the themes of nature, blood, and female sexuality converge. An early sonnet, for example, begins:

> She took the dappled partridge fleckt with blood,
> And in her hands the drooping pheasant bare,
> And by his feet she held the woolly hare,
> And like a master-painting where she stood,
> Lookt some new goddess of an English wood.

This powerful figure of female authority, bloody, dangerous, but curiously attractive, springs from the imagination of a young poet already moving toward a post-Words-worthian view of nature as "red in tooth and claw." In "The Palace of Art," the protagonist, withdrawing too deeply into self, approaching too closely the dark, secret springs of nature, comes "unawares" on "corpses three-months-old . . . that stood against the wall" and on "white-eyed phantasms weeping tears of blood." In the *Idylls*, the doom of the Round Table is sealed at the moment during "The Last Tournament" when, to defeat the bestial Red Knight, Arthur's men give themselves up to the almost erotic appeal of blood lust, when

>   swording right and left
> Men, women, on their sodden faces, [they] hurl'd
> Till all the rafters rang with woman-yells,
> And all the pavement streamed with massacre.

But the dismantling of the brotherhood had begun even earlier, as a direct result of the Grail quest. The blood-filled holy cup, itself a menstrual symbol, first appears in the *Idylls* to Percival's sister, a young nun in whose description the vessel seems almost explicitly a living female organ:

> Down the long beam stole the Holy Grail,
> Rose-red with beatings in it, as if alive,
> Till all the white walls of my cell were dyed
> With rosy colors leaping on the wall.
>   ("The Holy Grail")

It is when the Round Table knights abandon themselves to the visionary pursuit of this symbol of the "eternal feminine" that Camelot, literally "unmanned," begins to fall into ruin.

"Creator and destroyer," Robert M. Adams comments on the Victorian image of the femme fatale,

> but more fascinating in the second capacity than the first, woman for the late nineteenth century . . . is both sacred and obscene, sacred as redeeming man from culture, obscene as content with a merely appetitive existence that

declines inevitably from the high fever of Eros to the low fever of dissolution
and decay.   (185)

In the end, Arthur's dream of a natural community is destroyed, Tennyson suggests,
by the carnality to which such a dream must necessarily lead, is spoiled by an
irrepressible female libidinousness that, once released by the withdrawal of patrilineal authority, can be neither contained nor directed. The second half of the
Idylls is one long record of licentiousness: the faithless depravity of Gawain and
Ettarre, the crass sensuality of Tristram and Isolt, the open adultery of Lancelot
and Guinevere. "Thou hast spoilt the purpose of my life" we have already heard
Arthur declare bitterly to the queen at their last meeting, a key passage in the
long-standing controversy about the psychological and moral sophistication of the
Idylls. For if Christopher Ricks, among others, is right that in this speech Guinevere
is made "too much a scapegoat, [since] the doom of the Round Table seems to
antedate her adultery," he is surely wrong to find, in such an attack on her,
evidence of "a root confusion in Tennyson" (272). Rather, what the poem preem-
inently shows is that the confusion here is Arthur's. It is Arthur's naiveté about
the dynamics of the human psyche that dooms his ideal community from the start;
it is his own well-intentioned but foolish binding of his knights "by vows . . . the
which no man can keep" that threatens his dream long before the adultery of
Guinevere and Lancelot can precipitate its destruction.[20]

In his isolation from reality, the king resembles other self-authorizing post-
Renaissance heroes, from Faust to Frankenstein, who begin by creating the worlds
in which they live out of their own private visions and end by succumbing to the
dark natural forces they have raised but fail to understand or control. The solipsistic
isolation of such figures becomes their fate as well as their failing, their retribution
as well as their sin. For where the historical record provides individuals with a
context independent of themselves, a past and a future in which they need not
participate to believe, a variety of experiences unlike their own but just as real,
myth asserts the sovereignty of the eternal moment, which is forever the present,
and the ubiquitousness of the representative human, who is always the same,
without antecedents or heirs. It is into this reductive timelessness and silence of
myth that characters like Merlin and Arthur ultimately fall in the *Idylls* for having
cut their connections with patriarchal history.

Merlin, Tennyson tells us in the sixth idyll, derives his power from an ancient
volume that is the paradigmatic book of history, passed down through the generations
from one male magician to another. The first owner we hear of is a little, shriveled,
Pellam-like wizard whose strength comes from his rejection of sensuality in favor
of the intensest possible concentration on the text. (The seer's principal use of this
text is to help a local king exercise absolute control over his queen.) The book
then "comes down" to Merlin, who describes it as

> Writ in a language that has long gone by
>
> . . . .
>
> And every margin scribbled, crost, and cramm'd
> With comment, densest condensation, hard

> . . . .
> And none can read the text, not even I;
> And none can read the comment but myself;
> And in the comment did I find the charm.

Here is the perfect symbol of what we have been calling patrilineal continuity, continuity dependent on a bequeathed historical record that is both the ultimate source of male power and, with its antiquity and its accumulating burden of interpretation, a constant reminder of the belatedness of the present. Shut out of history by her gender, a vengeful Vivien determines to seduce Merlin from the satisfactions of male tradition with the blandishments of female sexuality. For a long while the old magician holds out against the woman, but in the end he yields, revealing to her the secret of the ultimate charm. The next moment, Vivien has turned the spell back on him, robbing him—significantly—of "name and fame," the two best gifts that patrilineal history can bestow on a man, and casting him into the eternal isolation of myth, "Closed in the four walls of a hollow tower / From which was no escape for evermore."[21]

In his final battle, Arthur suffers a fate much like Merlin's. Because he has received authorization from no father and conveyed it to no son, the king is trapped in the reflexiveness of the prophecy that has governed him all his life: "From the great deep to the great deep he goes." That same solipsistic reflexiveness characterizes Arthur's last hallucinatory battle against his sister's son, a war, he tells us,

> against my people and my knights.
> A king who fights his people fights himself.
> . . . .
> I perish by this people that I made.
> ("The Passing of Arthur")

The war is fought in "a death-white mist" in which the solid reality of the world proves an illusion, "For friend and foe were shadows in the mist, / And friend slew friend not knowing who he slew."

Ironically, the reign that began with the whole world doubting the legitimacy of the king ends with the king himself doubting it. "On my heart," says Arthur,

> hath fallen
> Confusion, till I know not what I am,
> Nor whence I am, nor whether I be king;
> Behold, I seem but king among the dead.

In the end—Tennyson summarizes the central theme of the *Idylls*—all certainty is impossible for a man who rejects the stability of patrilineal descent and seeks instead to derive his authority from himself, to build a community on the idealization of nature and female energy.

VI

The resemblance of this scene, in which "friend slays friend," to the equally confusing struggle of "ignorant armies" on "the darkling plain" in Matthew Arnold's "Dover Beach" reminds us that, in writing the *Idylls of the King,* Tennyson was participating in an elaborate symposium with his fellow Victorians on the troubling state of their world. But where Arnold's poem focuses on a particular moment in the history of that world, Tennyson's *Idylls* provide, in John D. Rosenberg's phrase, "the chronicle . . . of a whole civilization" (34) as it passes from the Romantic optimism of its first days—about which Wordsworth could exult, "Bliss was it in that dawn to be alive"—to the fin de siècle disillusionment of the last hours— which found, in Walter Pater's words, "each man keeping as a solitary prisoner, his own dream of a world." The springtime innocence and eagerness of the first idylls wonderfully convey the excitement of the Romantic rediscovery of nature, and the Arthurian credo of passionlessness embodies the early Victorian belief in the benevolence and controllability of that nature. But just as the Victorians' famous efforts to suppress female sexuality only succeeded in generating a grim and extensive sexual underground, so Arthur's naive manipulations of nature con- clude in the society of the Round Table being swept away on a great wave of carnality.

Despite the failure of the Arthurian assault on history, Tennyson persists at the end of the *Idylls,* as he does elsewhere, in seeking a rapprochement with myth. Thus, against the linear and historical implications of the king's famous valedictory, "The old order changeth, yielding place to new," the poet reiterates the traditional cyclical promise of Arthur's eventual return as *rex quondam rexque futurus.* In the same way, at the end of *In Memoriam* Tennyson sets the historical and progressive "one far-off, divine event / To which the whole creation moves" within a cycle of seasons. To be sure, the hero of "Locksley Hall" seems to offer the definitive disavowal of myth when he declares, "Better fifty years of Europe than a cycle of Cathay." But it is significant that the narrator of that poem lives long enough to discover how the inevitable alternation of "chaos and cosmos" in the universe renders even the most intense vision of historical progress trivial.

Such ambivalence about history, our starting point for this consideration of the *Idylls,* marks the history of the poem itself, a history that records the poet's entrapment in a familiar nineteenth-century dilemma, one with its own broader ramifications. Like Merlin, Tennyson is committed—since "first light[ing] upon Malory"—to the authority of a historical text of which he is his generation's principal interpreter.

> And none can read the comment but myself;
> And in the comment did I find the charm.

But no belated expositor such as he, no descendant of patriarchal exegetes, can hope to make the unimaginable backward leap through commentary to the mystery of the text itself. Indeed, it is the very weight of traditional commentary—"densest condensation, hard"—that renders such a leap impossible, precisely that burden of the past that unmans where it means to empower. For in exhausted latter days, as Merlin informs us, "None can read the text, not even I." Yet Tennyson's attempt, in the face of this exhaustion, to reject traditional sources in favor of a contemporary, ahistorical representation of Arthurian materials—his refusal, that is, to "remodel models"—courts another kind of weakness, risking, in the absence of patrilineal resonances, the domesticity and effeminacy of a "Morte d'Albert."

A similar ambivalence toward history characterizes the century for which Tennyson wrote. Already during the early decades Viconian cyclical theory was becoming influential, Thomas Carlyle was denouncing scientific reconstructions of the past as "tombstone history" and time as "a grand anti-magician and wonderhider," and the First Reform Act, Britain's bloodless version of the French Revolution, had dramatically rejected genealogy as society's sole authorizing principle. In the light of such reformist impulses, Tennyson's investigation of a natural community in the *Idylls of the King*, one in which the female energy of myth substitutes for the male energy of history, seems inevitable. Equally inevitable, however, is the failure of that community, given the growing Victorian disillusionment with the Romantic experiment.[22] For Carlyle, for instance, who in his own way shared the fate of Tennyson's Arthur, the magic creativity of *Sartor Resartus* unavoidably declined into the solipsistic self-imprisonment of the *Latter-Day Pamphlets*. Just as inescapably, the First Reform Act led to the Second and toward that "anarchy" which Matthew Arnold prophesied and deplored and of which the developing women's movement was seen by the Victorians as a powerful symbol. And, despite eager celebrations of myth, over this perceived decline brooded a sense of the enervating, irreversible historicity of things. Particularly in the *Idylls*, Tennyson depicts a disintegration of society from which there can be no reasonable expectation of a return. From his long, dark Arthurian speculation, Tennyson seems to be saying, the century can only move inexorably forward through fin de siècle hedonism into the fragmentation and alienation of a modernist waste land.

Notes

1. See, e.g., George Meredith's description of Arthur as a "crowned curate," quoted in Martin 423–24. "Tennyson was criticized," Mark Girouard writes, "both at the time and later for turning Malory's king and knights into pattern Victorian gentlemen" (184).

2. See also John Ruskin's comment to Tennyson about the *Idylls* in a letter of Sept. 1859: "So great power ought not to be spent on visions of things past but on the living present . . . . The intense, masterful and unerring transcript of an actuality . . . . seems to me to be the true task of the modern poet" (36:320–21).

3. The complete passage from *Middlemarch* reads: "[Dorothea's] full nature, like that river of which Cyrus broke the strength, spent itself in channels which had no great name on the earth. But the effect of her being on those around her was incalculably diffusive: for the growing good of the world is partly dependent on unhistoric acts; and that things

are not so ill with you and me as they might have been, is half-owing to the number who lived faithfully a hidden life, and rest in unvisited tombs" (613). In speaking of Theresa at the end of the novel, George Eliot implies that it is the girl's childish innocence, analogous to the innocence of her time, the made possible her great work. By contrast, the present is so burdened with knowledge of the past that "its strength is broken into channels," and people like Dorothea Brooke are effective precisely because they are "unhistoric." Were they to be historic—that is, memorable—they would only add to the burden of the next generation, become one more influence for the future to be anxious about. Their importance, then, derives from the fact that their lives are "hidden" and their tombs "unvisited." Note that unhistoric people are likelier to be women than men (history remembers more Cyruses than Theresas), women's "hidden" influence being "incalculably diffusive," like nature, rather than immediate and focused, like history. In this connection, consider the puns on Dorothea's "nature" and on her last name, closer in meaning to channel than to river.

4. See, e.g., National Socialism's twentieth-century exploitation of this nineteenth-century idea in support of its own revolutionary theories. "I, as a politician," Hitler is quoted by Hermann Rauschning, "need a conception that enables the order that has hitherto existed on an historic basis to be abolished and an entirely new and antihistoric order enforced" (229).

5. "The Revolution," writes Virginia Woolf of Mary Wollstonecraft, "was not merely an event that had happened outside her; it was an active agent in her own blood" (143).

6. G. P. Gooch writes that "in combating the French Revolution, Burke emphasized the continuity of historic life and the debt of every age to its predecessors" (9), just those patriarchal values under attack by the apocalyptic female energy Burke associated with the Revolution.

7. See John D. Rosenberg's discussion of Tennyson's deep interest in apocalyptic subjects, an interest evident as early as the poet's fifteenth year in the fragment "Armageddon" (14–19).

8. Indeed, the early nineteenth century found victory over Rome a particularly compelling metaphor. When Napoleon seized the crown from Pius VII at Reims and placed it on his own head, he was attacking the most venerable patriarchy in Europe, substituting for an "apostolic" descent of royal power a self-authorizing kingship that may well have influenced Tennyson's depiction of Arthur in the *Idylls*.

9. Tennyson himself refused to be tied down to a specific identification of the three queens; he responded to readers who saw them as Faith, Hope, and Charity that "they mean that and they do not . . . . They are much more" (H. Tennyson 2:127).

10. Some forty years earlier, Tennyson had dealt with this same fragmentation in "Tithonus." In that poem, he sets the Pellam-like figure of the aged male protagonist— unable to die, obliged to move always forward in time burdened more and more by his own past, his own history—against Aurora, the female representation of the dawn, a natural phenomenon who, existing out of time in Eliade's *illo tempore* and always circling back to her beginning, continually renews her youth. In the end, Tithonus's dearest wish is to awake from the nightmare of history, to which he had willfully consigned himself, and to reenter the restorative cycle of nature, even though that change can only be inaugurated by his own death.

11. That Arthur is himself dismayed at how the embodiment of those values in the Grail quest must necessarily destroy the Round Table brotherhood prefigures the king's later despair at the final collapse of his ideal.

12. See Jessie L. Weston's discussion of this symbol (72–76). See also Robert Stephen Hawker's contemporary "Quest of the Sangraal" (1863), where the poet writes about Joseph

of Arimathaea, keeper of the Grail, that "His home was like a garner, full of corn / and wine and oil: a granary of God" (184).

13.   "The timelessness of myth was one of its greatest attractions to the Victorians," writes James Kissane. "It was the realm of myths and legends that came closest to constituting an idealized past that could solace Tennyson's imagination as a kind of eternal presence" (129).

14.   If Lévi-Strauss does not explicitly equate culture and history, he clearly links the two through his association of culture with genealogy.

15.   See also Ward Hellstrom's comment that "if the *Idylls* fail to speak to the modern world, that failure is the result to a great degree of Tennyson's attempt to preserve a lost and perhaps ultimately indefensible ideal of womanhood" (134). As my own essay tries to establish, it is Arthur rather than Tennyson who futilely defends this ideal. I fully agree with Hellstrom, however, that "the woman question is more or less central to all the books of " 'The Round Table' " and even with his more daring assertion that it is "perhaps the most significant revolutionary question of the nineteenth century" (109).

16.   "In the *Idylls*, Tennyson takes up with complete seriousness, although not without irony, the question of woman's role in private and public life—a topic that in *The Princess* he treated half seriously, half satirically" (Eggers 144).

17.   Tennyson had also dealt with the issue in *The Princess*, where he dramatizes "a pattern of feminine identification in his portrayal of the Prince" (Christ 154). Such mildness would also be appropriate, of course, to the more conventional association of Arthur with Jesus. But the attack on mid-nineteenth-century Christianity for its effeminacy, already noted, suggests that the familiar image of Arthur as Christ and Tennyson's new depiction of him as female king were beginning to coincide.

18.   Margaret Homans makes a similar point, speaking of Arthur as "a victim of continuity: his origins, from which he has endeavored all his life to escape, have successfully reasserted the claim that the past makes on the future" (693).

19.   Interestingly, Robert B. Martin sees this issue reflected in what he calls the poet's "slackened language" in the *Idylls*, a neglect of grammatical cause and effect that "robs the characters of any appearance of *'real man'* because there is no feeling of behavior resulting from antecedents" (496; italics mine).

20.   Jerome Buckley comments that Arthur is "ineffective"in dealing with Lancelot and the queen "despite his ideal manhood, or perhaps because of it" (177).

21.   Henry Kozicki describes this passage as portraying "the lotos death of old historical form through its hero's withdrawal into self" (112). Kozicki's study comments usefully on Tennyson's vision of, and attitude toward, history during the course of his career.

22.   "With its lesson that the world is irredeemable," writes Clyde de L. Ryals, "the *Idylls of the King* seems to reflect much of the pessimism of nineteenth-century philosophy" (94).

Works Cited

Adams, Robert M. "Religion of Man, Religion of Woman." In *Art, Politics, and Will: Essays in Honor of Lionel Trilling*. Ed. Quentin Anderson et al. New York: Basic, 1977, 173–90.

Arnold, Matthew. Preface to *Poems* (1853). In *On the Classical Tradition*. Ed. R. H. Super. Ann Arbor: Univ. of Michigan Press, 1961.

Austen, Jane. *Northanger Abbey*. In the *Novels of Jane Austen*. Ed. R. W. Chapman. Vol. 5. London: Oxford Univ. Press, 1923.

Browning, Elizabeth Barrett. *The Poetical Works of Elizabeth Barrett Browning*. Ed. Ruth M. Adam. Boston: Houghton, 1974.

Buckley, Jerome. *Tennyson: The Growth of a Poet*. Cambridge: Harvard Univ. Press, 1960.

Burke, Edmond. *Reflections on the Revolution in France*. Ed. Thomas H. D. Mahoney. New York: Bobbs-Merrill, 1955.

Carlyle, Thomas. *Past and Present*. Ed. Richard D. Altick. Boston: Houghton, 1965.

Christ, Carol. "Victorian Masculinity and the Angel in the House." In *A Widening Sphere*. Ed. Martha Vicinus. Bloomington: Indiana Univ. Press, 1977. 146–62.

Cott, Nancy F. "Passionlessness: An Interpretation of Victorian Sexual Ideology, 1790–1850." *Signs* 4(1978):219–36.

Douglas, Ann. *The Feminization of American Culture*. New York: Knopf, 1977.

Eggers, J. Philip. *King Arthur's Laureate*. New York: New York Univ. Press, 1971.

Eliade, Mircea. *Cosmos and History*. New York: Harper, 1954.

———. *Mephistopheles and the Androgyne*. Trans. J.M. Cohen. New York: Sheed & Ward, 1965, 78–124.

Eliot, George. *Middlemarch*. Ed. Gordon S. Haight. Boston: Houghton, 1956.

Ellis, Havelock. *Studies in the Psychology of Sex*. 2nd ed. Philadelphia: F. A. Davis, 1913.

Gent, Margaret. " 'To Flinch from Modern Varnish': The Appeal of the Past to the Victorian Imagination." In *Victorian Poetry*. Ed. Malcolm Bradbury and David Palmer. Stratford-upon-Avon Studies 15. London: Edward Arnold, 1972, 11–35.

Girouard, Mark. *The Return to Camelot*. New Haven: Yale Univ. Press, 1981.

Gooch, G. P. *History and Historians of the Nineteenth Century*. London: Longmans, 1913.

Gray, J. M. *Man and Myth in Victorian England: Tennyson's "The Coming of Arthur."* Lincoln, Nebr.: Tennyson Society, 1969.

Harrison, Frederic. "The History Schools." In his *The Meaning of History*. 1894; rpt. New York: Macmillan, 1908, 118–38.

Hawker, Robert Stephen. "Quest of the Sangraal." In *The Cornish Ballads and other Poems*. Oxford, 1869, 180–203.

Hellstrom, Ward. *On the Poems of Tennyson*. Gainesville: Univ. of Florida Press, 1972.

Homans, Margaret. "Tennyson and the Spaces of Life." *ELH* 46(1979):693–709.

Joseph, Gerhard. *Tennysonian Love: The Strange Diagonal*. Minneapolis: Univ. of Minnesota Press, 1969.

Kincaid, James R. *Tennyson's Major Poems: The Comic and Ironic Patterns*. New Haven: Yale Univ. Press, 1975.

Kissane, James. "Tennyson: The Passion of the Past and the Curse of Time." In *Tennyson*. Ed. Elizabeth A. Francis. Englewood Cliffs, N.J.: Prentice-Hall, 1980, 108–32.

Kolodny, Annette. *The Lay of the Land*. Chapel Hill: Univ. of North Carolina Press. 1975.

Kozicki, Henry. *Tennyson and Clio: History in the Major Poems*. Baltimore: Johns Hopkins Univ. Press, 1979.

Lévi-Strauss, Claude. *The Elementary Structures of Kinship*. Boston: Beacon, 1969.

Martin, Robert B. *Tennyson: The Unquiet Heart*. New York: Oxford Univ. Press, 1980.

Neumann, Erich. *The Great Mother*. Princeton: Princeton Univ. Press, 1955.

Priestley, F. E. L. "Tennyson's *Idylls*." *University of Toronto Quarterly* 19(1949):35–49.

Rauschning, Hermann, ed. *Hitler Speaks*. London: Butterworth, 1939.

Ricks, Christopher. *Tennyson*. New York: Macmillan, 1972

Rosenberg, John D. *The Fall of Camelot: A Study of Tennyson's* Idylls of the King. Cambridge: Belknap-Harvard Univ. Press, 1973.

Ruskin, John. *The Works of John Ruskin*. Ed. E. T. Cook and Alexander Wedderburn. 39 vols. London: George Allen, 1909.

Ryals, Clyde de L. *From the Great Deep: Essays on* Idylls of the King. Athens: Ohio Univ. Press, 1967.

Schlesinger, Arthur, "The Role of Women in American History." In his *New Viewpoints in American History*. New York: Macmillan, 1921, 126–59.

Smith, Henry Nash. *The Virgin Land*. Cambridge: Harvard Univ. Press, 1950.

Sterling, John. Rev. of Tennyson's *Poems* (1842). *Quarterly Review* (Sept. 1842):385–416. Rpt. in *Tennyson: The Critical Heritage* Ed. John D. Jump. London: Routledge & Kegan Paul, 1967, 103–25.

Swinburne, Algernon Charles. *Under the Microscope*. In *Swinburne Replies*. Ed. Clyde K. Hyder. Syracuse, N.Y.: Syracuse Univ. Press, 1966, 33–87.

Tennyson, Alfred Lord. *Poems of Tennyson*. Ed. Jerome H. Buckley. Boston: Riverside, 1958.

Tennyson, Hallam. *Alfred Lord Tennyson: A Memoir by His Son*. 2 vols. London, 1897.

Weston, Jessie L. *From Ritual to Romance*. New York: Anchor-Doubleday, 1957.

Wollstonecraft, Mary. *An Historical and Moral View of the Origin and Progress of the French Revolution and the Effect It Had Produced in Europe*. In *A Wollstonecraft Anthology*. Ed. Janet M. Todd. Bloomington: Indiana Univ. Press, 1977, 125–41.

Woolf, Virginia. *The Second Common Reader*. New York: Harcourt, 1932.

10

Cage aux folles: Sensation and Gender in Wilkie Collins's *The Woman in White*

D. A. Miller

I

Nothing "boring" about the Victorian sensation novel: the excitement that seizes us here is as direct as the "fight-or-flight" physiology that renders our reading bodies, neither fighting nor fleeing, theaters of neurasthenia. The genre offers us one of the first instances of modern literature to address itself primarily to the sympathetic nervous system, where it grounds its characteristic adrenalin effects: accelerated heart rate and respiration, increased blood pressure, the pallor resulting from vasoconstriction, and so on. It is not, of course, the last, and no less current than the phenomenon is the contradictory manner in which, following in the Victorians' footsteps, we continue to acknowledge it.[1] On the one hand, a vulgar salesmanship unblinkingly identifies hyperventilation with aesthetic value, as though art now had no other aim or justification than its successful ability to rattle what the French would call, with anatomical precision, our *cage*. That the body is compelled to automatism, that the rhythm of reading is frankly addictive—such dreary evidence of involuntary servitude is routinely marshaled in ads and on back covers to promote entertainments whose Pavlovian expertise has become more than sufficient recommendation. On the other hand, an overnice literary criticism wishfully reassures us that these domineering texts, whose power is literally proved upon our pulses, are beneath notice. By a kind of Cartesian censorship, in which pulp-as-flesh gets equated with pulp-as-trash, the emphatic physicality of thrills in such literature allows us to hold them cheap. Accordingly, the sensation novel is relegated to the margins of the canon of approved genres, and on the infrequent occasions when it is seriously discussed, "sensation"—the modern nervousness that is as fundamental to this genre as its name—is the first thing to be dropped from the discussion.[2] What neither view of sensation fiction questions—what both views, it might be argued, become strategies for not questioning—is the natural immediacy of sensation itself. The celebration of sensation (as a physical experience to be enjoyed for its own sake) merely *receives* it; the censure of sensation (granting to it the obviousness of something about which there is nothing to say) refuses to *read* it. In either case, sensation is felt to occupy a natural site entirely outside meaning, as though in the breathless body signification expired.

To be sure, the silence that falls over the question of sensation seems first enjoined by the sensation novel itself, which is obsessed with the project's finding meaning—of staging the suspense of its appearance—in everything except the sensations that the unfolding of the project excites in us. Yet in principle the sensation novel must always at least imply a reading of these sensations, for the simple reason that it can mobilize the sympathetic nervous system only by giving it something to sympathize with. In order to make us nervous, nervousness must first be represented: in situations of character and plot that, both in themselves and in the larger cultural allusions they carry, make the operation of our own nerves significant in particular ways. The fiction elaborates a fantasmatics of sensation in which our reading bodies take their place from the start, and of which our physiological responses thus become the hysterical acting out. To speak of hysteria here, of course, is also to recall the assumption that always camouflages it—that what the body suffers, the mind needn't think. "So far as my own sensations were concerned, I can hardly say that I thought at all."[3] The efficacy of psychosomatisms as "defenses" presupposes a rigorously enforced separation in the subject between *psyche* and *soma*, and hysteria successfully breeches the body's autonomy only when this autonomy is felt to remain intact. Reading the sensation novel, our hystericized bodies "naturalize" the meanings in which the narrative implies them, but in doing so they also nullify these meanings. Incarnate in the body, the latter no longer seem part of a cultural, historical process of signification but instead dissolve into an inarticulable, merely palpable self-evidence. Thus, if every sensation novel necessarily provides an interpretation of the sensations to which it gives rise in its readers, the immediacy of these sensations can also be counted on to *disown* such an interpretation. It may even be that the nonrecognition that thus obtains between our sensations and their narrative thematization allows the sensation novel to "say" certain things for which our culture—at least at its popular levels—has yet to develop another language.

Wilkie Collins's *The Woman in White* (1860)—of all sensation novels the best known, and considered the best—seems at any rate an exemplary text for making this case. For what "happens" in this novel becomes fully clear and coherent only, I think, when one takes into account the novel's implicit reading of its own (still quite "effective") performative dimension and thus restores sensation to its textual and cultural mediations. For the reason given above, the attempt to do so must be prepared to seem rather "forced"—as unprovable as a connotation and as improbable as latency—but it is worth undertaking for more than a better understanding of this particular text. The ideological valences with which sensation characteristically combines in the novel do not of course absolutely transcend the second half of the Victorian period in which they are elaborated—as though the social significance of nervousness (itself a historical construct) were fixed once for all; but neither are they restricted to this period. Collins's novel continues to be not just thoroughly readable but eminently "writable" as well. If it is still capable of moving readers to the edge of their seats (and how sharp a sense of this edge may be is suggested when one character starts from his own seat "as if a spike had grown up from the ground through the bottom of [his] chair" [41]), this is because its particular staging of nervousness remains cognate with that of many of our own thrillers, printed or filmed. It thus offers a pertinent, if not exhaustive, demonstration of the value, meaning, and use that modern culture—which in this respect has by no means broken radically with Victorian culture—finds in the nervous state.

Without exception, such a state affects all the novel's principal characters, who are variously startled, affrighted, unsettled, chilled, agitated, flurried. All sooner or later inhabit the "sensationalized" body where the blood curdles, the heart beats violently, the breath comes short and thick, the flesh creeps, the cheeks lose their color. No one knows what is the matter with Mr. Fairlie, but "we all say it's on the nerves" (61), and in widely different ways his niece Laura is "rather nervous and sensitive" (63). The "nervous sensitiveness" (127) of her double and half-sister Anne Catherick, the Woman in White, issues in the aneurism that causes her death. Characters who are not constitutionally nervous become circumstantially so, in the unnerving course of events. Unsettled by the mystery surrounding Anne, fearful that Laura may be implicated in it, suspecting that he is himself being watched, Walter Hartright develops a "nervous contraction" about his lips and eyes (178), which he appears to have caught from Laura herself, whose "sweet, sensitive lips are subject to a slight nervous contraction" (75). At first "perfect self-possession" (209), Sir Percival Glyde degenerates after his marriage to Laura into "an unsettled, excitable manner . . . a kind of panic or frenzy of mind" (417). And Marian Halcombe, Laura's other half-sister, has already lost the "easy inborn confidence in herself and her position" (60) that initially characterized her by the time of the first anxious and "sadly distrustful" extract (184) from her diary. In the course of keeping that diary, of gathering the increasingly less equivocal evidence of a "plot" against Laura, she literally writes herself into a fever. It is a measure of Count Fosco's control over these characters that he is said to be "born without nerves" (376), though his "eternal cigarettes" (252) attest that even here nervousness is not so much missing as mastered, and mastered only insofar as its symptoms are masked in the banal practices of civilized society.

Nervousness seems the necessary "condition" in the novel for perceiving its real plot and for participating in it as more than a pawn. The condition is not quite sufficient, as the case of the willfully ignorant Mr. Fairlie shows, but otherwise those without the capacity to become nervous also lack the capacity to interpret events, or even to see that events require interpreting. The servants, for instance, also called (more accurately) "persons born without nerves" (69), are uniformly oblivious to what is or might be going on: the "unutterably tranquil" governess Mrs. Vesey (72), the maid who "in a state of cheerful stupidity" grins at the sight of Mrs. Catherick's wounded dog (229); the housekeeper Mrs. Michelson, whose

Christian piety prevents her from advancing "opinions" (381). It is not exactly that
the novel uses nervousness to mark middle-class status, since the trait fails to
characterize the "sanguine constitution" of Mr. Gilmore, the family lawyer, who
"philosophically" walks off his "uneasiness" about Laura's marriage (159). Rather
the novel makes nervousness a metonymy for reading, its cause or effect. No reader
can identify with unruffled characters like Gilmore or Mrs. Michelson, even when
they narrate parts of the story, because every reader is by definition committed to
a hermeneutic project that neither of these characters finds necessary or desirable.
Instead we identify with nerve-racked figures like Walter and Marian who carry
forward the activity of our own deciphering. We identify even with Anne Catherick
in her "nervous dread" (134), though she is never capable of articulating its object,
because that dread holds at least the promise of the story we will read. Nervousness
is our justification in the novel, as Mrs. Michelson's faith is hers, insofar as it
validates the attempt to read, to uncover the grounds for *being* nervous.

The association of nervousness with reading is complicated—not to say troubled—by its coincident, no less insistent or regular association with femininity.
However general a phenomenon, nervousness is always gendered in the novel as,
like Laura's headache symptom, an "essentially feminine malady" (59). Of the
novel's three characters who seem "born" nervous, two are women (Anne and
Laura) and the third, Mr. Fairlie, an effeminate. "I am nothing," the latter pronounces himself, "but a bundle of nerves dressed up to look like a man" (370).
No one, however, is much convinced by the drag, and Walter's first impression—
"He had a frail, languid-fretful, over-refined look—something singularly and un-
pleasantly delicate in its association with a man" (66)—never stands in need of
correction. Even in the less fey male characters, nervousness remains a signifier
of femininity. At best it declares Walter still "unformed," and Sir Percival's
imposture—that he is not, so to speak, the man he is pretending to be—is already
in a manner disclosed when Mrs. Michelson observes that "he seemed to be almost
as nervous and fluttered . . . as his lady herself" (403). Fosco too, Marian informs
us, "is as nervously sensitive as the weakest of us [women]. He starts at chance
noises as inveterately as Laura herself" (242).

The novel's "primal scene," which it obsessively repeats and remembers ("Anne
Catherick again!") as though this were the trauma it needed to work through,
rehearses the "orgins" of male nervousness in female contagion—strictly, in the
woman's touch. When Anne Catherick, in flight from the asylum where she has
been shut away, "lightly and suddenly" lays her hand on Walter Hartright's shoulder, it brings "every drop of blood in [his] body . . . to a stop" (47). Released
from—and with—the Woman, nervousness touches and enters the Man: Anne's
nervous gesture is at once sympathetically "caught" in Walter's nervous response
to it. Attempting to recover himself, Walter tightens his fingers round "the handle
of [his] stick," as if the touch—"from behind [him]" (47)—were a violation requiring
violent counteraction, and what was violated were a gender identification that

needed to be reaffirmed. Yet Anne Catherick impinges on him again: "The loneliness and helplessness of the woman touch me" (49). His formulation hopefully denies what is happening to him—Anne's weak femininity is supposed to evince *a contrario* his strong masculinity—but the denial seems only to produce further evidence of the gender slippage it means to arrest. Even in his classic gallantry, Walter somehow feels insufficiently manly, "immature": "The natural impulse to assist her and spare her got the better of the judgment, the caution, the worldly tact, which an older, wiser, and colder man might have summoned to help him in this strange emergency" (49). He is even "distressed by an uneasy sense of having done wrong" (54), of having betrayed his sex: "What had I done? Assisted the victim of the most horrible of all false imprisonments to escape; or cast loose on the wide world of London an unfortunate creature, whose actions it was my duty, and every man's duty, mercifully to control?" (55). Walter's protection has in fact suspended the control that is "every man's duty" to exercise over the activity of the neuropathic woman. Thanks to his help, Anne eludes a manifold of male guardians: the turnpike man at the entry gate of the city; the two men from the asylum including its director; the policeman who, significantly, is assumed to be at their disposal; and even Walter himself, who puts her into a cab, destination unknown. "A dangerous woman to be at large" (177): the female trouble first transmitted to Walter will extend throughout the thick ramifications of plot to excite sympathetic vibrations in Laura and Marian, and in Sir Percival and even Fosco as well. And not just in them. "The reader's nerves are affected like the hero's," writes Mrs. Oliphant in a contemporary review of the novel; in what I have called the novel's primal scene, this means that "the silent woman lays her hand upon our shoulder as well as upon that of Mr. Walter Hartright."[4] As the first of the novel's sensation effects *on us*, the scene thus fictionalizes the beginning of our physiological experience of the sensation novel as such. Our first sensation coincides with—is positively triggered by—the novel's originary account of sensation. Fantasmatically, then, we "catch" sensation from the neuropathic body of the Woman who, no longer confined or controlled in an asylum, is free to make our bodies resonate with—like—hers.

Every reader is consequently implied to be a version or extension of the Woman in White, a fact that entails particularly interesting consequences when the reader is—as the text explicitly assumes he is—male.[5] This reader willy-nilly falls victim to a hysteria in which what is acted out (desired, repressed) is an essentially female "sensation." His excitements come from—become—her nervous excitability; his rib cage, arithmetically Adam's, houses a woman's quickened respiration, and his heart beats to her skittish rhythm; even his pallor (which of course he cannot see) is mirrored back to him only as hers, the Woman in White's. This reader thus lends himself to elaborating a fantasy of *anima muliebris in corpore virili inclusa*— or as we might appropriately translate here, "a woman's breath caught in a man's body." The usual rendering, of course, is "a woman's soul trapped . . . ," and it will be recognized as nineteenth-century sexology's classic formulation (coined by Karl Ulrichs in the 1860s) for male homosexuality.[6] I cite it not just to anticipate the homosexual component given to readerly sensation by the novel, but also, letting the phrase resonate beyond Ulrichs's intentions, to situate this component among the others that determine its context. For if what essentially characterizes male homosexuality in this way of putting it is the woman-in-the-man, and if this "woman" in *inclusa,* incarcerated or shut up, her freedoms abridged accordingly, then homosexuality would be by its very nature homophobic: imprisoned in a carceral problematic that does little more than channel into the homosexual's "ontology" the social and legal sanctions that might otherwise be imposed on him. Meant to win a certain intermediate space for homosexuals, Ulrichs's formulation in fact ultimately colludes with the prison or closet drama—of keeping the "woman" well put away—that it would relegate to the unenlightened past. And homosexuals' souls are not the only ones to be imprisoned in male bodies; Ulrichs's phrase does perhaps far better as a general description of the condition of nineteenth-century women, whose "spirit" (whether understood as intellect, integrity, or sexuality) is massively interned in male corporations, constitutions, contexts. His metaphor thus may be seen to link or fuse (1) a particular fantasy about male homosexuality; (2) a homophobic defense against that fantasy; and (3) the male oppression of women that, among other things, extends that defense. All three meanings bear pointedly on Collins's novel, which is profoundly about enclosing and secluding the woman in male "bodies," among them institutions like marriage and madhouses. And the sequestration of the woman takes for its object not just women, who need to be put away in safe places or asylums, but men as well, who must monitor and master what is fantasized as the "woman inside" them.

II

Like *The Moonstone, The Woman in White* accords itself the status of a quasi-legal document.

> If the machinery of the Law could be depended on to fathom every case of suspicion, and to conduct every process of inquiry, with moderate assistance only from the lubricating influences of oil of gold, the events which fill these pages might have claimed their share of the public attention in a Court of Justice. But the Law is still, in certain inevitable cases, the pre-engaged servant of the long purse; and the story is left to be told, for the first time, in this place. As the Judge might once have heard it, so the Reader shall hear it now . . . . Thus, the story here presented will be told by more than one pen, as the story of an offence against the laws is told in Court by more than one witness—with the same object, in both cases, to present the truth always in its most direct and most intelligible aspect.(33)

The organizational device is a curious one, since nothing in the story ever appears to motivate it. Why and for whom does this story need to be thus told? At the end of the novel—after which Walter Hartright presumably gathers his narratives together—neither legal action nor even a paralegal hearing seems in the least required. And it is of course pure mystification to preface a mystery story with a claim to be presenting the truth "always in its most direct and most intelligible aspect." But the obvious gimmickry of the device offers only the crudest evidence of the limited pertinence of the legal model that the text here invokes. On the face of it, despite its conventionally bitter references to oil of gold and the long purse, the text is eager to retain the law—the juridical model of an inquest—for its own narrative. It simply proposes to extend this model to a case that it wouldn't ordinarily cover. The explicit ideal thus served would be a law that fathomed every case of suspicion and conducted every process of inquiry. But what law has ever done this, or wanted to? Certainly not the English law, which like all non-totalitarian legal systems is on principle concerned to limit the matters that fall under its jurisdiction. The desire to extend the law as totally as the text utopically envisions— to *every* case of suspicion and *every* process of inquiry—would therefore supersede the legal model to which, the better not to alarm us, it nominally clings. For the project of such a desire makes sense only in a world where suspicion and inquiry have already become everyday practices, and whose affinities lie less with a given legal code or apparatus than with a vast, multifaceted network of inquests-without- end. Under the guise of a pedantic, legalistic organization, the novel in fact aligns itself with extra-, infra-, and supralegal modern discipline.

Not, of course, that *The Woman in White* represents the world of discipline in the manner of either *Bleak House* or *Barchester Towers*. Its most important rela- tionship to this world, at any rate, does not come at the level of an "objective" portrayal, either of institutions (like Court of Chancery and the Detective Police in Dickens) or of less formal means of social control (like "moderate schism" and the norm in Trollope). It would be quite difficult to evolve a sociological under- standing of Victorian asylums from Collins's novel, which, voiding a lively con- temporary concern with the private madhouse, describes neither its structure nor the (medicinal? physical? psychological?) therapies that may or may not be practiced within it.[7] Anne never says, and Laura finds it too painfully confusing to recall, what goes on there. The asylum remains a very black "black box," the melodramatic site of "the most horrible of false imprisonments," where the sane middle class might mistakenly be sent. The asylum, in short, is available to representation mainly insofar as it has been *incorporated*: in Walter's "unsettled state" when he first learns that Anne is a fugitive from there, in Anne's nervous panic at the very word, in the difference between Laura's body before she enters the place and after she leaves, in the way we are invited to fill in the blank horror of what she cannot remember with the stuff of our own nightmares. What the example may be broadened to suggest is that the novel represents discipline mainly in terms of certain general isolated effects on the disciplinary *subject*, whose sensationalized body both dramatizes and facilitates his functioning as *the subject/object of continual supervision*.

These effects, together with the juridical metaphor under which they are first inscribed, are best pursued in the contradiction between the judge and the reader who is supposed to take his place. "As the Judge might once have heard [the story], so the Reader shall hear it now." The pronouncement, of course, confers on the latter role all the connotations of sobriety and even serenity attached to the former. That "wretches hang that jurymen may dine" will always give scandal to our Western mythology of justice, in which the judge—set above superstition, prejudice, "interest" of any kind—weighs the evidence with long and patient scruple before pronouncing sentence. Nothing, however, could be less judicial, or judicious, than the actual hermeneutic practice of the reader of this novel, whose technology of nervous stimulation—in many ways still the state of the art— has him repeatedly jumping to unproven conclusions, often literally jumping at them. Far from encouraging reflective calm, the novel aims to deliver "positive personal shocks of surprise and excitement" that so sensationalize the reader's body that he is scarcely able to reflect at all.[8] The novel's only character with strictly judicial habits of mind is the lawyer Gilmore, who judges only to misjudge. Hearing Sir Percival's explanation of his dealings with Anne Catherick, he says: "My function was of the purely judicial kind. I was to weigh the explanation we had just heard . . . and to decide honestly whether the probabilities, on Sir Percival's own showing, were plainly with him, or plainly against him. My own conviction was that they were plainly with him" (155). Characters who rely on utterly unlegal standards of evidence like intuition, coincidence, literary connotation get closer to what will eventually be revealed as the truth. In her first conversation with Walter, Anne Catherick nervously inquires about an unnamed baronet in Hampshire; Walter later learns that Laura is engaged to a baronet in Hampshire named Sir Percival Glyde. "Judging by the ordinary rules of evidence, I had not the shadow of a reason, thus far, for connecting Sir Percival Glyde with the suspicious words of inquiry that had been spoken to me by the woman in white. And yet, I did connect them" (101). Similarly, when after Sir Percival's explanation Gilmore wonders what excuse Laura can possibly have for changing her mind about him, Marian answers: "In the eyes of law and reason, Mr. Gilmore, no excuse, I dare say. If she still hesitates, and if I still hesitate, you must attribute our strange conduct, if you like, to caprice in both cases" (162). The competent reader, who does not weigh evidence so much as he simply assents to the ways in which it has been weighted, fully accepts the validity of such ungrounded connections and inexcusable hesitations: they validate, among other things, the sensations they make him feel. And this reader is capable of making what by the ordinary rules of evidence are comparably tenuous assumptions of his own. We can't know, just because Sir Percival's men are watching Somebody, and Walter may be being watched, that Walter is that Somebody, and yet we are convinced that we do know this. Or again, the loose seal on the letter that Marian recovers from the post-bag after she has seen Fosco hovering about it does not establish the fact that Fosco has opened and resealed her letter, but we take it firmly for granted nonetheless. Our judgments are often informed by no better than the silliest folk wisdom. When Laura's pet greyhound shrinks from Sir Percival, Gilmore considers it "a trifle" (156), though Nina later jumps eagerly enough into his own lap: in the strange court of justice over which we preside, her discrimination is unimpeachable evidence. Yet neither adhering to ordinary rules of evidence nor inhering in a decisive institutional context (except of course that provided by the conventions of this kind of novel), such "acts of judgment" are in fact only entitled to the considerably less authoritative status of *suspicions*, whose "uncertainty" in both these senses makes it easy to discredit them. Walter is the first to refer his hypotheses to their possible source in "delusion" and "monomania" (101, 105). Like the characters who figure him, the reader becomes—what a judge is never supposed to be—paranoid. From trifles and common coincidences, he suspiciously infers a complicated structure of persecution, an elaborately totalizing "plot."

What a judge is never supposed to be? Yet the most famous paranoid of modern times *was* a judge: the German jurist Daniel Paul Schreber, whose *Memoirs of My Nervous Illness* provided Freud's theory of paranoia with its major and most lurid example. Schreber's paranoia, we recall, was triggered precisely when, at Dresden, he entered on his duties as Senatspräsident. His case suggests that paranoia is "born" at the moment when the judge, without ceasing to be judge, has also become the accused, when he is both one and the other. It was, more than anything else, his homosexuality that put Schreber in this institutionally untenable position, since the law he was expected to administer would certainly include, as Guy Hocquenquengham has pointed out, interdictions against homosexuality itself.[9] Schreber's delusion does nothing so much as elaborate the paradoxical aspect of his actual situation as a judge who might well have to judge (others like) himself. The Rays of God, he hallucinates, having constituted his monstrosity (literally: by feminizing his constitution via the nerves), taunt him with it thus: "So *this* sets up to have been a Senatspräsident, this person who lets himself be f—d!"[10] In *The Woman in White*, another case of feminization via the nerves, Mrs. Michelson's article of unsuspecting faith—"Judge not that ye be not judged" (381)—postulates an inevitable slippage between subject and object whenever judgment is attempted. The slippage is in fact far more likely to occur when judgment, no longer governed by an institutional practice with established roles and rules of evidence, has devolved into mere suspicion. Unlike legal judgment, suspicion presupposes the reversibility of the direction in which it passes. The novel abounds with suspicious characters, in the telling ambiguity of the phrase, for what Anne, Walter, and Marian all suspect is that *they are themselves suspected*. Why else would Anne be pursued, Walter watched, Marian's correspondence opened? They are suspected, moreover, precisely *for being suspicious*. For Walter to notice that Anne's manner is "a little touched by suspicion" is already to suspect her, as she instantly recognizes ("Why do you suspect me?" [48]). Hence the urgency, as well as the futility, of the suspicious character's obsessive desire *not to excite suspicion* (260, 275, 293, 311, 325), since the act of suspecting always already implies the state of being suspect. The whole vertiginous game (in which I suspect him of suspecting me of suspecting him) is meant to ward off—but only by passing along—the violation of privacy that it thus at once promotes and resists. In what Roland Barthes would call the novel's symbolic code, this violation connotes the sexual attack whose possibility "haunts" the novel no less thoroughly than the virginal presence—insistent like a dare—of the Woman in White. What stands behind the vague fears of Anne and Walter during their first encounter; what subtends Mr. Fairlie's malicious greeting ("So glad to possess you at Limmeridge, Mr. Hartright" [66]); what Sir Percival sadistically fantasizes when he invites his wife to imagine her lover "with the marks of my horsewhip on his shoulders" (283); and what Fosco finally accomplishes when he reads Marian's *journal intime*—is virtual rape. We might consider what is implied or at stake in the fact that the head game of suspicion is always implicitly transcoded by the novel into the body game of rape.

Perhaps the most fundamental value that the Novel, as a cultural institution, may be said to uphold is privacy, the determination of an integral, autonomous, "secret" self. Novel reading takes for granted the existence of a space in which the reading subject remains safe from the surveillance, suspicion, reading, and rape of others. Yet this privacy is always specified as the freedom to read about characters who oversee, suspect, read, and rape one another. It is not just that, strictly private subjects, we read about violated, objectified subjects but that, in the very act of reading about them, we contribute largely to constituting them as such. We enjoy our privacy in the act of watching privacy being violated, in the act of watching that is already itself a violation of privacy. Our most intense identification with characters never blinds us to our ontological privilege over them: they will never be reading about *us*. It is built into the structure of the Novel that every reader must realize the definitive fantasy of the liberal subject, who imagines himself free from the surveillance that he nonetheless sees operating everywhere around him.

The sensation novel, however, submits this panoptic immunity to a crucial modification: it produces repeated and undeniable evidence—"on the nerves"—that we are perturbed by what we are watching. We remain unseen, of course, but not untouched: our bodies are rocked by the same "positive personal shocks" as the characters' are said to be. For us, these shocks have the ambivalent character of being both an untroubled pleasure (with a certain "male" adventurism we read the sensation novel in order to *have* them) and a less tame and more painful *jouissance* (with a certain "female" helplessness we often protest that we can't *bear* them, though we do when they keep on coming). The specificity of the sensation novel in nineteenth-century fiction is that it renders the liberal subject the subject of a *body*, whose fear and desire of violation displaces, reworks, and exceeds his constitutive fantasy of intact privacy. The themes that the liberal subject ordinarily defines himself against—by reading *about* them—are here inscribed into his reading body. Moreover, in *The Woman in White* this body is gendered: not only has its gender been *decided*, but also its gender identification is an active and determining *question*. The drama in which the novel writes its reader turns on the disjunction between his allegedly masculine gender and his effectively feminine gender identification (as a creature of "nerves"): with the result that his experience of sensation must include his panic at having the experience at all, of being in the position to have it. In this sense, the novel's initial assumption that its reader is male is precisely what cannot be assumed (or better, what stands most in need of "proof"), since his formal title—say, "a man"—is not or not yet a substantial entity—say, "a real man."

By far the most shocking moment in the reader's drama comes almost in the exact middle of the novel when the text of Marian's diary, lapsing into illegible fragments, abruptly yields to a postscript by the very character on whom its suspicions center. Not only has Count Fosco read Marian's "secret pages" (240), he lets her know it, and even returns them to her. In a fever that soon turns to typhus, Marian is in no condition even to take cognizance of this revelation, whose only immediate register is the reader's own body. Peter Brooks articulates our state of shock thus: "Our readerly intimacy with Marian is violated, our act of reading adulterated by profane eyes, made secondary to the villain's reading and indeed dependent on his permission."[11] It is not only, then, that Marian has been "raped," as both the Count's amorous flourish ("Admirable woman!" [258]) and her sub- sequent powerless rage against him are meant to suggest. We are "taken" too, taken by surprise, which is itself an overtaking. We are taken, moreover, from behind: from a place where, in the wings of the ostensible drama, the novelist disposes of a whole plot machinery whose existence—so long as it didn't oblige us by making creaking sounds (and here it is as "noiseless" as Fosco himself [242])—we never suspected. (We never suspected, though the novel has trained us to be nothing if not suspicious. Surprise—the recognition of what one "never suspected"—is precisely what the paranoid seeks to eliminate, but it is also what, in the event, he survives by reading as a frightening incentive: he can never be paranoid enough.) To being the object of violation here, however, there is an equally disturbing alternative: to identify with Fosco, with the novelistic agency of violation. For the Count's postscript only puts him in the position we already occupy. Having just finished reading Marian's diary ourselves, we are thus im- plicated in the sadism of his act, which even as it violates our readerly intimacy with Marian reveals that "intimacy" to be itself a violation. The ambivalent structure of readerly identification here thus condenses—as simultaneous but opposite ren- derings of the same powerful shock—homosexual panic and heterosexual violence.

This is the shock, however, that, having administered, the novel (like any good administration) will work to absorb. The shock in fact proves the point of transition between what the narrative will soothingly render as a *succession:* on one side, a passive, paranoid, homosexual feminization; on the other, an active, corroborative, heterosexual masculine protest. Marian alerts us to this succession ("Our endurance must end, and our resistance must begin" [321]), but only toward the end of her narrative, since the moment of "resistance" will need to be effectively sponsored not just by a male agent but by an indefectibly composed male discourse as well. The master narrator and actor in the second half of the novel is therefore Walter: no longer the immature Walter whose nerve-ridden opening narrative seemed— tonally, at any rate—merely continued in Marian's diary, but the Walter who has returned from his trials in Central America "a changed man": "In the stern school of extremity and danger my will had learnt to be strong, my heart to be resolute, my mind to rely on itself. I had gone out to fly from my own future. I came back to face it, as a man should" (427). Concomitantly, the helpless paranoia of the first half of the novel now seeks *to prove itself*, as Walter aggressively attempts to "force a confession" from Sir Percival and Fosco "on [his] own terms" (470). Shocks decline "dramatically" in both frequency and intensity (our last sensation: its absence) as characters and readers alike come to get answers to the question that sensation could never do more than merely pose of the event occasioning it— namely, "What did it mean?" (99). Foremost on the novel's agenda in its second half is the dissolution of sensation in the achievement of decided meaning. What the narrative must most importantly get straight is, from this perspective, as much certain sexual and gender deviances as the obscure tangles of plot in which they thrive. In short, the novel needs to realize the normative requirements of the heterosexual menage whose happy picture concludes it.

This conclusion, of course, marks the most banal moment in the text, when the sensation novel becomes least distinguishable from any other kind of Victorian fiction. Herein, one might argue, lies the "morality" of sensation fiction, in its ultimately fulfilled wish to abolish itself: to abandon the grotesque aberrations of character and situation that have typified its representation, which now coincides with the norm of the Victorian household. But the project, however successful, is nothing here if not drastic. In *Barchester Towers*, by contrast, the normative elements of heterosexual coupling—the manly husband, the feminine wife—are ready-to-hand early on, and the plot is mainly a question of overcoming various inhibitions and misunderstandings that temporarily prevent them from acknowledging their appropriateness for one another. In *The Woman in White*, however, these elements have to be "engendered" in the course of the plot through the most extreme and violent expedients. The sufficiently manly husband needs to have survived plague, pygmy arrows, and shipwreck in Central America, and the suitably feminine wife must have been schooled in a lunatic asylum, where she is half cretinized. Such desperate measures no doubt dramatize the supreme value of a norm for whose incarnation no price, including the most brutal aversion therapy, is considered too high to pay. But they do something else besides, something the Victorians, in thrall to this norm, suspected when they accused the sensation novel of immorality and that we, more laxly oppressed that they, are perhaps in a better position to specify. This is simply that, recontextualized in a "sensational" account of its genesis, such a norm risks appearing *monstrous:* as aberrant as any of the abnormal conditions that determine its realization.

III

"It ended, as you probably guess by this time, in his insisting on securing his own safety by shutting her up" (557). Male security in *The Woman in White* seems always to depend on female claustration. Sir Percival not only shuts up Anne in the asylum but successfully conspires with Fosco to shut up Laura there as well. In a double sense, he also shuts up Anne's mother, whose silence he purchases with a "handsome" allowance and ensures by insisting she not leave the town where she has been shamed and where therefore "no virtuous female friends would tempt [her] into dangerous gossiping at the tea-table" (554–55). Thanks to "the iron rod" that Fosco keeps "private" (224), Madame Fosco, who once "advocated the Rights of Women" (255), now lives in a "state of suppression" that extends to "stiff little rows of very short curls" on either side of her face and "quiet black or grey gowns, made high round the throat" (238–39). She walks in a favorite circle, "round and round the great fish pond" (290)—the Blackwater estate is in any case already "shut in—almost suffocated . . . by trees" (220)—as though she were taking yard exercise. The novel does not of course approve of these restraining orders, which originate in unambiguously criminal depravity, but as we will see it is not above exploiting them as the stick with which to contrast and complement the carrot of a far more ordinary and acceptable mode of sequestration.

Sandra M. Gilbert and Susan Gubar have argued that "dramatizations of imprisonment and escape are so all-pervasive in nineteenth-century literature by women that . . . they represent a uniquely female tradition in this period." Male carceral representations, "more consciously and objectively" elaborated, tend to be "metaphysical and metaphorical," whereas female ones remain "social and actual."[12] Yet at least in the nineteenth-century novel, the representation of imprisonment is too pervasive to be exclusively or even chiefly a female property, and too consistent overall to be divided between male and female authors on the basis of the distinctions proposed. On the one hand, Dickens's carceral fictions refer pointedly to actual social institutions, and there is little that is metaphysical in Trollope's rendering of social control: what little there is, in the form of "religion" or "Providence," merely sanctions the social mechanisms concretely at work. On the other hand, Charlotte Brontë's "dramatizations of imprisonment" do not deal with literal prisons at all, as Gilbert and Gubar themselves demonstrate. Insofar as these critics endorse a familiar series of oppositions (masculine/feminine = abstract/concrete = conscious/unconscious = objective/subjective) that, even graphically, keeps women behind a lot of bars, their attempt to isolate the essential paradigm of female writing unwittingly risks recycling the feminine mystique. We are nonetheless indebted to them for posing the question of the specific historical configuration, in the nineteenth-century English novel, of what might be called the "feminine carceral." As they plausibly show, this configuration centers on the representation, in varying degrees of alienation, of the "madwoman," and if this representation is not a uniquely female tradition, one readily grants that it is dominantly so. *The Woman in White*, however, with impressive ease incorporating the story of female "imprisonment and escape" (again, *anima muliebris inclusa*), suggests that there is a radical ambiguity about the "madwoman" that allows the feminist concerns she often voices to have already been appropriated in antifeminist ways. To the extent that novelists (or critics) underwrite the validity of female "madness" as virtually the only mode of its subject's authenticity, they inevitably slight the fact that it is also her socially given *role*, whose quasi-mandatory performance under certain conditions apotheosizes the familiar stereotypes of the woman as "unconscious" and "subjective" (read: irresponsible) that contribute largely to her oppression. The madwoman finds a considerable part of her truth—in the corpus of nineteenth-century fiction, at any rate—in being implicitly juxtaposed to the male *criminal* she is never allowed to be. If, typically, *he* ends up in the prison or its metaphorical equivalents, *she* ends up in the asylum or *its* metaphorical equivalents. (As a child perusing the shelves of a public library, I thought *The Woman in White* must be the story of a nurse: it at least proves to be the story of various women's subservience to "the doctor," to medical domination.) The distinction between criminal men (like Sir Percival and Fosco) and innocently sick women (like Anne and Laura) bespeaks a paternalism whose "chivalry" merely sublimates a system of constraints. In this light, the best way to read the madwoman would be not to derive the diagnosis from her social psychology ("Who wouldn't go crazy under such conditions?") but rather to drive her social psychology from the diagnosis: from the very category of madness that, like a fate, lies ever in wait to "cover"—account for and occlude—whatever behaviors, desires, or tendencies might be considered socially deviant, undesirable, or dangerous.

The achievement of blowing this cover belongs to *Lady Audley's Secret* (1862), the novel where, writing under the ambiguous stimulus of *The Woman in White*, Mary Elizabeth Braddon demonstrates that the madwoman's primary "alienation" lies in the rubric under which she is put down. Not unlike Anne Catherick, "always weak in the head" (554), Lady Audley appears to have been born with the "taint" of madness in her blood. She inherits the taint from her mother, whose own madness was in turn "an hereditary disease transmitted to her from her mother, who died mad." Passed on like a curse through—and as—the woman, madness virtually belongs to the condition of being female. But the novel is not so much concerned to conjoin madness and femininity, each the "truth" of the other, as to display how—under what assumptions and by what procedures—such a conjunction comes to be socially achieved. For in fact the text leaves ample room for doubt on the score of Lady Audley's "madness." Her acts, including bigamy, arson, and attempted murder, qualify as crimes in a strict legal sense, and they are motivated (like crime in English detective fiction generally) by impeccably rational considerations of self-interest. When her nephew Robert Audley at last detects her, however, he simply arranges for her to be pronounced "mad" and imprisoned accordingly in a *maison de santé* abroad. The "secret" let out at the end of the novel is not, therefore, that Lady Audley is a madwoman but rather that, *whether she is one or not*, she must be treated as such. Robert feels no embarrassment at the incommensurability thus betrayed between the diagnosis and the data that are supposed to confirm it; if need be, these data can be dispensed with altogether, as in the findings of the doctor ("experienced in cases of mania") whom he calls in for an opinion:

> "I have talked to the lady," [the doctor] said quietly, "and we understand each other very well. There is latent insanity! Insanity which might never appear; or which might appear only once or twice in a lifetime. It would be a *dementia* in its worst phase, perhaps; acute mania; but its duration would be very brief, and it would only arise under extreme mental pressure. The lady is not mad; but she has the hereditary taint in her blood. She has the cunning of madness, with the prudence of intelligence. I will tell you what she is, Mr. Audley. She is dangerous!"[13]

The doctor's double-talk ("the cunning of madness, with the prudence of intelligence") will be required to sanction two contradictory propositions: (1) Lady Audley is criminal, in the sense that her crimes must be punished; and (2) Lady Audley is not criminal, in the sense that neither her crimes nor her punishment must be made public in a male order of things. ("My greatest fear," Robert tells the doctor, "is the necessity of any exposure—any disgrace.") "Latent insanity, an insanity which might never appear" nicely meets the requirements of the case. At the same time that it removes the necessity for evidence (do Lady Audley's crimes manifest her latent insanity? or is it, quite independent of them, yet to make its appearance?), it adduces the grounds for confining her to a madhouse. Lady Audley is mad, then, only because she must not be criminal. She must not, in other words, be supposed capable of acting on her own diabolical responsibility and hence of publicly spoiling her assigned role as the conduit of power transactions between men.[14] Whatever doubts the doctor entertains in pronouncing her mad do not affect his certainty that she is, at all events, dangerous, and this social judgment entirely suffices to discount the ambiguities that the properly medical one need not bother to resolve.

Lady Audley's Secret thus portrays the woman's carceral condition as her fundamental and final truth. The novel's power as a revision of *The Woman in White* consists in its refusal of the liberal dialectic whereby the latter thinks to surpass this truth. Up to a certain point—say, up to the success of the conspiracy to confine Laura—Collins's novel is willing to tell the same story as Braddon's: of an incarceration whose patriarchal expediency takes priority over whatever humane considerations may or may not be invoked to rationalize it. (Anne's mental disorder, though real enough, is only a plausible pretext for confining her on other grounds, and Laura's confinement has no medical justification whatsoever.) But unlike Lady Audley, Lady Glyde *escapes* from her asylum, and fortunately has somewhere else to go. The asylum has an "alibi" in Limmeridge House (twice called an "asylum" in the text [367, 368]), where in the end Laura settles happily down with Walter. Whereas in the first movement of the novel the woman is shut up, in the second she is liberated, and it is rather the "feminine carceral" that is put away instead. Laura thus follows a common itinerary of the liberal subject in nineteenth-century fiction: she takes a nightmarish detour through the carceral ghetto on her way *home*, to the domestic haven where she is always felt to belong. Yet while her history plainly dichotomizes carceral and liberal spaces, the asylum that keeps one inside and the "asylum" that keeps others out, it also gives evidence of continuities and overlappings between them. If her situation as Mrs. Hartright throws domesticity into relief as relief indeed from the brutalities of the asylum, her state as Lady Glyde (at Sir Percival's "stifling" house [227]) merely anticipates the asylum, which in turn only perfects Sir Percival's control over her. The difference between the asylum-as-confinement and the asylum-as-refuge is sufficiently dramatic to make a properly enclosed domestic circle the object of both desire and— later—gratitude, but evidently it is also sufficiently precarious to warrant—as the means of maintaining it—a domestic self-discipline that must have internalized the institutional control it thereby forestalls. The same internment that renders Laura's body docile, and her mind imbecile, also fits her to incarnate the norm of the submissive Victorian wife. (Sir Percival might well turn in his grave to see his successor effortlessly reaping what, with nothing to show but acute frustration, *he* had sown.) Collins makes Laura's second marriage so different from her first that he has no reason to conceal the considerable evidence of its resemblance to what can be counted upon to remain its "opposite."

This evidence comes as early as when, virtually at first sight, Walter falls in love with Laura. "Think of her," he invites the reader who would understand his feelings, "as you thought of the first woman who quickened the pulses within you" (76). As here, so everywhere else his passion declares itself in the language of sensation: of thrill and chill (86); of pang and pain (96); of "sympathies" that, lying "too deep for words, too deep almost for thoughts," have been "touched" (76). Concomitantly, in the associative pattern we have already established, his sensationalized body puts him in an essentially feminine position. His "hardly-earned self-control" (90) is as completely lost to him as if he had never possessed it, and "aggravated by the sense of [his] own miserable weakness" (91), his situation becomes one of "helplessness and humiliation" (92)—the same hendiadys that Marian will apply to herself and Laura at Blackwater Park (272). This is all to say that, notwithstanding Walter's implication, Laura Fairlie is *not* the first woman to quicken his pulses but rather the object of a repetition compulsion whose origin lies in his (sensationalizing, feminizing) first encounter with the Woman in White. Walter replays this primal trauma, however, with an important difference that in principle marks out the path to mastering it. He moves from an identification with the woman to a desire for her, heterosexual choice replacing homosexual surprise. The woman is once more (or for the first time) the other, and the man, who now at least "knows what he wants," has to that extent taken himself in charge.

Yet the sensational features of Walter's desire necessarily threaten to reabsorb it in the identification against which it erects itself as a first line of defense. Something more, therefore, is required to stabilize his male self-mastery, something that Walter does *not* know that he wants. "Crush it," Marian counsels him, "Don't shrink under it like a woman. Tear it out; trample it under foot like a man!" (96). But the eventual recipient of this violence will be as much the object of Walter's passion as the passion itself. From the very beginning of his exposure to it, Laura's "charm" has suggested to him "the idea of something wanting":

> At one time it seemed like something wanting in *her*, at another, like something wanting in myself, which hindered me from understanding her as I ought. The impression was always strongest in the most contradictory manner, when she looked at me, or, in other words, when I was most conscious of the harmony and charm of her face, and yet, at the same time, most troubled by the sense of an incompleteness which it was impossible to discover. Something wanting, something wanting—and where it was, and what it was, I could not say. (76–77)

This is not (or not just) a Freudian riddle (Q.: What does a woman want? A.: What she is wanting), though even as such it attests the particular anxiety of the man responsible for posing it: who desires Laura "because" (= so that) she, not he, is wanting. For shortly afterward, with "a thrill of the same feeling which ran through [him] when the touch was laid upon [his] shoulder on the lonely highroad," Walter comes to see that the "something wanting" is "[his] own recognition of the ominous likeness between the fugitive from the asylum and [his] pupil at Limmeridge House" (86). Laura's strange "incompleteness" would thus consist in what has made this likeness imperfect—namely, that absence of "profaning marks" of "sorrow and suffering" which alone is said to differentiate her from her double (120). Accordingly, the Laura Walter most deeply dreams of loving proves to be none other than the Anne who has been put away. It is as though, to be quite perfect, his pupil must be taught a lesson: what is wanting—what Laura obscurely lacks and Walter obscurely wishes for—is her sequestration in the asylum.

Courtesy of Sir Percival and Fosco, the want will of course be supplied, but long before her actual internment Laura has been well prepared for it at Limmeridge House, where—on the grounds that her delicacy requires protection—men systematically keep their distance from her. Rather than deal with her directly, Sir Percival, Mr. Gilmore, Mr. Fairlie, Walter himself all prefer to have recourse to the mannish Marian, who serves as their intermediary. "I shrank," says Walter at one point, "I shrink still—from invading the innermost sanctuary of her heart, and laying it open to others, as I have laid open my own" (90) . His many such gallant pronouncements entail an unwillingness to *know* Laura, the better to affirm without interference the difference between him and her, man and woman. ("Me Tarzan, you Jane": notice how male solipsism overbears the very opposition that guarantees male difference. Laura is a closed sanctuary / Walter is an open book, but it is Walter here who empowers himself to decide, by his shrinking reticence, what Laura shall be.) More than anything else, this "respect" is responsible in the text for rendering Laura—even in terms of a genre that does not specialize in complex character studies—a psychological cipher. (An English translation of the French translation of the novel might be entitled, precisely, *The Woman as Blank*.) From turbid motives of her own, Marian is more than willing to do her part in drawing round Laura this *cordon sanitaire*. Like an efficient secretary in love with her boss, she spares Laura all troublesome importunities, and she is no less aggressive in forbidding an interview between Laura and Anne ("Not to be thought of for a moment" [131]) than in dispatching Walter from Limmeridge House "before more harm is done" (95). Laura's subsequent experience of the asylum only further justifies the imperative to isolate her. "The wrong that had been inflicted on her . . . must be redressed without her knowledge and without her help" (456). And now a self-evident opposition between parent and child is available to overdetermine what had been the all-too-doubtful difference between man and woman. "Oh, don't, don't, don't treat me like a child!" Laura implores, but Walter immediately takes the plea for more evidence of her childishness and accordingly gives her some pretend-work to do. When she asks him "as a child might have" whether he is as fond of her as he used to be, he reassures her that "she is dearer to [him] now than she had ever been in the past times" (458). His profession carries conviction, and no wonder, since his passion for her, now become a part-parental, part-pedophilic condescension, no longer makes him feel like a woman. Though the text takes perfunctory notice of "the healing influences of her new life" with Walter (576), these have no power to produce a Laura who in any way exceeds men's (literal or "liberal") incarcerating fantasies about her. It is not just, as the text puts it, that the mark of the asylum is "too deep to be effaced" but that it has always already effaced everything else.

The same could not be said of Marian Halcombe, whose far more "interesting" character represents the only significant variation on business-as-usual in the novel's gynaeceum. As the conspicuously curious case of a woman's body that gives all the signs of containing a man's soul, Marian figures the exact inversion of what we have taken to be the novel's governing fantasy. Yet we must not conceive of this inversion standing in opposition to what it inverts, as though it implied not just the existence of a rival set of matching *female* fears and fantasies but also the consequent assurance that, in the love and war between the sexes, all at least is fair: *così fan tutte*, too. No less than that of the woman-in-the-man, the motif of the man-in-the-woman is a function of the novel's anxious male imperatives ("Cherchez, cachez, couchez la femme") that, even as a configuration of resistance, it rationalizes, flatters, and positively encourages. Thus, however "phallic," "lesbian," and "male-identified" Marian may be considered at the beginning of the novel, the implicit structuring of these attributes is precisely what is responsible for converting her—if with a certain violence, then also with a certain ease—into the castrated, heterosexualized "good angel" (646) of the Victorian household at the end.

Our memorable first view of her comes in the disappointed appraisal of Walter's idly cruising eye:

> The instant my eyes rested on her, I was struck by the rare beauty of her form, and by the unaffected grace of her attitude. Her figure was tall, yet not too tall; comely and well-developed, yet nor fat; her head set on her shoulders with an easy, pliant firmness; her waist, perfection in the eyes of a man, for it occupied its natural place, it filled out its natural circle, it was visibly and delightfully undeformed by stays. She had not heard my entrance into the room; and I allowed myself the luxury of admiring her for a moment, before I moved one of the chairs near me, as the least embarrassing means of attracting her attention. She turned towards me immediately. The easy elegance of every movement of her limbs and body as soon as she began to advance from the far end of the room, set me in a flutter of expectation to see her face clearly. She left the window—and I said to myself, The lady is dark. She moved forward a few steps—and I said to myself, The lady is young. She approached nearer—and I said to myself (with a sense of surprise which words fail me to express), The lady is ugly!
>
> Never was the old conventional maxim, that Nature cannot err, more flatly contradicted—never was the fair promise of a lovely figure more strangely and startlingly belied by the face and head that crowned it. The lady's complexion was almost swarthy, and the dark down on her upper lip was almost a moustache. She had a large, firm, masculine mouth and jaw; prominent, piercing, resolute brown eyes; and thick, coal-black hair, growing unusually low down on her forehead. Her expression—bright, frank, and intelligent— appeared, while she was silent, to be altogether wanting in those feminine attractions of gentleness and pliability, without which the beauty of the handsomest woman alive is beauty incomplete. To see such a face as this set on shoulders that a sculptor would have longed to model—to be charmed by the modest graces of action through which the symmetrical limbs betrayed their beauty when they moved, and then to be almost repelled by the masculine form and masculine look of the features in which the perfectly shaped figure ended—was to feel a sensation oddly akin to the helpless discomfort familiar to us all in sleep, when we recognize yet cannot reconcile the anomalies and contradictions of a dream. (58–59)

Though the passage develops all the rhetorical suspense of a striptease, in which, as Barthes has written, "the entire excitation takes refuge in the hope of seeing the sexual organ," the place of the latter seems strangely occupied here by Marian's "head and face."[15] What Barthes calls the "schoolboy's dream" turns into a far less euphoric "sensation" of "helpless discomfort" when, at the climactic moment of unveiling, the woman's head virtually proves her a man in drag. Banal as this kind of revelation has become in our culture (where it is ritualized in a variety of spectacles, jokes, and folkloric anecdotes), it never ceases to be consumed, as here, "with a sense of surprise." The surprise would perhaps better be understood as a stubborn refusal to recognize how unsurprising it is that an obsessively phallocentric system of sexual difference, always and everywhere on the lookout for its founding attribute (if only in the case of women to make sure it isn't there), should sometimes, as though overcome by eyestrain, find this attribute even in its absence. Yet Walter's sense of surprise exceeds the more or less conscious ruse that serves to divorce his quasi-heterosexual identity from its quasi-homosexual genealogy. Surprise is also the text's figure for the violence of that double meta-morphosis which overtakes this identity and thus calls for such a ruse. Marian's sudden transformation from the object that Walter looks at into the subject whose "piercing" eyes might look back at him—look at his back—simultaneously entails the reverse transformation in him. In a context, then, where the positions of subject and object are respectively gendered as male and female, and where the relation between them is eroticized accordingly, the nature of Walter's surprise, "which words fail [him] to express," may go without saying. Necessarily, his recovery has recourse to the affect of *repulsion*, which will reinstate the distance that surprise has momentarily abolished between him and the amphibolous figure of the "mas-culine woman." Walter's recoil carries the "instinctive" proof—more than welcome after his unnerving encounter with the Woman in White—both of his competence in a male code of sexual signs (which Marian's monstrosity, far from compromising, offers the occasion for rehearsing and confirming) and of his own stable, unam-biguous position in that code (as a man who judges with "the eyes of a man"). On such a basis, he succeeds in containing his potentially disturbing vision within the assured comic effects ("The lady was ugly!") of a worldly raconteur to whom Marian's sexual anomalousness presents no threat of contagion.

For Marian's "masculine look" may be seen in two ways, not just as what poses the problem she embodies but also as what resolves it. Precisely in her "masculinity" she incarnates that wit which men familiarly direct against women who are "al-together wanting in those feminine attractions of gentleness and pliability." We notice, for a characteristic example of such wit, that someone—an erring Nature, if not the anxious drawing master who faithfully copies Nature's work—*has drawn a moustache on her*. However perturbed Walter may be that Marian lacks the lack, he is also plainly gratified to take inventory of the numerous phallic signs on her person, as though these could finally only mock the absence of the penile referent. The well-known anxiety attaching to male jokes about the "masculine woman" in no way extenuates the strategy that it energizes: which is to render the woman who is their target external to the system of sexual difference that gets along quite well without her. Unable to compete (when the chaps are down), she cannot be "male"; unable to attract (as though the derisive signs remained persuasive after all), neither can she be "female." What is thereby neutralized, in the root as well as derived sense of the word, is any sexuality—female and/or male—that cannot be reduced to either term of a phallic binarism.

Yet Walter's aggressive indifference to Marian as a relevant sexual counter is eventually belied when Count Fosco—who is as helpful in acting out the implications of Walter's fantasy here as he is in the case of Laura—takes a pronounced, even violent erotic interest in her. How does this ugly, neutered woman come to be targeted for what, as we have seen, the novel encodes as "rape"? We notice that Walter's portrait of Marian, though it abounds in phallic *signs*, nowhere offers a phallic *symbol*: only later, too late, will the novelist hand her "the horrid heavy man's umbrella" (235). Where, then, *is* the phallus so bountifully signified? If it isn't *on* Marian, whose unimpeachably curvilinear body (like the perfect waist that is its synecdoche) is "visibly and delightfully undeformed by stays," then it must be *in* her, the iron in the soul that manifests itself only through the soul's traditional windows: those "prominent, piercing, resolute brown eyes" with their "masculine look." (Even her moustache suggests that the masculine signs defacing her body have pushed through from within.) Psychoanalysis and the male adolescent alike are familiar with the castration fantasy in which (act one) the penis gets "locked" in the vagina during intercourse and (act two) having broken off, remains inside the female body. *Anima virilis in corpore muliebri inclusa:* Marian is not just the "dog" that no self-respecting male adolescent would be "caught with"; she is also— the "evidence" for act one of course being canine—the dog that he would not be caught *in*.[16] As the focus of fears of *male* incarceration, Marian's body becomes the operational theater for the two tactics of "men's liberation" that usually respond to these fears. She is firmly abandoned by Walter's erotic interest and forcibly seduced by Fosco's. The two tactics cohere in a single strategy, since perhaps the most important fantasy feature of rape is the reaffirmation of the rapist's unimpaired capacity to withdraw, the integrity of his body (if not his victim's) recovered intact. (Fosco, we recall, returns to Marian the journal he has indelibly signed, and she, evidently, is stuck with it.)[17] As its sexual variant, seduction-and-abandonment would thus in both senses of the word "betray" the constitutive myth of the liberal (male) subject, whose human rights must include the freedom, as he pleases, to come and go.

The meaning of Marian's "rape" is of course further determined by another, better-known figure of the *anima virilis:* the lesbian. "She will be *his* Laura instead of mine!" (207), writes Marian of the bride of Limmeridge—having taken the precaution, however, of promoting rather this faint-hearted marriage to Sir Percival than the obvious love match with Walter, as if already anticipating the consolation that an unhappy Lady Glyde will not fail to bring to her closet: "Oh, Marian! . . . promise you will never marry, and leave me. It is selfish to say so, but you are so much better off as a single woman—unless—unless you are very fond of your husband—but you won't be very fond of anybody but me, will you?" (235). Important as it is not to censor the existence of erotic feeling between women in the text (in any of the ways this can be done, including a certain way of acknowledging it),[18] it is perhaps more important to recognize that what would also get absorbed here under the name of lesbianism is a woman's unwillingness to lend her full cooperation to male appropriations of her, as though Marian's "gayness" were the only conceivable key to passages like the following: "Men! They are the enemies of our innocence and our peace—they drag us away from our parents' love and our sisters' friendship—they take us body and soul to themselves, and fasten our helpless lives to theirs as they chain up a dog to his kennel. And what does the best of them give us in return? Let me go, Laura—I'm mad when I think of it!" (203). In general, the "lesbianism" contextualized in *The Woman in White* amounts mainly to a male charge, in which the accusation is hard to dissociate from the excitation. In particular, the novel most effectively renders Marian "lesbian" in the sense that it makes her suffer the regular fate of the lesbian in male representations: who defiantly bides her time with women until the inevitable and irrevocable heterosexual initiation that she, unlike everyone else, may not have known that she always wanted. Once recalls this exchange from *Goldfinger*, after James Bond has seduced Pussy Galore: "He said, 'They told me you only liked women.' She said, 'I never met a man before.' "[19] Not dissimilarly, Marian's "half-willing, half-unwilling liking for the Count" (246)—what in a rape trial would be called her "complicity"—provides the novel's compelling, compulsive proof of the male erotic power that operates even and especially where it is denied. "I am almost afraid to confess it, even to these secret pages. The man has interested me, has attracted me, has forced me to like him" (240). Fosco's eyes "have at times a clear, cold, beautiful, irresistible glitter in them which forces me to look at him, and yet causes me sensations, when I do look, which I would rather not feel" (241, repeated almost verbatim on 287). Like Pussy Bonded, Marian Foscoed (hearing the metathesis in the name of the "wily Italian" [264], we need not even consider resorting to what Freud called Schreber's "shamefaced" elision) is a changed woman. If it is not her ultimate destiny to roll up the Count's endless cigarettes "with the look of mute submissive inquiry which we are all familiar with in the eyes of a faithful dog" (239), as she abjectly fantasizes, he has nonetheless well trained her to be another man's best friend. "What a woman's hands *are* fit for," she tells Walter, whom she entrusts with her avengement, "early and late, these hands of mine shall do. . . . It's my weakness that cries, not me. The house-work shall conquer it, if *I* can't" (453–54). The old signs of Marian's "masculinity"—the hands that were "as awkward as a man's" (253), the tears that came "almost like men's" (187)—now realize what had always been their implied potential to attest a "weakness" that (like the housework she takes on "as her own right") refeminizes her. In the novel's last image, almost exactly according to the proper Freudian resolution of *Penisneid*, Marian is able to "rise" only on condition that she "hold up" Walter's son and heir "kicking and crowing in her arms" (646). Almost exactly, but not quite, since the child is not of course her own. It is as though the woman whom Fosco "rapes" and the woman whom Walter "neuters" prove finally one and the same odd thing—as though, in other words, a woman's heterosexuality ("hetero-" indeed) were no sexuality of hers.

Even as the victim of terrific male aggression, however, Marian is simultaneously the beneficiary of considerable male admiration. Walter aptly imagines that she "would have secured the respect of the most audacious man breathing" (60), and apart from Fosco, who eventually embodies that hypothetical man, apart even from Walter, who at once finds in the ugly lady an old friend (59), the novelist himself unexceptionally portrays Marian as a "positive," immensely likable character. Demonstrably, then, *The Woman in White* accords a far warmer welcome to the fantasy of the man-in-the-woman (which, fully personified, the novel works through to a narrative resolution) than to the apparently complementary fantasy of the woman-in-the-man (which, as we have seen, the novel only broaches obscurely, in the blind spot of "nonrecognition" between textual thematics and male reading bodies). This is doubtless because the *anima virilis* includes, in addition to the aspects aforementioned, a male identification. "I don't think much of my own sex," Marian admits to Walter on their first meeting; "No woman does think much of her own sex, though few of them confess it as freely as I do" (60). As though misogyny were primarily a female phenomenon and as such justified the male phenomenon that ventriloquially might go without saying, Marian's voice becomes the novel's principal articulation of that traditional code according to which women are quarrelsome, chattering, capricious, superstitious, inaccurate, unable to draw or play billiards. For all the pluck that it inspires, Marian's male identification consistently vouches for her female dependency. Thus, determined "on justifying the Count's opinion of [her] courage and sharpness" (340), she bravely makes her night-crawl onto the caves of the house at Blackwater to overhear Fosco's conversation with Sir Percival. But—perhaps because, as the male-identified woman necessarily comes to think, her "courage was only a woman's courage after all" (341–42)—this determination obliges her to remove "the white and cumbersome parts of [her] underclothing" (342) and so to prepare herself for the violation that, on one way of looking at it, follows soon afterward but that, on another, has already succeeded. If the woman-in-the-man requires his *keeping her* inside him, the man-in-the-woman takes for granted her *letting him* inside her. The sexual difference that the former endangers, the latter reaffirms: by determining a single view of women—men's—to which women accede in the course of constructing a male-identified femininity. Fosco "flatters" Marian's vanity "by talking to [her] as seriously and sensibly as if [she were] a man" (245), and she more than returns the favor by addressing Fosco, Walter, and the male reader on the same premise, reassuring all concerned that even the woman who speaks as "freely" as a man remains the prolocutor of a masculist discourse that keeps her in place. Finally, therefore, Marian may be taken to suggest how the novel envisions that *female* reader whom, though it nominally ignores, it has always taken into practical account. For the same sensation effects that "feminize" the male reading body also (the quotation marks are still indispensable) "feminize" the female: with the difference that this feminization is construed in the one case to threaten sexual identity and in the other to confirm it. Implicitly, that is, the text glosses the female reader's sensationalized body in exactly the terms of Marian's erotic responsiveness to Fosco: as the corporal confession of a "femininity" whose conception is all but exhausted in providing the unmarked term in opposition to a thus replenished "masculinity." If only on its own terms (though, when one is trembling, these terms may be hard to shake), the sensation novel constitutes proof of women's inability, as Marian puts it, to "resist a man's tongue when he knows how to speak to them" (278) and especially, we might add with Marian emblematically in mind, when he knows how to speak through them.

IV

Precisely insofar as it does not fail, the project of confining or containing the woman cannot succeed in achieving narrative quiescence or closure. Safely shut up in the various ways we have considered, women cease being active participants in the drama that nonetheless remains to be played out (for over a hundred pages) "man to man." For when the text produces the configuration of incarcerated femininity, it simultaneously cathects the congruent configuration of phobic male homoeroticism: thus, for instance, its "paradoxical" rendering of Fosco, who is at once "a man who could tame anything" (239) and "a fat St. Cecilia masquerading in male attire" (250). Accordingly, the novel needs to supplement its misogynistic plot with a misanthropic one, in which it will detail the frightening, even calamitous consequences of unmediated relations between men, thereby administering to its hero an aversion therapy calculated to issue in a renunciation of what Eve Kosofsky Sedgwick has called "male homosocial desire," or in a liberation from what—with a more carceral but no less erotic shade of meaning—we might also call male bonds.[20] After Sedgwick's demonstration that men's desire for men is the very motor of patriarchally given social structures, it might seem implausible even to entertain the possibility of such a renunciation or liberation, which would amount to a withdrawal from the social *tout court*. Yet this is apparently what the endings of many nineteenth-century novels paradigmatically stage: the hero's thoroughgoing disenchantment with the (homo)social, from which he is resigned to isolate himself. By and large, nineteenth-century fiction is no less heavily invested than Sedgwick's analysis of it in luridly portraying the dysphoric effects—particularly on men— of homosocial desire, and this fact must raise the question of the status of such effects within the general rhetorical strategy of the fiction that cultivates them. If, for example, *The Woman in White* obligingly constitutes a "pathology" of male homosocial desire, this is not because the novel shares, say, Sedgwick's ambition to formulate a feminist/gay critique of homophobically patriarchal structure; but neither is it because the novel so naively embraces this structure that it recounts-without-counting its psychological costs. Rather, as we will see, the novel puts its homosocial pathology in the service of promoting a homosocial cure: a cure that has the effect of a renunciation of men's desire for men only because, in this treated form, and by contrast, such desire exists in a "normal" or relatively silent state.

The novel's most obvious specimen of an abnormal male homosocial *Bund*— the one it adduces at the end, as though at last to consolidate the freely floating homoerotics of the text and thus to name and contain them—is that secret Italian political association which (Walter is quite correct in saying) is "sufficiently individualized" for his purposes if he calls it, simply, "The Brotherhood" (595). The novel tolerates this exotic freemasonry on two ideological conditions, which, if they were not so inveterately combined in a policy of quarantine, might otherwise strike us as incompatible. On the one hand, The Brotherhood owes its existence to the political adolescence of Italy (595–96), to which, in case the point is lost, Pesca correlates his own immaturity when he became a member (597). The advanced nation as well as the enlightened parent may rest assured imagining that The Brotherhood is only a phase that in the normal course of political or personal development will be superseded. Yet on the other hand, no possible course of development can retrieve someone once he has been admitted into this society of fellows and bears its "secret mark," which, like his membership, lasts for life (596). Strange as it may be for Walter to learn that some one of his best friends belongs to the secret fraternity, the revelation occasions no alarm (lest, for instance, an attempt be made to initiate *him*), since the pathos of Pesca's case is well cultivated by Pesca himself, who admits to suffering still from those youthful impulses ("I try to forget them—and they will not forget *me!*" [642]), which forever condemn him to consort in such dubious company. (In the usual distribution of roles, Walter's mother, but not his sullenly nubile sister, has welcomed Pesca into the household.) A congenial point is borne in the activities of The Brotherhood itself, whose in-house purges are the "outside" world's best protection against it. Walter's sword need never cross with Fosco's—a mercy given the impressive estimates we are invited to make of the "length" of the latter (611)—in the duel that "other vengeance" has rendered unnecessary (642). The Brotherhood has mortally called the Count to "the day of reckoning" (642)—not for his offenses against Walter but for his all-too promiscuous fraternizing within and without its organization. The wound struck "exactly over his heart" (643) hints broadly at the "passional" nature of the crime in which—for which—Fosco is murdered. Thus, at the exhibition of his naked and knifed corpse (the former "Napoleon" [241] now, as it were, the dead Marat, and the rueful Parisian morgue, also as it were, the gayer continental baths), we hear the curator's familiarly excited double discourse, in which a flushed moralism never quite manages to pacify the sheer erotic fascination that hence remains available to incite it: "There he lay, unowned, unknown, exposed to the flippant curiosity of a French mob! There was the dreadful end of that long life of degraded ability and heartless crime! Hushed in the sublime repose of death, the broad, firm, massive face and head fronted us so grandly that the chattering Frenchwomen about me lifted their hands in admiration, and cried in shrill chorus, 'Ah, what a handsome man!' " (643).

"And all men kill the thing they love": what is often taken for Wilde's gay depressiveness (though in Reading Gaol, what else is left to intelligence but to read its prison?) provides a not-so-oddly apt formula for the novel's pathology of male bonds, whose godforsaken expression coincides with its providential punishment in death. (Besides the murder of Fosco, we may cite the "suicide" of his boon companion: it is no accident that, having locked himself in the vestry, Sir Percival accidentally sets it on fire.) A couple of reasons obtain for bringing out, as I have pseudo-anachronistically been doing, the continuities between the novel's representation of "brotherhood" and our media's no less sensational staging of male homosexuality. One would be to begin measuring the extent to which nineteenth-century culture has contributed to the formation of the context in which an un-closeted gayness is popularly determined. (Thus, the homophobic virulence that dispreads in response to AIDS is "only" the most recent, extreme, and potentially catastrophic figure of an interpretative framework that has preceded the disease by well over a century.) Another would be to recognize that if our culture can only "think" male homosexual desire within a practice of aversion therapy, this is because—for a long while and with apparently greater efficiency—it has routinely subjected male homosocial desire to the same treatment.

Representationally, this treatment consists of a diptych in which the baleful images of homosocial apocalypse on one panel confront a comparatively cheering family portrait on the other. The fact that Fosco and Sir Percival are both married is far from making them what *The Woman in White* understands by family men. For as the novel's final tableau makes abundantly clear, what is distinctively cheering about the family portrait is less the connection between husband and wife (Marian, not Laura, holds up his son to Walter's charmed gaze) than the bond between father and son. Thus, the aim of what we have called aversion therapy is not to redirect men's desire for men onto women but, through women, onto boys: that is, to privatize homosocial desire within the middle-class nuclear family, where it takes the "normal" shape of an oedipal triangle. Yet the twinned projects whose achievement the novel makes *precede* the establishment of a family curiously correspond to what, at least since Freud's summation of nineteenth-century culture, we may recognize as the family's own defining injunctions: (1) shut up the woman— or, in the rivalry between father and son of which she is the object, keep mother from becoming the subject of a desire of her own; and (2) turn from the man— or, in that same rivalry, develop an aversion therapy for home use. The foundation of the Hartright family, therefore, cannot put an end to the brutalities of its prehistory, nor will these brutalities have dialectically prepared the way for a civilizing familialism, since the violent workings of an oedipal family organization (Sir Percival is a much older man than Walter, and so forth) have implicitly generated the narrative that this organization is explicitly constituted to conclude. At the end, then, the novel has merely discovered its beginning, in the family matrix where such violence has acquired its specific structure and whence it has made its fearful *entrée dans le monde*. "And there is more where that came from," if only because where that came from is also where that eventually returns. As though refusing to cease shocking us, even where it least surprises us, *The Woman in White* "ends" only by recurring to that family circle which will continue to relay—with no end in sight—a plot that still takes many people's breath away.[21]

V

A note on the author's body: shortly after I began writing this essay, the muscles on my shoulders and back went into spasm. Referring this pain to other matters (excessive working out, an affair of the heart) than the work on which it continually interrupted my progress, I consulted physical and psychological therapists. Only when the former at last pronounced that a rib was out of place (which may have been what the latter was getting at when he diagnosed, on the insurance form, a personality disorder), was I willing to entertain the possibility that I had become, in relation to my own writing, an improbably pat case of hysteria. Now that a practiced hand has put the fugitive rib back into its cage, my spine tingles to have borne out my assumption of that "nonrecognition" which evidently also obtains between the somatics of writing and what is written about. I am less pleased (though still thrilled) to understand that, on the same assumption, what dumbfounds me also lays the foundation for my dumbness: too stupid to utter what has already been said in the interaction between body and text, and in the traces of that interaction within body or text; and too mute to do more than designate the crucial task of identifying in this writing the equivocal places where "sensation" has gone, not to say love.

Notes

1. A valuable survey of Victorian responses to sensation fiction may be found in Elizabeth K. Helsinger, Robin Lauterbach Sheets, and William Veeder, *The Woman Question: Society and Literature in Britain and America, 1837–1883*, 3 vols. (New York: Garland, 1983), 3:122–44

2. The omission is well exemplified in a recent article by Patrick Brantlinger entitled "What Is 'Sensational' About the Sensation Novel?" *Nineteenth-Century Fiction* 37 (June 1982): 1–28. Having posed the crucial question, the author elides its most obvious answer— namely, the somatic experience of sensation itself—by at once proceeding to considerations of "content" (murder, adultery, bigamy) and generic "mixture" (domestic realism, Gothic romance, and so on).

3. Wilkie Collins, *The Woman in White*, ed. Julian Symons (Harmondsworth: Penguin, 1974), p. 47. Subsequent references to the novel are to this edition and are cited parenthetically in the text by page number.

4. Mrs. [Margaret] Oliphant, "Sensation Novels," *Blackwood's Magazine* 91 (May 1862), reprinted in Norman Page, ed., *Wilkie Collins: The Critical Heritage* (London: Routledge and Kegan Paul, 1974), pp. 118–19.

5. For example, Walter, the master narrator who solicits the others' narratives and organizes them into a whole, speaks of Laura to the reader: "Think of her as you thought of the first woman who quickened the pulses within you" (76). The same identification is also sustained implicitly, as in the equation between the reader and a judge (33). As Veeder documents, Victorian discussion emphasized the dangers that sensation fiction posed to the *female* reader, as though a perilous natural affinity linked sensation to her all-too-excitable body. Positing a male reader, *The Woman in White* has the advantage of allowing us to show what ulteriorly determined the Victorian concern with protecting "the woman" from "her" own susceptibilities.

6. See Jeffrey Weeks, *Coming Out: Homosexual Politics in Britain, From the Nineteenth Century to the Present* (London: Quarter Books, 1977), pp. 26–27. It does not seem altogether a historical "irony" that this intrinsically ambiguous notion—so useful to the apologists for homosexuality in the late nineteenth and early twentieth centuries—should popularly survive today as part of the mythological rationale for "vulgar" homophobia, which draws on an equally vulgar misogyny to oppress gay men. It may also be pertinent here to note that turn-of-the-century sexology almost universally agreed on "a marked tendency to nervous development in the [homosexual] subject, not infrequently associated with nervous maladies" (Edward Carpenter, *The Intermediate Sex* [1908], in *Selected Writings* [London: Gay Men's Press, 1984], 1:209). Criticizing Krafft-Ebing for continuing to link homosexuality with " 'an hereditary neuropathic or psychopathic tendency'—*neuro(psycho)-pathische Belastung*," Carpenter remarks that "there are few people in modern life, perhaps none, who could be pronounced absolutely free from such a *Belastung!*" (210). His ostensible point— that nervous disorders are far too widespread in modern life to be the distinctive mark of homosexuals, whose "neuropathic tendency" would bespeak rather a social than a metaphysical fatality—is still (mutatis mutandis) worth making. Yet in a discursive formation that insistently yokes male homosexuality and neuropathology (in the femininity common to both), his observation might also be taken to conclude that this homosexuality *too* (if principally in its reactive, homophobic form) is a general modern phenomenon.

7. See William Ll. Parry-Jones, *The Trade in Lunacy: A Study of Private Madhouses in England in the Eighteenth and Nineteenth Centuries* (Toronto: University of Toronto Press, 1972).

8. Mrs. Oliphant, in Page, *Wilkie Collins*, p. 112.

9. Guy Hocquenghem, *Homosexual Desire*, trans. Daniella Dangoor (London: Allison and Busby, 1978), pp. 42–43.

10. Quoted in Sigmund Freud, "Psycho-Analytic Notes on an Autobiographical Account of Paranoia," in *The Standard Edition of the Complete Works of Sigmund Freud*, ed. James Strachey, 24 vols. (London: Hogarth Press and the Institute of Psycho-Analysis, 1953–74), 12:20.

11. Peter Brooks, *Reading for the Plot* (New York: Knopf, 1984), p. 169.

12. Sandra M. Gilbert and Susan Gubar, *The Madwoman in the Attic* (New Haven: Yale University Press, 1979), pp. 85–86.

13. Mary Elizabeth Braddon, *Lady Audley's Secret* (New York: Dover, 1974), p. 249.

14. A Victorian reviewer, W. Fraser Ray, criticizes the characterization of Lady Audley thus: "In drawing her, the authoress may have intended to portray a female Mephistopheles; but if so, she should have known that a woman cannot fill such a part"; "Sensation Novelists: Miss Braddon," *North British Review* 43 (1865), quoted in Veeder, *The Woman Question*, p. 127. Ray might have spared himself the trouble (nor to mention, in our hindsight, the embarrassment of failing to read the text that nonetheless proves quite capable of reading

him), since his objection merely rehearses the same principle that, within the novel, Robert Audley victoriously carries in having Lady Audley confined.

15. Roland Barthes, *The Pleasure of the Text*, trans. Richard Miller (New York: Hill and Wang, 1975), p. 10.

16. The novel's elaborate canine thematics more than justify this slang usage, which of course postdates it. Marian's first lesson at Blackwater Park, for instance, involves being instructed in the destiny of dogs there. A housemaid thus accounts to her for the wounded dog found in the boathouse: "Bless you, miss! Baxter's the keeper, and when he finds strange dogs hunting about, he takes and shoots 'em. It's keeper's dooty, miss. I think that dog will die. Here's where he's been shot, ain't it? That's Baxter's doings, that is. Baxter's doings, miss, and Baxter's dooty" (229). "Baxter's" doings indeed: if the keeper is little more than a name in the novel, the name nonetheless contains almost all the elements in the novel's representation of female containment. For one thing, the suffix *-ster* originally designates a specifically feminine agency (in Old English a *baxter* means a female baker): whence perhaps Baxter's violence, as though he were protesting the femininity latently inscribed in his name. For another, in the context of the novel's insistence on "the touch from behind," the name would also signify the person who handles (its gender inflection keeps us from quite saying: man-handles) the hinder part of the body.

17. In this context one must read Fosco's dandiacal lament after the episode where— "to the astonishment of all the men" who watch him—he successfully intimidates "a chained bloodhound—a beast so savage that the very groom who feeds him keeps out of his reach": "Ah! my nice waistcoat! . . . Some of that brute's slobber has got on my pretty clean waistcoat!" (243–44).

18. For example: "Does [Marian] . . . have Lesbian tendencies?" the editor of the Penguin edition boldly speculates, before prudently concluding that "it is doubtful whether such thoughts were in Collins's mind" (15). The response, which rationalizes its titillation as a sophisticated willingness to call things by their names and then rationalizes its disavowal of that titillation (and of those names) as scholarly caution, typifies the only acknowledgment that homoeroticism, female or male, is accustomed to receive in the criticism of nineteenth-century fiction. Here it does little more than faithfully reproduce—"Mind that dog, sir!" (243)—the novel's own equivocal structuring of the evidence for Marian's lesbianism. One may observe in passing how a similar fidelity entails that the editor who can mention lesbianism must fall entirely silent on the *male* homoerotics of the novel (see p. 209 below for why this should be so).

19. Ian Fleming, *Goldfinger* (1959; New York: Berkley Books, 1982), p. 261.

20. Readers of Eve Kosofsky Sedgwick's *Between Men: English Literature and Male Homosocial Desire* (New York: Columbia University Press, 1985) will recognize how nearly its concerns touch on those of this chapter.

21. Like the woman's, or the homosexual's, or (for she has figured in both roles) Marian's: "Let Marian end our Story" (646), but—these are the text's last words, as well as Walter's— what follows is dead silence.

11

"Kiss Me with Those Red Lips": Gender and Inversion in Bram Stoker's *Dracula*

Christopher Craft

When Joseph Sheridan Le Fanu observed in *Carmilla* (1872) that "the vampire is prone to be fascinated with an engrossing vehemence resembling the passion of love" and that vampiric pleasure is heightened "by the gradual approaches of an artful courtship," he identified clearly the analogy between monstrosity and sexual desire that would prove, under a subsequent Freudian stimulus, paradigmatic for future readings of vampirism.[1] Modern critical accounts of *Dracula*, for instance, almost universally agree that vampirism both expresses and distorts an originally sexual energy. That distortion, the representation of desire under the defensive mask of monstrosity, betrays the fundamental psychological ambivalence identified by Franco Moretti when he writes that "vampirism is an excellent example of the identity of desire and fear."[2] This interfusion of sexual desire and the fear that the moment of erotic fulfillment may occasion the erasure of the conventional and integral self informs both the central action in *Dracula* and the surcharged emotion of the characters about to be kissed by "those red lips."[3] So powerful an ambivalence, generating both errant erotic impulses and compensatory anxieties, demands a strict, indeed an almost schematic formal management of narrative material. in *Dracula* Stoker borrows from Mary Shelley's *Frankenstein* and Robert Louis Stevenson's *Dr. Jekyll and Mr. Hyde* a narrative strategy characterized by a predictable, if variable, triple rhythm. Each of these texts first invites or admits a monster, then entertains and is entertained by monstrosity for some extended duration, until in its closing pages it expels or repudiates the monster and all the disruption that he/she/it brings.[4]

Obviously enough, the first element in this triple rhythm corresponds formally to the text's beginning or generative moment, to its need to produce the monster, while the third element corresponds to the text's terminal moment, to its need both to destroy the monster it has previously admitted and to end the narrative that houses the monster. Interposed between these antithetical gestures of admission and expulsion is the gothic novel's prolonged middle,[5] during which the text affords its ambivalence a degree of play intended to produce a pleasurable, indeed a thrilling anxiety. Within its extended middle, the gothic novel entertains its resident demon—is, indeed, entertained by it—and the monster, now ascendent in its strength, seems for a time potent enough to invert the "natural" order and overwhelm the comforting closure of the text. That threat, of course, is contained and finally nullified by the narrative requirement that the monster be repudiated and the world of normal relations restored; thus, the gesture of expulsion, compensating for the original irruption of the monstrous, brings the play of monstrosity to its predictable close. This narrative rhythm, whose tripartite cycle of admission-entertainment-expulsion enacts sequentially an essentially simultaneous psychological equivocation, provides aesthetic management of the fundamental ambivalence that motivates these texts and our reading of them.

While such isomorphism of narrative method obviously implies affinities and similarities among these different texts, it does not argue identity of meaning. However similar *Frankenstein, Dr. Jekyll and Mr. Hyde,* and *Dracula* may be, differences nevertheless obtain, and these differences bear the impress of authorial, historical, and institutional pressures. This essay therefore offers not a reading of monstrosity in general, but rather an account of Bram Stoker's particular articulation of the vampire metaphor in *Dracula,* a book whose fundamental anxiety, an equivocation about the relationship between desire and gender, repeats, with a monstrous difference, a pivotal anxiety of late Victorian culture. Jonathan Harker, whose diary opens the novel, provides *Dracula's* most precise articulation of this anxiety. About to be kissed by the "weird sisters" (64), the incestuous vampiric daughters who share Castle Dracula with the Count, a supine Harker thrills to a double passion:

> All three had brilliant white teeth, that shone like pearls against the ruby of their voluptuous lips. There was something about them that made me uneasy, *some longing and at the same time some deadly fear.* I felt in my heart a wicked, burning desire that they would kiss me with those red lips. (51: emphasis added)

Immobilized by the competing imperatives of "wicked desire" and "deadly fear," Harker awaits an erotic fulfillment that entails both the dissolution of the boundaries of the self and the thorough subversion of conventional Victorian gender codes, which constrained the mobility of sexual desire and varieties of genital behavior by according to the more active male the right and responsibility of vigorous appetite, while requiring the more passive female to "suffer and be still." John Ruskin, concisely formulating Victorian conventions of sexual difference, provides us with a useful synopsis: "The man's power is active, progressive, defensive. He is eminently the doer, the creator, the discoverer, the defender. His intellect is for speculation and invention: his energy for adventure, for war, and for conquest. . . ." Woman, predictably enough, bears a different burden: "She must be enduringly, incorruptibly, good: instinctively, infallibly wise—wise, not for self-development, but for self-renunciation . . . wise, not with the narrowness of insolent and loveless pride, but with the passionate gentleness of an infinitely variable, because infinitely applicable, modesty of service—the true changefulness of woman."[6] Stoker, whose vampiric women exercise a far more dangerous "change-fulness" than Ruskin imagines, anxiously inverts this conventional pattern, as virile Jonathan Harker enjoys a "feminine" passivity and awaits a delicious pen-etration from a woman whose demonism is figured as the power to penetrate. A swooning desire for an overwhelming penetration and an intense aversion to the demonic potency empowered to gratify that desire compose the fundamental mo-tivating action and emotion in *Dracula*.

This ambivalence, always excited by the imminence of the vampiric kiss, finds its most sensational representation in the image of the Vampire Mouth, the central and recurring image of the novel: "There was a deliberate voluptuousness which was both thrilling and repulsive . . . I could see in the moonlight the moisture shining on the red tongue as it lapped the white sharp teeth" (52). That is Harker describing one of the three vampire women at Castle Dracula. Here is Dr. Steward's description of the Count: "His eyes flamed red with devilish passion; the great nostrils of the white aquiline nose opened wide and quivered at the edges; and the white sharp teeth, behind the full lips of the blood-dripping mouth, champed together like those of a wild beast" (336). As the primary site of erotic experience in *Dracula*, this mouth equivocates, giving the lie to the easy separation of the masculine and the feminine. Luring at first with an inviting orifice, a promise of red softness, but delivering instead a piercing bone, the vampire mouth fuses and confuses what Dracula's civilized nemesis, Van Helsing and his Crew of Light,[7] works so hard to separate—the gender-based categories of the penetrating and the receptive, or, to use Van Helsing's language, the complementary categories of "brave men" and "good women." With its soft flesh barred by hard bone, its red crossed by white, this mouth compels opposites and contrasts into a frightening unity, and it asks some disturbing questions. Are we male or are we female? Do we have penetrators or orifices? And if both, what does that mean? And what about our bodily fluids, the red and the white? What are the relations between blood and semen, milk and blood? Furthermore, this mouth, bespeaking the subversion of the stable and lucid distinctions of gender, is the mouth of all vampires, male and female.

Yet we must remember that the vampire mouth is first of all Dracula's mouth, and that all subsequent versions of it (in *Dracula* all vampires other than the Count are female)[8] merely repeat as diminished simulacra the desire of the Great Original, that "father or furtherer of a new order of beings" (360). Dracula himself, calling his children "my jackals to do my bidding when I want to feed," identifies the systematic creation of female surrogates who enact his will and desire (365). This should remind us that the novel's opening anxiety, its first articulation of the vampiric threat, derives from Dracula's hovering interest in Jonathan Harker; the sexual threat that this novel first evokes, manipulates, sustains, but never finally represents is that Dracula will seduce, penetrate, drain another male. The suspense and power of *Dracula*'s opening section, of that phase of the narrative which we have called the invitation to monstrosity, proceeds precisely from this unfulfilled sexual ambition. Dracula's desire to fuse with a male, most explicitly evoked when Harker cuts himself shaving, subtly and dangerously suffuses this text. Always postponed and never directly enacted, this desire finds evasive fulfillment in an important series of heterosexual displacements.

Dracula's ungratified desire to vamp Harker is fulfilled instead by his three vampiric daughters, whose anatomical femininity permits, because it masks, the silently interdicted homoerotic embrace between Harker and the Count. Here, in a displacement typical both of this text and the gender-anxious culture from which it arose, an implicitly homoerotic desire achieves representation as a monstrous heterosexuality, as a demonic inversion of normal gender relations. Dracula's daughters offer Harker a feminine form but a masculine penetration:

> Lower and lower went her head as the lips went below the range of my mouth and chin and seemed to fasten on my throat. . . . I could feel the soft, shivering touch of the lips on the supersensitive skin of my throat, and the hard dents of two sharp teeth, just touching and pausing there. I closed my eyes in a langorous ecstasy and waited—waited with a beating heart. (52)

This moment, constituting the text's most direct and explicit representation of a male's desire to be penetrated, is governed by a double deflection: first, the agent of penetration is nominally and anatomically (from the mouth down, anyway) female; and second, this dangerous moment, fusing the maximum of desire and the maximum of anxiety, is poised precisely at the brink of penetration. Here the "two sharp teeth," just "touching" and "pausing" there, stop short of the transgression which would unsex Harker and toward which this text constantly aspires and then retreats: the actual penetration of the male.

This moment is interrupted, this penetration denied. Harker's pause at the end of the paragraph ("waited—waited with a beating heart"), which seems to anticipate an imminent piercing, in fact anticipates not the completion but the interruption of the scene of penetration. Dracula himself breaks into the room, drives the women away from Harker, and admonishes them: "How dare you touch him, any of you? How dare you cast eyes on him when I had forbidden it? Back, I tell you all! This man belongs to me" (53). Dracula's intercession here has two obvious effects: by interrupting the scene of penetration, it suspends and disperses throughout the text the desire maximized at the brink of penetration, and it repeats the threat of a more direct libidinous embrace between Dracula and Harker. Dracula's taunt, "This man belongs to me," is suggestive enough, but at no point subsequent to this moment does Dracula kiss Harker, preferring instead to pump him for his knowledge of English law, custom, and language. Dracula, soon departing for England, leaves Harker to the weird sisters, whose final penetration of him, implied but never represented, occurs in the dark interspace to which Harker's journal gives no access.

Hereafter *Dracula* will never represent so directly a male's desire to be penetrated; once in England Dracula, observing a decorous heterosexuality, vamps only women, in particular Lucy Westenra and Mina Harker. The novel, nonetheless, does not dismiss homoerotic desire and threat; rather it simply continues to diffuse and displace it. Late in the text, the Count himself announces a deflected homoeroticism when he admonishes the Crew of Light thus: "My revenge is just begun! I spread it over the centuries, and time is on my side. Your girls that you all love are mine already; and *through them you and others shall yet be mine* . . ." (365; italics added). Here Dracula specifies the process of substitution by which "the girls that you all love" mediate and displace a more direct communion among males. Van Helsing, who provides for Lucy transfusions designed to counteract the dangerous influence of the Count, confirms Dracula's declaration of surrogation; he knows that once the transfusions begin, Dracula drains from Lucy's veins not her blood, but rather blood transferred from the veins of the Crew of Light: "even we four who gave our strength to Lucy it also is all to him [*sic*]" (244). Here, emphatically, is another instance of the heterosexual displacement of a desire mobile enough to elude the boundaries of gender. Everywhere in this text such desire seeks a strangely deflected heterosexual distribution; only through women may men touch.

The representation of sexuality in *Dracula*, then, registers a powerful ambivalence in its identification of desire and fear. The text releases a sexuality so mobile and polymorphic that Dracula may be best represented as bat or wolf or floating dust; yet this effort to elude the restrictions upon desire encoded in traditional conceptions of gender then constrains that desire through a series of heterosexual displacements. Desire's excursive mobility is always filtered in *Dracula* through the mask of a monstrous or demonic heterosexuality. Indeed, Dracula's mission in England is the creation of a race of monstrous women, feminine demons equipped with masculine devices. This monstrous heterosexuality is apotropaic for two reasons: first, because it masks and deflects the anxiety consequent to a more direct representation of same sex eroticism; and second, because in imagining a sexually aggressive woman as a demonic penetrator, as a usurper of a prerogative belonging "naturally" to the other gender, it justifies, as we shall see later, a violent expulsion of this deformed femininity.

In its particular formulation of erotic ambivalence, in its contrary need both to liberate and constrain a desire indifferent to the prescriptions of gender by figuring such desire as monstrous heterosexuality, *Dracula* may seem at first idiosyncratic, anomalous, merely neurotic. This is not the case, *Dracula* presents a characteristic, if hyperbolic, instance of Victorian anxiety over the potential fluidity of gender roles,[9] and this text's defensiveness toward the mobile sexuality it nonetheless wants to evoke parallels remarkably other late Victorian accounts of same sex eroticism, of desire in which the "sexual instincts" were said to be, in the words of John Addington Symonds, "improperly correlated to [the] sexual organs."[10] During the last decades of the nineteenth century and the first of the twentieth,

English writers produced their first sustained discourse about the variability of sexual desire, with a special emphasis upon male homoerotic love, which had already received indirect and evasive endorsement from Tennyson in "In Memoriam" and from Whitman in the "Calamus" poems. The preferred taxonomic label under which these writers categorized and examined such sexual desire was not, as we might anticipate, "homosexuality" but rather "sexual inversion," a classificatory term involving a complex negotiation between socially encoded gender norms and a sexual mobility that would seem at first unconstrained by those norms. Central polemical texts contributing to this discourse include Symonds's *A Problem in Greek Ethics* (1883), and his *A Problem in Modern Ethics* (1891); Havelock Ellis's *Sexual Inversion*, originally written in collaboration with Symonds, published and suppressed in England in 1897, and later to be included as volume 2 of Ellis's *Studies in the Psychology of Sex* (1901); and Edward Carpenter's *Homogenic Love* (1894) and his *The Intermediate Sex* (1908). Admittedly polemical and apologetic, these texts argued, with considerable circumspection, for the cultural acceptance of desire and behavior hitherto categorized as sin, explained under the imprecise religious term "sodomy,"[11] and repudiated as "the crime *inter Christianos non nominandum*."[12] Such texts, urbanely arguing an extremist position, represent a culture's first attempt to admit the inadmissible, to give the unnamable a local habitation and a name, and as Michel Foucault has argued, to put sex into discourse.[13]

"Those who read these lines will hardly doubt what passion it is that I am hinting at," wrote Symonds in the introduction to *A Problem in Modern Ethics*, a book whose subtitle—*An Inquiry into the Phenomenon of Sexual Inversion, Addressed Especially to Medical Psychologists and Jurists*—provides the OED *Supplement* with its earliest citation (1896) for "inversion" in the sexual sense. Symonds's coy gesture, his hint half-guessed, has the force of a necessary circumlocution. Symonds, Ellis, and Carpenter struggled to devise, and then to revise, a descriptive language untarnished by the anal implications, by suggestions of that "circle of extensive corruption,"[14] that so terrified and fascinated late Victorian culture. Symonds "can hardly find a name that will not seem to soil" his text "because the accomplished languages of Europe in the nineteenth century provide no term for this persistant feature of human psychology without importing some implication of disgust, disgrace, vituperation." This need to supply a new term, to invent an adequate taxonomic language, produced more obscurity than clarity. A terminological muddle ensued, the new names of the unnameable were legion: "homosexuality," "sexual inversion," "intermediate sex," "homogenic love," and "uranism" all coexisted and completed for terminological priority. Until the second or third decade of this century, when the word "homosexuality," probably because of its medical heritage, took the terminological crown, "sexual inversion"—as word, metaphor, taxonomic category—provided the basic tool with which late Victorians investigated, and constituted, their problematic desire. Symonds, more responsible than any other writer for the establishment of "inversion" as Victorian England's preferred term for same sex eroticism, considered it a "convenient phrase" "which does not prejudice the matter under consideration." Going further, he naively claimed that "inversion" provided a "neutral nomenclature" with which "the investigator has good reason to be satisfied.[15]

Symonds's claim of terminological neutrality ignores the way in which conventional beliefs and assumptions about gender inhabit both the label "inversion" and the metaphor behind it. The exact history of the word remains obscure (the *OED Supplement* defines sexual inversion tautologically as "the inversion of the sex instincts" and provides two perfunctory citations) but it seems to have been employed first in English in an anonymous medical review of 1871; Symonds later adopted it to translate the account of homoerotic desire offered by Karl Ulrichs, an "inverted" Hanoverian legal official who wrote in the 1860s in Germany "a series of polemical, analytical, theoretical, and apologetic pamphlets" endorsing same sex eroticism.[16] As Ellis explains it, Ulrichs "regarded uranism, or homosexual love, as a congenital abnormality by which a female soul had become united with a male body—*anima muliebris in corpore virili inclusa*."[17] The explanation for this improper correlation of anatomy and desire is, according to Symonds's synopsis of Ulrichs in *Modern Ethics*, "to be found in physiology, in that obscure department of natural science which deals with the evolution of sex."[18] Nature's attempt to differentiate "the indeterminate ground-stuff" of the foetus—to produce, that is, not merely the "male and female organs of procreation" but also the "corresponding male and female appetites"—falls short of complete success: "Nature fails to complete her work regularly and in every instance. Having succeeded in differentiating a male with full-formed sexual organs from the undecided foetus, she does not always effect the proper differentiation of that portion of the physical being in which resides the sexual appetite. There remains a female soul in a male body." Since it holds nature responsible for the "imperfection in the process of development," this explanation of homoerotic desire has obvious polemical utility; in relieving the individual of moral responsibility for his or her anomalous development, it argues first for the decriminalization and then for the medicalization of inversion. According to this account, same sex eroticism, although statistically deviant or abnormal, cannot then be called unnatural. Inverts or urnings or homosexuals are therefore "abnormal, but natural, beings"; they constitute the class of "the naturally abnormal." Symonds, writing to Carpenter, makes his point succinctly: "The first thing is to force people to see that the passions in question have their justification in nature."[19]

As an extended psychosexual analogy to the more palpable reality of physical hermaphroditism, Ulrichs's explanation of homoerotic desire provided the English polemicists with the basic components for their metaphor of inversion, which never relinquished the idea of a misalignment between inside and outside, between desire and the body, between the hidden truth of sex and the false sign of anatomical gender. ("Inversion," derived from the Latin verb *vertere*, "to turn," means literally to turn in, and the *OED* cites the following meaning from pathology: "to turn outside in or inside out.") This argument's intrinsic doubleness—its insistence of the simultaneous inscription within the individual of two genders, one anatomical and one not, one visible and one not—represents an accommodation between contrary impulses of liberation and constraint, as conventional gender norms are subtilized and manipulated but never fully escaped. What this account of same sex eroticism cannot imagine is that sexual attraction between members of the same gender may be a reasonable and natural articulation of a desire whose excursiveness is simply indifferent to the distinctions of gender, that desire may not be gendered intrinsically as the body is, and that desire seeks its objects according to a complicated set of conventions that are culturally and institutionally determined. So radical a reconstitution of notions of desire would probably have been intolerable even to an advanced reading public because it would threaten the moral priority of the heterosexual norm, as the following sentence from Ellis suggests: "It must also be pointed out that the argument for acquired or suggested inversion logically involves the assertion that normal sexuality is also acquired or suggested."[20] Unable or unwilling to deconstruct the heterosexual norm, English accounts of sexual inversion instead repeat it; desire remains, despite appearances, essentially and irrevocably heterosexual. A male's desire for another male, for instance, is from the beginning assumed to be a feminine desire referable not to the gender of the body (*corpore virili*) but rather to another invisible sexual self composed of the opposite gender (*anima muliebris*). Desire, according to this explanation, is always already constituted under the regime of gender—to want a male cannot not be a feminine desire, and vice versa—and the body, having become an unreliable signifier, ceases to represent adequately the invisible truth of desire, which itself never deviates from respectable heterosexuality. Thus the confusion that threatens conventional definitions of gender when confronted by same sex eroticism becomes merely illusory. The body, quite simply, is mistaken.

Significantly, this displaced repetition of heterosexual gender norms contains within it the undeveloped germ of a radical redefinition of Victorian conventions of feminine desire. The interposition of a feminine soul between erotically associated males inevitably entails a certain feminization of desire, since the very site and source of desire for males is assumed to be feminine (*anima muliebris*). Implicit in this argument is the submerged acknowledgment of the sexually independent woman, whose erotic empowerment refutes the conventional assumption of feminine passivity. Nonetheless, this nascent redefinition of notions of feminine desire remained largely unfulfilled. Symonds and Ellis did not escape their culture's phallocentrism, and their texts predictably reflect this bias. Symonds, whose sexual and aesthetic interests pivoted around the "pure & noble faculty of understanding & expressing manly perfection,"[21] seems to have been largely unconcerned with feminine sexuality; his seventy-page *A Problem in Greek Ethics*, for instance, offers only a two-page "parenthetical investigation" of lesbianism. Ellis, like Freud, certainly acknowledged sexual desire in women, but nevertheless accorded to masculine heterosexual desire an ontological and practical priority: "The female responds to the stimulation of the male at the right moment just as the tree responds to the stimulation of the warmest days in spring."[22] (Neither did English law want to recognize the sexually self-motivated woman. The Labouchère Amendment to the Criminal Law Amendment Act of 1885, the statute under which Oscar Wilde was convicted of "gross indecency," simply ignored the possibility of erotic behavior between women.) In all of this we may see an anxious defense against recognition of an independent and active feminine sexuality. A submerged fear of the feminization of desire precluded these polemicists from fully developing their own argumentative assumption of an already sexualized feminine soul.

Sexual inversion, then, understands homoerotic desire as misplaced heterosexuality and configures its understanding of such desire according to what George Chauncey has called "the heterosexual paradigm," an analytical model requiring that all love repeat the dyadic structure (masculine/feminine, husband/wife, active/passive) embodied in the heterosexual norm.[23] Desire between anatomical males requires the interposition of an invisible femininity, just as desire between anatomical females requires the mediation of a hidden masculinity. This insistent ideology of heterosexual mediation and its corollary anxiety about independent feminine sexuality return us to *Dracula*, where all desire, however mobile, is fixed within a heterosexual mask, where a mobile and hungering woman is represented as a monstrous usurper of masculine function, and where, as we shall see in detail, all erotic contacts between males, whether directly libidinal or thoroughly sublimated, are fulfilled through a mediating female, through the surrogation of the other, "correct," gender. Sexual inversion and Stoker's account of vampirism, then, are symmetrical metaphors sharing a fundamental ambivalence. Both discourses, aroused by a desire that wants to elude or flaunt the conventional prescriptions of gender, constrain that desire by constituting it according to the heterosexual paradigm that leaves conventional gender codes intact. The difference between the two discourses lies in the particular articulation of that paradigm. Sexual inversion, especially as argued by Symonds and Ellis, represents an urbane and civilized accommodation of the contrary impulses of liberation and constraint. Stoker's vampirism, altogether more hysterical and hyperbolic, imagines mobile desire as monstrosity and then devises a violent correction of that desire; in *Dracula* the vampiric abrogation of gender codes inspires a defensive reinscription of the stabilizing distinctions of gender. The site of that ambivalent interplay of desire and its correction, of mobility and fixity, is the text's prolonged middle, to which we now turn.

Engendering Gender

> *Our strong game will be to play our masculine against her feminine.*
> —Stoker, THE LAIR OF THE WHITE WORM

The portion of the gothic novel that I have called the prolonged middle, during which the text allows the monster a certain dangerous play, corresponds in *Dracula* to the duration beginning with the Count's arrival in England and ending with his flight back home, this extended middle constitutes the novel's prolonged moment of equivocation, as it entertains, elaborates, and explores the very anxieties it must later expel in the formulaic resolution of the plot. The action within this section of *Dracula* consists, simply enough, in an extended battle between two evidently masculine forces, one identifiably good and the other identifiably evil, for the allegiance of a woman (two women actually—Lucy Westenra and Mina Harker nee Murray).[24] This competition between alternative potencies has the apparent simplicity of a black and white opposition. Dracula ravages and impoverishes these women. Van Helsing's Crew of Light restores and "saves" them. As Dracula conducts his serial assaults upon Lucy, Van Helsing, in a pretty counterpoint of penetration, responds with a series of defensive transfusions; the blood that Dracula takes out Van Helsing then puts back. Dracula, isolated and disdainful of community, works alone; Van Helsing enters this little English community, immediately assumes authority, and then works through surrogates to cement communal bonds. As critics have noted, this pattern of opposition distills readily into a competition between antithetical fathers. "The vampire Count, centuries old," Maurice Richardson wrote twenty-five years ago, "is a father figure of huge potency" who competes with Van Helsing, "the good father figure."[25] The theme of alternate paternities is, in short, simple, evident, unavoidable.

This oscillation between vampiric transgression and medical correction exercises the text's ambivalence toward those fundamental dualisms—life and death, spirit and flesh, male and female—which have served traditionally to constrain and delimit the excursions of desire. As doctor, lawyer, and sometimes priest ("The Host. I brought it from Amsterdam. I have an indulgence."), Van Helsing stands as the protector of the patriarchal institutions he so emphatically represents and as the guarantor of the traditional dualisms his religion and profession promote and authorize.[26] His largest purpose is to reinscribe the dualities that Dracula would muddle and confuse. Dualities require demarcations, inexorable and ineradicable lines of separation, but Dracula, as a border being who abrogates demarcations, makes such distinctions impossible. He is *nosferatu*, neither dead nor alive but somehow both, mobile frequenter of the grave and boudoir, easeful communicant of exclusive realms, and as such as he toys with the separation of the living and the dead, a distinction critical to physician, lawyer, and priest alike. His mobility and metaphoric power deride the distinction between the spirit and flesh, another of Van Helsing's sanctified dualisms. Potent enough to ignore death's terminus, Dracula has a spirit's freedom and mobility, but that mobility is chained to the most mechanical of appetites: he and his children rise and fall for a drink and for nothing else, for nothing else matters. This con- or inter-fusion of spirit and appetite, of eternity and sequence, produces a madness of activity and a mania of unceasing desire. Dracula lives an eternity of sexual repetition, a lurid wedding of desire and satisfaction that parodies both.

But the traditional dualism most vigorously defended by Van Helsing and most subtly subverted by Dracula is, of course, sexual: the division of being into gender, either male or female. Indeed, as we have seen, the vampiric kiss excites a sexuality so mobile, so insistent, that it threatens to overwhelm the distinctions of gender, and the exuberant energy with which Van Helsing and the Crew of Light counter Dracula's influence represents the text's anxious defense against the very desire it also seeks to liberate. In counterposing Dracula and Van Helsing, Stoker's text simultaneously threatens and protects the line of demarcation that insures the intelligible division of being into gender. This ambivalent need to invite the vampiric kiss and then to repudiate it defines exactly the dynamic of the battle that constitutes the prolonged middle of this text. The field of this battle, of this equivocal competition for the right to define the possible relations between desire and gender, is the infinitely penetrable body of a somnolent woman. This interposition of a woman between Dracula and Van Helsing should not surprise us; in England, as in Castle Dracula, a violent wrestle between males is mediated through a feminine form.

The Crew of Light's conscious conception of women is, predictably enough, idealized—the stuff of dreams. Van Helsing's concise description of Mina may serve as a representative example: "She is one of God's women fashioned by His own hand to show us men and other women that there is a heaven we can enter, and that its light can be here on earth" (226). The impossible idealism of this conception of women deflects attention from the complex and complicitous interaction within this sentence of gender, authority, and representation. Here Van Helsing's exegesis of God's natural text reifies Mina into a stable sign or symbol ("one of God's women") performing a fixed and comfortable function within a masculine sign system. Having received from Van Helsing's exegesis her divine impress, Mina signifies both a masculine artistic intention ("fashioned by His own hand") and a definite didactic purpose ("to show us men and other women" how to enter heaven), each of which constitutes an enormous constraint upon the significative possibilities of the sign or symbol that Mina here becomes. Van Helsing's reading of Mina, like a dozen other instances in which his interpretation of the sacred determines and delimits the range of activity permitted to women, encodes woman with a "natural" meaning composed according to the textual imperatives of anxious males. Precisely this complicity between masculine anxiety, divine textual authority, and a fixed conception of femininity—which may seem benign enough in the passage above—will soon be used to justify the destruction of Lucy Westenra, who, having been successfully vamped by Dracula, requires a corrective penetration. To Arthur's anxious importunity "Tell me what I am to do," Van Helsing answers: "Take this stake in your left hand, ready to place the point over the heart, and the hammer in your right. Then when we begin our prayer for the dead—I shall read him; I have here the book, and the others shall follow— strike in God's name . . ." (259). Here four males (Van Helsing, Seward, Holmwood, and Quincey Morris) communally read a masculine text (Van Helsing's mangled English even permits Stoker the unidiomatic pronominalization of the genderless text: "I shall read him"),[27] in order to justify the fatal correction of Lucy's dangerous wandering, her insolent disregard for the sexual and semiotic constraint encoded in Van Helsing's exegesis of "God's women."

The process by which women are construed as signs determined by the interpretive imperatives of authorizing males had been brilliantly identified some fifty years before the publication of *Dracula* by John Stuart Mill in *The Subjection of Women*. "What is now called the nature of women," Mill writes, "is an extremely artificial thing—the result of forced repression in some directions, unnatural stimulation in others."[28] Mill's sentence, deftly identifying "the nature of women" as an "artificial" construct formed (and deformed) by "repression" and "unnatural stimulation," quietly unties the lacings that bind something called "woman" to something else called "nature." Mill further suggests that a correct reading of gender becomes almost impossible, since the natural difference between male and female is subject to cultural interpretation: ". . . I deny that anyone knows, or can know, the nature of the two sexes, as long as they have only been seen in their present relation to one another," Mill's agnosticism regarding "the nature of the sexes" suggests the societal and institutional quality of all definitions of the natural, definitions which ultimately conspire to produce "the imaginary and conventional character of women."[29] This last phrase, like the whole of Mill's essay, understands and criticizes the authoritarian nexus that arises when a deflected or transformed desire ("imaginary"), empowered by a gender-biased societal agreement ("conventional"), imposes itself upon a person in order to create a "character." "Character" of course functions in at least three senses: who and what one "is," the role one plays in society's supervening script, and the sign or letter that is intelligible only within the constraints of a larger sign system. Van Helsing's exegesis of "God's women" creates just such an imaginary and conventional character. Mina's body/character may indeed be feminine, but the signification it bears is written and interpreted solely by males. As Susan Hardy Aiken has written, such a symbolic system takes "for granted the role of women as passive objects or signs to be manipulated in the grammar of privileged male interchanges."[30]

Yet exactly the passivity of this object and the ease of this manipulation are at question in *Dracula*. Dracula, after all, kisses these women out of their passivity and so endangers the stability of Van Helsing's symbolic system. Both the prescriptive intention of Van Helsing's exegesis and the emphatic methodology (hypodermic needle, stake, surgeon's blade) he employs to insure the durability of his interpretation of gender suggest the potential unreliability of Mina as sign, an instability that provokes an anxiety we may call fear of the mediatrix. If, as Van Helsing admits, God's women provide the essential mediation ("the light can be here on earth") between the divine but distant patriarch and his earthy sons, the God's intention may be distorted by its potentially changeable vehicle. If woman-as-signifier wanders, then Van Helsing's whole cosmology, with its founding dualisms and supporting texts, collapses. In short, Van Helsing's interpretation of

Mina, because endangered by the proleptic fear that his mediatrix might destabilize and wander, necessarily imposes an *a priori* constraint upon the significative possibilities of the sign "Mina." Such an authorial gesture, intended to forestall the semiotic wandering that Dracula inspires, indirectly acknowledges woman's dangerous potential. Late in the text, while Dracula is vamping Mina, Van Helsing will admit, very uneasily, that "Madam Mina, our poor, dear Madam Mina is changing" (384). The potential for such a change demonstrates what Nina Auerbach has called this woman's "mysterious amalgam of imprisonment and power."[31]

Dracula's authorizing kiss, like that of a demonic Prince Charming, triggers the release of the latent power and excites in these women a sexuality so mobile, so aggressive, that it thoroughly disrupts Van Helsing's compartmental conception of gender. Kissed into a sudden sexuality,[32] Lucy grows "voluptuous" (a word used to describe her only during the vampiric process), her lips redden, and she kisses with a new interest. This sexualization of Lucy, metamorphosing woman's "sweetness" to "adamantine, heartless cruelty, and [her] purity to voluptuous wantonness" (252), terrifies her suitors because it entails a reversal or inversion of sexual identity; Lucy, now toothed like the Count, usurps the function of penetration that Van Helsing's moralized taxonomy of gender reserves for males. *Dracula*, in thus figuring the sexualization of woman as deformation, parallels exactly some of the more extreme medical uses of the idea of inversion. Late Victorian accounts of lesbianism, for instance, superscribed conventional gender norms upon sexual relationships to which those norms were anatomically irrelevant. Again the heterosexual norm proved paradigmatic. The female "husband" in such a relationship was understood to be dominant, appetitive, masculine, and "cogenitally inverted"; the female "wife" was understood to be quiescent, passive, only "latently" homosexual, and, as Havelock Ellis argued, unmotivated by genital desire.[33] Extreme deployment of the heterosexual paradigm approached the ridiculous, as George Chauncey explains:

> The early medical case histories of lesbians thus predictably paid enormous attention to their menstrual flow and the size of their sexual organs. Several doctors emphasized that their lesbian patients stopped menstruating at an early age, if they began at all, or had unusually difficult and irregular periods. They also inspected the woman's sexual organs, often claiming that inverts had unusually large clitorises, which they said the inverts used in sexual intercourse as a man would his penis.[34]

This rather pathetic hunt for the penis-in-absentia denotes a double anxiety: first, that the penis shall not be erased, and if it is erased, that it shall be reinscribed in a perverse simulacrum; and second, that all desire repeat, even under the duress of deformity, the heterosexual norm that the metaphor of inversion always assumes. Medical professionals had in fact no need to pursue this fantasized amazon of the clitoris, this "unnatural" penetrator, so vigorously, since Stoker, whose imagination was at least deft enough to displace that dangerous simulacrum to an isomorphic orifice, had by the 1890s already invented her. His sexualized women are men too.

Stoker emphasizes the monstrosity implicit in such abrogation of gender codes by inverting a favorite Victorian maternal function. His New Lady Vampires feed at first only on small children, working their way up, one assumes, a demonic pleasure thermometer until they may feed at last on full-blooded males. Lucy's dietary indiscretions evoke the deepest disgust from the Crew of Light:

> With a careless motion, she flung to the ground, callous as a devil, the child that up to now she had clutched strenuously to her breast, growling over it as a dog growls over a bone. The child gave a sharp cry, and lay there moaning. There was a cold-bloodedness in the act which wrung a groan from Arthur, when she advanced to him with outstretched arms and a wanton smile, he fell back and hid his face in his hands.
>
> She still advanced, however, and with a langorous, voluptuous grace, said:
> "Come to me Arthur. Leave those others and come to me. My arms are hungry for you. Come, and we can rest together. Come, my husband, come!" (253–254)

Stoker here gives us a *tableau mordant* of gender inversion: the child Lucy clutches "strenuously to her breast" is not being fed, but is being fed upon. Furthermore, by requiring that the child be discarded that the husband may be embraced, Stoker provides a little emblem of this novel's anxious protestation that appetite in a woman ("My arms are hungry for you") is a diabolic ("callous as a devil") inversion of natural order, and of the novel's fantastic but futile hope that maternity and sexuality be divorced.

The aggressive mobility with which Lucy flaunts the encasements of gender norms generates in the Crew of Light a terrific defensive activity, as these men race to reinscribe, with a series of pointed instruments, the line of demarcation which enables the definition of gender. To save Lucy from the mobilization of desire, Van Helsing and the Crew of Light counteract Dracula's subversive series of penetrations with a more conventional series of their own, that sequence of transfusions intended to provide Lucy with the "brave man's blood" which "is the best thing on earth when a woman is in trouble" (180). There are in fact four transfusions, which begin with Arthur, who as Lucy's accepted suitor has the right of first infusion, and include Lucy's other two suitors (Dr. Seward, Quincey Morris) and Van Helsing himself. One of the established observations of *Dracula* criticism is that these therapeutic penetrations represent displaced marital (and martial) penetrations; indeed, the text is emphatic about this substitution of medical for sexual penetration. After the first transfusion, Arthur feels as if he and Lucy "had been really married and that she was his wife in the sight of God" (209); and Van Helsing, after his donation, calls himself a "bigamist" and Lucy "this so sweet maid . . . a polyandrist" (211–212). These transfusions, in short, are sexual (blood substitutes for semen here)[35] and constitute, in Nina Auerbach's superb phrase, "the most convincing epithalamiums in the novel."[36]

These transfusions represent the text's first anxious reassertion of the conventionally masculine prerogative of penetration; as Van Helsing tells Arthur before the first transfusion, "You are a man and it is a man we want" (148). Countering the dangerous mobility excited by Dracula's kiss, Van Helsing's penetrations restore to Lucy both the stillness appropriate to his sense of her gender and "the regular breathing of healthy sleep," a necessary correction of the loud "stertorous" breathing, the animal snorting, that the Count inspires. This repetitive contest (penetration, withdrawal; penetration, infusion), itself an image of *Dracula's* ambivalent need to evoke and then to repudiate the fluid pleasures of vampiric appetite, continues to be waged upon Lucy's infinitely penetrable body until Van Helsing exhausts his store of "brave men," whose generous gifts of blood, however efficacious, fail finally to save Lucy from the mobilization of desire.

But even the loss of this much blood does not finally enervate a masculine energy as indefatigable as the Crew of Light's, especially when it stands in the service of a tradition of "good women whose lives and whose truths may make good lesson [*sic*] for the children that are to be" (222). In the name of those good women and future children (very much the same children whose throats Lucy is now penetrating), Van Helsing will repeat, with an added emphasis, his assertion that penetration is a masculine prerogative. His logic of corrective penetration demands an escalation, as the failure of the hypodermic needle necessitates the stake. A woman is better still than mobile, better dead than sexual:

> Arthur took the stake and the hammer, and when once his mind was set on action his hands never trembled nor even quivered. Van Helsing opened his missal and began to read, and Quincey and I followed as well as we could. Arthur placed the point over the heart, and as I looked I could see its dint in the white flesh. Then he struck with all his might.
>
> The Thing in the coffin writhed; and a hideous, blood-curdling screech came from the opened red lips. The body shook and quivered and twisted in wild contortions; the sharp white teeth clamped together till the lips were cut and the mouth was smeared with a crimson foam. But Arthur never faltered. He looked like the figure of Thor as his untrembling arm rose and fell, driving deeper and deeper the mercy-bearing stake, whilst the blood from the pierced heart welled and spurted up around it. His face was set, and high duty seemed to shine through it; the sight of it gave us courage, so that our voices seemed to ring through the little vault.
>
> And then the writhing and quivering of the body became less, and the teeth ceased to champ, and the face to quiver. Finally it lay still. The terrible task was over. (258–259)

Here is the novel's real—and the woman's only—climax, its most violent and misogynistic moment, displaced roughly to the middle of the book, so that the sexual threat may be repeated but its ultimate success denied: Dracula will not win Mina, second in his series of English seductions. The murderous phallicism of this passage clearly punishes Lucy for her transgression of Van Helsing's gender code, as she finally receives a penetration adequate to insure her future quiescence. Violence against the sexual woman here is intense, sensually imagined, ferocious in its detail. Note, for-instance, the terrible dimple, the "dint in the white flesh," that recalls Jonathan Harker's swoon at Castle Dracula ("I could feel . . . the hard dents of the two sharp teeth, just touching and pausing there") and anticipates the technicolor consummation of the next paragraph. That paragraph, masking murder as "high duty," completes Van Helsing's penetrative therapy by "driving deeper and deeper the mercy-bearing stake." One might question a mercy this destructive, this fatal, but Van Helsing's actions, always sanctified by the patriarchal textual tradition signified by "his missal," manage to "restore Lucy to us as a holy and not an unholy memory" (258). This enthusiastic correction of Lucy's monstrosity provides the Crew of Light with a double reassurance: it effectively exorcises the threat of a mobile and hungering feminine sexuality, and it counters the homo-eroticism latent in the vampiric threat by reinscribing (upon Lucy's chest) the line dividing the male who penetrates and the woman who receives. By disciplining Lucy and restoring each gender to its "proper" function, Van Helsing's pacification program compensates for the threat of gender indefinition implicit in the vampiric kiss.

The vigor and enormity of this penetration (Arthur driving the "round wooden stake," which is "some two and a half or three inches thick and about three feet long," resembles "the figure of Thor") do not bespeak merely Stoker's personal or idiosyncratic anxiety but suggest as well a whole culture's uncertainty about the fluidity of gender roles. Consider, for instance, the following passage from Ellis's contemporaneous *Studies in the Psychology of Sex*. Ellis, writing on "The Mechanism of Detumescence" (i.e., ejaculation), employs a figure that Stoker would have recognized as his own:

> Detumescence is normally linked to tumescence. Tumescence is the piling on of the fuel; detumescence is the leaping out of the devouring flame whence is lighted the torch of life to be handed on from generation to generation. The whole process is double yet single; it is exactly analogous to that by which a pile is driven into the earth by the raising and the letting go of a heavy weight which falls on the head of the pile. In tumescence the organism is slowly wound up and force accumulated; in the act of detumescence the accumulated force is let go and by its liberation the sperm-bearing instrument is driven home.[37]

Both Stoker and Ellis need to imagine so homely an occurrence as penile penetration as an event of mythic, or at least seismographic, proportions. Ellis's pile driver, representing the powerful "sperm-bearing instrument," may dwarf even Stoker's already outsized member, but both serve a similar function: they channel and finally "liberate" a tremendous "accumulated force" that itself represents a trans- or supra-natural intention. Ellis, employing a Darwinian principle of interpretation to explain that intention, reads woman's body (much as we have seen Van Helsing do) as a natural sign—or, perhaps better, as a sign of nature's overriding repro- ductive intention:

> There can be little doubt that, as one or two writers have already suggested, the hymen owes its development to the fact that its influence is on the side of effective fertilization. It is an obstacle to the impregnation of the young female by immature, aged, or feeble males. *The hymen is thus an anatomical expression of that admiration of force which marks the female in her choice of a mate.* So regarded, it is an interesting example of the intimate matter in which sexual selection is really based on natural selection.[38] (italics added)

Here, as evolutionary teleology supplants divine etiology and as Darwin's texts assume the primacy Van Helsing would reserve for God's, natural selection, not God's original intention, becomes the interpretive principle governing nature's text. As a sign or "anatomical expression" within that text, the hymen signifies a woman's presumably natural "admiration of force" and her invitation to "the sperm-bearing instrument." Woman's body, structurally hostile to "immature, aged, or feeble males," simply begs for "effective fertilization." Lucy's body, too, reassures the Crew of Light with an anatomical expression of her admiration of force. Once fatally staked, Lucy is restored to "the so sweet that was." Dr. Seward describes the change:

> There in the coffin lay no longer the foul Thing that we had so dreaded and grown to hate that the work of her destruction was yielded to the one best entitled to it, but Lucy as we had seen her in her life, with her face of unequalled sweetness and purity. . . . One and all we felt that the holy calm that lay like sunshine over the wasted face and form was only an earthly token and symbol of the calm that was to reign for ever. (259)

This post-penetrative peace[39] denotes not merely the final immobilization of Lucy's body, but also the corresponding stabilization of the dangerous signifier whose wandering had so threatened Van Helsing's gender code. Here a masculine in- terpretive community ("One and all we felt") reasserts the semiotic fixity that allows Lucy to function as the "earthly token and symbol" of eternal beatitude, of the heaven we can enter. We may say that this last penetration is doubly efficacious; in a single stroke both the sexual and the textual needs of the Crew of Light find a sufficient satisfaction.

Despite its placement in the middle of the text, this scene, which successfully pacifies Lucy and demonstrates so emphatically the efficacy of the technology Van Helsing employs to correct vampirism, corresponds formally to the scene of ex- pulsion, which usually signals the end of the gothic narrative. Here, of course, this scene signals not the end of the story but the continuation of it, since Dracula will now repeat his assault on another woman. Such displacement of the scene of expulsion requires explanation. Obviously this displacement subserves the text's anxiety about the direct representation of eroticism between males: Stoker simply could not represent so explicitly a violent phallic interchange between the Crew of Light and Dracula. In a by now familiar heterosexual mediation, Lucy receives the phallic correction that Dracula deserves. Indeed, the actual expulsion of the Count at novel's end is a disappointing anticlimax. Two rather perfunctory knife strokes suffice to dispatch him, as *Dracula* simply forgets the elaborate ritual of correction that vampirism previously required. And the displacement of this scene performs at least two other functions: first, by establishing early the ultimate efficacy of Van Helsing's corrective technology, it reassures everyone—Stoker, his characters, the reader—that vampirism may indeed be vanquished, that its sexual threat, however powerful and intriguing, may be expelled; and second, in doing so, in establishing this reassurance, it permits the text to prolong and repeat its flirtation with vampirism, its ambivalent petition of that sexual threat. In short, the displacement of the scene of expulsion provides a heterosexual locale for Van Helsing's demonstration of compensatory phallicism, while it also extends the duration of the text's ambivalent play.

This extension of the text's flirtation with monstrosity, during which Mina is threatened by but not finally seduced into vampirism, includes the novel's only explicit scene of vampiric seduction. Important enough to be twice presented, first by Seward as spectator and then by Mina as participant, the scene occurs in the Harker bedroom, where Dracula seduces Mina while "on the bed lay Jonathan Harker, his face flushed and breathing heavily as if in a stupor." The Crew of Light bursts into the room; the voice is Dr. Seward's:

> With his left hand he held both Mrs. Harker's hands, keeping them away with her arms at full tension; his right hand gripped her by the back of the neck, forcing her face down on his bosom. Her white nightdress was smeared with blood, and a thin stream trickled down the man's bare breast, which was shown by his torn-open dress. The attitude of the two had a terrible resemblance to a child forcing a kitten's nose into a saucer of milk to compel it to drink. (336)

In this initiation scene Dracula compels Mina into the pleasure of vampiric appetite and introduces her to a world where gender distinctions collapse, where male and female bodily fluids intermingle terribly. For Mina's drinking is double here, both a "symbolic act of enforced fellation"[40] and a lurid nursing. That this is a scene of enforced fellation is made even clearer by Mina's own description of the scene a few pages later; she adds the graphic detail of the "spurt":

> With that he pulled open his shirt, and with his long sharp nails opened a vein in his breast. When the blood began to spurt out, he took my hands in one of his, holding them tight, and with the other seized my neck and pressed

my mouth to the wound, so that I must either suffocate or swallow some of the—Oh, my God, my God! What have I done? (343)

That "Oh, my God, my God!" is deftly placed: Mina's verbal ejaculation supplants the Count's liquid one, leaving the fluid unnamed and encouraging us to voice the substitution that the text implies—this blood is semen too. But this scene of fellation is thoroughly displaced. We are at the Count's breast, encouraged once again to substitute white for red, às blood becomes milk: "the attitude of the two had a terrible resemblance to a child forcing a kitten's nose into a saucer of milk." Such fluidity of substitution and displacement entails a confusion of Dracula's sexual identity, or an interfusion of masculine and feminine functions, as Dracula here becomes a lurid mother offering not a breast but an open and bleeding wound. But if the Count's sexuality is double, then the open wound may be yet another displacement (the reader of *Dracula* must be as mobile as the Count himself). We are back in the genital region, this time a woman's, and we have the suggestion of a bleeding vagina. The image of red and voluptuous lips, with their slow trickle of blood, has, of course, always harbored this potential.

We may read this scene, in which anatomical displacements and the confluence of blood, milk, and semen forcefully erase the demarcation separating the masculine and the feminine, as *Dracula*'s most explicit representation of the anxieties excited by the vampiric kiss. Here *Dracula* defines most clearly vampirism's threat of gender indefinition. Significantly, this scene is postponed until late in the text. Indeed, this is Dracula's last great moment, his final demonstration of dangerous potency; after this, he will vamp no one. The novel, having presented most explicitly its deepest anxiety, its fear of gender dissolution, now moves mechanically to repudiate that fear. After a hundred rather tedious pages of pursuit and flight, *Dracula* perfunctorily expels the Count. The world of "natural" gender relations is happily restored, or at least seems to be.

A Final Dissolution

If my last sentence ends with an equivocation, it is because *Dracula* does so as well; the reader should leave this novel with a troubled sense of the difference between the forces of darkness and the forces of light. Of course the plot of *Dracula*, by granting ultimate victory to Van Helsing and a dusty death to the Count, emphatically ratifies the simplistic opposition of competing conceptions of force and desire, but even a brief reflection upon the details of the war of penetrations complicates this comforting schema. A perverse mirroring occurs, as puncture for puncture the Doctor equals the Count. Van Helsing's doubled penetrations, first the morphine injection that immobilizes the woman and then the infusion of masculine fluid, repeat Dracula's spatially doubled penetrations of Lucy's neck. And that morphine injection, which subdues the woman and improves her receptivity, curiously imitates the Count's strange hypnotic power; both men prefer to immobilize a woman before risking a penetration.[41] Moreover, each penetration announces through its displacement this same sense of danger. Dracula enters at the neck, Van Helsing at the limb; each evades available orifices and refuses to submit to the dangers of vaginal contact. The shared displacement is telling: to make your own holes is an ultimate arrogance, an assertion of penetrative prowess that nonetheless acknowledges, in the flight of its evasion, the threatening power imagined to inhabit woman's available openings. Woman's body readily accommodates masculine fear and desire, whether directly libidinal or culturally refined. We may say that Van Helsing and his tradition have polished teeth into hypodermic needles, a cultural refinement that masks violations as healing. Van Helsing himself, calling his medical instruments "the ghastly paraphernalia of our beneficial trade," employs an adjectival oxymoron (ghastly/beneficial) that itself glosses the troubled relationship between paternalism and violence (146). The medical profession licenses the power to penetrate, devises a delicate instrumentation, and defines canons of procedure, while the religious tradition, with its insistent idealization of women, encodes a restriction on the mobility of desire (who penetrates whom) and then licenses a tremendous punishment for the violation of the code.

But it is all penetrative energy, whether re-fanged or refined, and it is all libidinal; the two strategies of penetration are but different articulations of the same primitive force. *Dracula* certainly problematizes, if it does not quite erase, the line of separation signifying a meaningful difference between Van Helsing and the Count. In other words, the text itself, in its imagistic identification of Dracula and the Crew of Light, in its ambivalent propensity to subvert its own fundamental differences, sympathizes with and finally domesticates vampiric desire; the uncanny, as Freud brilliantly observed, always comes home. Such textual irony, composed of simultaneous but contrary impulses to establish and subvert the fundamental differences between violence and culture, between desire and its sublimations, recalls Freud's late speculations on the troubled relationship between the id and the superego (or ego ideal). In the two brief passages below, taken from his late work *The Ego and the Id*, Freud complicates the differentiation between the id and its unexpected effluent, the superego:

> There are two paths by which the contents of the id can penetrate into the ego. The one is direct, the other leads by way of the ego ideal.

And:

> From the point of view of instinctual control, of morality, it may be said of the id that it is totally non-moral, of the ego that it strives to be moral, and of the super-ego that it can be supermoral and then becomes as cruel as only the id can be.[42]

It is so easy to remember the id as a rising energy and the superego as a suppressive one, that we forget Freud's subtler argument. These passages, eschewing as too facile the simple opposition of the id and superego, suggest instead that the id and the superego are variant articulations of the same primitive energy. We are already familiar with the "two paths by which the contents of the id penetrate the ego." "The one is direct," as Dracula's penetrations are direct and unembarrassed, and the other, leading "by way of the ego ideal," recalls Van Helsing's way of repression and sublimation. In providing an indirect path for the "contents of the id" and in being "as cruel as only the id can be," the superego may be said to be, in the words of Leo Bersani, "the id which has become its own mirror."[43] This mutual reflectivity of the id and superego, of course, constitutes one of vampirism's most disturbing features, as Jonathan Harker, standing before his shaving glass, learns early in the novel: "This time there could be no error, for the man was close to me, and I could see him over my shoulder. But there was no reflection of him in the mirror! The whole room behind me was displayed: but there was no sign of a man in it, except myself" (37). The meaning of this little visual allegory should be clear enough: Dracula need cast no reflection because his presence, already established in Harker's image, would be simply redundant; the monster, indeed, is no one "except myself." A dangerous sameness waits behind difference; tooth, stake, and hypodermic needle, it would seem, all share a point.

This blending or interfusion of fundamental differences would seem, in one respect at least, to contradict the progress of my argument. We have, after all, established that the Crew of Light's penetrative strategy, subserving Van Helsing's ideology of gender and his heterosexual account of desire, counters just such interfusions with emphatic inscriptions of sexual difference. Nonetheless, this penetrative strategy, despite its purposive heterosexuality, quietly erases its own fundamental differences, its own explicit assumptions of gender and desire. It would seem at first that desire for connection among males is both expressed in and constrained by a traditional articulation of such fraternal affection, as represented in this text's blaring theme of heroic or chivalric male bonding. The obvious male bonding in *Dracula* is precipitated by action—a good fight, a proud ethic, a great victory. Dedicated to a falsely exalted conception of woman, men combine fraternally to fulfill the collective "high duty" that motivates their "great quest" (261). Van Helsing, always the ungrammatical exegete, provides the apt analogy: "Thus we are ministers of God's own wish. . . . He have allowed us to redeem one soul already, and we go out as the old knights of the Cross to redeem more" (381). Van Helsing's chivalric analogy establishes this fraternity within an impeccable lineage signifying both moral rectitude and adherence to the limitation upon desire that this tradition encodes and enforces.

Yet beneath this screen or mask of authorized fraternity a more libidinal bonding occurs as male fluids find a protected pooling place in the body of a woman. We return, for a last time, to those serial transfusions which, while they pretend to serve and protect "good women," actually enable the otherwise inconceivable interfusion of the blood that is semen too. Here displacement (a woman's body) and sublimation (these are medical penetrations) permit the unpermitted, just as in gang rape men share their semen in a location displaced sufficiently to divert the anxiety excited by a more direct union. Repeating its subversive suggestion that the refined moral conceptions of Van Helsing's Crew of Light express obliquely an excursive libidinal energy, an energy much like the Count's, *Dracula* again employs an apparently rigorous heterosexuality to represent anxious desire for a less conventional communion. The parallel here to Dracula's taunt ("Your girls that you all love are mine already; and through them you . . . shall be mine") is inescapable; in each case Lucy, the woman in the middle, connects libidinous males. Here, as in the Victorian metaphor of sexual inversion, an interposed difference—an image of manipulable femininity—mediates and deflects an otherwise unacceptable appetite for sameness. Men touching women touch each other, and desire discovers itself to be more fluid than the Crew of Light would consciously allow.

Indeed, so insistent is this text to establish this pattern of heterosexual mediation that it repeats the pattern on its final page. Jonathan Harker, writing in a postscript that compensates clearly for his assumption at Castle Dracula of a "feminine" passivity, announces the text's last efficacious penetration:

> Seven years ago, we all went through the flames; and the happiness of some of us since then is, we think, well worth the pain we endured. It is an added joy to Mina and to me that our boy's birthday is the same day as that on which Quincey Morris died. His mother holds, I know, the secret belief that some of our brave friend's spirit has passed into him. His bundle of names links all our little band of men together; but we call him Quincey. (449)

As offspring of Jonathan and Mina Harker, Little Quincey, whose introduction so late in the narrative insures his emblematic function, seemingly represents the restoration of "natural" order and especially the rectification of conventional gender roles. His official genesis is, obviously enough, heterosexual, but Stoker's prose quietly suggests an alternative paternity: "His bundle of names links all our little band of men together." This is the fantasy child of those sexualized transfusions, son of an illicit and nearly invisible homosexual union. This suggestion, reinforced by the preceding pun of "spirit," constitutes this text's last and subtlest articulation of its "secret belief" that "a brave man's blood" may metamorphose into "our brave friend's spirit." But the real curiosity here is the novel's last-minute displacement, its substitution of Mina, who ultimately refused sexualization by Dracula, for Lucy, who was sexualized, vigorously penetrated, and consequently destroyed. We may say that Little Quincey was luridly conceived in the veins of Lucy Westenra and then deftly relocated to the purer body of Mina Harker. Here, in the last of its many displacements, *Dracula* insists, first, that successful filiation implies the expulsion of all "monstrous" desire in women and, second, that all desire, however mobile and omnivorous it may secretly be, must subject itself to the heterosexual configuration that alone defined the Victorian sense of the normal. In this regard, Stoker's fable, however hyperbolic its anxieties, represents his age. As we have seen, even polemicists of same sex eroticism like Symonds and Ellis could not imagine such desire without repeating within their metaphor of sexual inversion the basic structure of the heterosexual paradigm. Victorian culture's anxiety about desire's potential indifference to the prescriptions of gender produces everywhere a predictable repetition and a predictable displacement: the heterosexual norm repeats itself in a mediating image of femininity—the Count's vampiric daughters, Ulrichs's and Symonds's *anima muliebris*, Lucy Westenra's penetrable body—that displaces a more direct communion among males. Desire, despite its propensity to wander, stays home and retains an essentially heterosexual and familial definition. The result in *Dracula* is a child whose conception is curiously immaculate, yet disturbingly lurid: child of his fathers' violations. Little Quincey, fulfilling Van Helsing's prophecy of "the children that are to be," may be the text's emblem of a restored natural order, but his paternity has its unofficial aspect too. He is the unacknowledged son of the Crew of Light's displaced homoerotic union, and his name, linking the "little band of men together," quietly remembers that secret genesis.

Notes

1. Joseph Sheridan Le Fanu, *Carmilla*, in *The Best Ghost Stories of J. S. Le Fanu* (New York: Dover, 1964), p. 337; this novella of lesbian vampirism, which appeared first in Le Fanu's *In A Glass Darkly* (1872), predates *Dracula* by twenty-five years.

2. Franco Moretti, *Signs Taken for Wonders* (Verso, 1983), p. 100.

3. Bram Stoker, *Dracula* (New York, 1979), p. 51. All further references to *Dracula* appear within the essay in parentheses.

4. The paradigmatic instance of this triple rhythm is Mary Shelley's *Frankenstein*, a text that creates—bit by bit, and stitch by stitch—its resident demon, then equips that demon with a powerful Miltonic voice with which to petition both its creator and the novel's readers, and finally drives its monster to polar isolation and suicide. Stevenson's *Dr. Jekyll and Mr. Hyde* repeats the pattern: Henry Jekyll's chemical invitation to Hyde corresponds to the gesture of admission; the serial alternation of contrary personalities constitutes the ambivalent play of the prolonged middle; and Jekyll's suicide, which expels both the monster and himself, corresponds to the gesture of expulsion.

5. Readers of Tzvetan Todorov's *The Fantastic* (Ithaca: Cornell University Press, 1975) will recognize that my argument about the gothic text's extended middle derives in part from his idea that the essential condition of fantastic fiction is a duration characterized by readerly suspension of certainty.

6. John Ruskin, *Sesame and Lilies* (New York, 1974), pp. 59–60.

7. This group of crusaders includes Van Helsing himself, Dr. John Seward, Arthur Holmwood, Quincey Morris, and later Jonathan Harker; the title Crew of Light is mine, but I have taken my cue from Stoker: Lucy, *lux*, light.

8. Renfield, whose "zoophagy" precedes Dracula's arrival in England and who is never vamped by Dracula, is no exception to this rule.

9. The complication of gender roles in *Dracula* has of course been recognized in the criticism. See, for instance, Stephanie Demetrakopoulos, "Feminism, Sex Role Exchanges,

and Other Subliminal Fantasies in Bram Stoker's *Dracula*," *Frontiers*, 2 (1977), pp. 104–113. Demetrakopoulos writes: "These two figures I have traced so far—the male as passive rape victim and also as violator-brutalizer—reflect the polarized sex roles and the excessive needs this polarizing engendered in Victorian culture. Goldfarb recounts the brothels that catered to masochists, sadists, and homosexuals. The latter aspect of sexuality obviously did not interest Stoker. . . ." I agree with the first sentence here and, as this essay should make clear, emphatically disagree with the last.

10. John Addington Symonds, *A Problem in Modern Ethics* (London, 1906), p. 74.

11. The semantic imprecision of the word "sodomy" is best explained by John Boswell, *Christianity, Social Tolerance, and Homosexuality* (Chicago: University of Chicago Press, 1980), pp. 91–116. "Sodomy," notes Boswell, "has connoted in various times and various places everything from ordinary heterosexual intercourse in an atypical position to oral sexual contact with animals" (93).

12. This is the traditional Christian circumlocution by which sodomy was both named and unnamed, both specified in speech and specified as unspeakable. It is the phrase, according to Jeffrey Weeks, "with which Sir Robert Peel forbore to mention sodomy in Parliament," quoted in Weeks, *Coming Out* (London: Quartet Books, 1977), p. 14.

13. Michel Foucault, *The History of Sexuality* (New York, 1980). My argument agrees with Foucault's assertion that "the techniques of power exercised over sex have not obeyed a principle of rigorous selection, but rather one of dissemination and implantation of polymorphous sexualities" (12). Presumably members of the same gender have been copulating together for uncounted centuries, but the invert and homosexual were not invented until the nineteenth century.

14. I cite this phrase, spoken by Mr. Justice Wills to Oscar Wilde immediately after the latter's conviction under the Labouchère Amendment to the Criminal Law Amendment Act of 1885, as an oblique reference to the orifice that so threatened the homophobic Victorian imagination; that Wilde was never accused of anal intercourse (only oral copulation and mutual masturbation were charged against him) seems to me to confirm, rather than to undermine this interpretation of the phrase. Wills's entire sentence reads: "And that you, Wilde, have been the centre of a circle of extensive corruption of the most hideous kind among young men, it is equally impossible to doubt"; quoted in H. Montgomery Hyde, *The Trials of Oscar Wilde* (New York, 1962), p. 272. The Labouchère Amendment, sometimes called the blackmailer's charter, punished "any act of gross indecency" between males, whether in public or private, with two years' imprisonment and hard labor. Symonds, Ellis, and Carpenter argued strenuously for the repeal of this law.

15. Symonds, *A Problem in Modern Ethics*, p. 3.

16. Symonds, *A Problem in Modern Ethics*, p. 84. To my knowledge, the earliest English instance of "inversion" in this specific sense is the phrase "Inverted Sexual Proclivity" from *The Journal of Mental Science* (October, 1871), where it is used anonymously to translate Carl Westphal's neologism *die conträre Sexualempfindung*, the term that would dominate German discourse on same gender eroticism. I have not yet been able to date precisely Symonds's first use of "inversion."

17. Havelock Ellis, *Sexual Inversion*, volume 2 of *Studies in the Psychology of Sex* (Philadelphia: F. A. Davis, 1906), p. 1.

18. This and the two subsequent quotations are from Symonds's *A Problem in Modern Ethics*, pp. 86, 90, and 85 respectively.

19. Symonds's letter to Carpenter, December 29, 1893, in *The Letters of John Addington Symonds*, volume 3, eds. H. M. Shueller and R. L. Peters (Detroit, 1969), p. 799; also quoted in Weeks, *Coming Out*, p. 54.

20. Ellis, *Sexual Inversion*, p. 182.

21. Symonds in *Letters*, volume 2, p. 169.

22. Ellis, quoted in Weeks, *Coming Out*, p. 92.

23. George Chauncey, Jr., "From Sexual Inversion to Homosexuality: Medicine and the Changing Conceptualization of Female Deviance," *Salmagundi*, 58–59 (1982), pp. 114–146.

24. This bifurcation of woman is one of the text's most evident features, as critics of *Dracula* have been quick to notice. See Phyllis Roth, "Suddenly Sexual Women in Bram Stoker's *Dracula*," *Literature and Psychology*, 27 (1977), p. 117, and her full-length study *Bram Stoker* (Boston, 1982). Roth, in an argument that emphasizes the pre-Oedipal element in *Dracula*, makes a similar point: ". . . one recognizes that Lucy and Mina are essentially the same figure: the Mother. Dracula is, in fact, the same story told twice with different outcomes." Perhaps the most extensive thematic analysis of this split in Stoker's representation of women is Carol A. Senf's "*Dracula*: Stoker's Response to the New Woman," *Victorian Studies*, 26 (1982), pp. 33–39, which sees this split as Stoker's "ambivalent reaction to a topical phenomenon—the New Woman."

25. Maurice Richardson, "The Psychoanalysis of Ghost Stories," *The Twentieth Century*, 166 (1959), pp. 427–428.

26. On this point see Demetrakopoulos, "Feminism, Sex Role Exchanges," p. 104.

27. In this instance at least Van Helsing has an excuse for his ungrammatical usage; in Dutch, Van Helsing's native tongue, the noun *bijbel* (Bible) is masculine.

28. John Stuart Mill, *The Subjection of Women* in *Essays on Sex Equality*, ed. Alice Rossi (Chicago: University of Chicago Press, 1970), p. 148.

29. Mill, *The Subjection of Women*, p. 187.

30. Susan Hardy Aiken, "Scripture and Poetic Discourse in *The Subjection of Women*," *PMLA*, 98 (1983), p. 354.

31. Nina Auerbach, *Woman and the Demon: The Life of a Victorian Myth* (Cambridge: Harvard University Press, 1982), p. 11.

32. Roth, "Suddenly Sexual Women," p. 116.

33. An adequate analysis of the ideological and political implications of the terminological shift from "inversion" to "homosexuality" is simply beyond the scope of this essay, and the problem is further complicated by a certain imprecision or fluidity in the employment by these writers of an already unstable terminology. Ellis used the word "homosexuality" under protest and Carpenter, citing the evident bastardy of any term compounded of one Greek and one Latin root, preferred the word "homogenic." However, a provisional if oversimplified discrimination between "inversion" and "homosexuality" may be useful: "true" sexual inversion, Ellis argued, consists in "sexual instinct turned by *inborn constitutional abnormality* toward persons of the same sex" (*Sexual Inversion*, p. 1; italics added), whereas homosexuality may refer to same sex eroticism generated by spurious, circumstantial (*faute de mieux*), or intentionally perverse causality. The pivotal issue here is will or choice: the "true" invert, whose "abnormality" is biologically determined and therefore "natural," does not choose his/her desire but is instead chosen by it; the latent or spurious homosexual, on the other hand, does indeed choose a sexual object of the same gender. Such a taxonomic distinction (or, perhaps better, confusion) represents a polemical and political compromise that allows, potentially at least, for the medicalization of congenital inversion and the criminalization of willful homosexuality. I repeat the caution that my description here entails a necessary oversimplification of a terminological muddle. For a more complete and particular

analysis see Chauncey, "From Sexual Inversion," pp. 114–146; for the applicability of such a taxonomy to lesbian relationships see Ellis, *Sexual Inversion*, pp. 131–141.

34. Chauncey, "From Sexual Inversion," p. 132.

35. The symbolic interchangeability of blood and semen in vampirism was identified as early as 1931 by Ernest Jones in *On the Nightmare* (London, 1931), p. 119: "in the unconscious mind blood is commonly an equivalent for semen. . . ."

36. Auerbach, *Woman and the Demon*, p. 22.

37. Havelock Ellis, *Erotic Symbolism*, volume 5 of *Studies in the Psychology of Sex*, p. 142.

38. Ellis, *Erotic Symbolism*, p. 140.

39. Roth correctly reads Lucy's countenance at this moment as "a thank you note" for the corrective penetration; "Suddenly Sexual Women," p. 116.

40. C. F. Bentley, "The Monster in the Bedroom: Sexual Symbolism in Bram Stoker's *Dracula*," *Literature and Psychology*, 22 (1972), p. 30.

41. Stoker's configuration of hypnotism and anaesthesia is not idiosyncratic. Ellis, for instance, writing at exactly this time, conjoins hypnosis and anaesthesia as almost identical phenomena and subsumes them under a single taxonomic category: "We may use the term 'hypnotic phenomena' as a convenient expression to include not merely the condition of artificially-produced sleep, or hypnotism in the narrow sense of the term, but all those groups of psychic phenomena which are characterized by a decreased control of the higher nervous centres, and increased activity of the lower centres." The quality that determines membership in this "convenient" taxonomy is, to put matters baldly, a pelvis pumped up by the "increased activity of the lower centres." Ellis, in an earlier footnote, explains the antithetical relationship between the "higher" and "lower" centers: "The persons best adapted to propagate the race are those with the large pelves, and as the pelvis is the seat of the great centres of sexual emotion the development of the pelvis and its nervous and vascular supply involves the greater heightening of the sexual emotions. At the same time the greater activity of the cerebral centres enables them to subordinate and utilise to their own ends the increasingly active sexual emotions, so that reproduction is checked and the balance to some extent restored." The pelvic superiority of women, necessitated by an evolutionary imperative (better babies with bigger heads require broader pelves), implies a corresponding danger—an engorged and hypersensitive sexuality that must be actively "checked" by the "activity of the cerebral centres" so that "balance" may be "to some extent restored." Hypnotism and anaesthesia threaten exactly this delicate balance, and especially so in women because "the lower centres in women are more rebellious to control than those of men, and more readily brought into action." Anaesthesiology, it would seem, is not without its attendant dangers: "Thus chloroform, ether, nitrous oxide, cocaine, and possibly other anaesthetics, possess the property of exciting the sexual emotions. Women are especially liable to these erotic hallucinations during anaesthesia, and it has sometimes been almost impossible to convince them that their subjective sensations have had no objective cause. Those who have to administer anaesthetics are well aware of the risks they may thus incur." Ellis's besieged physician, like Stoker's master monster and his monster master, stands here as a male whose empowerment anxiously reflects a prior endangerment. What if this woman's lower centers should take the opportunity—to use another of Ellis's phrases—"of indulging in an orgy"? Dracula's kiss, Van Helsing's needle and stake, and Ellis's "higher centres" all seek to modify, constrain, and control the articulation of feminine desire. (But, it might be counter-argued, Dracula comes precisely to excite such an orgy, not to constrain one. Yes, but with an important qualification: Dracula's kiss, because it authorizes only repetitions of itself, clearly articulates the destiny of feminine desire: Lucy will only do

what Dracula has done before.) Havelock Ellis, *Man and Woman* (New York: Scribner, 1904), pp. 299, 73, 316, and 313 respectively. I have used the fourth edition; the first edition appeared in England in 1895.

42.   Sigmund Freud, *The Ego and the Id* (New York: Norton, 1960), pp. 44–45.

43.   Leo Bersani, *Baudelaire and Freud* (Berkeley: University of California Press, 1977), p. 92.

12

The Beast in the Closet: James and the Writing of Homosexual Panic

Eve Kosofsky Sedgwick

I. Historicizing Male Homosexual Panic

At the age of twenty-five, D.H. Lawrence was excited about the work of James M. Barrie. He felt it helped him understand himself and explain himself. "*Do* read Barrie's *Sentimental Tommy* and *Tommy and Grizel*," he wrote Jessie Chambers. "They'll help you understand how it is with me. I'm in exactly the same predicament."[1]

Fourteen years later, though, Lawrence placed Barrie among a group of writers whom he considered appropriate objects of authorial violence. "What's the good of being hopeless, so long as one has a hob-nailed boot to kick [them] with? *Down with the Poor in Spirit!* A war! But the Subtlest, most intimate warfare. Smashing the face of what one *knows* is rotten."[2]

It was not only in the intimate warfares of one writer that the years 1910 to 1924 marked changes. But Lawrence's lurch toward a brutal, virilizing disavowal of his early identification with Barrie's sexually irresolute characters reflects two rather different trajectories: first, of course, changes in the historical and intellectual context within which British literature could be read; but second, a hatingly crystallized literalization, as *between* men, of what had been in Barrie's influential novels portrayed as exactly "the Subtlest, most intimate warfare" *within* a man. Barrie's novel sequence was also interested, as Lawrence was not, in the mutilating effects of this masculine civil war on women.

I argue that the Barrie to whom Lawrence reacted with such volatility and finally with such virulence was writing out of a post-Romantic tradition of fictional meditations on the subject specifically of male homosexual panic. The writers whose work I adduce here include—besides Barrie—Thackeray, George Du Maurier, and Henry James: an odd mix of big and little names. The cheapnesses and compromises of this tradition will, however, turn out to be as important as its freshest angularities, since one of the functions of a tradition *is* to create a path-of-least-resistance (or at the last resort, a pathology-of-least-resistance) for the expression of previously inchoate material.

An additional problem: This tradition was an infusing rather than a generically distinct one in British letters, and it is thus difficult to discriminate it with confidence or to circumscribe it within the larger stream of nineteenth-century fictional writing. But the tradition is worth tracing partly on that very account, as well: the difficult questions of generic and thematic embodiment resonate so piercingly with another set of difficult questions, those precisely of sexual definition and embodiment. The supposed oppositions that characteristically structure this writing—the respectable "versus" the bohemian, the cynical "versus" the sentimental, the provincial "versus" the cosmopolitan, the anesthetized "versus" the sexual—seem to be, among other things, recastings and explorations of another pseudo-opposition that had come by the middle of the nineteenth century to be cripplingly knotted into the guts of British men and, through them, into the lives of women. The name of this pseudo-opposition, when it came to have a name, was homosexual "versus" heterosexual.

Recent sexual historiography by, for instance, Alan Bray in his *Homosexuality in Renaissance England* suggests that until about the time of the Restoration, homophobia in England, while intense, was for the most part highly theologized, was anathematic in tone and structure, and had little cognitive bite as a way for people to perceive and experience their own and their neighbors' actual activities.[3] Homosexuality "was not conceived as part of the created order at all," Bray writes, but as "part of its dissolution. And as such it was not a sexuality in its own right, but existed as a potential for confusion and disorder in one undivided sexuality."[4] If sodomy was the most characteristic expression of anti-nature or the anti-Christ itself, it was nevertheless, or perhaps for that very reason, not an explanation that sprang easily to mind for those sounds from the bed next to one's own—or even for the pleasures of one's own bed. Before the end of the eighteenth century, however, Bray shows, with the beginnings of a crystallized male homosexual role and male homosexual culture, a much sharper-eyed and acutely psychologized secular homophobia was current.

I have argued (in *Between Men: English Literature and Male Homosocial Desire*) that this development was important not only for the persecutory regulation of a nascent minority population of distinctly homosexual men but also for the regulation of the male homosocial bonds that structure *all* culture—at any rate, all public or heterosexual culture.[5] This argument follows Lévi-Strauss in defining culture itself, like marriage, in terms of a "total relationship of exchange . . . not established between a man and a woman, but between two groups of men, [in which] the woman figures only as one of the objects in the exchange, not as one of the partners";[6] or follows Heidi Hartmann in defining patriarchy itself as "*relations between men,* which have a material base, and which, though hierarchical, establish or create interdependence and solidarity among men that enable them to dominate women."[7] To this extent, it makes sense that a newly active concept—a secular, psychologized homophobia—that seemed to offer a new proscriptive or descriptive purchase on the whole continuum of male homosocial bonds, would be a pivotal and embattled concept indeed.

Bray describes the earliest legal persecutions of the post-Restoration gay male subculture, centered in gathering places called "molly houses," as being random and, in his word, "pogrom"-like in structure.[8] I would emphasize the specifically terroristic or exemplary workings of this structure: because a given homosexual man could not know whether or not to expect to be an object of legal violence, the legal enforcement had a disproportionately wide effect. At the same time, however, an opening was made for a subtler strategy in response, a kind of ideological pincers-movement that would extend manyfold the impact of this theatrical enforcement. As *Between Men* argues, under this strategy (or, perhaps better put, in this space of strategic potential),

> not only must homosexual men be unable to ascertain whether they are to be the objects of "random" homophobic violence, but no man must be able to ascertain that he is not (that his bonds are not) homosexual. In this way, a relatively small exertion of physical and legal compulsion potentially rules great reaches of behavior and filiation.
>
> So-called "homosexual panic" is the most private, psychologized form in which many . . . western men experience their vulnerability to the social pressure of homophobic blackmail.[9]

Thus, at least since the eighteenth century in England and America, the continuum of male homosocial bonds has been brutally structured by a secularized and psychologized homophobia, which has excluded certain shiftingly and more or less arbitrarily defined segments of the continuum from participating in the overarching male entitlement—in the complex web of male power over the production, reproduction, and exchange of goods, persons, and meanings. I argue that the historically shifting, and precisely the arbitrary and self-contradictory, nature of the way *homosexuality* (along with its predecessor terms) has been defined in relation to the rest of the male homosocial spectrum has been an exceedingly potent and embattled locus of power over the entire range of male bonds, and perhaps especially over those that define themselves, not *as* homosexual, but *as against* the homosexual. Because the paths of male entitlement, especially in the nineteenth century, required certain intense male bonds that were not readily distinguishable from the most reprobated bonds, an endemic and ineradicable state of what I am calling male homosexual panic became the normal condition of the male heterosexual entitlement.

Some consequences and corollaries of this approach to male relationships should perhaps be made more explicit. To begin with, as I suggested earlier, the approach is not founded on an essential differentiation between "basically homosexual" and "basically heterosexual" men, aside from the historically small group of consciously and self-acceptingly homosexual men, who are no longer susceptible to homosexual panic as I define it here. If such compulsory relationships as male friendship, mentorship, admiring identification, bureaucratic subordination, and heterosexual rivalry all involve forms of investment that force men into the arbitrarily mapped, self-contradictory, and anathema-riddled quicksands of the middle distance of male homosocial desire, then it appears that men enter into adult masculine entitlement only through acceding to the permanent threat that the small space they have cleared for themselves on this terrain may always, just as arbitrarily and with just as much justification, be punitively and retroactively foreclosed.

The result of men's accession to this double bind is, first, the acute *manipulability*, through the fear of one's own "homosexuality," of acculturated men; and second, a reservoir of potential for *violence* caused by the self-ignorance that this regime constitutively enforces. The historical emphasis on homophobic enforcement in the armed services in, for instance, England and the United States supports this analysis. In these institutions, where both men's manipulability and their potential for violence are at the highest possible premium, the *pre*scription of the most intimate male bonding and the *pro*scription of (the remarkably cognate) "homosexuality" are both stronger than in civilian society—are, in fact, close to absolute.

My specification of widespread, endemic male homosexual panic as a post-Romantic phenomenon rather than as coeval with the beginnings, under homophobic pressure, of a distinctive male homosexual culture a century or so earlier, has to do with (what I read as) the centrality of the paranoid Gothic[10] as the literary genre in which homophobia found its most apt and ramified embodiment. Homophobia found in the paranoid Gothic a genre of its own, not because the genre provided a platform for expounding an already-formed homophobic ideology—of course, it did no such thing—but through a more active, polylogic engagement of "private" with "public" discourses, as in the wildly dichotomous play around solipsism and intersubjectivity of a male paranoid plot like that of *Frankenstein*. The transmutability of the intrapsychic with the intersubjective in these plots where one man's mind could be read by that of the feared and desired other; the urgency and violence with which these plots reformed large, straggly, economically miscellaneous families such as the Frankensteins in the ideologically hypostatized image of the tight Oedipal family; and then the extra efflorescence of violence with which the remaining female term in these triangular families was elided, leaving, as in *Frankenstein*, a residue of two potent male figures locked in an epistemologically indissoluble clench of will and desire—through these means, the paranoid Gothic powerfully signified, at the very moment of crystallization of the modern, capitalism-marked Oedipal family, the inextricability from that formation of a strangling double bind in male homosocial constitution. Put another way, the usefulness of Freud's formulation, in the case of Dr. Schreber, that paranoia in men results from the repression of their homosexual desire,[11] has nothing to do with a classification of the paranoid Gothic in terms of "latent" or "overt" "homosexual" "types," but everything to do with the foregrounding, under the specific, foundational historic conditions of the early Gothic, of intense male homosocial desire as at once the most compulsory and the most prohibited of social bonds.

To inscribe that vulgar classification supposedly derived from Freud on what was arguably the founding moment of the world view and social constitution that he codified would hardly be enlightening. Still, the newly formulated and stressed "universal" imperative/prohibition attached to male homosocial desire, even given that its claim for universality already excluded (the female) half of the population, nevertheless required, of course, further embodiment and specification in new taxonomies of personality and character. These taxonomies would mediate between the supposedly classless, "personal" entities of the ideological fictions and the particular, class-specified, economically inscribed lives that they influenced; and at the same time, the plethoric and apparently comprehensive pluralism of the taxonomies occluded, through the illusion of choice, the overarching existence of the double bind that structured them all.

Recent gay male historiography, influenced by Foucault, has been especially good at unpacking and interpreting those parts of the nineteenth-century systems of classification that clustered most closely around what current taxonomies construe as "the homosexual." The "sodomite," the "invert," the "homosexual," the "heterosexual" himself, all are objects of historically and institutionally explicable construction.[12] In the discussion of male homosexual *panic*, however—the treacherous middle stretch of the modern homosocial continuum, and the terrain from whose wasting rigors *only* the homosexual-identified man is at all exempt—a different and less distinctly sexualized range of categories needs to be opened up. Again, however, it bears repeating that the object of doing that is not to arrive at a more accurate or up-to-date assignment of "diagnostic" categories, but to understand better the broad field of forces within which masculinity—and thus, *at least* for men, humanity itself—could (can) at a particular moment construct itself.

I want to suggest here that with Thackeray and other early and mid-Victorians, a character classification of "the bachelor" came into currency, a type that for some men both narrowed the venue, and at the same time startlingly desexualized the question, of male sexual choice.[13] Later in the century, when a medical and social-science model of "the homosexual man" had institutionalized this classification for a few men, the broader issue of endemic male homosexual panic was again up for grabs in a way that was newly redetached from character taxonomy and was more apt to be described narratively, as a decisive moment of choice in the developmental labyrinth of the generic individual (male). As the unmarried gothic hero had once been, the bachelor became once again the representative man: James wrote in his 1881 *Notebook*, "I take [London] as an artist and as a bachelor; as one who has the passion of observation and whose business is the study of human life."[14] In the work of writers like Du Maurier, Barrie, and James, among others, male homosexual panic was acted out as a sometimes agonized sexual anesthesia that was damaging to both its male subjects and its female nonobjects. The paranoid Gothic itself, a generic structure that seemed to have been domesticated in the development of the bachelor taxonomy, returned in some of these works as a formally intrusive and incongruous, but strikingly persistent, literary element.[15]

II. Meet Mr. Batchelor

> *"Batchelor, my elderly Tiresias, are you turned into a lovely young lady par hasard?"*
> *"Get along, you absurd Trumperian professor!" say I.*
>
> —*Thackeray*[16]

In Victorian fiction, it is perhaps the figure of the urban bachelor, especially as popularized by Thackeray, who personifies the most deflationary tonal contrast to the eschatological harrowings and epistemological doublings of the paranoid Gothic. Where the Gothic hero had been solipsistic, the bachelor hero is selfish. Where the Gothic hero had raged, the bachelor hero bitches. Where the Gothic hero had been suicidally inclined, the bachelor hero is a hypochondriac. The Gothic hero ranges from euphoria to despondency—the bachelor hero, from the eupeptic to the dyspeptic.

Structurally, moreover, whereas the Gothic hero had personified the concerns and tones of an entire genre, the bachelor is a distinctly circumscribed and often a marginalized figure in the books he inhabits. Sometimes, like Archie Clavering, Major Pendennis, and Jos Sedley, he is simply a minor character; but even when he is putatively the main character, like Surtees's hero "Soapey" Sponge, he more often functions as a clotheshorse or comic place-marker in a discursive plot.[17] The bachelor hero can only be mock-heroic: not merely diminished and parodic himself, he symbolizes the diminution and undermining of certain heroic and totalizing possibilities of generic embodiment. The novel of which the absurd Jos Sedley is not the hero is a novel *without* a hero.

It makes sense, I think, to see the development of this odd character the bachelor, and his dissolutive relation to romantic genre, as, among other things, a move toward the recuperation as character taxonomy of the endemic double bind of male homosexual panic that had been acted out in the paranoid Gothic as plot and structure. This recuperation is perhaps best described as, in several senses, a domestication. Most obviously, in the increasingly stressed nineteenth-century bourgeois dichotomy between domestic female space and extrafamilial, political and economic male space, the bachelor is at least partly feminized by his attention to and interest in domestic concerns. (At the same time, though, his intimacy with clubland and bohemia gives him a special passport to the world of men, as well.) Then, too, the disruptive and self-ignorant potential for violence in the Gothic hero is replaced in the bachelor hero by physical timidity and, often, by a high valuation on introspection and by (at least partial) self-knowledge. Finally, the bachelor is housebroken by the severing of his connections with a discourse of genital sexuality.

The first-person narrators of much of Thackeray's later fiction are good examples of the urban bachelor in his major key. Even though the Pendennis who narrates *The Newcomes* and *Philip* is supposedly married, his voice, personality, and tastes are strikingly similar to those of the archetypal Thackeray bachelor, the narrator of his novella *Lovel the Widower* (1859)—a man called, by no coincidence at all, Mr. Batchelor. (Of course, Thackeray's own ambiguous marital status—married, but to an inveterately sanitarium-bound, psychotically depressed woman—facilitated this slippage in the narrators whom Thackeray seemed to model on himself.) Mr. Batchelor is, as James says of Olive Chancellor, unmarried by every implication of his being. He is compulsively garrulous about marital prospects, his own (past and present) among others, but always in a tone that points, in one way or another, to the absurdity of the thought. For instance, his hyperbolic treatment of an early romantic disappointment is used both to mock and undermine the importance to him of that incident, and at the same time, by invidious comparison, to discredit in advance the seriousness of any later involvement:

> Some people have the small-pox twice; *I do not*. In my case, if a heart is broke, it's broke: if a flower is withered, it's withered. If I choose to put my grief in a ridiculous light, why not? why do you suppose I am going to make a tragedy of such an old, used-up, battered, stale, vulgar, trivial every-day subject as a jilt who plays with a man's passion, and laughs at him, and leaves him? Tragedy indeed! Oh, yes! poison—black-edged note-paper— Waterloo Bridge—one more unfortunate, and so forth! No: if she goes, let her go!—*si celeres quatit pennas*, I puff the what-d'ye-call-it away! (Ch. 2)

The plot of *Lovel*—slight enough—is an odd local station on the subway from *Liber Amoris* to Proust. Mr. Batchelor, when he lived in lodgings, had had a slightly tender friendship with his landlady's daughter Bessy, who at that time helped support her family by dancing in a music hall. A few years later, he gets her installed as governess in the home of his friend Lovel, the widower. Several men in the vicinity are rivals for Bessy's affections: the local doctor, the shrewd autodidact butler, and, halfheartedly, Batchelor himself. When a visiting bounder attacks Bessy's reputation and her person, Batchelor, who is eavesdropping on the scene, fatally hesitates in coming to her defense, suddenly full of doubts about her sexual purity ("Fiends and anguish! he had known her before" [Ch. 5]) and his own eagerness for marriage. Finally it is the autodidact butler who rescues her, and Lovel himself who marries her.

If the treatment of the romantic possibilities that are supposedly at the heart of *Lovel* has a tendency to dematerialize them almost before they present themselves, the treatment of certain other physical pleasures is given an immediacy that seems correspondingly heightened. In fact, the substantiality of physical pleasure is explicitly linked to the state of bachelorhood.

> To lie on that comfortable, cool bachelor's bed. . . . Once at Shrublands I heard steps pacing overhead at night, and the feeble but continued wail of

> an infant. I wakened from my sleep, was sulky, but turned and slept again.
> Biddlecombe the barrister I knew was the occupant of the upper chamber.
> He came down the next morning looking wretchedly yellow about the cheeks,
> and livid round the eyes. His teething infant had kept him on the march all
> night. . . . He munched a shred of toast, and was off by the omnibus to
> chambers. I chipped a second egg; I may have tried one or two other nice
> little things on the table (Strasbourg pâté I know I never can resist, and am
> convinced it is perfectly wholesome). I could see my own sweet face in the
> mirror opposite, and my gills were as rosy as any broiled salmon. (Ch. 3)

Unlike its sacramental, community-building function in Dickens, food in Thackeray—even good food— is most apt to signify the bitterness of dependency or
inequality. The exchange value of food and drink, its expensiveness or cheapness
relative to the status and expectations of those who partake, the ostentation or
stinginess with which it is doled out, or the meanness with which it is cadged,
mark out for it a shifty and invidious path through each of Thackeray's books,
including this one. The rounded Pickwickian self-complacency of the rosy-gilled
bachelor at breakfast is, then, all the more striking by contrast. In Thackeray's
bitchy art where, as in James's, the volatility of the perspective regularly corrodes
both the object and the subject of perception, there are moments when the bachelor
hero, exactly through his celibacy and selfishness, can seem the only human particle
atomized enough to plump through unscathed.

Sometimes unscathed; never unscathing. Of course one of the main pleasures
of reading this part of Thackeray's oeuvre is precisely its feline gratuitousness of
aggression. At odd moments we are apt to find kitty's unsheathed claws a millimeter
from our own eyes. "Nothing, dear friend, escapes your penetration: if a joke is
made in your company, you are down upon it instanter, and your smile rewards
the wag who amuses you: so you knew at once. . . . " (Ch. 1). When one bachelor
consults another bachelor about a third bachelor, nothing is left but ears and
whiskers.

> During my visit to London, I had chanced to meet my friend Captain Fitzb—
> dle, who belongs to a dozen clubs, and knows something of every man in
> London. "Know anything of Clarence Baker?" "Of course I do," says Fitz;
> "and if you want any *renseignement,* my dear fellow, I have the honor to
> inform you that a blacker little sheep does not trot the London *pavé.* . . .
> know anything of Clarence Baker! My dear fellow, enough to make your hair
> turn white, unless (as I sometimes fondly imagine) nature has already per-
> formed that process, when of course I can't pretend to act upon mere hair-
> dye." (The whiskers of the individual who addressed me, innocent, stared
> me in the face as he spoke, and were dyed of the most unblushing purple.)
> . . . " . . . . From the garrison towns where he has been quartered, he has
> carried away not only the hearts of the milliners, but their gloves, haber-
> dashery, and perfumery." (Ch. 4)

If, as I am suggesting, Thackeray's bachelors created or reinscribed as a personality
type one possible path of response to the strangulation of homosexual panic, their

basic strategy is easy enough to trace: a preference of atomized male individualism to the nuclear family (and a corresponding demonization of women, especially of mothers); a garrulous and visible refusal of anything that could be interpreted as genital sexuality, toward objects male or female; a corresponding emphasis on the pleasures of the other senses; and a well-defended social facility that freights with a good deal of magnetism its proneness to parody and to unpredictable sadism.

I must say that this does not strike me as a portrait of an exclusively Victorian human type. To refuse sexual choice, in a society where sexual choice for men is both compulsory and always self-contradictory, seems, at least for educated men, still often to involve invoking the precedent of this nineteenth-century persona—not Mr. Batchelor himself perhaps, but generically, the self-centered and at the same time self-marginalizing bachelor he represents. Nevertheless, this person *is* highly specified as a figure of the nineteenth-century metropolis. He has close ties with the *flâneurs* of Poe, Baudelaire, Wilde, Benjamin. What is most importantly specified is his pivotal class position between the respectable bourgeoisie and bohemia—a bohemia that, again, Thackeray in the Pendennis novels half invented for English literature and half merely housetrained.

Literally, it was Thackeray who introduced both the word and the concept of bohemia to England from Paris.[18] As a sort of reserve labor force and a semiporous, liminal space for vocational sorting and social rising and falling, bohemia could seemingly be entered from any social level; but, at least in these literary versions, it served best the cultural needs, the fantasy needs, and the needs for positive and negative self-definition of an anxious and conflicted bourgeoisie. Except to homosexual men, the idea of "bohemia" seems before the 1890s not to have had a distinctively gay coloration. In these bachelor novels the simple absence of an enforcing family structure was allowed to perform its enchantment in a more generalized way; and the most passionate male comradeship subsisted in an apparently loose relation to the erotic uses of a common pool of women. It might be more accurate, however, to see the flux of bohemia as the *temporal* space where the young, male bourgeois literary subject was required to navigate his way through his "homosexual panic"—seen here as a *developmental* stage—toward the more repressive, self-ignorant, and apparently consolidated status of the mature bourgeois *paterfamilias*.

Among Thackeray's progeny in the exploration of bourgeois bachelors in bohemia, the most self-conscious and important are Du Maurier, Barrie, and—in a book like *The Ambassadors*—James. The filiations of this tradition are multiple and heterogeneous. For instance, Du Maurier offered James the plot of *Trilby* years before he wrote the novel himself.[19] Or again, Little Bilham in *The Ambassadors* seems closely related to Little Billee, the hero of *Trilby*, a small girlish-looking Left Bank art student. Little Billee shares a studio with two older, bigger, more virile English artists, whom he loves deeply—a bond that seems to give erotic point to Du Maurier's use of the Thackeray naval ballad from which Du Maurier, in turn, had taken Little Billee's name.

> There was gorging Jack and guzzling Jimmy,
> And the youngest he was little Billee.
> Now when they got as far as the Equator
> They's nothing left but one split pea.
>
> Says gorging Jack to guzzling Jimmy,
> "I am extremely hungaree."
> To gorging Jack says guzzling Jimmy,
> "We've nothing left, us must eat we."
>
> Says gorging Jack to guzzling Jimmy,
> "With one another we shouldn't agree!
> There's little Bill, he's young and tender,
> We're old and tough, so let's eat he.
>
> "Oh! Billy, we're going to kill and eat you,
> So undo the button of your chemie. . . ."[20]

As one moves past Thackeray toward the turn of the century, toward the ever greater visibility across class lines of a medicalized discourse of—and newly punitive assaults on—male homosexuality, however, the comfortably frigid campiness of Thackeray's bachelors gives way to something that sounds more inescapably like panic. Mr. Batchelor had played at falling in love with women, but felt no urgency about proving that he actually could. For the bachelor heroes of *Trilby* and *Tommy and Grizel*, though, even that renunciatory high ground of male sexlessness has been strewn with psychic landmines.

In fact, the most consistent keynote of this late literature is exactly the explicitly thematized sexual anesthesia of its heroes. In each of these fictions, moreover, the hero's agonistic and denied sexual anesthesia is treated as being *at the same time* an aspect of a particular, idiosyncratic personality type *and also* an expression of a great Universal. Little Billee, for instance, the hero of *Trilby*, attributes his sudden inability to desire a woman to "a pimple" inside his "bump of" "fondness"— "for that's what's the matter with me—a pimple—just a little clot of blood at the root of a nerve, and no bigger than a pin's point!"[21] In the same long monologue, however, he again attributes his lack of desire, not to the pimple, but on a far different scale to his status as Post-Darwinian Man, unable any longer to believe in God. "Sentimental" Tommy, similarly, the hero of Barrie's eponymous novel and also of *Tommy and Grizel*, is treated throughout each of these astonishingly acute and self-hating novels both as a man with a crippling moral and psychological defect and as the very type of the great creative artist.

III. Reading James Straight

James's "The Beast in the Jungle" (1902) is one of the bachelor fictions of this period that seems to make a strong implicit claim of "universal" applicability through heterosexual symmetries, but that is most movingly subject to a change of Gestalt and of visible saliencies as soon as an assumed heterosexual male norm is at all interrogated. Like *Tommy and Grizel,* the story is of a man and a woman who have a decades-long intimacy. In both stories, the woman desires the man but the man fails to desire the woman. In fact—in each story—the man simply fails to desire at all. Sentimental Tommy desperately desires to feel desire; confusingly counterfeits a desire for Grizel; and, with all the best intentions, finally drives her mad. John Marcher, in James's story, does not even know that desire is absent from his life, nor that May Bartram desires him, until after she has died from his obtuseness.

To judge from the biographies of Barrie and James, each author seems to have made erotic choices that were complicated enough, shifting enough in the gender of their objects, and, at least for long periods, kept distant enough from *éclaircissement* or physical expression, to make each an emboldening figure for a literary discussion of male homosexual panic.[22] Barrie had an almost unconsummated marriage, an unconsummated passion for a married woman (George Du Maurier's daughter!), and a lifelong uncategorizable passion for her family of sons. James had—well, exactly that which we now all know that we know not. Oddly, however, it is simpler to read the psychological plot of *Tommy and Grizel*—the horribly thorough and conscientious ravages on a woman of a man's compulsion to pretend he desires her—into the cryptic and tragic story of James's involvement with Constance Fenimore Woolson, than to read it directly into any incident of Barrie's life. It is hard to read Leon Edel's account of James's sustained (or repeated) and intense, but peculiarly furtive,[23] intimacies with this deaf, intelligent American woman author who clearly loved him, without coming to a grinding sense that James felt he had with her above all something, sexually, to prove. And if it is hard to read about what seems to have been her suicide without wondering whether the expense of James's heterosexual self-probation—an expense, one envisions if one has Barrie in mind, of sudden "generous" "yielding" impulses in him and equally sudden revulsions—was not charged most intimately to this secreted-away companion of so many of his travels and residencies. If this is true, the working-out of his denied homosexual panic must have been only the more grueling for the woman in proportion to James's outrageous gift and his moral magnetism.

If something like the doubly destructive interaction I am sketching here did in fact occur between James and Constance Fenimore Woolson, then its structure has been resolutely reproduced by virtually all the critical discussion of James's writing. James's mistake here, biographically, seems to have been in moving blindly from a sense of the good, the desirability, of love and sexuality, to the automatic imposition on himself of a specifically *hetero*sexual compulsion. (I say "imposition on himself," but of course he did not invent the heterosexual specificity of this compulsion—he merely failed, at this point in his life, to resist it actively.) The easy assumption (by James, the society, and the critics) that sexuality and heterosexuality are always exactly translatable into one another is, obviously, homophobic. Importantly, too, it is deeply heterophobic: it denies the very possibility of *difference* in desires, in objects. One is no longer surprised, of course, at the repressive blankness on these issues of most literary criticism; but for James, in whose life the pattern of homosexual desire was brave enough and resilient enough to be at last biographically inobliterable, one might have hoped that in criticism of his work the possible differences of different erotic paths would not be so ravenously subsumed under a compulsorily—and hence, never a truly "hetero"—heterosexual model. With strikingly few exceptions, however, the criticism has actively repelled any inquiry into the asymmetries of gendered desire.

It is possible that critics have been motivated in this active incuriosity by a desire to protect James from homophobic misreadings in a perennially repressive sexual climate. It is possible that they fear that, because of the asymmetrically marked structure of heterosexual discourse, *any* discussion of homosexual desires or literary content will marginalize him (or them?) as, simply, *homosexual*. It is possible that they desire to protect him from what they imagine as anachronistically "gay" readings, based on a late twentieth-century vision of men's desire for men that is more stabilized and culturally compact than James's own. It is possible that they read James himself as, in his work, positively refusing or evaporating this element of his eros, translating lived homosexual desires, where he had them, into written heterosexual ones so thoroughly and so successfully that the difference *makes* no difference, the transmutation leaves no residue. Or it is possible that, believing—as I do—that James often, though not always, attempted such a disguise or transmutation, but reliably left a residue both of material that he did not attempt to transmute and of material that could be transmuted only rather violently and messily, some critics are reluctant to undertake the "attack" on James's candor or artistic unity that could be the next step of that argument. Any of these critical motives would be understandable, but their net effect is the usual repressive one of elision and subsumption of supposedly embarrassing material. In dealing with the multiple valences of sexuality, critics' choices should not be limited to crudities of disruption or silences of orthodox enforcement.

Even Leon Edel, who traced out *both* James's history with Constance Fenimore Woolson *and* some of the narrative of his erotic desires for men, connects "The Beast in the Jungle" to the history of Woolson,[24] but connects neither of these to the specificity of James's—or of any—sexuality. The result of this hammeringly tendentious blur in virtually all the James criticism is, for the interpretation of "The Beast in the Jungle," seemingly in the interests of showing it as universally applicable (e.g., about "the artist"), to assume without any space for doubt that the moral point of the story is not only that May Bartram desired John Marcher but that John Marcher *should have desired* May Bartram.

Tommy and Grizel is clearer-sighted on what is essentially the same point. "*Should have desired*," that novel graphically shows, not only is nonsensical as a moral judgment but is the very mechanism that enforces and perpetuates the mutilating charade of heterosexual exploitation. (James's compulsive use of Woolson, for instance.) Grizel's tragedy is not that the man she desires fails to desire her—which would be sad, but, the book makes clear, endurable—but that he pretends to desire her, and intermittently even convinces himself that he desires her, when he does not.

Impressively, too, the clarity with which *Tommy and Grizel* conveys this process and its ravages seems *not* to be dependent on a given, naive, or monolithic idea of what it would mean for a man to "really" desire someone. On that issue the novel seems to remain agnostic—leaving open the possibility that there is some rather different quantity that is "real" male desire, or alternatively that it is only more and less intermittent infestations of the same murderous syndrome that fuel any male eros at all. That the worst violence of heterosexuality comes with the male *compulsion to desire* women and its attendant deceptions of self and other, however, Barrie says quite decisively.

Tommy and Grizel is an extraordinary, and an unjustly forgotten, novel. What has dated it and keeps it from being a great novel, in spite of the acuteness with which it treats male desire, is the—one can hardly help saying Victorian—mawkish opportunism with which it figures the desire of women. Permissibly, the novel's real imaginative and psychological energies focus entirely on the hero. Impermissibly—and here the structure of the novel itself exactly reproduces the depredations of its hero—there is a moralized pretense at an equal focus on a rounded, autonomous, imaginatively and psychologically invested female protagonist, who however—far from being novelistically "desired" in herself—is really, transparently, created in the precise negative image of the hero, created to be the single creature in the world who is most perfectly fashioned to be caused the most exquisite pain and intimate destruction by him and him only. The fit is excruciatingly seamless. Grizel is the daughter of a mad prostitute, whose legacies to her—aside from vitality, intelligence, imagination—have been a strong sensuality and a terror (which the novel highly valorizes) of having that sensuality stirred. It was acute of Barrie to see that this is the exact woman—were such a woman possible—who, appearing strong and autonomous, would be most unresistingly annihilable precisely by Tommy's two-phase rhythm of sexual come-on followed by repressive frigidity, and his emotional geology of pliant sweetness fundamented by unyielding compulsion. But the prurient exactitude of the female fit, as of a creature bred for sexual sacrifice without resistance or leftovers, drains the authority of the novel to make an uncomplicit judgment of Tommy's representative value.

Read in this context, "The Beast in the Jungle" looks—from the point of view of female desire—potentially revolutionary. Whoever May Bartram is and whatever she wants (I discuss this more later), clearly at least the story has the Jamesian negative virtue of not pretending to present her rounded and whole. She is an imposing character, but—*and*—a bracketed one. James's bravura in manipulating point of view lets him dissociate himself critically from John Marcher's selfishness—from the sense that there is no *possibility* of a subjectivity other than Marcher's own—but lets him leave himself in place of that selfishness finally an *askesis*, a particular humility of point of view as being *limited* to Marcher's. Of May Bartram's history, of her emotional determinants, of her erotic structures, the reader learns very little; we are permitted, if we pay attention at all, to *know* that we have learned very little. Just as, in Proust, it is always open to any minor or grotesque character to turn out at any time to have a major artistic talent with which, however, the novel does not happen to busy itself, so "The Beast in the Jungle" seems to give the reader permission to imagine some female needs and desires and gratifications that are not structured exactly in the image of Marcher's or of the story's own laws.

It is only the last scene of the story—Marcher's last visit to May Bartram's grave—that conceals or denies the humility, the incompleteness of the story's presentation of her subjectivity. This is the scene in which Marcher's sudden realization that *she* has felt and expressed desire for *him* is, as it seems, answered in an intensely symmetrical, "conclusive" rhetorical clinch by the narrative/authorial prescription: "The escape would have been to love her; then, *then* he would have lived."[25] The paragraph that follows, the last in the story, has the same climactic, authoritative (even authoritarian) rhythm of supplying Answers in the form of symmetrical supplementarities. For this single, this conclusive, this formally privileged moment in the story—this resolution over the dead body of May Bartram—James and Marcher are presented as coming together, Marcher's revelation underwritten by James's rhetorical authority, and James's epistemological askesis gorged, for once, beyond recognition, by Marcher's compulsive, ego-projective certainties. In the absence of May Bartram, the two men, author/narrator and hero, are reunited at last in the confident, shared, masculine knowledge of what she Really Wanted and what she Really Needed. And what she Really Wanted and Really Needed show, of course, an uncanny closeness to what Marcher Really (should have) Wanted and Needed, himself.

Imagine "The Beast in the Jungle" without this enforcing symmetry. Imagine (remember) the story with May Bartram alive.[26] Imagine a possible alterity. And the name of alterity is not *always* "woman." What if Marcher himself had other desires?

IV. The Law of the Jungle

> Names . . . *Assingham—Padwick—*
> *Lutch—Marfle—Bross—Crapp—*
> *Didcock—Wichells—*Putchin—*Brind—*
> *Coxeter—Coxster* . . . *Dickwinter*
> . . . *Jakes* . . . *Marcher—*
> —(James, Notebook, *1901*)

There has so far seemed no reason, or little reason, why what I have been calling "male homosexual panic" could not just as descriptively have been called "male heterosexual panic"—or, simply, "male sexual panic." Although I began with a structural and historicizing narrative that emphasized the pre- and proscriptively defining importance of men's bonds with men, potentially including genital bonds, the books I have discussed have not, for the most part, seemed to center emotionally or thematically on such bonds. In fact, it is, explicitly, a male panic in the face of *hetero*sexuality that many of these books most describe. It is all very well to insist, as I have done, that homosexual panic is necessarily a problem only, but endemically, of nonhomosexual-identified men; nevertheless the lack in these books of an embodied male-homosexual thematics, however inevitable, has had a dissolutive effect on the structure and texture of such an argument. Part, although only part, of the reason for the lack was historical: it was only close to the end of the nineteenth century that a cross-class homosexual role and a consistent ideologically full thematic discourse of male homosexuality became entirely visible, in developments that were publicly dramatized in—though far from confined to—the Wilde trials.

In "The Beast in the Jungle," written at the threshold of the new century, the possibility of an embodied male-homosexual thematics has, I would like to argue, a precisely liminal presence. It is present as a—as a very particular, historicized—thematics of absence, and specifically of the absence of speech. The first (in some ways the only) thing we learn about John Marcher is that he has a "secret" (358), a destiny, a something unknown in his future. "You said," May Bartram reminds him, "you had from your earliest time, as the deepest thing within you, the sense of being kept for something rare and strange, possibly prodigious and terrible, that was sooner or later to happen" (359). I would argue that to the extent that Marcher's secret has *a* content, that content is homosexual.

Of course the extent to which Marcher's secret has anything that could be called a content is, not only dubious, but in the climactic last scene actively denied. "He had been the man of his time, *the* man, to whom nothing on earth was to have happened" (401). The denial that the secret has a content—the assertion that its content is precisely a lack—is a stylish and "satisfyingly" Jamesian formal gesture. The apparent gap of meaning that it points to is, however, far from being a genuinely empty one; it is no sooner asserted than filled to a plenitude with the most orthodox of ethical enforcements. To point rhetorically to the emptiness of the secret, "the nothing that is," is, in fact, oddly, *the same gesture* as the attribution to it of a compulsory content about heterosexuality—of the content specifically, "He should [have] desire[d] her."

> *She* was what he had missed. . . . The fate he had been marked for he had met with a vengeance—he had emptied the cup to the lees; he had been the man of his time, *the* man, to whom nothing on earth was to have happened. That was the rare stroke—that was his visitation. . . . This the companion of his vigil had at a given moment made out, and she had then offered him the chance to baffle his doom. One's doom, however, was never baffled, and on the day she told him his own had come down she had seen him but stupidly stare at the escape she offered him.
>
> The escape would have been to love her; then, *then* he would have lived. (401)

The "empty" meaning of Marcher's unspeakable doom is thus necessarily, specifically heterosexual; it refers to the perfectly specific absence of a prescribed heterosexual desire. If critics, eager to help James moralize this ending, persist in claiming to be able to translate freely and without residue from that (absent) heterosexual desire to an abstraction of all possibilities of human love, there are, I think, good reasons for trying to slow them down. The totalizing, insidiously symmetrical view that the "nothing" that is Marcher's unspeakable fate is necessarily a mirror image of the "everything" he could and should have had is, specifically, in an *oblique* relation to a very different history of meanings for assertions of the erotic negative.

The "full" meaning of that unspeakable fate, on the other hand, comes from the centuries-long historical chain of substantive uses of space-clearing negatives to void and at the same time to underline the possibility of male homosexual genitality. The rhetorical name for this figure is *preterition*. Unspeakable, Unmentionable, *nefandam libidinem*, "that sin which should be neither named nor committed,"[27] the "detestable and abominable sin, amongst Christians not to be named,"

> Whose vice in special, if I would declare,
> It were enough for to perturb the air,

"things fearful to name," "the obscene sound of the unbeseeming words,"

> A sin so odious that the fame of it
> Will fright the damned in the darksome pit,[28]

"the Love that dare not speak its name,"[29]—such *were* the speakable nonmedical terms, in Christian tradition, of the homosexual possibility for men. The marginality of these terms' semantic and ontological status as substantive nouns reflected and shaped the exiguousness—but also, the potentially enabling secrecy—of the "possibility." And the newly specifying, reifying medical and penal public discourse of the male homosexual role, in the years around the Wilde trials, far from retiring or obsolescing these preteritive names, seems instead to have packed them more firmly and distinctively with homosexual meaning.[30]

John Marcher's "secret" (358), "his singularity" (366), "the thing she knew, which grew to be at last, with the consecration of the years, never mentioned between them save as 'the real truth' about him" (366), "the abyss" (375), "his queer consciousness" (378), "the great vagueness" (379), "the secret of the gods" (379), "what ignominy or what monstrosity" (379), "dreadful things . . . I couldn't name" (381): the ways in which the story refers to Marcher's secret fate have the same quasi-nominative, quasi-obliterative structure.

There are, as well, some "fuller," though still highly equivocal, lexical pointers to a homosexual meaning: "The rest of the world of course thought him *queer*, but she, she only, knew how, and above all why, queer; which was precisely what enabled her to dispose the concealing veil in the right folds. She took his *gaiety* from him—since it had to pass with them for gaiety—as she took everything else. . . . She traced his unhappy *perversion* through reaches of its course into which he could scarce follow it" (367; emphasis added). Still, it is mostly in the reifying grammar of periphrasis and preterition—"such a cataclysm" (360), "the great affair" (360), "the catastrophe" (361), "his predicament" (364), "their real truth" (368), "his inevitable topic" (371), "all that they had thought, first and last" (372), "horrors" (382), something "more monstrous than all the monstrosities we've named" (383), "all the loss and all the shame that are thinkable" (384)—that a homosexual meaning becomes, to the degree that it does become, legible. "I don't focus it. I can't name it. I only know I'm exposed" (372).

I am convinced, however, that part of the point of the story is that the reifying effect of periphrasis and preterition on this particular meaning is, if anything, *more* damaging than (though not separable from) its obliterative effect. To have succeeded—which was not to be taken for granted—in cracking the centuries-old code by which the-articulated-denial-of-articulability always had the possibility of meaning two things, of meaning either (heterosexual) "nothing" or "homosexual meaning," would also always have been to assume one's place in a discourse in which there was *a* homosexual meaning, in which all homosexual meaning meant a single thing. To crack a code and enjoy the reassuring exhilarations of knowingness is to buy into the specific formula, "We Know What That Means." (I assume it is this mechanism that makes even critics who know about the male-erotic pathways of James's personal desires appear to be so untroubled about leaving them out of accounts of his writing.[31] As if this form of desire were the most calculable, the simplest to add or subtract or allow for in moving between life and art!) But if, as I suggested in Section I, men's accession to heterosexual entitlement has, for these modern centuries, always been on the ground of a cultivated and compulsory denial of the *un*knowability, of the arbitrariness and self-contradictoriness, of homosexual/heterosexual definition, then the fearful or triumphant interpretive formula "We Know What That Means" seems to take on an odd centrality. First, it is a lie. But second, it is the particular lie that animates and perpetuates the mechanism of homophobic male self-ignorance and violence and manipulability.

It is worth, then, trying to discriminate the possible plurality of meanings behind the unspeakables of "The Beast in the Jungle." To point, as I argue that the narrative itself points and as we have so far pointed, simply to *a* possibility of "homosexual meaning," is to say worse than nothing—it is to pretend to say one thing. But even on the surface of the story, the secret, "*the* thing," "the thing she knew," is discriminated, first of all discriminated temporally. There are at least two secrets: Marcher feels that he knows, but has never told anyone but May Bartram (secret number one) that he is reserved for some very particular, uniquely rending fate in the future, whose nature is (secret number two) unknown to himself. Over the temporal extent of the story, both the balance, between the two characters, of cognitive mastery over the secrets' meanings, and the temporal placement, between future and past, of the second secret, shift; it is possible, in addition, that the actual content (if any) of the secrets changes with these temporal and cognitive changes, if time and intersubjectivity are of the essence of the secrets.

Let me, baldly, then, spell out my hypothesis of what a series of "full"—that is, homosexually tinged—meanings for the Unspeakable might look like for this story, differing both over time and according to character.

For John Marcher, let us hypothesize, the future secret—the secret of his hidden fate—importantly includes, though it is not necessarily limited to, the possibility of something homosexual. For *Marcher*, the presence or possibility of a homosexual meaning attached to the inner, the future secret, has exactly the reifying, totalizing, and blinding effect we described earlier in regard to the phenomenon of the Unspeakable. Whatever (Marcher feels) may be to be discovered along those lines, it is, in the view of his panic, *one* thing, and the worst thing, "the superstition of the Beast" (394). His readiness to organize the whole course of his life around the preparation for it—the defense against it—remakes his life monolithically in the image of *its* monolith of, in his view, the inseparability of homosexual desire, yielding, discovery, scandal, shame, annihilation. Finally, he has "but one desire left": that *it* be "decently proportional to the posture he had kept, all his life, in the threatened presence of it" (379).

This is how it happens that the outer secret, the secret of having a secret, functions, in Marcher's life, precisely as *the closet*. It is not a closet in which there is a homosexual man, for Marcher is not a homosexual man. Instead, however, it is the closet of, simply, the homosexual secret—the closet of imagining *a* homosexual secret. Yet it is unmistakable that Marcher lives as one who is *in the closet*. His angle on daily existence and intercourse is that of the closeted person,

> the secret of the difference between the forms he went through—those of his little office under government, those of caring for his modest patrimony, for his library, for his garden in the country, for the people in London whose invitations he accepted and repaid—and the detachment that reigned beneath them and that made of all behaviour, all that could in the least be called behaviour, a long act of dissimulation. What it had come to was that he wore a mask painted with the social simper, out of the eye-holes of which there looked eyes of an expression not in the least matching the other features. This the stupid world, even after years, had never more than half-discovered. (367–78)

Whatever the content of the inner secret, too, it is one whose protection requires, for him, a playacting of heterosexuality that is conscious of being only window dressing. "You help me," he tells May Bartram, "to pass for a man like another" (375). And "what saves us, you know," she explains, "is that we answer so completely to so usual an appearance: that of the man and woman whose friendship has become such a daily habit—or almost—as to be at last indispensable" (368–69). Oddly, they not only appear to be but are such a man and woman. The element of deceiving the world, of window dressing, comes into their relationship *only* because of the compulsion he feels to invest it with the legitimating stamp of visible, institutionalized genitality: "The real form it should have taken on the basis that stood out large was the form of their marrying. But the devil in this was that the very basis itself put marrying out of the question. His conviction, his apprehension, his obsession, in short, wasn't a privilege he could invite a woman to share; and that consequence of it was precisely what was the matter with him" (365).

Because of the terrified stultification of his fantasy about the inner or future secret, Marcher has, until the story's very last scene, an essentially static relation to and sense of both these secrets. Even the discovery that the outer secret is already shared with someone else, and the admission of May Bartram to the community it creates, "the dim day constituted by their discretions and privacies" (363), does nothing to his closet but furnish it—camouflage it to the eyes of outsiders, and soften its inner cushioning for his own comfort. In fact, the admission of May Bartram importantly *consolidates and fortifies* the closet for John Marcher.

In my hypothesis, however, May Bartram's view of Marcher's secrets is different from his and more fluid. I want to suggest that—while it is true that she feels desire for him—her involvement with him occurs originally on the ground of her understanding that he is imprisoned by homosexual panic; and her interest in his closet is not at all in helping him fortify it but in helping him dissolve it.

In this reading, May Bartram from the first sees, correctly, that the possibility of Marcher's achieving a genuine ability to attend to a woman—sexually or in any other way—depends as an absolute precondition on the dispersion of his totalizing, basilisk fascination with and terror of homosexual possibility. It is only through his coming out of the closet—whether as *a homosexual man,* or as a man with a less exclusively defined sexuality that nevertheless admits the possibility of desires for other men—that Marcher could even begin to perceive the attention of a woman as anything other than a terrifying demand or a devaluing complicity. The truth of this is already evident at the beginning of the story, in the surmises with which Marcher first meets May Bartram's allusion to something (he cannot remember what) he said to her years before: "The great thing was that he saw in this no vulgar reminder of any 'sweet' speech. The vanity of women had long memories, but she was making no claim on him of a compliment or a mistake. With another woman, a totally different one, he might have feared the recall possibly even of some imbecile 'offer' " (356). The alternative to this, however, in his eyes, is a different kind of "sweetness," that of a willingly shared confinement: "her knowledge . . . began, even if rather strangely, to taste sweet to him" (358). "Somehow the whole question was a new luxury to him—that is from the moment she was in possession. If she didn't take the sarcastic view she clearly took the sympathetic, and that was what he had had, in all the long time, from no one whomsoever. What he felt was that he couldn't at present have begun to tell her, and yet could profit perhaps exquisitely by the accident of having done so of old" (358). So begins the imprisonment of May Bartram in John Marcher's closet—an imprisonment that, the story makes explicit, is founded on his inability to perceive or value her as a person beyond her complicity in his view of his own predicament.

The conventional view of the story, emphasizing May Bartram's interest in liberating, unmediatedly, Marcher's heterosexual possibilities, would see her as unsuccessful in doing so until too late—until the true revelation that comes, however, only after her death. If what needs to be liberated is in the first place Marcher's potential for homosexual desire, however, the trajectory of the story must be seen as far bleaker. I hypothesize that what May Bartram would have liked for Marcher, the narrative she wished to nurture for him, would have been a progress from a vexed and gaping self-ignorance around his homosexual possibilities to a self-knowledge of them that would have freed him to find and enjoy a sexuality of whatever sort emerged. What she sees happen to Marcher, instead, is the "progress" that the culture more insistently enforces: the progress from a vexed and gaping self-ignorance around his homosexual possibilities, to a completed and rationalized and wholly concealed and accepted one. The moment of Marcher's full incorporation of his erotic self-ignorance is the moment at which the imperatives of the culture cease to enforce him, and he becomes instead the enforcer of the culture.

Section 4 of the story marks the moment at which May Bartram realizes that, far from helping dissolve Marcher's closet, she has instead and irremediably been permitting him to reinforce it. It is in this section and the next, too, that it becomes explicit in the story that Marcher's fate, what was to have happened to him and did happen, involves a change in him from being the suffering object of a Law or judgment (of a doom in the original sense of the word) to being the embodiment of that Law.

If the transition I am describing is, in certain respects, familiarly Oedipal, the structuring metaphor behind its description here seems to be oddly alimentative. The question that haunts Marcher in these sections is whether what he has thought of as the secret of his future may not be, after all, in the past; and the question of passing, of who is passing through what or what is passing through whom, of what residue remains to *be* passed, is the form in which he compulsively poses his riddle. Is the beast eating him, or is he eating the beast? "It hasn't passed you by," May Bartram tells him. "It has done its office. It has made you its own" (389). "It's past. It's behind," she finally tells him, to which he replies, "*Nothing*, for me, is past; nothing *will* pass till I pass myself, which I pray my stars may be as soon as possible. Say, however, . . . that I've eaten my cake, as you contend, to the last crumb—how can the thing I've never felt at all be the thing I was marked out to feel?" (391). What May Bartram sees, that Marcher does not, is that the process of incorporating—of embodying—the Law of masculine self-ignorance, is the one that has the least in the world to do with feeling.[32] To gape at and, rebelliously, be forced to swallow the Law is to feel; but to have it finally stick to one's ribs, become however incongruously a part of one's own organism, is then to perfect at the same moment a new hard-won insentience of it and an assumption of (or subsumption by) an identification with it. May Bartram answers Marcher's question, "You take your 'feelings' for granted. You were to suffer your fate. That was not necessarily to know it" (391). Marcher's fate is to cease to suffer fate, and, instead, to become it. May Bartram's fate, with the "slow fine shudder" that climaxes her ultimate appeal to Marcher, is herself to swallow this huge, bitter bolus with which *she* can have *no* deep identification, and to die of it—of what is, to her, knowledge, not power. "So on her lips would the law itself have sounded" (389). Or, tasted.

To end a reading of May Bartram with her death, to end with her silenced forever in that ultimate closet, "her" tomb that represents (to Marcher) *his fate*, would be to do to her feminine desire the same thing I have already argued that James M. Barrie, unforgivably, did to Grizel's. That is to say, it leaves us in danger of figuring May Bartram, or more generally the woman in heterosexuality, as only the exact, heroic supplement to the murderous enforcements of male homophobic/homosocial self-ignorance. "The Fox," Emily Dickinson wrote, "fits the Hound."[33] It would be only too easy to describe May Bartram as the fox that most irreducibly fits this particular hound. She seems the woman (don't we all know them?) who has not only the most delicate nose for but the most potent attraction toward men who are at crises of homosexual panic . . .—Though for that matter, won't most women admit that an arousing nimbus, an excessively refluent and dangerous maelstrom of eroticism, somehow attends men in general at such moments, even otherwise boring men?

If one is to avoid the Barrie-ism of describing May Bartram in terms that reduce her perfectly to the residue-less sacrifice John Marcher makes to his Beast, it might be by inquiring into the difference of the paths of her own desire. What does she want—not for him, but for herself—from their relationship? What does she actually get? To speak less equivocally from my own eros and experience, there is a particular relation to truth and authority that a mapping of male homosexual panic offers to a woman in the emotional vicinity. The fact that male heterosexual entitlement in (at least modern Anglo-American) culture depends on a perfected but always friable self-ignorance in men as to the significance of their desire for other men, means that it is always open to women to know something that it is much more dangerous for any nonhomosexual-identified man to know. The ground of May Bartram's and John Marcher's relationship from the first is that she has the advantage of him, cognitively: she remembers, as he does not, where and when and with whom they have met before, and most of all she remembers his "secret" from a decade ago while he forgets having told it to her. This differential of knowledge affords her a "slight irony," an "advantage" (353)—but one that he can at the same time use to his own profit as "the buried treasure of her knowledge," "this little hoard" (363). As their relationship continues, the sense of power and of a marked, rather free-floating irony about May Bartram becomes stronger and stronger, even in proportion to Marcher's accelerating progress toward self-ignorance and toward a blindly selfish expropriation of her emotional labor. Both the care and the creativity of her investment in him, the imaginative reach of her fostering his homosexual potential as a route back to his truer perception of herself, are forms of gender-political resilience in her as well as of love. They are forms of excitement, too, of real though insufficient power, and of pleasure.

In the last scene of the "The Beast in the Jungle," John Marcher becomes, in this reading, not the finally self-knowing man who is capable of heterosexual love, but the irredeemably self-ignorant man who embodies and enforces heterosexual compulsion. In this reading, that is to say, May Bartram's prophecy to Marcher that "You'll never know now" (390) is *a true one*.

Importantly for the homosexual plot, too, the final scene is also the only one in the entire story that reveals or tests the affective quality of Marcher's perception of another man. "The shock of the face" (399)—this is, in the last scene, the beginning of what Marcher ultimately considers "the most extraordinary thing that had happened to him" (400). At the beginning of Marcher's confrontation with this male figure at the cemetery, the erotic possibilities of the connection between the men appear to be all open. The man, whose "mute assault" Marcher feels "so deep down that he winced at the steady thrust," is mourning profoundly over "a grave apparently fresh," but (perhaps only to Marcher's closet-sharpened suspicions?) a slightest potential of Whitmanian cruisiness seems at first to tinge the air, as well.

> His pace was slow, so that—and all the more as there was a kind of hunger in his look—the two men were for a minute directly confronted. Marcher knew him at once for one of the deeply stricken . . . nothing lived but the deep ravage of the features he showed. He *showed* them—that was the point; he was moved, as he passed, by some impulse that was either a signal for sympathy or, more possibly, a challenge to an opposed sorrow. He might already have been aware of our friend . . . What Marcher was at all events conscious of was in the first place that the image of scarred passion presented to him was conscious too—of something that profaned the air; and in the second that, roused, startled, shocked, he was yet the next moment looking after it, as it went, with envy. (400–401)

The path traveled by Marcher's desire in this brief and cryptic non-encounter reenacts a classic trajectory of male entitlement. Marcher begins with the possibility of *desire for* the man, in response to the man's open "hunger" ("which," afterward, "still flared for him like a smoky torch" [401]). Deflecting that desire under a fear of profanation, he then replaces it with envy, with an *identification with* the man in that man's (baffled) desire for some other, female, dead object. "The stranger passed, but the raw glare of his grief remained, making our friend wonder in pity what wrong, what wound it expressed, what injury not to be healed. What had the man *had*, to make him by the loss of it so bleed and yet live?" (401).

What had the man *had?* The loss by which a man *so bleeds and yet lives* is, is it not, supposed to be the castratory one of the phallus figured as mother, the inevitability of whose sacrifice ushers sons into the status of fathers and into the control (read both ways) of the Law. What is strikingly open in the ending of "The Beast in the Jungle" is how central to that process is man's desire for man—and the denial of that desire. The imperative that there *be* a male figure to take this place is the clearer in that, at an earlier climactic moment, in a female "shock of the face," May Bartram has presented to Marcher her own face, in a conscious revelation that was far more clearly of desire.

> It had become suddenly, from her movement and attitude, beautiful and vivid to him that she had something more to give him; her wasted face delicately shone with it—it glittered almost as with the white lustre of silver in her expression. She was right, incontestably, for what he saw in her face was the truth, and strangely, without consequence, while their talk of it as dreadful was still in the air, she appeared to present it as inordinately soft. This, prompting bewilderment, made him but gape the more gratefully for her revelation, so that they continued for some minutes silent, her face shining at him, her contact imponderably pressing, and his stare all kind but all expectant. The end, none the less, was that what he had expected failed to come to him. (386)

To the shock of the female face, Marcher is not phobic but simply numb. It is only by turning his desire for the male face into an envious identification with male loss that Marcher finally comes into *any* relation to a woman—and then it is a relation through one dead woman (the other man's) to another dead woman of his own. That is to say, it is the relation of *compulsory* heterosexuality.

When Lytton Strachey's claim to be a conscientious objector was being examined, he was asked what he would do if a German were to try to rape his sister. "I should," he is said to have replied, "try and interpose my own body."[34] Not the gay self-knowledge but the heterosexual, self-ignorant acting out of just this fantasy ends "The Beast in the Jungle." To face the gaze of the Beast would have been, for Marcher, to dissolve it.[35] To face the "kind of hunger in the look" of the grieving man—to explore at all into the sharper lambencies of that encounter—would have been to dissolve the closet. Marcher, instead, to the very end, turns his back—re-creating a double scenario of homosexual compulsion and heterosexual compulsion. "He saw the Jungle of his life and saw the lurking Beast; then, while he looked, perceived it, as by a stir of the air, rise, huge and hideous, for the leap that was to settle him. His eyes darkened—it was close; and, instinctively turning, in his hallucination, to avoid it, he flung himself, face down, on the tomb" (402).

Notes

This essay has profited—though not as fully as I wish I had been able to make it do—from especially helpful readings by Maud Ellmann, Neil Hertz, H. A. Sedgwick, D. A. Miller, and Ruth Bernard Yeazell.

1. Lawrence to Jessie Chambers, Aug. 1910, *The Collected Letters of D. H. Lawrence*, ed. Harry T. Moore (London: W. H. Heinemann, 1962), 1: 63.

2. Lawrence to Rolf Gardiner, Aug. 9, 1924, in Moore, ed., *Collected Letters*, 2: 801.

3. Alan Bray, *Homosexuality in Renaissance England* (London: Gay Men's Press, 1982), chs. 1–3. Note the especially striking example on pp. 68–69, 76–77.

4. Bray, *Homosexuality*, p. 25.

5. Eve Kosofsky Sedgwick, *Between Men: English Literature and Male Homosocial Desire* (New York: Columbia University Press, 1985), pp. 83–96.

6. Claude Lévi-Strauss, *The Elementary Structures of Kinship* (Boston: Beacon Press, 1969), p. 115; also quoted and well discussed in Gayle Rubin, "The Traffic in Women: Notes Toward a Political Economy of Sex," in *Toward an Anthropology of Women*, ed. Rayna Reiter (New York: Monthly Review Press, 1975), pp. 157–210.

7. Heidi Hartmann, "The Unhappy Marriage of Marxism and Feminism: Towards a More Progressive Union," in *Women and Revolution: A Discussion of the Unhappy Marriage of Marxism and Feminism*, ed. Lydia Sargent (Boston: South End Press, 1981), p. 14; emphasis added.

8. Bray, *Homosexuality*, ch. 4.

9. Sedgwick, *Between Men*, pp. 88–89.

10. By "paranoid Gothic" I mean Romantic novels in which a male hero is in a close, usually murderous relation to another male figure, in some respects his "double," to whom he seems to be mentally transparent. Examples of the paranoid Gothic include, besides *Frankenstein*, Ann Radcliffe's *The Italian*, William Godwin's *Caleb Williams*, and James Hogg's *Confessions of a Justified Sinner*. This tradition is discussed more fully in my *Between Men*, chs. 5 and 6.

11. Sigmund Freud, "Psycho-Analytic Notes on an Autobiographical Account of a Case of Paranoia (Dementia Paranoides)," in *The Standard Edition of the Complete Psychological Works of Sigmund Freud*, trans. and ed. James Strachey et al. (London: Hogarth Press, 1953–73), 12: 143–77.

12. On this see, along with Bray, *Homosexuality*, such works as John Boswell, *Christianity, Social Tolerance, and Homosexuality: Gay People in Western Europe from the Beginning of the Christian Era to the Fourteenth Century* (Chicago: University of Chicago Press, 1980); Jonathan Katz, *A Gay/Lesbian Almanac* (New York: Thomas Y. Crowell Co., 1982); Jeffrey Weeks, *Coming Out: Homosexual Politics in Britain from the Nineteenth Century to the Present* (London: Quartet Books, 1977); and Weeks, *Sex, Politics, and Society: The Regulation of Sexuality since 1800* (London: Longman & Co., 1981).

13. For more on bachelors see Fredric Jameson, *Wyndham Lewis: Fables of Aggression* (Berkeley and Los Angeles: University of California Press, 1979), ch. 2; also, cited in Jameson, Jean Borie, *Le Célibataire français* (Paris: Le Sagittaire, 1976); and Edward Said, *Beginnings* (New York: Basic Books, 1975), pp. 137–52.

14. F. O. Matthiessen and Kenneth B. Murdock, eds., *The Notebooks of Henry James* (New York: Oxford University Press, 1947), p. 28.

15. Bachelor literature in which the paranoid Gothic—or more broadly, the supernatural—makes a reappearance includes, besides Du Maurier's *Trilby*, George Eliot's *The Lifted Veil*, Robert Louis Stevenson's *Dr. Jekyll and Mr. Hyde*, numerous Kipling stories such as "In the Same Boat," and numerous James stories such as "The Jolly Corner."

16. *Lovel the Widower*, in *Works of Thackeray* (New York: National Library, n.d.), 1: ch. 1. Subsequent references to this novel are to this edition and are cited parenthetically in the text by chapter number.

17. In, respectively, Trollope's *The Claverings* and Thackeray's *Pendennis* and *Vanity Fair*; "Soapey" Sponge is in R. S. Surtees's *Mr. Sponge's Sporting Tour*.

18. Richard Miller, *Bohemia: The Protoculture Then and Now* (Chicago: Nelson-Hall Co., 1977), p. 58.

19. *Notebooks of James*, Matthiessen and Murdock, eds., pp. 97–98.

20. "Ballads," *Works of Thackeray*, 6: 337.

21. George Du Maurier, *Trilby* (New York: Harper & Bros., 1922), p. 271.

22. The effect of emboldenment should be to some extent mistrusted—not, I think, because the attribution to these particular figures of a knowledge of male homosexual panic is likely to be wrong, but because it is so much easier to be so emboldened about men who are arguably homosexual in (if such a thing exists) "basic" sexual orientation; while what I am arguing is that panic is proportioned not to the homosexual but to the nonhomosexual-identified elements of these men's characters. Thus, if Barrie and James are obvious authors with whom to *begin* an analysis of male homosexual panic, the analysis I am offering here must be inadequate to the degree that it does not work just as well—even better—for Joyce, Milton, Faulkner, Lawrence, Yeats.

23. Leon Edel, *Henry James: The Middle Years: 1882–1895*, vol. 3 of *The Life of Henry James* (New York: J. B. Lippincott, Co., 1962; repr., Avon Books, 1978), makes clear that these contacts—coinciding visits to some cities and shared trips to others (e.g., 3: 94), "a special rendezvous" in Geneva (3: 217), a period of actually living in the same house (3: 215–17)—were conducted with a consistent and most uncharacteristic extreme of secrecy. (James seems also to have taken extraordinary pains to destroy every vestige of his correspondence with Woolson.) Edel cannot, nevertheless, imagine the relationship except as "a continuing 'virtuous' attachment"; "That this pleasant and *méticuleuse* old maid may have nourished fantasies of a closer tie does not seem to have occurred to him at this time. If it had, we might assume he would have speedily put distance between himself and her" (3: 217). Edel's hypothesis does nothing, of course, to explain the secrecy of these and other meetings.

24. Edel, *Life of James*, vol. 4, *The Master: 1910–1916*, pp. 132–40.

25. "The Beast in the Jungle," in *The Complete Tales of Henry James*, ed. Leon Edel (London: Rupert Hart-Davis, 1964), 11:401. All subsequent references to this work are to this edition and are cited parenthetically in the text by page number.

26. Interestingly, in the 1895 germ of (what seems substantially to be) "The Beast in the Jungle," in James's *Notebooks*, p. 184, the woman outlives the man. "It's *the woman's sense of what might [have been] in him* that arrives at the intensity. . . . *She is his Dead Self: he is alive in her and dead in himself*—that is something like the little formula I seem to *entrevoir*. He himself, the man, must, *in* the tale, also materially die—die in the flesh as he has died long ago in the spirit, the *right* one. Then it is that his lost treasure revives most—no longer *contrarié* by his material existence, existence in his false self, his wrong one."

27. Quoted in Boswell, *Christianity*, p. 349 (from a legal document dated 533) and p. 380 (from a 1227 letter from Pope Honorious III).

28. Quoted in Bray, *Homosexuality*—the first two from p. 61 (from Edward Coke's *Institutes* and Sir David Lindsay's *Works*), the next two from p. 62 (from William Bradford's *Plimouth Plantation* and Guillaume Du Bartas's *Divine Weeks*), and the last from p. 22, also from Du Bartas.

29.   Lord Alfred Douglas, "Two Loves," from *The Chameleon*, quoted in Byron R. S. Fone, *Hidden Heritage: History and the Gay Imagination* (New York: Irvington Publishers, 1981), p. 196.

30.   For a striking anecdotal example of the mechanism of this, see Beverley Nichols, *Father Figure* (New York: Simon and Schuster, 1972), pp. 92–99.

31.   Exceptions that I know of include Georges-Michel Sarotte's discussions of James in *Like a Brother, Like a Lover: Male Homosexuality in the American Novel and Theater from Herman Melville to James Baldwin,* trans. Richard Miller (New York: Doubleday & Co./Anchor, 1978); Richard Hall, "Henry James: Interpreting an Obsessive Memory," *Journal of Homosexuality* 8, no. 3/4 (Spring/Summer 1983): 83–97; and Robert K. Martin, "The 'High Felicity' of Comradeship: A New Reading of Roderick Hudson," *American Literary Realism* 11 (Spring 1978): 100–108.

32.   A fascinating passage in James's *Notebooks*, p. 318, written in 1905 in California, shows how a greater self-knowledge in James, and a greater acceptance and *specificity* of homosexual desire, transform this half-conscious enforcing rhetoric of anality, numbness, and silence into a much richer, pregnant address to James's male muse, an invocation of fisting-as-*écriture:*

> I sit here, after long weeks, at any rate, in front of my arrears, with an inward accumulation of material of which I feel the wealth, and as to which I can only invoke my familiar demon of patience, who always comes, doesn't he?, when I call. He is here with me in front of this cool green Pacific— he sits close and I feel his soft breath, which cools and steadies and inspires, on my cheek. Everything sinks in: nothing is lost; everything abides and fertilizes and renews its golden promise, making me think with closed eyes of deep and grateful longing when, in the full summer days of L[amb] H[ouse], my long dusty adventure over, I shall be able to [plunge] my hand, my arm, *in*, deep and far, and up to the shoulder—into the heavy bag of remembrance—of suggestion—of imagination—of art— and fish out every little figure and felicity, every little fact and fancy that can be to my purpose. These things are all packed away, now, thicker than I can penetrate, deeper than I can fathom, and there let them rest for the present, in their sacred cool darkness, till I shall let in upon them the mild still light of dear old L[amb] H[ouse]—in which they will begin to gleam and glitter and take form like the gold and jewels of a mine.

33.   *Collected Poems of Emily Dickinson*, ed. Thomas H. Johnson (Boston: Little, Brown & Co., 1960), p. 406.

34.   Lytton Strachey, quoted in Michael Holroyd, *Lytton Strachey: A Critical Biography* (London: W. H. Heinemann, 1968), 2: 179.

35.   Ruth Bernard Yeazell makes clear the oddity of having Marcher turn his back on the Beast that is supposed, at this moment, to represent his self-recognition (in *Language and Knowledge in the Late Novels of Henry James* [Chicago: University of Chicago Press, 1976], pp. 37–38.)

13

Virile Womanhood:
Olive Schreiner's Narratives of
a Master Race

Carol L. Barash

"We take all labor for our province."

Olive Schreiner, *Woman and Labor*

Preferring male to female friendship, considering herself different from other women, and keeping her distance from organized feminism, Olive Schreiner seems an unlikely candidate to have written the "bible" of the British women's suffrage movement. But militant suffragists read Schreiner's *Woman and Labor* (1911) to one another in prison, they quoted it frequently, and assimilated its tone and language to a wide range of writings on gender, morality, and sexuality. Even those who disagreed with Schreiner's views on motherhood and heterosexuality were forced to respond to her powerful Darwinian prose. At the same time, Schreiner was unable to complete her two most ambitious feminist works: an introduction to Mary Wollstonecraft's *Vindication of the Rights of Woman* and a novel criticizing marriage and prostitution that was published posthumously by her husband as *From Man to Man* (1927). Schreiner's strongest personal and narrative ambivalences—woman as pure and maternal, maternity as central to the salvation of the human race—helped to shape the militants' rhetoric and symbolism of gender and remain problems central to contemporary feminism.

While some feminists in the United States have reclaimed Schreiner's as a lost feminist voice (Gubar, 1983) or discussed her life as that of a tragic heroine (Showalter, 1982), others, particularly in South Africa, sense that Schreiner's limits were political ones, that her vision was ameliorative and colonialist (Jacobsen, 1971), structurally if not ideologically racist. Nadine Gordimer claims, "[Schreiner's] tragedy as a writer was that in the end she was unable to put the best she had—the power of her creative imagination—to the service of her original thought, fiercely profound convictions, and political and human insights" (Smith and Maclennan, 1983: 18). Schreiner's incantatory Darwinian rhetoric is stronger than the novels that contain it; her writing attempts to reveal necessary political change but cannot embody those hopes in fiction. However, such narrative limits can also be read as political truths: stories don't change until the social order changes; the act of writing political fiction involves straining against social constructs, enabling them to change. By discussing Schreiner's fiction as the interplay of personal and political situation and narrative form, I hope to describe her later, overtly political writing as part of a continuum of creative works, and her ideological concerns as problems of interaction and communication, that is, as attempts to narrate, and in the process of narrating to create, a changed world.[1]

Born in 1855 in Cape Colony, South Africa, Olive Emilie Albertina Schreiner was the ninth of Rebecca Lyndall and Gottlob Schreiner's twelve children. She believed that the death of her younger sister catalyzed her break with her parents' German Protestantism and her move toward free thought and mysticism: "I cannot conceive of either birth or death, or anything but simple changes in the endless existence. . . . I first had this feeling with regard to death clearly when my favorite little sister died when I was nine years old" (Cronwright-Schreiner, 1924a: 219). This very physical desire for transcendence and unity informs *The Story of an African Farm* (1883), where it is elaborated in relation to, and limited by abiding in, a female body. Schreiner also linked her sense of women as other to her love of her sister and to her sister's death: "I sometimes think my great love for women and girls, *not* because they are myself, but because they are *not* myself, comes from my love to her" (Cronwright-Schreiner, 1924a: 274). We can read an ambivalent lesbian fantasy behind Schreiner's "love" for other women; she describes women as sexually other, as objects of curiosity, power, and often disdain. Schreiner enacted this objectification and scientific examination of other women, a pattern of defining herself by way of but in contrast to them, when she sought out and lived among prostitutes while writing *From Man to Man*.

When Schreiner left home to work as a governess, she began writing novels. At age seventeen, the Bible, Emerson, and nineteenth-century science were her major influences. Before discussing the novels it is helpful to understand Schreiner's peculiar, almost skew relationship to the English literary tradition. Schreiner spoke of her attraction to scientific theory in sexual terms. Repeatedly she was both empowered by men's writing and overwhelmed by the literalness of its presence. She read Herbert Spencer's *First Principles* (1862) as a young girl and described him as a doctor who had cured her broken leg: "Once it is set one may be said to have no more need of the doctor, nevertheless one always walks on his leg. . . . He helped me to believe in a unity underlying all nature; that was a great thing" (Cronwright-Schreiner, 1924b: 82–83). Similarly, once Schreiner began to imbibe Darwin, his writing took her over completely, so that while she was enabled to imagine independent thought she ceased thinking independently. The impact of Darwin is seen in everything from Rebekah's fascination with biological and moral evolution in *From Man to Man* to the arguments for racial development and eugenics in *Woman and Labor* and Schreiner's other political writings.

In *Darwin's Plots: Evolutionary Narrative in Darwin, George Eliot, and Nineteenth-Century Fiction* (1983), Gillian Beer describes how evolutionary discourse shapes the narrative patterns of many Victorian novels. One way to understand Schreiner's fiction is to rethink these Darwinian patterns from her colonial point of view. Where a novelist like George Eliot can elaborate Darwin's story of female sexual selection by narrating from the point of view of the colonial power (Beer: 210–235), Schreiner has recourse to long-term, feminist evolution only by denying her situation as a white woman, descended from but not a member of the European elite governing the country of her birth. As the young Rebekah demonstrates while memorizing a long Victorian poem in *From Man to Man*, certain language only makes sense from the dominant point of view: "I could understand it all except 'For-Empire' and 'far-renown.'—I don't know what 'far-renown' is—or 'for-empire'—" (p. 25).

Schreiner seems to construct her sense of sexual status[2] by way of a potentially racist turn in Darwin's diction: at times the words "race" and "species" are synonymous (as in "the human race") but at other times racial "varieties" become subordinate to the needs of the dominant or white "species." As Gordimer shows so well in *July's People* (1981), white women in South Africa are both colonizer and colonized, and like Maureen in that novel experience this political self-division as both self-hatred and racism. The force of Schreiner's prose comes in part from trying to address two very different audiences: the white colonial rulers in England and the many colored, colonized people of South Africa. In all her writing Schreiner uses allegory—both the narrative structure and the language of the Bible—to bridge this gap; in *From Man to Man* and *Woman and Labor* she develops an empowering but nonetheless problematic notion of timeless maternal strengths to compensate for the powerlessness she feared to be women's biological lot.

In four years as a governess, Schreiner wrote drafts of three novels: *Undine* (1928), *The Story of an African Farm*, and *From Man to Man*. Schreiner's fiction clusters around a matrix of emotions—loss and betrayal in love, women's alienation and guilt—to which Schreiner returned time and time again without resolving them in narrative. We can see what Freud calls a repetition compulsion in Schreiner's repeated use of her own and her mother's names (Em and Lyndall in *African Farm*, Rebekah in *Man to Man*) and in the reappearance of outsiders who, like Waldo's and Rebekah's, bring transcendental wisdom or, like Lyndall's and Bertie's, engulf the heroine and overdetermine her demise by introducing an irresistible but devastating male sexuality (Freud, 1914). But in Schreiner's case we can also rethink Freud in more local, and more political, terms. In the refusal to relinquish her pain and in the desire to transform it into something permanently beautiful and true are rooted both the intensity and the limitations of Schreiner's best work. Schreiner insists in *Woman and Labor* that one learns from suffering and that women's greater pain in bearing, raising, and losing children makes them more qualified to govern human affairs (pp. 178–179). Schreiner's fiction of transcendent femaleness, enabling in its promise of a distinctly female sexuality and stultifying in its biologism, was bequeathed by Victorian science.

Published under the Emersonian pseudonym Ralph Iron, *The Story of an African Farm* was Schreiner's best-known work; it made her instantly notorious in London's intellectual circles. At the center of the novel, Lyndall leaves home seeking an education in knowledge and experience, but discovers that her girls' "finishing school" tries to squelch everything she likes in herself in an effort to make her submissive and helpless. Lyndall's explanation of her entrapment in womanhood is a powerful articulation of what we now call the cultural construction of gender:

> We all enter the world little plastic beings, with so much natural force, perhaps, but for the rest—blank; and the world tells us what we are to be, and shapes us by the ends it sets before us. To you it says—*Work!* and to us it says—*Seem!* To you it says—As you approximate to man's highest ideal of God, as your arm is strong and your knowledge great, and the power to labor is with you, so you shall gain all that human heart desires. To us it says—Strength shall not help you, nor knowledge, nor labor. You shall gain what men gain, but by other means. And so the world makes men and women. (p. 175)

Later, responding to her unnamed lover's proposal, Lyndall adds:

> [Y]our hands and your voice are like the hands and the voice of any other man. . . . You call into activity one part of my nature; there is a higher part that you know nothing of, that you never touch. If I married you, afterwards it would arise and assert itself, and I should hate you always, as I do now sometimes. (p. 224)

But Lyndall's feminist rhetoric is at odds with the novel's plot. Without explanation, Lyndall destroys herself by capitulating to the unnamed man who wishes only to master her. She becomes pregnant but the child dies, and the pain of losing this newborn daughter stalks her through her own slow death.

Although there is no explicit reason for Lyndall's sudden reversal, her seeming self-destruction, we can understand the novel as ideological, in a dynamic sense, if we explore how sexual difference operates as both an enabling and a limiting fiction. The novel has two major sections—childhood and adulthood—which are also marked by contrasts of innocence and experience, belief and despair. These two narratives are separated by a long, meditative passage, "Times and Seasons," about the birth and growth of belief and told by the first-person plural, "we." Schreiner told her brother that the two central characters, Lyndall and Waldo, were both herself, and it is this nonlinear passage which most strongly links the imagery of their shared transcendentalism. The language in this section is particularly sexual, with conversion figured as male orgasm:

> After hours and nights of frenzied fear of the supernatural desire to appease the power above, a fierce quivering excitement in every inch of nerve and

blood-vessel, there comes a time when nature cannot endure longer, and the spring long bent recoils. We sink down emasculated. Up creeps the deadly delicious calm. (pp. 129–130)

Just as religious mysticism is figured in terms of male sexuality, we learn about religious doubt through the central male character. The narrator claims sympathy with Waldo's spiritual suffering as if it is not marked by gender: "There are some of us who in after years say to Fate, 'Now deal us your hardest blow, give us what you will; but let us never again suffer as we suffered when we were children' " (p. 29). The narrator's "we" provides a fictive unity, an allegory of transcendence that is deconstructed by the novel's fierce economy of gender possibilities. As Lyndall's experience shows, the mystic desire for unity must be lived in a world in which actively heterosexual women become child-bearing rather than spiritual adults.

For the male characters in *African Farm* the desire for a union between male and female spheres is unconscious but profound. Waldo twice thinks of his intellectual creations as offspring (pp. 93, 144). They take nine months each to produce, and he feels bereft when they are stolen from him. Similarly, when Gregory Rose dons women's clothing and tends Lyndall in her delirium, the narrator claims that he is a better nurse than many trained women. In Schreiner's Darwinian symbolism of gender it is possible, even necessary, for men to learn the powers of compassion and nurturing, yet impossible for even the most feminist woman to think freely or to work. Explaining the difference between Spencer's and Darwin's use of the term "sexual selection," a nineteenth-century critic illuminates how *African Farm* is built around the Darwinian man and the Spencerian woman: "For [Herbert] Spencer, the development of woman is early arrested by procreative functions. In short, Darwin's man is as it were an evolved woman, and Spencer's woman an arrested man" (quoted in Beer, 1983: 214).

In proceeding from doubt to transcendence, male characters draw upon the utopian, cross-cultural matrix of belief voiced by the feminist Lyndall and central to *Woman and Labor*. Waldo's god nurtures him as a mother would: " 'The presence of God'; a sense of a good, strong something folding him round" (p. 84). Just before Waldo dies, the narrator allows him a revelation of an explicitly maternal Nature to replace the "old Hebrew God": "When the old desire is crushed, then the Divine compensation of Nature is made manifest, She shows herself to you. So near she draws you, that the blood seems to flow from her to you, through a still uncut cord: you feel the throb of her life" (p. 285).

Lyndall's belief system links maternity with images of spiritual power from a variety of cultures—"A Hindoo philosopher . . . a troop of Bacchanalians . . . a mother giving bread and milk to her children" (pp. 201–202); her sense of potential power fuses images from both male and female spheres of Victorian sexuality. Yet she is happiest with Waldo, in whose presence she imaginatively cancels gender: "When I am with you I never know that I am a woman and you are a man; I only know that we are both things that think" (p. 197). However, when Lyndall enacts the sexual potential of her mysticism, she must choose between work and love, and a series of socially proscribed roles—lover, mistress, unwed mother, fallen woman—collapses around her frail body and its powerful plans. Lyndall's tiny hands and feet are marks of her failure, of centuries of confinement and servitude which she is far too weak, and seemingly masochistic, to overcome. In all of Schreiner's heroines there are gaps between their best vision of a new society and their entrapment in a Victorian world of separate men's and women's spheres which marks biology as destiny.

Again, in *From Man to Man*, a novel Schreiner worked on all her life but never completed, we find visionary rhetoric voiced by Rebekah, a woman who will not sever herself from a marriage she knows to be inadequate and self-defeating, a husband she knows to be unfaithful. This is a very Darwinian bind: although the individual knows that culture changes over time, in a single lifetime culture is experienced as fixed. *From Man to Man, or Perhaps Only* was meant to be a radically feminist novel, one that explored a series of miserable marriages and challenged Darwin by showing the connections between Victorian marriage and prostitution. Schreiner's most sustained work on *From Man to Man* developed out of her friendships with Karl Pearson and Havelock Ellis and her involvement in the Men and Women's Club, an elite London group that met weekly to discuss what they called "the Woman Question": the changing relationship between men and women resulting from the Married Women's Property Act, women's entrance into the professions, and socialists' interest in women's relationship to both work and child-bearing. Schreiner was frequently thwarted at the Men and Women's Club, and although she longed for interaction with other women, she did not seek them out as intellectual equals (Walkowitz, 1986).

From Man to Man is framed by an introduction, "A Note on the Genesis of the Book," and a concluding note, all apologetically added by Schreiner's husband. Among these notes is a letter to Havelock Ellis in which Schreiner states the novel's purpose: "I have always built upon the fact that *From Man to Man* will help other people, for it will help to make men more tender to women, because they will understand them better; it will make some women more tender to others; it will comfort some women by showing them that others have felt as they do." This ambitious, conciliatory mission seems to have been incapacitating. Each time Schreiner approached completion of *From Man to Man* she silenced herself, just as the novel's heroine does, by massively editing, rearranging the plot, or otherwise destroying her own manuscript. But even the unfinished version of *From Man to Man* points to an extremely imaginative political novel. What were spiritual problems in *African Farm* become moral and intellectual problems in *From Man to Man*; the novel is most importantly about two sisters, and about the relationship between women.

The novel is dedicated "to My Little Sister Ellie Who died aged eighteen months, when I was nine years old. Also to My Only Daughter. Born on the 30th April, and died the 1st May. She never lived to know she was a woman." It opens with five-year-old Rebekah listening to her mother's labor pains: "The little mother lay in the agony of childbirth. . . . The mother groaned" (p. 3). As in *African Farm*, the story grows out of early childhood events, but here the central characters are both women, and the chapters are accordingly titled "The Child's Day" and "The Woman's Day." The novel shows both sustaining and competitive relationships between women, including the language and beliefs of Boer and African servants as well as those of the main characters. It is a sign of Rebekah's moral strength that she raises the mulatto child of her husband and his mistress as one of her own. *From Man to Man*, as it stands, is an attempt to integrate two separate stories, told from the points of view of the two sisters, Bertie and Rebekah.

Unlike Lyndall, whose hero is Napoleon, Rebekah calls herself the "little Queen Victoria of South Africa" (p. 15) and imagines writing "a book something like the Bible" (p. 23). She studies biology with her father, runs the house and raises Bertie in place of her weak mother. She marries not for love or passion but because of a primordial "hunger" to have children, "a voice from that primal depth of nature which, before man was man, called beast to beast and kind to kind" (p. 57). Rebekah's strengths evolve from her lifelong desire to support and to nurture others. She rarely sleeps, remaining close to her children's nursery in a study no bigger than a closet where she retreats to books as children or lovers:

> From her shelves, the bindings of her books looked down at her, each one a little brown face that seemed to love her. Behind each was hidden the mind of some human creature which at some time had touched her own . . . each one was there because at some time she had lived close to it and it had penetrated her. (p. 149)

We see the personal danger in Rebekah's caring instinct when she cannot leave her unfaithful husband because she imagines that she is his mother rather than his wife: "If I had had a son and he had loved another woman not his wife, and he had come and laid his head on my breast and told me about it, would I not have sympathized with him and tried to help him to find a way that was truthful and open?" (p. 245).

Rebekah's private writings—a diary and two long letters she writes to her husband—form the core of the novel. This hallucinatory writing is like the "Times and Seasons" passage of *African Farm*, but more woman-identified and more Darwinian. Rebekah describes marriage and prostitution as two types of a sexual arrangement in which a man legally possesses a woman. She backs away from saying that in marriage both the woman's body and her brain are owned by the man: " 'He puts his hand in among the finest cords of her being and rends and tears them if he will . . . it isn't only her body a woman gives a man—' (This paragraph Rebekah had not finished and had scratched out)" (p. 250). But Rebekah's evolutionary narrative is often both trivializing and racist, relying more on the Victorian iconography of prostitution than on the experience of real prostitutes with whom Schreiner was familiar.[3]

> Which is fairer and more akin to the ideals toward which humanity seems to move?—the little Bushman in his open cave on the mountain brow, etching away into the rock . . . or a swell-chinned ragged woman staggering out of

a public-house in one of our centers of civilization, while the man who made the drink dwells in high places? (p. 181)

In language that likens motherhood to Christ's suffering, Rebekah traces "mother-love" from amoebas to humans:

> Love becomes incarnate in the female mammal feeding her young from her breast—this is my blood which I give for the life of the world—through all nature, life and growth and evolution are possible only because of mother-love. . . . Man individually and as a race is possible on earth only because, not for weeks or months but for years, love and the guardianship of the strong over the weak has existed. (p. 185)

Rebekah's instincts for love and "guardianship" lead her, often without conscious choice, to discover the truth. Thinking of her husband "as one thinks of one's little child," she goes to join him in bed only to discover that he is outside in the servant's hut. After this discovery Rebekah experiences no anger, but fills a waste-paper basket with "pages of paper, wholly or partially covered with writing and then torn up" (pp. 221–224). The death of Rebekah's ideals leads her to silence herself but it mysteriously strengthens what can only be called "instinct." In a scene that reverses the end of *Jane Eyre*, she experiences "a sudden feeling . . . that [she] must go to Muizenberg" and races there to discover her husband making love with their neighbor Mrs. Drummond (pp. 241–243). Finally, the more egal-itarian desire between Rebekah and Mr. Drummond is poured into his search for Bertie, who has fallen into prostitution and is dying of syphilis.

The most interesting twist of plot involves Rebekah's buying a farm and beginning an independent life with her children. For a time she switches from writing to work as a means to break away from her husband. Like Lyndall's sense of freedom outside of culturally constructed gender, Rebekah imagines herself and her husband as "two free souls." But in her massively edited letter to him these souls are most often gendered, "just like two men" (pp. 266–275). As in *Woman and Labor* a sexual division not only of labor but also of language is built into Schreiner's evolutionary model. The most important parts of Rebekah's story—her powerful experience of her body as fecund and child-bearing, and the moral force that evolves from her commitment to others—remain private knowledge. Although she believes that society needs these maternal powers she cannot integrate them into a public discourse about sexuality.

The important events in Bertie's story are even less narratable than those in Rebekah's. Schreiner's original vision was to link marriage and prostitution struc-turally in *From Man to Man;* however, in the published manuscript this connection is attempted by an unbelievable, Calvinist conclusion. Called Baby Bertie because she never grows up, Rebekah's sister is seduced by her tutor, than abandoned by the man she loves when she tells him about this earlier sexual encounter. Rebekah describes Bertie as a less developed, dependent type of woman:

Some women with complex, many-sided natures, if love fails them and one half of their nature dies, can still draw a kind of broken life through the other. . . . But Bertie and such as Bertie have only one life possible, the life of the personal relations; if that fails them, all fails. (pp. 92–93)

As much as she is seduced by cruel men Bertie is seduced by her desire for sensual experience, which unlike Rebekah she cannot experience vicariously through books. She marries a rich Jew (*From Man to Man* is patently anti-semitic) who locks her in an apartment in the city where she grows obese and raises kittens like children. Completely passive and powerless, Bertie slowly becomes a prostitute. In the projected final scene of the novel, Bertie's deathbed was to have been tended by Rebekah, who oversees her conversion. The failed plot of *From Man to Man* highlights the limits of maternal ideology; written as a political tract, *Woman and Labor* is a much less critical articulation of an evolutionary system that deifies biological motherhood.

Woman and Labor extends Mary Wollstonecraft's (1792; rpt 1975) plea for equality from the world of education to the world of economics and production, claiming that women's access to work of equal quality at equal wages with men will end a long period of decay and infuse new vigor into the moral order. The most important similarity between Wollstonecraft and Schreiner—their belief that women have been rendered social "parasites"—also points to the major differences between the two theorists. Schreiner wanted both to vindicate the suffrage movement and the wide range of public and professional activities being undertaken by "New Women," and to respond to those (including herself) who feared the New Women cared only for their own advancement and would no longer protect, nurture, and give birth. According to Schreiner, "sex-parasitism" was the interdependence of "passive" women, who relied on men's money and praise, and "licentious" men who paid women for the use of their bodies and for their subordination. Prostitutes and upper-class women were equally implicated as "the most deadly microbe which can make its appearance on the surface of any social organism" (p. 81). Schreiner links prostitutes and upper-class women by seeing them both from the point of view of the male consumer, that is, as sexual objects but not as powerless sexual dependents.

Like many late nineteenth-century writers, including Engels (1884; trans. and rpt 1978) and Bachofen (rpt 1967), Schreiner idealizes a matriarchal age when motherhood was worshipped as the source of human life (p. 28). In all these writers, a sexual division of labor is projected onto a Golden Age when women and women's culture were central to all human affairs. Through a series of sudden changes, Schreiner traces human society from this matriarchal time through industrialization to the present. Ironically, this series of technological and ideological crises—the arrival of organized agriculture, cottage industry, and capitalism—both moves away from and justifies women's privileged maternal status. Schreiner uses "labor" to mean both work for wages and child-bearing. Entrance into all fields of work will enable women to refuse vanity and prostitution, and as mothers to lead a moral cleansing of the race.

Putting forward a series of essentially incompatible analogies, Schreiner argues that the struggle for women's equality is a fundamentally different struggle from socialist demands for equal wages. In long, rhythmic sentences, she claims first that the women's movement is formed like a child in the womb (p. 142), then that social change is like a cathedral, built by numerous generations of workers, each having "carried on his duties and month by month toiled at carving his own little gargoyle or shaping the traceries of his own little oriel window, without any complete vision" (p. 144). Next, the women's movement is like Moses' vision of the "Land of Promise"; and finally, linking the work of New Women to these other multi-generational struggles, Schreiner is trapped between a vision of women warriors and failed artists. She returns to the cathedral builders; this time they are women and feminists, but they fail:

> [They] labor on patiently year after year at some poor little gargoyle of a Franchise Bill . . . [They] carve away all their lives to produce a corbel of some new and beautiful condition in sexual relations, in the end to find it break under the chisel. . . . It is through the labors of these myriad toilers, each working in her own minute sphere, with her own small outlook, and out of endless failures and miscarriages, that at last the enwidened and beautiful relations of woman to life must rise. (p. 146)

The New Women of *Woman and Labor* are like all of Schreiner's heroines; they speak passionately for a vision that will someday come, but they and their creations are imperfect, arrested, dwarfed.

In contrast, Schreiner describes "Teutonic woman" as the source of all powerful women, be they European or African, ancient or modern. "Teutonic womanhood" is an extremely phallic type:

> We who lead in this movement to-day are of that old, old Teutonic womanhood, which twenty centuries ago plowed its march through European forests . . . which marched with the Cimbri to Italy . . . which peopled Scandinavia, and penetrated to Britain . . . We have in us the blood of a womanhood that was never bought and never sold . . . who stood side by side with the males they loved in peace or war, and whose children . . . sucked manhood from their breasts, and even through their fetal existence heard a brave heart beat above them. (p. 148)

When Schreiner calls these women "virile," she draws on both the usual meanings—masculine, adult, or strong—and an obsolete meaning—nubile, ready for child-bearing. These two meanings come together when she says that Teutonic women were "virile and could give birth to men" (p. 91). Placed after images of "aborted" and "miscarried" creations, these women who can create sons compensate narratively for the imaginative births of feminist daughters who fail in the present moment.

As Schreiner noted English women no longer asserting their "overmastering hunger" to bear children, she used native South African women as the template to project her Golden Age of sexual harmony and lost maternal values; they alone feel the drumbeat of that eternal motherhood in the twentieth-century (p. 5). This myth of common descent was a way to gloss over vast race and class differences to prove middle-class women "maternal," even if they chose not to have children, by way of other women's literal maternity. Schreiner's racial primitivism, like sociobiology or biblical allegory, is a way to avoid confronting gender as a cultural construct that mediates between ideal and real. The belief in archetypal maternity and its blurring of history into a set of trans-temporal values obviates the need for political change in the present while justifying the rule and reproduction of "virile" white men and women, those already in power. Crossing Darwin's models of racial determinism and female sexual selection creates a heterosexual determinism that glorifies motherhood without changing the world into which women and men bear children. Darwin's ideals, based on warfare and domination, are not antipathetic but inextricably linked to Schreiner's belief in timeless maternal values. Schreiner was incapable of tolerating a world which was rent into shards of pain and conflict. But the price of her belief in unity was often a capitulation to the patterns of white male dominance, a need to experience power from the point of view of patriarchy's reproductive needs.

The strongest reading of *Woman and Labor* is to call it an extended allegory, a dreamlike evocation of a time when men and women "shall eat of the tree of knowledge together . . . [and] they shall together raise about them an Eden nobler than any the Chaldean dreamed of; an Eden created by their own labor and made beautiful by their own fellowship" (p. 298). This strong, biblical language had the power to mobilize thousands of British women, to help them imagine their lives as potentially powerful, dramatic, and lush. At its most radical, *Woman and Labor* claims that women's joint participation in the work force will change not only gender configurations—how society construes maleness and femaleness—but also sexuality, desire, and the relationships between and among men and women. But by collapsing the complexities of culturally constructed gender and sexuality into the biological duality of sex, Schreiner cancels our power to choose and our desire for change, which may be in all its manifold varieties our most persistent and powerful desire.

Notes

Longer versions of this paper were presented at the "Feminist Reconstructions of the Self and Society" Colloquium, Douglass College, Rutgers University, February 1985, and at the National Women's Studies Association Conference, University of Washington, June 1985. I would also like to thank Polly Beals, Elaine Showalter, and Judith Walkowitz for generous discussions of an earlier draft.

1. For theoretical discussions of the relationship between ideology, gender, and language, see Barrett (1980) and Williams (1977).

2.   I take this term from Ortner and Whitehead (1981: 8), where they discuss how gender figures in and works against other cultural understandings of power and identity. See Davin (1978) for an account of the problem in Schreiner's historical context.

3.   See Walkowitz (1980) for an excellent discussion of the myths and realities of prostitution in Victorian England.

References

Appleman, Philip. 1979. *Darwin*. Norton Critical Edition, New York.

Bachofen, J. J. 1967. *Myth, Religion, and Mother Right, Selected Writings of J . J . Bachofen*. Trans. Ralph Manheim. Princeton University Press, Princeton.

Barash, Carol. Forthcoming. "Olive Schreiner." In Schlueter, Paul and June, eds. *British Women Writers*. Ungar, New York.

Barrett, Michèle. 1980. *Women's Oppression Today: Problems in Marxist Feminist Analysis*. Verso, London.

Beer, Gillian. 1983. *Darwin's Plots: Evolutinary Narrative in Darwin, George Eliot, and Nineteenth-Century Fiction*. Routledge & Kegan Paul, London.

Cronwright-Schreiner, S. C. 1924a. *The Letters of Olive Schreiner*. T. Fisher Unwin, London.

Cronwright-Schreiner, S. C. 1924b. *The Life of Olive Schreiner*. T. Risher Unwin, London.

Davin, Anna. 1978. "Imperialism and motherhood," *History Workshop J*. 5: 9–65.

Engels, Frederick. 1884; trans. and rpt 1978. *The Origin of the Family, Private Property, and the State*. Foreign Languages Press, Peking.

First, Ruth and Ann Scott. 1980. *Olive Schreiner, A Biography*. Schocken, New York.

Freud, Sigmund. 1914: English edn 1958. "Remembering, repeating, and working through." *Standard Edition of the Complete Psychological Works of Sigmund Freud*, Vol. XII, pp. 147–156. Hogarth, London.

Gordimer, Nadine. 1981. *July's People*. Viking, New York.

Gubar, Susan. 1983. "Patricides and Parasites: The 'Bandaged Moments' of Olive Schreiner." Paper delivered to the Modern Languages Association, New York.

Jacobson, Dan. 1971. "Introduction." *The Story of an African Farm*. Penguin, Harmondsworth.

Ortner, Sherry B. and Harriet Whitehead. 1981. *Sexual Meanings: The Cultural Construction of Gender and Sexuality*. Cambridge University Press, Cambridge.

Schreiner, Olive. 1883; rpt 1976. *The Story of an African Farm*. Schocken, New York.

Schreiner, Olive. 1892. *Dreams*. Roberts Brothers, Boston.

Schreiner, Olive. 1911. *Woman and Labor*. Frederick Stokes, New York.

Schreiner, Olive. 1927; rpt 1977. *From Man to Man, or Perhaps Only*. Academy Press, Chicago.

Schreiner, Olive. 1928. *Undine*. Harper and Brothers, New York and London.

Showalter, Elaine. 1977. *A Literature of Their Own*. Princeton University Press, Princeton.

Showalter, Elaine. 1982. "Olive Schreiner: A Biography." *Tulsa St. Women's Lit*. 1 (1): 104–109.

Smith, Malvern V. W. and Don Maclennan. 1983. *Olive Schreiner and After: Essays on Southern African Literature in Honour of Guy Butler*. David Phillip, Cape Town.

Vicinus, Martha. 1985. *Independent Women: Work and Community for Single Women, 1850–1920*. University of Chicago Press, Chicago.

Walkowitz, Judith R. 1980. *Prostitution and Victorian Society: Women, Class, and the State*. Cambridge University Press, Cambridge.

Walkowitz, Judith R. 1986. "Science, feminism and romance: the Men and Women's Club, 1885–89." *History Workshop J*. 21: 36–59.

Williams, Raymond. 1977. *Marxism and Literature*. Oxford University Press, New York.

Wollstonecraft, Mary. 1792; rpt 1975. *A Vindication of the Rights of Woman*. Norton, New York.

14

Soldier's Heart:
Literary Men, Literary Women, and
the Great War

Sandra M. Gilbert

> This great war . . . is Nature's vengeance—is God's vengeance upon
> the people who held women in subjection, and by doing that have
> destroyed the perfect, human balance.
> [Christabel Pankhurst, *The Suffragette*]

> I rose—because He sank—
> I thought it would be opposite—
> But when his power dropped—
> My Soul grew straight.
> [Emily Dickinson, Poem 616]

Battle of the Sexes

As we have all been told over and over again, World War I was not just the war
to end wars; it was also the war of wars, a paradigm of technological combat which,
with its trenches and zeppelins, its gases and mines, has become a diabolical
summary of the idea of modern warfare—Western science bent to the service of
Western imperialism, the murderous face of Galileo revealed at last. That this
apocalyptic Great War involved strikingly large numbers of men as well as shock-
ingly powerful technological forces, moreover, has always been understood to
intensify its historical significance. The first modern war to employ now familiar
techniques of conscription and classification in order to create gigantic armies on
both sides, World War I, as we have all been taught, virtually completed the
Industrial Revolution's construction of anonymous dehumanized man, that impotent
cipher who is frequently thought to be the twentieth century's most characteristic
citizen. Helplessly entrenched on the edge of No Man's Land, this faceless being
saw that the desert between him and his so-called enemy was not just a metaphor
for the technology of death and the death dealt by technology, it was also a symbol
for the state, whose nihilistic machinery he was powerless to control or protest.

Fearfully assaulted by a deadly bureaucracy on the one side, and a deadly technocracy on the other, he was No Man, an inhabitant of the inhumane new era and a citizen of the unpromising new land into which this war of wars had led him.[1]

Of course, as we have also been taught, these many dark implications of World War I had further implications for twentieth-century literature. As Malcolm Bradbury puts it, "Many critics have seen the war as . . . the apocalypse that leads the way into Modernism [and] as violation, intrusion, wound, the source of psychic anxiety [and] generational instability."[2] From Lawrence's paralyzed Clifford Chatterley to Hemingway's sadly emasculated Jake Barnes to Eliot's mysteriously sterile Fisher King, moreover, the gloomily bruised modernist anti-heroes churned out by the war suffer specifically from sexual wounds, as if, having traveled literally or figuratively through No Man's Land, all have become not just No Men, nobodies, but *not* men, *un*men. That twentieth-century Everyman, the faceless cipher, their authors seem to suggest, is not just publicly powerless, he is privately impotent.

Obviously, however, such effects of the Great War were in every case gender-specific problems, problems only men could have. Never having had public power, women could hardly become more powerless than they already were. As for private impotence, most late Victorian young girls were trained to see such "passionlessness" as a virtue rather than a failure.[3] Yet women, too, lived through these years, and many modernist writers seem to suggest that, oddly enough, women played an unusually crucial part in the era. In D. H. Lawrence's 1915 "Eloi, Eloi, Lama Sabachthani?" for instance—a representative, if somewhat feverish, wartime poem—the unmanning terrors of combat lead not just to a generalized sexual anxiety but also to a sexual anger directed specifically against the female, as if the Great War itself were primarily a climactic episode in some battle of the sexes that had already been raging for years. Drawing upon the words Christ cried out as he died on the cross, the creator of Clifford Chatterley here presents the war metaphorically as a perverse sexual relationship that becomes a blasphemous (homo)sexual crucifixion.[4] As battle rages and death attacks, the speaker assumes in turn the terrifying roles of rapist and victim, deadly groom and dying bride. Lawrence's perversely revisionary primal scene is made even more terrible, however, by the voyeuristic eyes of a woman who peers "through the rents/In the purple veil" and peeps "in the empty house like a pilferer." Like the gaze of the Medusa, her look seems somehow responsible for male sufferings.

Can this be because the war, with its deathly parody of sexuality, somehow suggests female conquest? Because wives, mothers, and sweethearts were safe on the home front, did the war appear in some peculiar sense their fault, a ritual of sacrifice to their victorious femininity? At the center of his poem, Lawrence places a rhetorical question which seems to imply as much: "Why do the women follow us, satisfied,/Feed on our wounds like bread, receive our blood/Like glittering seed upon them for fulfilment?" Through a paradox that is at first almost imcomprehensible, the war that has traditionally been defined as an apocalypse of masculinism seems here to have led to an apotheosis of femaleness. If we reflect upon this point, however, we must inevitably ask a set of questions about the relations between the sexes during this war of wars. What part, after all, *did* women play in the Great War? How did men perceive that role? More specifically, what connections might there be between the wartime activities of women and the sense of sexual wounding that haunts so many male modernist texts? Most importantly did women themselves experience the wound of the war in the same way that their sons and lovers did?

If we meditate for a while on the sexual implications of the Great War, we must certainly decide, to begin with, that it is one of those classic cases of dissonance between official, male-centered history and unofficial female history about which Joan Kelly has written so tellingly.[5] For not only did the apocalyptic events of this war have a very different meaning for men and women, such events were in fact very different for men and women, a point understood almost at once by an involved contemporary like Vera Brittain, who noted about her relationship with her soldier fiancé that the war put "a barrier of indescribable experience between men and the women whom they loved. . . . Quite early I realized [the] possibility of a permanent impediment to understanding."[6] The nature of the barrier thrust between Brittain and her fiancé, however, may have been even more complex than she herself realized, for the impediment preventing a marriage of their true minds was constituted, as we shall see, not only by his altered experience but by hers. Specifically, I will argue here that as young men became increasingly alienated from their prewar selves, increasingly immured in the muck and blood of No Man's Land, women seemed to become, as if by some uncanny swing of history's pendulum, even more powerful. As nurses, as mistresses, as munitions workers, bus drivers, or soldiers in the "land army," even as wives and mothers, these formerly subservient creatures began to loom malevolently larger, until it was possible for a visitor to London to observe in 1918 that "England was a world of women—women in uniforms,"[7] or, in the words of a verse by Nina Macdonald, "Girls are doing things/They've never done before . . . All the world is topsy-turvy/Since the War began."[8]

"*All the world is topsy-turvy/Since the War began*"; that phrase is a crucial one, for the reverses and reversals of No Man's Land fostered in a number of significant ways the formation of a metaphorical country not unlike the queendom Charlotte Perkins Gilman called Herland, and the exhilaration (along with the anxiety) of that state is as dramatically rendered in wartime poems, stories, and memoirs by women as are the very different responses to the war in usually better-known works by men. Sometimes subtly and subversively, sometimes quite explicitly, writers from Alice Meynell to Radclyffe Hall explored the political and economic revolution by which the Great War at least temporarily dispossessed male citizens of the patriarchal primacy that had always been their birthright while granting women access to both the votes and the professions that they had never before possessed. Similarly, a number of these artists covertly or overtly celebrated the release of female desires. In addition, many women writers recorded drastic (re)visions of society that were also, directly or indirectly, inspired by the revolutionary state in which they were living. For, as Virginia Woolf put it in a crucial passage from *Three Guineas,* "So profound was [the] unconscious loathing" of the daughters of educated (and uneducated) men for "the education" in oppression which all women had received, that while most "consciously desired [the advancement of] 'our splendid Empire,' " many "unconsciously desired" the apocalypse of "our splendid war."[9]

Not surprisingly, however, the words as well as the deeds of these women reinforced their male contemporaries' sense that "All the world is topsy-turvy/Since the War began" and thus intensified the misogynist resentment with which male writers defined this Great War as an apocalyptic turning point in the battle of the sexes. Not surprisingly either, therefore, the sexual gloom expressed by so many men as well as the sexual glee experienced by so many women ultimately triggered profound feelings of guilt in a number of women: to the guilt of the female survivor with her fear that "a barrier of indescribable experience" had been thrust between the sexes, there was often added a half-conscious fear that the woman survivor might be in an inexplicable way a perpetrator of some unspeakable crime. Thus, the invigorating sense of revolution, release, reunion, and re-vision with which the war paradoxically imbued so many women eventually darkened into reactions of anxiety and self-doubt as Herland and No Man's Land merged to become the Nobody's Land T. S. Eliot was to call "death's dream kingdom."[10]

Revolution

From the first, of course, as Paul Fussell has shown, World War I fostered characteristically modernist irony in young men, inducting them into "death's dream kingdom" by revealing exactly how spurious were their visions of heroism, and— by extension—history's images of heroism.[11] Mobilized and marched off to the front, idealistic soldiers soon found themselves *im*mobilized, even buried alive, in trenches of death that seemed to have been dug along the remotest margins of civilizations. Here, as Eric Leed has brilliantly observed, all the traditional categories of experience through which the rational cultured mind achieves its hegemony over the irrationality of nature were grotesquely mingled, polluting each other as if in some Swiftian fantasy.[12] Of his "hero," George Winterbourne, for instance, Richard Aldington tells us (in *Death of a Hero*) that "he lived among smashed bodies and human remains in an infernal cemetery,"[13] while Robert Graves (in *Goodbye to All That*) describes snatching his "fingers in horror from where I had planted them on the slimy body of an old corpse."[14] Even Vera Brittain, safe for a while at home, observes that when the filthy clothes of her dead fiancé were returned from the front, "the mud of France which covered them [seemed] saturated with dead bodies."[15] No wonder, then, that before his death her Roland had written her bitterly about his spiritual metamorphosis and his radical alienation from the "normal" world she now seemed to inhabit without him; "I feel a barbarian, a wild man of the woods [and] you seem to me rather like a character in a book or someone one has dreamt of and never seen."[16]

"A wild man of the woods": the phrase is significant, for entering the polluted realm of the trenches, young men like Roland understood themselves to have been exiled from the very culture they had been deputized to defend. From now on, their only land was No Man's Land, a land that *was not*, a country of the impossible and the paradoxical. Here, Leed remarks, "The retirement of the combatant into the soil produced a landscape suffused with ambivalence. . . . The battlefield was 'empty of men' and yet it was saturated with men."[17] Inevitably, such sinister invisibility combined with such deadly *being* created a sense of what Freud called the *unheimlich*, the uncanny. Yet of course No Man's Land was real in its bizarre unreality, and to become a denizen of that unreal kingdom was to become, oneself, unreal. Practically speaking, moreover, such a feeling of unreality or uncanniness was actually realistic. As Graves notes, "The average life expectancy of an infantry subaltern on the Western Front was, at some stages of the War, only about three months,"[18] so that a universal sense of doom, often manifesting itself as a *desire* for death, forced the "wild man" soldier to ask, with the speaker of one of D. H. Lawrence's poems, "Am I Lost?/Has death set me apart/Beforehand?/Have I crossed/ That border?/Have I nothing in this dark land?"[19] Catapulted over the frontiers of civilization, the men of war had been transformed into dead-alive beings whose fates could no longer be determined according to the rules that had governed Western History from time immemorial (see fig. 1).

Figure 1. Hospitalized veterans in England

With no sense of inherited history to lose, on the other hand, women in the terrible war years of 1914–18 would seem to have had, if not everything, at least something to gain: a place in public history, a chance, even, to make history. Wrote one former suffragist, "I knew nothing of European complications and cared less. . . . I asked myself if any horrors could be greater than the horrors of peace— the sweating, the daily lives of women on the streets. . . ."[20] Ultimately, such revolutionary energy and resolute feminism, together with such alienation from officially important events, was to lead to a phenomenon usefully analyzed by Nina Auerbach: "Union among women . . . is one of the unacknowledged fruits of war," and particularly during World War I, there was "a note of exaltation at the Amazonian countries created by the war, whose military elation spread from the suffrage battle to the nation at large."[21] For, of course, when their menfolk went off to the trenches to be literally and figuratively shattered, the women on the home front literally and figuratively rose to the occasion and replaced them in farms and factories. The propagandist Jessie Pope's "War Girls," moreover, records the exuberance with which these women settled into "Amazonian countries." "Strong, sensible and fit,/They're out to show their grit," this writer exclaims approvingly, adding—as if in anticipation of Woolf—an important qualifier: "*No longer caged and penned up,*/They're going to keep their end up" (italics mine).[22] Picture after picture from the Imperial War Museum's enormous collection of photos portraying "Women at War" illustrates her points. Liberated from parlors and petticoats alike, trousered "war girls" beam as they shovel coal, shoe horses, fight fires, drive buses, chop down trees, make shells, dig graves. Similarly, American women found that war, in the words of Harriet Stanton Blatch, "make[s] the blood course through the veins" because, by compelling "women to work," it sends them "over the top . . . up the scaling-ladder, and out into 'All Man's Land' " (see fig. 2).[23]

Though it may be a coincidence, then, there is ironic point to the fact that Charlotte Perkins Gilman's *Herland*, with its vision of a female utopia created by a cataclysm that wiped out all the men, was published in Gilman's feminist journal *Forerunner* in 1915, and at least one feminist noted the accuracy of a cartoon in *Punch* depicting two women who "did not think the war would last long—it was too good to last."[24] As David Mitchell observes, "When the time came for demobilisation," many women "wept at the ending of what they now saw as the happiest and most purposeful days of their lives."[25] For despite the massive tragedy that the war represented for an entire generation of young men—and for their grieving wives, mothers, daughters, and sisters—it also represented the first rupture with a socioeconomic history that had heretofore denied most women chances at first-class jobs—and first-class pay.

To be sure, that denial persisted for a time. At the beginning of the war only a very small proportion of those women in Great Britain who registered as volunteers for war service were given employment. By the end of the war, however, the number of working women had increased by almost 50 percent, and 700,000 of the women employed had directly replaced men in the work force.[26] Replacing men, moreover,

Figure 2. Women's Land Army Workers in England

these women finally received the kind of pay only men had earned in the past, so that many a working-class girl could join in the sardonic good cheer expressed by the speaker of Madeline Ida Bedford's "Munition Wages": "Earning high wages? Yus,/Five quid a week./A woman, too, mind you,/I calls it dim sweet" (see fig. 3).[27] Many a middle- or upper-class woman, too, could rejoice with Dr. Caroline Matthews, who asserted that because her medical services were needed at last, "Life was worth living in those days,"[28] or triumph with the novelist Edith Wharton, who claimed "the honour of having founded the first paying work-room in Paris," an *ouvroir* for "wives, widows, and young girls without near relatives in the army," and who filed for safekeeping the program of a 1917 New York bazaar for war relief called "Hero Land," which excitedly (and efficiently) offered "the greatest spectacle the world has ever known" in response to "the greatest need the world has ever known."[29]

Inevitably, however, the enthusiasm and efficiency with which women of all ranks and ages filled in the economic gaps men had left behind reinforced the soldiers' sickened sense that the war had drastically abrogated most of the rules that had always organized Western culture. From the first, after all, it had seemed to the man at the front that his life and limbs were forfeit to the comforts of the *home* front, so that civilians, male and female, were fictive inhabitants of a world that had effectively insulated itself from the trenches' city of dreadful night. Aldington's George Winterbourne goes to see his wife and his mistress, but "they were gesticulating across an abyss";[30] seventeen-year-old John Kipling, dead at

Figure 3. British recruitment poster (for women)

the front by the time he was eighteen, writes to Rudyard Kipling, his war-propagandist father, that "you people at home don't realize how spoilt you are"; and, enraged at the smugness of civilians, Siegfried Sassoon sits in a music hall and thinks, "I'd like to see a Tank come down the stalls,/Lurching to rag-time tunes, or 'Home, sweet Home.' "[31]

Ultimately, though, this barely veiled hostility between the front and the home front, along with the exuberance of the women workers who had succeeded to (and in) men's places, suggested that the most crucial rule the war had overturned was the rule of patrilineal succession, the founding law of patriarchal society itself. For as the early glamor of battle dissipated and Victorian fantasies of historical heroism gave way to modernist visions of irony and unreality, it became clear that this war to end all wars necessitated a sacrifice of the sons to the exigencies of the fathers—and the mothers, wives, and sisters. Even a patriotic bestseller like Ernest Raymond's 1922 *Tell England* implies, eerily, that in the new dispensation of war, sons are no longer the inheritors of their families' wealth, they *are* their families' wealth, a currency of blood that must be paid out indefinitely in order to keep the world safe, not for democracy, but for old men and women of all ages. "Eighteen, by jove!" says a comfortable colonel to some schoolboys he is encouraging to enlist. "England's wealth used to consist in other things. Nowadays you boys are the richest thing she's got."[32] Similarly, in "The Parable of the Old Man and the Young," Wilfred Owen retells the tale of "Abram" and Isaac to dramatize the generational conflict that, along with a sexual struggle, he and so many other soldiers like him saw as one of the darkest implications of the Great War.[33]

That such a generational conflict was not just associated with but an integral part of the sexual struggle fostered by the war is made very clear in a poem by Alice Meynell, a long-time suffrage fighter, who accurately foresaw that through one of the grimmer paradoxes of history the Great War might force recalcitrant men to grant women, the stereotypical peacemakers, a viable inheritance in patriarchal society. In fact, her "A Father of Women" seems almost to explain the sexual anxiety of D. H. Lawrence, who actually lived with her family during part of the war, for the speaker of this verse answers some of the questions Lawrence had asked in "Eloi, Eloi, Lama Sabachthani?": "Our father works in us./The daughters of his manhood. Not undone/Is he, not wasted, though transmuted thus,/And though he left no son."[34] She goes on to tell "The million living fathers of the War" that they should finally "Approve, accept, know [us] daughters of men,/Now that your sons are dust." Ostensibly so calm and sympathetic, her last phrase can be read almost as a taunt, though it is certain she did not intend it that way. You have killed your sons, she seems to say, your daughters will inherit the world.

A devout Catholic and a "poet's poet," Meynell was clearly no war propagandist, yet some readers might well have felt that such a revolutionary vision of patriarchy "transmuted" by war aligned her with more frankly militaristic women writers. And of these there was a considerable number, a phenomenon which would also have reinforced male sexual anger by implying that women were eager to implore men to make mortal sacrifices by which they themselves would ultimately profit. For while their brothers groped through the rubble of No Man's Land for fragments to shore against the ruins of a dying culture, countless women manned the machines of state, urging more men to go off to battle. Robert Graves reprints a famous, indeed infamous, piece of propaganda in the form of a letter from a "little mother" who argued that women should gladly "pass on the human ammunition" of sons to the nation and declared ambiguously that "we will emerge stronger women to carry on the glorious work [their] memories have handed down to us."[35] Similarly, "Women of Britain Say *'Go!'* " proclaimed one of the War Office's best-known posters (see fig. 4), and the female censoriousness implicit in that slogan was made explicit by the fact that at times the vigorous, able-bodied "war girls," who had once been judged wanting by even the weakest of young men, became frighteningly judgmental about their male contemporaries. Speaking with some disgust about "the instinct of pugnacity . . . that [is] so strong in women," Bernard Shaw describes "civilized young women handing white feathers to all young men who are not in uniform."[36] Metaphorically speaking, moreover, popular women writers like Jessie Pope and Mrs. Humphrey Ward (in England) as well as more serious artists like May Sinclair (in England) or Edith Wharton and Willa Cather (in the United States) distributed white feathers to large audiences of noncombatant readers. "Who's for the trench—/Are you, my laddie?" asked Jessie Pope in her jingoistic "The Call";[37] May Sinclair described "the ecstasy" of battle in *The Tree of Heaven,* and Edith Wharton depicted the satisfactions of having "a son at the front" in her novel of that name.[38] It is no wonder, then, that Wilfred Owen's bitterly antiwar "Dulce et Decorum Est" with its violent imagery of gas-caused "vile, incurable sores on innocent tongues" was originally entitled "To Jessie Pope" and then "To A Certain Poetess" before its author decided, instead, on a bleak allusion to Horace's "Dulce et decorum est/Pro patria mori."[39] In the words of women propagandists as well as in the deeds of feather-carrying girls, the classical Roman's noble *patria* must have seemed to become a sinister, death-dealing *matria*.

Even the most conventionally angelic of women's wartime ministrations, however, must have suggested to many members of both sexes that, while men were now invalid and maybe in-valid, their sisters were triumphant survivors and destined inheritors. Certainly both the rhetoric and the iconography of nursing would seem to imply some such points. To be sure, the nurse presents herself as a servant of her patient. "Every task," writes Vera Brittain of her days as a VAD, "had for us . . . a sacred glamour."[40] Yet in works by both male and female novelists the figure of the nurse ultimately takes on a majesty which hints that she is mistress rather than slave, goddess rather than supplicant. After all, when men are immobilized and dehumanized, it is only these women who possess the old (matriarchal) formulas for survival. Thus, even while memoirists like Brittain express "gratitude" for the "sacred glamour" of nursing, they seem to be pledging allegiance to a *secret* glamor—the glamor of an expertise which they will win from their patients. "Towards the men," recalls Brittain, "I came to feel an almost adoring

Figure 4. British recruitment poster (for men)

gratitude . . . for the knowledge of masculine functioning which the care of them gave me."[41]

Not surprisingly, this education in masculine functioning that the nurse experiences as a kind of elevation is often felt by her male patient as exploitation; her evolution into active, autonomous, transcendent subject is associated with his devolution into passive, dependent, immanent medical object. In *A Farewell to Arms* Hemingway's Frederic Henry clearly responds with a surface delight to being cared for and about by Catherine Barclay. Yet there is, after all, something faintly sinister in her claim that he *needs* her to make "unpleasant" preparations for an operation on his wounded knee and something frighteningly possessive in her assertion that "I get furious if [anyone else] touch[es] you." Similarly, in *The Sun Also Rises* Hemingway's Jake Barnes, consoled by the nymphomaniac Brett Ashley as he lies limply on his bed, cannot forget that she "was a V.A.D. in a hospital I was in during the war" and fell in love with him because "she only wanted what she couldn't have," a line that ambiguously implies a form of perverse penis envy as well as a species of masochistic desire.[42] More openly, Lawrence writes in "The Ladybird" about a wounded middle European prisoner who tells a visiting English Lady with whom he is falling in love that she must "let me wrap your hair around my hands like a bandage" because "I feel I have lost my manhood for the time being."[43] Hopelessly at the mercy of his aristocratic nurse, this helpless alien adumbrates wounded males who also appear in works by women—for example, the amnesiac hero of Rebecca West's *The Return of the Soldier*, whom a former girlfriend restores by gathering his "soul" in "her soul,"[44] and Lord Peter Wimsey, in Dorothy Sayers's *Busman's Honeymoon*, who is so haunted by memories of the war that he confesses to his bride that "you're my corner and I've come to hide."[45]

Where nurses imagined by men often do seem to have a sinister power, however, the nurses imagined by women appear, at least at first, to be purely restorative, positively (rather than negatively) maternal. The "grey nurse" whom Virginia Woolf describes in a notoriously puzzling passage in *Mrs. Dalloway* is thus a paradigm of her more realistically delineated sisters. Knitting steadily while Peter Walsh dozes, she seems "like the champion of the rights of sleepers" who responds to "a desire for solace, for relief." Yet even she is not an altogether positive figure. Like "The Greatest Mother in the World" depicted in Alonzo Earl Foringer's 1918 Red Cross War Relief poster—an enormous nurse cradling a tiny immobilized male on a doll-sized stretcher (see fig. 5)—Woolf's grey nurse evokes a parodic *pietà* in which the Virgin Mother threatens simultaneously to anoint and annihilate her long-suffering son, a point Woolf's imaginary male dreamer accurately grasps when he prays "let me walk straight on to this great figure, who will . . . mount me on her streamers and let me blow to nothingness with the rest."[46] Does male death turn women nurses on? Do figures like the pious Red Cross mother experience bacchanalian satisfaction as, in Woolf's curiously ambiguous phrase, they watch their male patients, one-time oppressors, "blow [up] to nothingness with the rest?"

Red Cross
Christmas
Roll Call
Dec. 16-23ʳᵈ

The
GREATEST MOTHER
in the WORLD

Figure 5. American Red Cross

A number of texts by men and women alike suggest that the revolutionary socio-economic transformations wrought by the war's "topsy turvy" role reversals did bring about a release of female libidinal energies, as well as a liberation of female anger, which men usually found anxiety-inducing and women often found exhilarating.

Release, (Re)union, (Re)vision

On the subject of erotic release, a severely political writer like Vera Brittain is notably restrained. Yet even she implies, at least subtextually, that she experienced some such phenomenon, for while she expresses her "gratitude" to the men from whom she learned about "masculine functioning," she goes on to thank the war that delivered their naked bodies into her hands for her own "early release from . . . sex-inhibitions."[47] Significantly, too, as if to confirm the possibility that Brittain did receive a wartime sex education, Eric Leed records the belief of some observers that "women in particular 'reacted to the war experience with a powerful increase in libido.' "[48] Was the war a festival of female misrule in which the collapse of a traditional social structure "permitted," as Leed also puts it, "a range of personal contacts that had been impossible in [former lives] where hierarchies of status ruled?"[49] Certainly the testimony of male artists would seem to suggest such a notion. In their different ways, for example, notorious heroines like Hemingway's Catherine Barclay and his Brett Ashley are set sexually free by the war, as are Lawrence's famous Connie Chatterley, his Ivy Bolton, and his Bertha Coutts, all of whom contribute to the impotence of his Clifford Chatterley and the anxiety of his Oliver Mellors.[50] In *Death of a Hero*, moreover, Richard Aldington is explicit about what he sees as the grotesque sexual permission the war has given such women. Speaking of George Winterbourne's mother, he remarks that "the effect of George's death on her temperament was . . . almost wholly erotic." Similarly, Elizabeth and Fanny, George's wife and mistress, are "terribly at ease upon the Zion of sex, abounding in masochism, Lesbianism, sodomy, etcetera."[51] Comparable allegations against the deadlines of female desire are leveled in a number of Lawrence's stories, notably "Tickets Please" and "Monkey Nuts." In the first, a bacchanalian group of girl tram conductors band together to enact a ritual scene of reverse rape on a tram inspector with the significant Lawrentian name of John Thomas, while in the second, a girl in the land army decides to seduce a passive young soldier and manifests the power of her perverse erotic will by putting "a soft pressure" on his waist that makes "all his bones rotten."[52]

Significantly, however, where men writers primarily recounted the horrors of unleashed female sexuality and only secondarily recorded the more generalized female excitement that energized such sexuality, women remembered, first, the excitement of the war and, second (but more diffusely), the sensuality to which such excitement led. Thus, where most male writers—at least after their earliest dreams of heroism had been deflated—associated the front with paralysis and pollution, many female writers imagined it as a place of freedom, ruefully comparing what they felt was their own genteel immobilization with the exhilaration of military mobility. In her "Many Sisters to Many Brothers," Rose Macaulay articulated their envy of the soldier's liberation from the dreariness of the home and the home front: "Oh it's you that have the luck, out there in blood and muck."[53] To women who managed to get to the front, moreover, the war did frequently offer the delight of (female) mobilization rather than the despair of (male) immobilization. After all, for nurses and ambulance drivers, women doctors and women messengers, the phenomenon of modern battle was very different from that experienced by entrenched combatants. Finally given a chance to take the wheel, these post-Victorian girls raced motorcars along foreign roads like adventurers exploring new lands, while their brothers dug deeper into the mud of France (see fig. 6). Retrieving the wounded and the dead from deadly positions, these once-decorous daughters had at last been allowed to prove their valor, and they swooped over the wastelands of the war with the energetic love of Wagnerian Valkyries, their mobility alone transporting countless immobilized heroes to safe havens.

It is no wonder, then, that even the roar of the guns seems often to have sounded in their ears like a glamorously dramatic rather than a gloomily dangerous counterpoint to adventure, and no wonder that even combat's bloodier aspects sometimes appeared to them like what Lawrence called "glittering seed" instead of wounding shrapnel. Thinking wistfully of an ambulance unit in Belgium that she has had to leave, May Sinclair summarizes this ambiguously apocalyptic "joy of women in

Figure 6. A motor dispatch rider of the WRNS (Women's Royal Naval Service)

wartime" as a vision of high-speed travel through a world in the process of violent transformation. "You go," she tells her former mates in the Munro Corps, "under the thunder of the guns . . ./And where the high towers are broken/And houses crack like the staves of a thin crate."[54] Elsewhere, Sinclair confides about the excitement of combat that "[you think] 'What a fool I would have been if I hadn't come. I wouldn't have missed this run for the world.' "[55] Just as enthusiastically, VADs, drivers, and nurses like Vera Brittain and Violetta Thurstan testify to "the exhilaration" of their departure from England, the "diversion" of bombings, the "thrill in the knowledge that we were actually in a country invaded by the enemy," and the "great fun!" of life at the front.[56]

If the testimony of these memoirists sounds inhumane or actually inhuman, it is worth remembering that most are in some sense recounting their feeling that the Great War was the first historical event to allow (indeed, to require) them to use their abilities and to be of use, to escape the private "staves" of houses as well as the patriarchal oppression of "high towers" and to enter the public realm of roads, records, maps, machines. Thus, even a pacifist like Virginia Woolf, who advised during the thirties that in the next war women should "refuse . . . to make munitions or nurse the wounded," was in *Three Guineas* to cite a passage about the glamor of the Spanish Civil War fighter Amalia Bonilla that describes this "amazon" who killed five men as a " 'fauve' of an unknown species."[57] It is quite likely, moreover, that such a vision of "an unknown species" explains the apparently naive envy of male combatants expressed by women like Macaulay; just as likely, it explains what seemed to some readers the equally naive or even pernicious propaganda implicit not only in the writings of poetasters like Pope but also in the works of serious novelists like Sinclair and Cather. Certainly Sinclair's account in *The Tree of Heaven* of the "exquisite moments of extreme danger" experienced by her heroes reflects a transference to men of the liberation she herself experienced when she worked in Belgium with the Munro Corps.[58] Similarly, when in *One of Ours* Cather celebrates Claude Wheeler's escape from rural Nebraska to wartime France—noting that "to be alive, to be conscious, to have one's faculties, was to be in the war" and associating the European cataclysm with the idea that now "the old . . . cages would be broken open for ever"—her vision of the doomed young man's good fortune is surely a way of dreaming her own release from the deadening decorum of the provincial prairie town where she herself had always longed to be a sturdy "Willie" rather than a submissive Willa.[59]

For many women, moreover, but perhaps in particular for lesbian women like Cather, whose inability to identify with conventional "femininity" had always made their gender a problem to them, the war facilitated not just a liberation from the constricting trivia of parlors and petticoats but an unprecedented transcendence of the profounder constraints imposed by traditional sex roles. Most dramatically, this transcendence is described in Radclyffe Hall's two crucial postwar fictions— her short story entitled "Miss Ogilvy Finds Herself" and her more famous *The Well of Loneliness*. In the first, the aging lesbian Miss Ogilvy remembers, as she is being demobilized, that her ambulance was "the merciful emblem that had set [her] free," and mourns the breaking up of the "glorious" all-female unit she has led.[60] Similarly, Stephen Gordon, the "invert" heroine of *The Well*, feels at the outset of the war like "a freak abandoned on a kind of no-man's-land" (and Hall's metaphor is significant) but soon finds herself paradoxically metamorphosed into a member of a new women's battalion "that would never again be disbanded." For, explains Hall, "war and death" had finally, ironically, given "a right to life" to lesbians like Stephen, women who refused the traditions of femininity and the conventions of heterosexuality alike.[61]

To be sure, specifically erotic release was frequently associated with such a right to life, for Vera Brittain's sex education was complemented by the romantic permission given, in various degrees, to heterosexual characters like Miranda in Katherine Anne Porter's "Pale Horse, Pale Rider" and to lesbian heroines like Miss Ogilvy and Stephen Gordon. In the first work, Porter's protagonist, falling in love with a young soldier, meditates happily on the "miracle of being two persons named Adam and Miranda" who are "always in the mood for dancing."[62] As for Miss Ogilvy, she goes off on a vacation where Hall grants her a dream of unleashed desire in which, transformed into a powerful primitive man, she makes love to a beautiful young woman, enthralled by the "ripe red berry sweet to the taste" of the female body.[63] Similarly, Stephen Gordon meets her lover, Mary Llewelyn, when they are sister drivers in the allegorically named "Breakspeare" ambulance unit, and after the war they too achieve a "new and ardent fulfillment" on a honeymoon in Spain.[64] Not coincidentally, perhaps, lesbian writers like Amy Lowell and Gertrude Stein produced some of their most ecstatic erotica during the war years. Lowell's "Two Speak Together," for instance, a tribute to her lover/companion Ada Russell, appeared in the same 1919 volume with her darkly elegiac "Dreams in War Time," while "Lifting Belly," Stein's most famous encoded celebration of lesbian sexuality, was composed, according to Richard Kostelanetz, between 1915 and 1917, the same years in which, in *The Autobiography of Alice B. Toklas*, she recounts her ambivalently cheerful experiences of the war.[65] Recording "real life," moreover, Vita Sackville-West wrote of how her love for Violet Trefusis was finally consummated in April 1918 when Violet came down to the Nicolson establishment at Long Barn because "the air-raids frightened her." As Vita tells the story, her own "exuberance"—"I had just got clothes like the women-on-the-land were wearing, and in the unaccustomed freedom of breeches and gaiters I went into wild spirits"—finally made the "under-current" of sexuality between the two too strong to resist. It is no wonder, then, that after the war, when the pair eloped to Paris, Vita "dressed as a boy" with "a khaki bandage round [her] head" to impersonate a wounded soldier named Julian, and no wonder either that, despite the irony of having been liberated by such an equivocal costume, she later recalled that she had "never been so happy since."[66]

Perhaps more important than the female eroticism that the war energized, however, was the more diffusely emotional sense of sisterhood its "Amazonian countries" inspired in nurses and VADs, land girls and tram conductors. As if to show the positive aspect of the bacchanalian bonding Lawrence deplores in his "Tickets, Please," women like Vera Brittain, May Sinclair, and Violetta Thurstan remembered how their liberation into the public realm from the isolation of the private house allowed them to experience a female (re)union in which they felt "the joys of companionship to the full . . . in a way that would be impossible to conceive in an ordinary world."[67] For Radclyffe Hall, too, the battalion of sisters "formed in those terrible years" consisted of "great-hearted women . . . glad . . . to help one another to shoulder burdens."[68] In a variation of this theme, Winifred Holtby told in *The Crowded Street* how her alienated heroine, Muriel Hammond, finally achieved a purposeful life through the friendship of Delia Vaughan, a feminist activist (modeled in part on Vera Brittain, as Muriel is on Holtby herself) whose fiancé was killed in the war. Not insignificantly, moreover, Holtby also dedicated this celebration of sisterly companionship to another of her close friends, Jean McWilliam, with whom she lived as a member of the WAAC in France in 1918.[69]

It is also of course true that, as Wilfred Owen's poems testify time and again, and as Paul Fussell has brilliantly demonstrated, the Great War produced for many men a "front-line experience replete with what we can call the homoerotic."[70] From Herbert Read, who wishes one of his dead soldiers to be kissed not by worms "but with the warm passionate lips/of his comrade here," to Owen himself, who sends his "identity disc" to a "sweet friend," imploring "may thy heart-beat kiss it, night and day," male combatants frequently feel for each other "a love passing the love of women."[71] Indeed, as Leed observes, "the comradeship of the front" was to create the crucial postwar phenomenon of veterans as "liminal" men who have nothing in common with anyone but each other.[72] Significantly, however, where the liberating sisterhood experienced by women was mostly untainted by hostility to men—where it was in fact frequently associated with admiration for male soldiers or identification with male heroism—the combatants' comradeship seems as often to have been energized by a disgust for the feminine as it was by a desire for the masculine. The war between the front and the home front, that is, issued in an inextricable tangle of (male) misogyny and (male) homosexuality, so that Owen, say, reproaches female "Love" while praising beautiful "lads."[73]

The male comradeship fostered by the isolated communities of the trenches, moreover, was continually countered and qualified by rifts between men that were not just accidental but essential consequences of the war. Most obviously, the No Man's Land that stretched between allies and enemies symbolized the fragmentation of what Sigmund Freud called the "wider fatherland" in which, as Freud sorrowfully noted, European men no longer dwelt, though they had "moved unhindered" in it before the war.[74] "Strange Meeting," perhaps Owen's most famous poem, stunningly dramatizes this disintegration of male love, with its vision of brotherly doubles meeting in a "dull tunnel" where one tells the other, in a paradox that summarizes the perils of patriarchal bonding, "I am the enemy you killed, my friend."[75] But even Lawrence, that notorious celebrant of "blood brotherhood," balances his depiction in *Kangaroo* of the "half-mystical" homoerotic friendship between Richard Lovat Somers and the young Cornish farmer John Thomas with a portrayal of the horror Somers experiences when military doctors, as part of an army physical, "handl[e] his private parts," a trauma so indelible that by the end of "The Nightmare" of the war Somers feels "broken off from his fellow-men . . . without a people, without a land."[76]

But if the war forced men like Lawrence, Freud, and Owen to qualify their dreams of brotherhood by confronting the reality of No Man's Land and imagining themselves as nightmare citizens "without a land," it liberated women not only to delight in the reality of the workaday Herland that was wartime England or America but also to imagine a revisionary worldwide Herland, a utopia arisen from the ashes of apocalypse and founded on the revelation of a new social order. In a range of genres—poems and polemics, extravagant fantasies and realistic fictions—women writers articulated this vision repeatedly, throughout the war and postwar years. Gertrude Atherton's popular fantasy, *The White Morning*, for instance, told a utopian tale of the takeover of Germany by a female army. Amazonian as Woolf's Amalia Bonilla, their leader, Gisela, flies over Munich, noting with satisfaction that the city is "packed with women" who are "armed to the teeth" and carrying "a white flag with a curious device sketched in crimson: a hen in successive stages of evolution" into an "eagle [whose] face, grim, leering, vengeful, pitiless, was unmistakably that of a woman." In less detail, but just as dramatically, Dorothy Harrison, one of the protagonists of Sinclair's *The Tree of Heaven*, has a mysterious epiphany when she is confined at Hollowell Prison as part of the prewar suffrage battle, an epiphany that turns out to be a proleptic vision of how women will get the vote in "some big, tremendous way that'll make all this fighting and fussing seem the rottenest game,"[77] Similarly, Eleanor Pargiter in Woolf's *The Years* thinks that because of the war things seemed "to be freed from some surface hardness" so that, as German planes raid London, she and her companions raise a toast "to the New World!"[78] Finally, For H. D., looking back at World War I through the palimpsestic ruins of World War II, the crucible of battle in *Helen in Egypt* reproduces Helen and Achilles as androgynous "New Mortals" while in *Trilogy* it offers both the poem's narrator and one of her characters a vision of reality transformed and transfigured by the resurrection of a female Atlantis.[79]

For many women, of course, such intimations of social change were channeled specifically through the politics of pacifism. From Olive Schreiner, whose meditation on "Woman and War" had argued that the mothers of the race have a special responsibility as well as a special power to oppose combat, to Charlotte Perkins Gilman, whose Herland was an Edenically peaceable garden because its author believed women to be naturally nonviolent, feminist activists had long claimed that, in the words of Crystal Eastman, "woman suffrage and permanent peace will go together."[80] Indeed, like the trade unionist Mrs. Raymond Robins, whose opinions were otherwise very different, Eastman had confidence that "it is the first hour in history for the women of the world. This is the woman's age!"[81] Precisely because these thinkers were uniformly convinced of woman's unique ability to encourage and enforce peace, however, there is sometimes an edge of contempt for men implicit in their arguments. But it is in Virginia Woolf's *Three Guineas*, the postwar era's great text of pacifist feminism, that such hostility to men comes most dramatically to the surface, in the form of violent antipatriarchal fantasies paradoxically embedded in an ostensibly nonviolent treatise on the subject of "how to prevent war." Perhaps, Woolf even hints in an early draft of this New Womanly book of revelation, the devastation wrought by war is a punishment (for men) exactly fitted not only to the crime of (masculine) war making but to other (masculine) crimes: "We should say let there be war. We should go on earning our living. We should say it is a ridiculous and barbarous but perhaps necaary little popgun. The at-would be a help. Then we should live ourselves the sight of happiness is very make you envious" [sic].[82] Even in the more subdued final version of *Three Guineas*, moreover, she seizes upon the imperative to prevent war as an excuse for imagining a conflagration that would burn down the old male-structured colleges of "Oxbridge," representative of all oppressive cultural institutions, and substitute instead an egalitarian and feminist "new college, [a] poor college" where "the arts of ruling, of killing, of acquiring land and capital" would not be taught.[83]

Later in *Three Guineas*, moreover, Woolf rebels even against the rhetoric of writers like Schreiner and Eastman, observing sardonically that "pacifism is enforced upon women" because they are not in any case allowed to offer their services to the army. Thus, most radically, she puts forward her famous proposal that "the daughters of educated men" should refuse to join with their brothers in working either for war *or* peace, but should instead found a "Society of Outsiders" based on the principle that "as a woman, I have no country. As a woman I want no country. As a woman my country is the whole world."[84] To be sure, Woolf recommends as part of this proposal a passive resistance to patriarchal militarism significantly similar to that advocated by many other feminist pacifists. But at the same time, with its calculated ex-patriotism and its revisionary vows of "indifference" to the uncivilized hierarchies of "our" civilization, her Society of Outsiders constitutes perhaps the most fully elaborated feminist vision of a secret apocalyptic Herland existing simultaneously within and without England's "splendid Empire," a righteous and rightful woman's state energized by the antiwar passions the war produced in women. In some part of herself, therefore, Woolf may well have shared the apocalyptic delight that Hesione Hushabye bizarrely expresses when bombs begin falling at the end of Bernard Shaw's *Heartbreak House:* "Did you hear the explosions? And the sound in the sky: it's splendid: it's like an orchestra: it's like Beethoven."[85] As patriarchal culture self-destructs, those it has subordinated can't help feeling that the sacrifices implied by "the sound in the sky" might nevertheless hold out the hope of a new heaven and a new earth.

Not surprisingly, then, even as they mourned the devastation of the war, a number of women writers besides Woolf felt that not only their society but also their art had been subtly strengthened, or at least strangely inspired, by the deaths and defeats of male contemporaries. Vera Brittain notes that when her fiancé, Roland, was killed, "His mother began to write, in semi-fictional form, a memoir of his life," and adds that she herself was filled "with longing to write a book about Roland."[86] In *A Son at the Front*, the tale of an artist-father whose art is mysteriously revitalized by the death of his soldier son, Edith Wharton offers an encoded description of a similar transformation of a dead man into an enlivening muse.[87] More frankly, Katherine Mansfield confides to her journal after the death of her brother, "Chummie," that through his muselike intervention she has been vouchsafed a "mysterious" and "floating" vision of "our undiscovered country," a transfigured land not unlike the state imagined by apocalyptic feminists from Schreiner to Woolf, in which the dead "Chummie" represents "the new man."[88] What issued from such ambivalent moments of inspiration, moreover, was her best set of stories—the New Zealand tales, "Prelude" and "At the Bay." Finally, in perhaps the most notable instance of female inspiration empowered by male desperation, H. D. writes in her roman à clef, *Bid Me to Live*, how the various defeats of her husband (Richard Aldington) and her male muse (D. H. Lawrence) transformed her autobiographical heroine, Julia, into a "witch with power. A wise woman . . . [a] seer, a see-er."[89] No wonder, then, that when she later looked back on her experiences in two wars she revised and reversed the imagery Lawrence had used in his "Eloi, Eloi, Lama Sabachthani?" "Am I bridegroom of War, war's paramour?" Lawrence's speaker had asked, and H. D. seems almost to have wanted to answer him directly. Tracing her own growth in an unpublished memoir called "Thorn Thicket," she declares mystically that "the war was my husband."[90] And at the very least, if the war was not her husband, it was her muse—as it was Woolf's, Mansfield's, Wharton's, and many other women's.

Reaction

Given the fact that the war functioned in so many different ways to liberate women— offering a revolution in economic expectations, a release of passionate energies, a (re)union of previously fragmented sisters, and a (re)vision of social and aesthetic dreams—it seems clear that more than simple patriotism caused some leaders of the women's movement quite early to recognize a connection between feminist aspirations and military effects. In 1915, for instance, *The Suffragette*, the newspaper of the English Women's Social and Political Union, was renamed *Britannia*, with a new dedication: "For King, for Country, for Freedom." At last, it must have seemed, women could begin to see themselves as coextensive with the state, and with a female state at that, a Britannia, not a Union Jack. And as we know, the female intuition expressed in that renaming was quite accurate; in 1918, when World War I was over, there were eight and a half million European men dead, and there had been thirty seven and a half million male casualties, while all the women in England over the age of thirty were finally, after a sixty-two-year struggle, given the vote. Not too much later all the women in America over the age of twenty-one achieved the same privilege. For four years, moreover, a sizable percentage of the young men in England had been imprisoned in trenches and uniforms, while the young women in England had been at liberty in farm and factory. Paradoxically, in fact, the war to which so many men had gone in the hope of becoming heroes ended up emasculating them, depriving them of autonomy, confining them as closely as any Victorian women had been confined. As if in acknowledgment of this, Leed tells us, doctors noted that "the symptoms of shell-shock were precisely the same as those of the most common hysterical disorders of peacetime, though they often acquired new and more dramatic names in war: 'the burial-alive neurosis,' 'gas neurosis,' 'soldier's heart,' 'hysterical sympathy with the enemy' . . . what had been predominantly a disease of women before the war became a disease of men in combat."[91]

Because women developed a very different kind of "soldier's heart" in these years, however, "wearing the pants" in the family or even "stepping into his shoes" had finally become a real possibility for them. Yet of course that triumph was not without its darker consequences for feminism. Because male artists believed even more strongly than their sisters did that soldiers had been sacrificed so that some gigantic female could sleep surrounded by, in Wilfred Owen's words, a "wall of boys on boys and dooms on dooms";[92] because they believed, with Hemingway, that a Lady Brett was a sort of monstrous antifertility goddess to whose powers the impotent bodies of men had ceaselessly to be offered up; because, finally, with Lawrence they "feared" the talents of liberated "poetesses" like H. D. at least as much as they admired them, the literature of the postwar years was marked by an "anti-feminism" which, in the words of Rebecca West, was "strikingly the correct fashion . . . among . . . the intellectuals."[93]

Inevitably, however, many women writers themselves internalized the misogyny that actuated such antifeminism. Heroines like Hall's Miss Ogilvy and her Stephen Gordon, for instance, who had been briefly freed by the war, ultimately succumb to the threat of a reconstituted status quo. Miss Ogilvy dies almost directly as a result of the sexual "dying" that climaxes her dream of erotic fulfillment, and Stephen Gordon is assaulted by "rockets of pain" which signal "l'heure de notre mort" as she surrenders Mary Llewelyn to the male lover who she decides is Mary's rightful spouse.[94] Just as theatrically, Gisela in *The White Morning* realizes that she has murdered a man she loves when "all feeling ebbed . . . out of her" because she was merely "the chosen instrument" of woman's revolution, and Katherine Mansfield, even while she is inspired to art by her dead brother/muse, speculates that she too is "just as much dead as he is" and wonders "why don't I commit suicide?" The guilt of the survivor implicit in such imaginings, moreover, is specifically articulated by one former nurse who defines her culpable numbness in a dreadful confession: "She [a nurse] is no longer a woman. She is dead already, just as I am . . . a machine inhabited by a ghost of a woman—soulless, past redeeming."[96] Most theatrically, perhaps, Katherine Anne Porter expresses in "Pale

Horse, Pale Rider" this nurse's feeling (and what might have been a universal female sense) that if men are sick, they must have fallen ill because women are sickening. After her heroine, Miranda, down with influenza, has had a terrifying dream about her lover, Adam, in which "he lay dead, and she still lived," she learns that her disease has contaminated him, and indeed, he has died and she has lived, kept going by a "fiery motionless particle [which] set itself . . . to survive . . . in its own madness of being."[97]

It is not surprising, then, that—repressed by what was still after all a male-dominated community and reproached by their own consciences—many women retreated into embittered unemployment or guilt-stricken domesticity after World War I. "Generally speaking, we war women are a failure,"confesses a character in Evadne Price's *Women of the Aftermath*. "We had a chance to make ourselves solid in the working market/ . . . and came a hell of a cropper in most cases."[98] To be sure, as J. Stanley Lemons and others observe, women's "peacetime levels [of employment] were [still] significantly higher than the pre-war situation."[99] Nothing would ever be the same again. But no war would ever function, either, the way this Great War had, as a battle of the sexes which initiated "the first hour in history for the women of the world." World War II certainly was to be as much a war against women civilians as it was against male combatants, with a front indistinguishable from the home front. As Virginia Woolf anticipated in *Three Guineas*, in fact, it was to be a war whose jackbooted Nazis, marching for the Fatherland, enacted the ultimate consequences of patriarchal oppression, so that Sylvia Plath, protesting against her imprisonment in "daddy's" black shoe, would fear that "I may be a bit of a Jew."[100] In 1944, moreover, in her war-shadowed "Writing on the Wall," H. D. was to return to Radclyffe Hall's definition of "no-man's-land" as a "waste land" for "inverts" (Hall) and "hysterical women" (H. D.) while more recently, in a revision of the metaphor that Hall's Stephen Gordon temporarily transcended, Linda Pastan was to see her own body as a "no man's land" over which sons and husbands battle, and in 1981 Adrienne Rich was to publish a poem which despairingly declared that "there is no no man's land," by which she clearly means that there is still no Herland.[101] With Rich, all of these women would understand themselves to be participants in an ongoing "war of the images" whose possibly apocalyptic dénouement has not yet really been revealed, though the combats of the early twentieth century offered enduring possibilities of vengeance and victory, female anxiety and feminist ecstasy.

Notes

This essay is an abbreviated version of a chapter in "No Man's Land: The Place of the Woman Writer in the Twentieth Century," a sequel to *The Madwoman in the Attic* which I am writing in collaboration with Susan Gubar, to whose inspiration and advice I am very much indebted throughout the piece. The essay also incorporates and elaborates upon some material originally presented in my "Costumes of the Mind: Transvestism as Metaphor in

Modern Literature," *Critical Inquiry* 7, no. 2 (Winter 1980): 391–417, and I wish to thank the editors for permission to reprint these passages. In addition, I am grateful to Elaine Showalter, Elliot Gilbert, Garrett Stewart, and the members of the Summer Seminar for College Teachers that Susan Gubar and I codirected in 1981, all of whom have given me useful advice and essential support. Also, I want in particular to thank Gayle Greene (at Scripps College) and David Savage (at Lewis and Clark College), who shared with me two brilliant student papers by Tamara Jones (Scripps) and Elizabeth Cookson (Lewis and Clark), projects whose revisionary research renews my confidence in the contribution women's studies has made to the undergraduate curriculum. Finally, all illustrations in this essay are reproduced with the kind permission of the Imperial War Museum in London.

1.   On the war's dark psychological consequences for men, major texts include Paul Fussell, *The Great War and Modern Memory* (New York: Oxford University Press, 1975); and Eric Leed, *No Man's Land: Combat and Identity in World War I* (New York: Cambridge University Press, 1979).

2.   Malcolm Bradbury. "The Denuded Place: War and Form in *Parade's End* and *U.S.A.* in *The First World War in Fiction*, ed. Holger Klein (London: Macmillan, 1976), pp. 193–94.

3.   See Nancy Cott, "Passionlessness: An Interpretation of Victorian Sexual Ideology, 1790–1850," *Signs: Journal of Women in Culture and Society* 4, no. 2 (Winter 1978): 219–36.

4.   D. H. Lawrence. *The Complete Poems*, ed. Vivian de Sola Pinto and F. Warren Roberts (New York: Penguin Books, 1977), pp. 741–43. For similar, though more subdued expressions of the sexual anger the war evoked, see Wilfred Owen's "Greater Love" and his "The Last Laugh," in *The Collected Poems of Wilfred Owen* (New York: New Direction Publishing Corp., 1965), pp. 41, 59; and Siegfried Sassoon's "Glory of Women," in his *Selected Poems* (London: Faber & Faber, 1968), p. 28. On Lawrence's wartime experience, see Paul Delany, *D. H. Lawrence's Nightmare* (New York: Basic Books, 1978).

5.   Joan Kelly-Gadol, "Did Women Have a Renaissance?" in *Becoming Visible: Women in European History*, ed. Renate Bridenthal and Claudia Koonz (Boston: Houghton Mifflin Co., 1977), pp. 137–64.

6.   Vera Brittain, *Testament of Youth* (London: Fontana/Virago, 1979), p. 143.

7.   Harriet Stanton Blatch, quoted in Nina Auerbach, *Communities of Women* (Cambridge, Mass.: Harvard University Press, 1978), p. 162.

8.   Nina Macdonald, "Sing a Song of War-Time," in *Scars upon My Heart: Women's Poetry and Verse of the First World War*, ed. Catherine Reilly (London: Virago, 1981), p. 69 (hereafter cited as *Scars*).

9.   Virginia Woolf, *Three Guineas* (New York: Harcourt, Brace & Co., 1938), p. 39.

10.   T. S. Eliot, "The Hollow Men," in *Selected Poems of T. S. Eliot* (1925; reprint ed., New York: Harcourt, Brace & World, 1964), pp. 77–80.

11.   Fussell (n. 1 above), pp. 3–35.

12.   Leed (n. 1 above), pp. 18–19.

13.   Richard Aldington, *Death of a Hero* (London: Chatto & Windus, 1929), p. 429.

14.   Robert Graves, *Goodbye to All That* (1929; reprint ed., New York: Doubleday & Co., 1957), p. 130.

15.   Brittain (n. 6 above), pp. 252–53.

16.   Brittain (n. 6 above), p. 216.

17. Leed, p. 20.

18. Graves, p. 59.

19. Lawrence (n. 4 above), pp. 748–49.

20. Mabel Darmer, quoted in David Mitchell, *Women on the Warpath: The Story of the Women of the First World War* (London: Jonathan Cape, 1966), p. 161.

21. Auerbach (n. 7 above), p. 187.

22. Jessie Pope, "War Girls," in *Scars* (n. 8 above), p. 90.

23. Blatch is quoted in J. Stanley Lemons, *The Woman Citizen: Social Feminism in the 1920s* (Urbana: University of Illinois Press, 1973), p. 15.

24. Mitchell (n. 20 above), p. 380.

25. Mitchell (n. 20 above), p. 380.

26. See Gail Braybon, *Women Workers in the First World War: The British Experience* (London: Croom Helm, 1981), pp. 46–47; and Mary Cadogan and Patricia Craig, *Women and Children First: The Fiction of Two World Wars* (London: Gollancz, 1978), pp. 32–33. For further information, see Mitchell (n. 20 above) and Maurine Weiner Greenwald, *Women, War and Work: The Impact of World War I on Women Workers in the United States* (Westport, Conn.: Greenwood Press, 1980).

27. Madeline Ida Bedford, "Munitions Wages," in *Scars* (n. 8 above), p. 7.

28. Caroline Matthews, *Experiences of a Woman Doctor in Serbia* (London: Mills & Boon, 1916), p. 72, quoted in Elizabeth Cookson, "The Forgotten Women: British Nurses, VADs, and Doctors across the Channel" (unpublished paper), p. 17 (hereafter cited as "Forgotten Women").

29. Wharton's notes on her *ouvroir* and other charities, as well as her program for "Hero Land," are held at the Beinecke Library, Yale University, New Haven, Connecticut.

30. Aldington (n. 13 above), p. 259.

31. John Kipling's unpublished letter of September 19, 1915, is held at the Rare Book Room, University of Sussex, Brighton, Sussex, England; Sassoon (n. 4 above), p. 17.

32. Quoted in Cadogan and Craig (n. 26 above), p. 92.

33. Owen (n. 4 above), p. 42.

34. Alice Meynell. "A Father of Women," in *Salt and Bitter and Good*, ed. Cora Kaplan (London: Paddington, 1975), pp. 187–89.

35. Graves (n. 14 above), pp. 229–30.

36. Bernard Shaw, quoted in Woolf, *Three Guineas* (n. 9 above), p. 182. It is worth noting, however, that Woolf believes Shaw was exaggerating.

37. Jessie Pope, "The Call," in *Scars* (n. 8 above), p. 88.

38. Max Sinclair, "Victory," in *The Tree of Heaven* (London: Cassell, 1917), n. 323; Edith Wharton, *A Son at the Front* (New York: Charles Scribner's Sons, 1923). For a sardonically masculinist view of women's propagandizing, see Aldous Huxley, "The Farcical History of Richard Greenow," in *Limbo* (New York: Doran, 1920).

39. Owen (n. 4 above), pp. 55–56.

40. Brittain (n. 6 above), p. 210.

41. Brittain (n. 6 above), pp. 165–66.

42. Ernest Hemingway, *A Farewell to Arms* (1929; reprint ed., New York: Bantam Books, 1949), p. 76; *The Sun Also Rises* (New York: Charles Scribner's Sons, 1926); pp. 38, 31.

43. D. H. Lawrence, "The Ladybird," in *Four Short Novels* (New York: Viking Press, 1923), p. 57.

44. Rebecca West, *The Return of the Soldier* (1918; reprint ed., London: Virago, 1980), p. 144.

45. Dorothy L. Sayers, *Busman's Honeymoon* (1937; reprint ed., New York: Avon Books, 1968), p. 316.

46. Virginia Woolf, *Mrs. Dalloway* (New York: Harcourt, Brace & Co., 1925), pp. 85–87.

47. Brittain (n. 6 above), pp. 165–66.

48. Leed (n. 1 above), p. 47.

49. Leed (n. 1 above), p. 45.

50. It seems significant that in *Lady Chatterley's Lover* Ivy Bolton becomes Clifford's perversely sexual nurse and significant too that Mellor's estranged wife Bertha has the same name as one of the war's principal guns—the "Big Bertha."

51. Aldington (n. 13 above), pp. 12, 19.

52. D. H. Lawrence, *The Complete Short Stories*, 3 vols. (1922; reprint ed., New York: Penguin Books, 1976), 2:343–44, 373.

53. Rose Macaulay, "Many Sisters to Many Brothers," in *Scars* (n. 8 above), p. xxxv.

54. Lorine Pruette's comment on "the joy of women in wartime" is quoted in Lemons (n. 23 above), p. 15; May Sinclair, cited in Mitchell (n. 20 above), p. 129.

55. May Sinclair, "The War of Liberation: From a Journal," *English Review*, no. 20–24 (June–July 1915), pp. 170–71, quoted in "Forgotten Women" (n. 28 above), p. 13.

56. Brittain (n. 6 above), p. 292; Mrs. St. Clair Stobart, "A Woman in the Midst of War," *Ladies Home Journal* (January 1915), p. 5; B. G. Mure, "A Side Issue of the War," *Blackwood's* (October 1916), p. 446; *A War Nurse's Diary* (New York: Macmillan Publishing Co., 1918), p. 59; all quoted in "Forgotten Woman" (n. 28 above), pp. 12–13.

57. Woolf, *Three Guineas* (n. 9 above), pp. 177–78.

58. Sinclair, *The Tree of Heaven* (n. 38 above), pp. 346–47.

59. Willa Cather, *One of Ours* (New York: Alfred A. Knopf, Inc., 1923), pp. 446, 291.

60. Radclyffe Hall, "Miss Ogilvy Finds Herself," in *Miss Ogilvy Finds Herself* (London: Heinemann, 1934), pp. 3, 4.

61. Radclyffe Hall, *The Well of Loneliness* (London: Cape, 1928), pp. 315, 319.

62. Katherine Anne Porter, "Pale Horse, Pale Rider," in *Pale Horse, Pale Rider* (1936; reprint ed., New York: Modern Library, Inc., 1939), p. 198.

63. Hall, "Miss Ogilvy Finds Herself," p. 34.

64. Hall, *Well of Loneliness*, p. 366.

65. Amy Lowell, *The Complete Poetical Works* (1919; reprint ed., Boston: Houghton Mifflin Co., 1955), pp. 209–18, 237–41; Gertrude Stein, "The War," in *The Autobiography of Alice B. Toklas*, in *The Selected Writings of Gertrude Stein* (1933; reprint ed., New York:

Vintage, 1972), pp. 135–81; Stein, "Lifting Belly," in *The Yale Gertrude Stein,* ed. Richard Kostelanetz (New Haven, Conn.: Yale University Press, 1980).

66. Nigel Nicolson, *Portrait of a Marriage* (London: Weidenfield & Nicolson, 1973), pp. 105, 112.

67. Violetta Thurstan, *Field Hospital and Flying Column: Being the Journal of an English Nursing Sister in Belgium and Russia* (London: Putnam's, 1915), p. 174, quoted in "Forgotten Women" (n. 28 above), p. 16.

68. Hall, *Well of Loneliness,* p. 336.

69. Winifred Holtby, *The Crowded Street* (1924; reprint ed., London: Virago, 1981).

70. Fussell (n. 1 above), p. 272.

71. Fussell (n. 1 above), p. 274; Owen (n. 4 above), p. 106.

72. Leed (n. 1 above), p. 200.

73. Owen (n. 4 above), p. 41. For the homoerotic significance of "lads," see Fussell (n. 1 above), pp. 282–85.

74. Sigmund Freud, "Reflections upon War and Death," in *Character and Culture* (New York: P. F. Collier, Inc., 1963), pp. 109–13.

75. Owen (n. 4 above), pp. 35–36.

76. D. H. Lawrence, *Kangaroo* (New York: Viking Press, 1923), pp. 261, 265.

77. Gertrude Atherton, *The White Morning* (New York: Stokes, 1918), pp. 165, 147, 146; Sinclair, *The Tree of Heaven,* p. 142. Atherton's novel was brought to my attention by Tamara Jones, "The Mud in God's Eye: World War I in Women's Novels" (unpublished paper), pp. 86–96.

78. Virginia Woolf, *The Years* (New York: Harcourt, Brace & Co., 1937), pp. 287, 292.

79. H. D., *Helen in Egypt* (New York: New Directions Publishing Corp., 1961), p. 300; H. D., *Trilogy* (1944–46; reprint ed., New York: New Directions Corp., 1973), p. 153.

80. Crystal Eastman, "Now I Dare Do It," in *Crystal Eastman on Women and Revolution,* ed. Blanche Cook (New York: Oxford University Press, 1978), p. 240; see also Olive Schreiner, "Woman and War," in *Woman and Labor* (London: Unwin, 1911); and Charlotte Perkins Gilman's comments on the Great War in the excerpt from *With Her in Ourland* included in Ann J. Lane, ed., *The Charlotte Perkins Gilman Reader* (New York: Pantheon Books, 1980).

81. Robins is quoted in Lemons, *The Woman Citizen* (n. 23 above), p. 20.

82. This Woolf manuscript is in the Berg Collection, New York Public Library, New York, and is quoted by permission of Quentin Bell.

83. Woolf, *Three Guineas* (n. 9 above), p. 103.

84. Woolf, *Three Guineas* (n. 9 above), p. 197, 109.

85. Bernard Shaw, *Bernard Shaw's Plays,* ed. Warren S. Smith (1919; reprint ed., New York: W. W. Norton & Co., 1970), p. 147.

86. Brittain (n. 6 above), pp. 251–52.

87. Wharton (n. 38 above), pp. 423, 426. Willa Cather records a similar (and similarly encoded) empowerment of the living by the wartime dead in *The Professor's House* (New York: Vintage, 1925), where the sacrificed Tom Outland gives meaning to Professor Peter's existence.

88. Katherine Mansfield, *The Journals of Katherine Mansfield* (1927; reprint ed., New York: Alfred A. Knopf, Inc., 1954), pp. 43–45, 49.

89. H. D., *Bid Me to Live* (New York: Grove Press, 1960), pp. 145–46.

90. The manuscript of H. D.'s "Thorn Thicket" is held at the Beinecke Library, Yale University, New Haven, Connecticut, and is quoted by permission of Perdita Schaffner.

91. Leed (n. 1 above), p. 163.

92. Owen (n. 1 above), p. 102.

93. Lawrence, *Kangaroo* (n. 76 above), p. 253; Rebecca West, "Autumn and Virginia Woolf," in *Ending in Earnest: A Literary Log* (New York: Arno Press, 1971), pp. 212–13.

94. Hall, *Well of Loneliness* (n. 61 above), pp. 511, 507.

95. Atherton (n. 77 above), pp. 133, 145; Mansfield (n. 88 above), p. 38.

96. Mary Borden, *The Forbidden Zone* (London: Heinemann, 1929), pp. 59–60, quoted in "Forgotten Women" (n. 28 above), p. 9.

97. Porter (n. 62 above), pp. 242, 253.

98. Quoted in Cadogan and Craig (n. 26 above), p. 47.

99. Lemons (n. 23 above), p. 22.

100. Sylvia Plath, "Daddy," Ariel (New York: Harper & Row Publishers, 1965), p. 50.

101. H. D., *Tribute to Freud* (New York: McGraw-Hill Book Co., 1975), p. 77; Linda Pastan, "In the Old Guerilla War," in *The Five Stages of Grief* (New York: W. W. Norton & Co., 1978); Adrienne Rich, "The Images," in *A Wild Patience Has Taken Me This Far* (New York: W. W. Norton & Co., 1981), pp. 3–5.

15

Writing War Poetry Like a Woman

Susan Schweik

Like the military itself, traditionally the most overtly male of preserves, the canon of the poetry of war presented in recent bibliographies or anthologies is especially and intensely androcentric. In the modern war poem as it is usually defined, the experience of the masculine soldier and the voice of the masculine author predominate. A reader of didactic discussions of war poetry written during the Second World War might therefore be surprised at the frequency with which American literary critics held up a text written by a woman as the single, paradigmatic, exemplary war poem: Marianne Moore's "In Distrust of Merits." W. H. Auden, for instance, called "In Distrust" "the best of . . . all" war poems of World War II.[1] Moore was so lionized on the American home front, her poem so praised, that Randall Jarrell began his famous critical answer to "In Distrust" with a mock-apologetic "Miss Moore is reviewed not as a poet but as an institution," going on to cite, acerbically, a reviewer who had called Moore "the greatest living poet" and then demanded that she be "placed in Fort Knox for the duration."[2]

The uses of Moore as institution, for the duration, deserve closer study than Jarrell's ironies might suggest; they shed light on assumptions prevalent in both the 1940s and the 1980s about what "war" means, what "war poetry" means, and where "woman" stands in relation to both. In the following pages, I shall be concerned specifically with how Moore's work invokes and attempts to revoke traditional formulations of sexual difference in wartime, and with how Jarrell's responses undertake a related task. I shall also be concerned, more broadly, with constructions of gender in theoretical controversies during the early forties over the criteria by which war poetry should be judged, particularly over standards of authorial credibility. These arguments matter because they set terms which still tend to define the parameters of current aesthetic and political evaluations of the war poem—values shared by texts as magisterial as the recent *Oxford Book of War Poetry* and as adversarial as collections of poems by Vietnam War protesters or veterans. But a look back to the volatile home-front debates about the decorum of the growing subgenre of war poetry reveals not only what most contemporary anthologists and critics of war literature have inherited from the Second World War period but also what they have attempted to discard or repress: the active presence of women *as subjects* in the discourse of war.

In the forties, many critics seized on "In Distrust of Merits" as a way of reforming the canon of war poetry, a canon till then largely shaped by the masculine "soldier poems" of British Great War poets such as Wilfred Owen and Siegfried Sassoon. First World War soldier poetry had, of course, never been a stable commodity; it could never be guaranteed to be written by a genuine soldier from a genuine trench, as Robert Graves's pointed summary of the tradition, written in 1948, makes clear:

> When war poetry became a fashion in 1915, a good deal of it was written imitatively by civilians who regretted that age or unfitness prevented them from also 'making the supreme sacrifice.' . . . Also, many soldiers wrote as though they had seen more of the war than they really had. Robert Nichols, for instance, whose brief service in France . . . was ended by sickness . . . scored a great success . . . as a crippled warrior, reading . . . to University and women's club audiences.[3]

These falsehoods only go to prove, rather than render suspicious, the power of the standards for war poems which became normative in the university and the women's club during and after the Great War. Within the developing tradition of war poetry, those poems were privileged which were, or seemed to be, rooted in the original ground of men's literal combat experience. War poems should be backed, as Sassoon described Owen's work, by the authority of experience of the infantry soldier.[4]

In World War II, however, that lonely masculine authority of experience—the bitter authority derived from direct exposure to violence, injury, and mechanized terror—was rapidly dispersing among general populations. Graves notes, with some discomfort, that the Second World War soldier "cannot even feel that his rendezvous with death is more certain than that of his Aunt Fanny, the firewatcher."[5] American culture was, obviously, characterized by far greater disjunctions between male and female "experience" of war than the British blitz society Graves describes, and the modern tradition of soldier poetry, with its ironic emphasis on unmendable gaps between the soldier author and the civilian reader, retained its strong influence. Still, public discussions of war and literature in the United States dwell frequently on the new conjunctions between civilians and soldiers, front and home front, and men and women, focusing on their shared morale or effort as well as on their common deprivation and vulnerability.

In a war newly perceived as "total," Moore's work could exemplify the power of a representative civilian voice. It could also represent modernism provisionally embracing realist and didactic functions, coming round to correcting earlier trends toward self-referentiality. Thus Richard Eberhart, arguing in his introduction to a well-known anthology of war poetry that "the spectator, the contemplator, the opposer of war have their hours with the enemy no less than uniformed combatants," praises Moore for abandoning the "complacencies of the peignoir" to write "In Distrust of Merits."[6] His phrasing links Moore with another civilian war poet, Wallace Stevens; by dressing Moore in Stevens's peignoir in order to show her doffing it, he represents her as a formerly feminine object of desire who has emerged from the coquetries of her sex into a new, superior, gender-free authority. Now, Eberhart argues, "the bloodshed of which she writes has caused her to break through the decorative surface of her verse" to a "different kind of utterance." For Eberhart, the poem's value lies in its violation of Moore's usual mannered aestheticism. She "breaks through" a feminine surface, as if puncturing skin, but the result is not a wound but a mouth: a "different kind of utterance," in which "the meaning has dictated the sincerity."[7] Oscar Williams, in the preface to a comparable anthology, also reads the poem as a model of transparent earnestness, offering it as a solution to the problem of Edna St. Vincent Millay, the "bad" woman war poet who is excoriated in these discussions as often as Moore is extolled. Describing one of Millay's war poems as "a sentimental piece of verse written by an American civilian, designed to be read by . . . people themselves out of danger because they are protected by a wall of living young flesh, much of which will be mangled," Williams contrasts Moore's "In Distrust of Merits":

> But with true poets the poetry is in the pity . . .

> I ask the reader to study closely a war poem peculiarly fitted to illustrate my present thesis. It is also written by a woman, a civilian. "In Distrust of Merits," by Marianne Moore, is the direct communication of honest feeling by one ready to search her own heart to discover the causes of war and accept her full share of responsibility for its effects.[8]

Moore's poem was indeed "peculiarly fitted to illustrate" Williams's anxious argument for a civilian war poetry, a pure "heart" which could express the "pity" of war—Owen's famous dictum—with no more false sentiment and no more indirection than a soldier poet would bring to the subject. As peculiarly fitted for illustration as the poem was, however, it could not transcend the intensities of the debates in which it was held up as an example, and it could not render the disputations over literary representation of war any less likely or necessary. "In Distrust of Merits" is no less didactic, no less overtly ideological, and no less a marked product of its own time than the patriotic poetry Millay wrote under the guidance of the Writers' War Board. Later readers, in fact, may well be more struck by what Moore's and Millay's war poems have in common than by the ways in which they diverge. Contemporary critics of Moore's work tend to dismiss "In Distrust" if they do not ignore it entirely; one of Moore's most sympathetic readers, Bonnie Costello, expresses her distaste in terms which might be used to define Millay's war work: the poem's conventional pronouncements "show too much the pressure of news."[9] This "too much," the offhand signal of shared evaluative norms, adumbrates for Costello's contemporary audience—one composed, presumably, largely of literary critics—a familiar set of postwar aesthetic values. A good poem— that is, a poem unpressured, or pressured just enough—will be cleanly universal and timeless, where "In Distrust" bears too obviously the imprints of an immediate historical and cultural context; it will be neutral, where "In Distrust" is polemical; it will enact poetically, where "In Distrust" spouts off oratorically; it will address an elite readership, where "In Distrust" invites the same kind of attention as the *Saturday Evening Post*.

But in another context—that, for instance, of forums organized during World War II to express and to prove American high culture's commitment to the war effort—a poem may be more likely to be judged uncompelling if it lacks ideological commitment and fails to appeal to a mass audience, if it shows too little "the pressure of news." We can sense the force of the strong demand during the war years for a literature which was overtly topical and politically engaged in Elizabeth Bishop's anxious words to the publisher of her first book of poems in 1945: "The fact that none of these poems deal directly with the war . . . will, I am afraid, leave me open to reproach."[10] Open to reproach then and now, either for its overt political commitment or for its lack of it, an obvious reminder of shifting standards of literary value and of the ideological constitution of poetry, the war poem of the forties often proves embarrassing. It is no surprise that Moore herself, in 1961, dismisses "In Distrust of Merits": "It is sincere but I wouldn't call it a poem . . . . As form, what has it? It is just a protest."[11]

During the forties, critics and anthologists like Williams and Eberhart encouraged their readers to understand Moore's poem as a firm resolution of wartime aesthetic crises. But we need not look later than the war period itself for evidence of "pressure" on and in the poem. Moore's private worksheets point to her own engagement with "In Distrust" as a field of dynamic and unresolved tensions, not to the poem's status as the one calm eye at the core of a storm. And Randall Jarrell's public critique of "In Distrust of Merits" declares a crisis of representation which, Jarrell argues, Moore's poem not only fails to assuage but also exacerbates. For both Moore and Jarrell, the conflicts of writing and reading about war which "In Distrust" provokes arise, particularly, around notions of sexual difference; for both of them, not least of the pressures the poem showed too much was the pressure of gender.

By Moore's own account, "In Distrust" did indeed originate out of the "pressure of the news": she once said that her incentive for writing the poem was a newspaper photograph of a dead soldier.[12] That image remains in the finished poem, flickering at its center: "O / quiet form upon the dust, I cannot/look and yet I must."[13] Like another battlefield image in another Moore war poem, "Keeping Their World Large"—"That forest of white crosses! My eyes won't close to it"—the scene of the dead soldier both repels and compels attention (*CP*, p. 145). These images draw the eye with hypnotic, irrational power and hold it there, trapped in its helpless, frightened gaze at the nightmare facts the pictures represent. Unlike other cultural artifacts represented in dozens of other Moore poems, these printed battle scenes elicit a strong resistance or an inability to attend to them carefully; the eyes try unsuccessfully to close, the face to swerve away.[14] In general, as Costello notes, Moore "is always observing while she is making observations."[15] But this poem seems to represent the process by which its author works as a constant struggle against evasion: here, it suggests, I am always fighting against the desire *not* to observe while I make measured assertions about the meaning of warfare.

Moore's letters and workbooks in the years preceding the publication of "In Distrust of Merits" reveal the force and shape of that struggle. Several developing ideas about war laid the groundwork for the poem's arguments. In 1939, Moore wrote to her brother, who was a naval chaplain on a ship in the Pacific, that in the process of reading Reinhold Niebuhr she had come to the conclusion that "intolerance is at work in us all *in all* countries,—that we ourselves 'persecute' Jews and Negroes & submit to wrongful tyranny. Or at least feel 'superior' in sundry ways."[16] Earlier, in her conversation notebook in June of 1938, Moore had observed: "In ancient times, people (barbarous) razed cities and murdered the innocent. One is faint before it and these people are with us now. One does not feel detached by one's horror—even if they are not of our country. They are *we*. They are of our kind."[17] This sense of war as a self-reflecting fight against personal intolerance shows up in the decisive ending, borrowed from a sermon, of an earlier poem, "The Labors of Hercules," in which one of the almost impossible labors is "to convince snake-charming controversialists / that one keeps on knowing . . . that the German is not a Hun" (*CP*, p. 53). It appears, too, in the "promise we make to the fighting" in "In Distrust of Merits": "We'll / never hate black, white, red, yellow, Jew, / Gentile, Untouchable."

We can trace in the notebooks the ongoing development of an idea of "inwardness" which becomes the central principle of "In Distrust": much of this idea, as Laurence Stapleton has determined, derives from and revises conversations Moore had with her mother. On 23 July 1942, she notes down in her reading diary the crucial phrase, "There never was a war that was not inward"; in the same entry, the climactic end of the poem is worked out: "I inwardly did nothing. / O Iscariot-like crime! / Beauty is everlasting / and dust is for a time"; and an entry on 22 March 1943 explains the crime more explicitly than it is defined in the published version of the poem: "Black white red yellow mixed Jew gentile and untouchable— they're begging and I inwardly did nothing . . . . " On a later page, in an undated entry, Moore further explores the value of inward action and inwardness, setting down the following: "Outstanding. Futile word. No indwelling."[18] This comment may be read as a partial gloss on the title of the poem: "merits," which are to be distrusted, are external, static signs of what a culture determines to be "outstanding"; successful "indwelling" struggle, in contrast, secret, dynamic and uncategorizable, cannot be signified in fixed medals or badges. Outward wars, in which men urged to be outstanding try to outstand each other, are caused, so the major argument of "In Distrust" goes, by a failure of each of us to exercise a continual inward struggle against the imperious and aggressive aspects of our own selves. Only by vigilantly practicing a form of inward warfare can we avoid external catastrophe.[19] "It is a violence from within that protects us from a violence without": Moore quotes Stevens approvingly in a wartime review of his work she entitled

"There Is a War That Never Ends," adding that Stevens "and the soldier are one."[20] If Stevens was a soldier poet, Moore might be one too, fighting in an ongoing conflict which was no less vital for being intellectual, spiritual, and figurative rather than bodily and literal.

Stevens's concept of inward war offers the imagination and its supreme fictions alone as a way of understanding, transcending, and solving world conflict. Moore's offers more orthodox Christian consolations as well and incorporates ideas of Christian spiritual warfare, as expressed in such conversation notes as the following: "It is not that we fear to have the body struck down from the soul that we hate war, but because man is not complete unless he has the power of peace in his soul" (14 August 1937); "The one good of war is that it brings people in their helplessness to pray. It keeps people from being satisfied with an indolent peace . . . "(2 November 1935).[21] In "In Distrust," Moore will develop this idea of sacred and inward spiritual warfare in language which openly declares its ties to the authoritative rhetoric of Scripture ("O / Star of David, star of Bethlehem . . . ").

But for every self-confident aphorism which generates a legitimate meaning for the war or imposes some kind of order upon it, we can locate others in the notebooks which demonstrate Moore's hesitation and anxiety. Moore can speak emphatically about the symbolic war within, but when she turns to the particular manifestations of the war without—its battles and body counts, the daily events which filled the pages of the newspapers—her voice assumes a deferent and nervous tone. "I:?" reads a mysterious note in the conversation diary for August 1937, continuing, "was the nobly fought for nothing. If they aren't killed they come back maimed or ["considerably weakened" is crossed out here] and disabled prospectively." In September 1940: "May those who fight in squadrons have a vision. We are sending them to their death." In the spring of 1943, amid several pages of scattered notes for the poem, the war within is first figured positively—"how does one resist invasion / but by resistance inwardly?"—but then loses its power, becoming a trap or cage: "Prisoner of inwardness."[22]

A nearby passage exemplifies the difficulty of Moore's struggle to authorize her own voice as representative and universal: "(may) humbly but with—confidence (may as one.) Say OUR."[23] Moore, I believe, is exploring here, amid considerable self-doubt and self-interrogation, the possibility of assuming the voice of a collective "we," a pronoun which would function, as John Ellis has suggested it does in wartime film documentaries, to articulate a nation, or the whole world, "as both actor and observer, enunciator and addressee."[24] "Say our," she orders herself—or recalls someone else's order—after speaking in muted parentheses. But for Moore, who is well aware of distinctions which cannot be entirely erased between herself as American civilian and the young male soldiers whose anonymous forms filled news photographs, the urge to "say our" may be a difficult, dangerous, and even reprehensible ambition. The line which begins, in a preliminary version of "In Distrust of Merits," "*we* are fighting fighting fighting" becomes, in the chastened final version, "they are fighting fighting fighting."[25] "All too literally," goes the epigraph of her "Keeping Their World Large," "their flesh and their spirit are our shield" (*CP*, p. 145). The "our" here is a limited, indebted pronoun. The poet who is a civilian and a woman can write of figurative war with aplomb, but of all too literal warfare she is wary and unsure, and she feels herself all too literally to be speaking passively, helplessly. In the context of the war, can a protected American woman "say our"?

"The difficulty is one of language," Moore wrote in one of her reading notebooks, copying a passage from Alexander G. Clifford's *Conquest of North Africa, 1940–1943*. "The facts of modern warfare are outside normal human experience and strictly speaking only the facts of normal human experience are reproductive in words."[26] She went on to write out sections of a review of the book by Colonel Joseph I. Greene: "He shows the highly observant [*sic*] of details that have a special meaning in war: Few things have a smaller comparative secondhand value than battle." These passages, taken together, allow us to differentiate between two kinds of difficulty which, Moore felt, complicated and vexed the representations of war in her poems. One is a universal difficulty inherent in all language, which shapes its vocabulary, according to Clifford's argument, out of an everyday human consensus; it therefore can never "reproduce" modern warfare because modern warfare, by definition, renders the "known" world abnormal and unknowable, completely resistant to mimesis. The other is a difficulty specific to the protected American, who can bring to her war poem no telling details derived from her own experience and who can only describe battle "secondhand," in inadequate comparisons. If the difficulty is one of language, it is also one of gender, of age, of all other specific cultural, psychological, and biographical contexts which determine the exact place of a civilian woman writer.

Women, of course, acted and suffered in the most direct ways in the war of 1939–1945, many American women among them. At the same time, many American men, even many American soldiers, experienced the war no more directly than their average female counterparts.[27] Several well-known soldier poets of the Second World War—Randall Jarrell and Richard Eberhart, for instance—did not actively participate in combat. In the end, though, Jarrell's actual distance from the "front lines" matters very little, while Moore's matters very much. Jarrell and Eberhart were "men as men," speaking for men, and therefore had imaginative right to the voice of the soldier, the terrain of the "front." Cynthia Enloe has described how "society's bastion of male identity," the military, "believes it must categorise women as peripheral, as serving safely at the 'rear' on the 'home front.' Women *as women* must be denied access to 'the front,' to 'combat.' . . . The military has to constantly redefine 'the front' and 'combat' as wherever 'women' are not."[28] Marianne Moore, writing from where women were, wrote inevitably about war within a situation of lack and absence, within a sense of herself as peripheral rather than central. Williams, Eberhart, and Auden might tout "In Distrust" as a universal war poem, but it, and all Moore's writing on war, show marked evidence of the specific stresses which result when an American woman writes a Second World War poem *as a woman*.

In "In Distrust of Merits," the tension between moral self-confidence on the one hand and felt or feared inadequacy on the other is pronounced and strenuous. Half in distrust of merits, half in defense of them, suspicious of herself but awed and moved by Allied soldiers, speaking in a voice half subdued and half like the gyroscope's fall in another Moore poem, "trued by regnant certainty" (*CP*, p. 134), Moore engages in what Geoffrey Hartman has called her "dialogue of one, an ironic crossfire of statement that continually denies and reasserts the possibility of a selfless assertion of the self":[29]

> Strengthened to live, strengthened to die for
>   medals and positioned victories?
> They're fighting, fighting, fighting the blind
>   man who thinks he sees—
> who cannot see that the enslaver is
> enslaved; the hater, harmed. O shining O
>   firm star, O tumultuous
>   ocean lashed till small things go
>   as they will, the mountainous
>   wave makes us who look, know
>
> depth. Lost at sea before they fought! O
>   star of David, star of Bethlehem,
> O black imperial lion
>   of the Lord—emblem
> of a risen world—be joined at last, be
> joined. There is hate's crown beneath which all is
>   death; there's love's without which none
>   is king; the blessed deeds bless
>   the halo. As contagion
>   of sickness makes sickness,
>
> contagion of trust can make trust. They're
>   fighting in deserts and caves, one by
> one, in battalions and squadrons;
>   they're fighting that I
> may yet recover from the disease, My
> Self; some have it lightly; some will die. "Man's
>   wolf to man" and we devour
>   ourselves. The enemy could not
>   have made a greater breach in our
>   defenses . . . .

Who is the subject of the first two lines of the poem? An "I"? a "she" or a "he"? an "us"? ("Say our.") Only after some uncertainty are we brought to a decisive distance from the active third-person subjects of the poem. The strengthened ones turn out to be "they" alone, the "they" of the professional army in distant places, surveyed as if by telescopic lens, "lost at sea before they fought," or "fighting in deserts and caves, one by / one, in battalions and squadrons," "Some / in snow, some on crags, some in quicksands."

These stylized summations of the various landscapes of combat are the poem's most "literal" moments. Moore strives here to represent the intractable, actual conditions of Second World warfare but does so in the language of the newsreel. More often, however, the war represented in "In Distrust" is entirely disengaged from history, becoming a figurative or archetypal war of wars rather than a specific historical event labeled "Second" and "World." The enemy has both a relatively literal status and a more predominantly allegorical one within this poem. For instance, the "blind / man who thinks he sees— / who cannot see that the enslaver is / enslaved" and who later is described as "small dust of the earth / that walks so arrogantly" may refer to Hitler or Mussolini or Hirohito, or to any men who live in and fight for a nation-state whose dominant ideologies are "fascist" or "militarist," but he also stands for an archetypal Everyman and Everywoman. Very much like Orgoglio or Archimago in *The Faerie Queene*, he represents an interior spiritual danger, Blindness and Aggression and Pride, while the speaking "I" and the "we" that the "I" addresses stand, like Spenserian allegorical heroes, for the self which must struggle with its own inward enemies in order to achieve and maintain a patient self-knowledge. Moore's narrative of spiritual trial recounts an essential, universal struggle within all selves for perfection of the soul and accounts for warfare as both a part of that struggle and the result of its lapses: "I must / fight till I have conquered in myself what / causes war." The poem's world is a world of inward emblems in which all selves have the opportunity to choose, and continually work toward, the archetypal qualities they wish to incorporate and embody: "There is hate's crown beneath which all is / death; there's love's without which none / is king; the blessed deeds bless / the halo."

At several crucial points in "In Distrust of Merits," however, the speaker's emblematic certainty dissolves, and the voice becomes edgy and mistrustful of itself and its surroundings. The formless force of the tidal wave which, apparently, has sunk a military ship near the start of the poem "makes us who look, know / depth," Moore writes—but whether the depth we discover is a new inward, spiritual dimension of ourselves or simply the terrifying flux of an uncontrolled and uncontrollable world ("O tumultuous / ocean lashed till small things go / as they will") we cannot be sure. At other moments, the speaker's voice more openly undermines and disables itself. Earlier I quoted one of the poem's most determined liberal morals: "We'll / never hate black, white, red, yellow, Jew, / Gentile, Untouchable." In context, this message, set off by quotation marks, retains its power, but the speaker severely undercuts her own authority:

> We
> vow, we make this promise
>
> to the fighting—it's a promise—"We'll
>   never hate black, white, red, yellow, Jew,
> Gentile, Untouchable." We are
>   not competent to
> make our vows. With set jaw they are fighting,
>   fighting, fighting . . .

Here the promise is first subtly questioned in Moore's use of the pat phrase, "it's a promise," a colloquial form of emphasis which, like "without a doubt" or "really," subverts its own assurances by being overly reassuring. A more open interrogation follows, as the speaker's voice entirely discredits itself and its collective audience: "we are not competent." Inability to vow, in a world which demands strong action and speech, constitutes a desperate handicap; moreover, this vision of the self as unstable and ineffective is inimical to the vision of the ultimately capable self which must be implicit in the "spiritual warfare" narrative in other parts of "In Distrust of Merits." Although the self in any "inward warfare" plot must have serious weaknesses to combat, it must as well have access to competence—an access in serious question here.

Other moments of high moral certitude in the poem are followed by other instances of equally radical self-distrust. The assertion that "there never was a war that was / not inward" ends "I must / fight till I have conquered in myself what / causes war, *but I would not believe it*" (my italics). Moore asserts her moral and then withdraws, anxiously, painfully. The next lines—"I˙inwardly did nothing. / O Iscariot-like crime!"—suggest a reading which aligns itself with the tradition of spiritual warfare narrative: "I would not believe it," in the past imperfect tense, can be read as a statement of self-castigation following a confession of a crime which can only now be atoned for ("I would not believe it then"). But it can also be interpreted as "I refuse to believe it now—I continue to be recalcitrant"; here, again, doubt and resistance threaten to replace confidence and preclude continuation of the redemptive spiritual warfare plot. "They are fighting," Moore writes in stanza five, " . . . that / hearts may feel and not be numb. / It cures me; or am I what / I can't believe in?" The extremity of personal doubt here, which goes beyond the requisite moral self-suspicion of the spiritual warrior, calls into question the veracity and validity of the war poem which it interrupts.

Or am I what I can't believe in? This kind of self-questioning may certainly be an attempt to put into literary practice the kind of humility Moore advocates in "In Distrust of Merits." But it also seems to be a response to her distance from the violence of which she is attempting to make sense. "If these great patient / dyings," she writes, "—all these agonies / and wound-bearings and bloodshed— / can teach us how to live, these / dyings were not wasted." *If* they can teach us, she says, not "they can teach us." The affirmations of meaning and purgations of suffering here are conditional, fragile, subject to denial from within the poem itself—a poem with "distrust" in its very title. We can feel the language straining in this passage, with its overblown "wound-bearings," an abstract euphemism atypical of Moore's style. When Americans safe on our own continent attempt to write about war, Cary Nelson has argued, "our own physical security makes the language flat and unconvincing. We have no historical ground for sympathetic identification; such words will not come to us."[30] In "In Distrust of Merits," Moore calls for such words to come to her, but she also, at key points, dramatizes her own failure to find them.

The poem is interspersed throughout with wholehearted, ringing assertions of piety that are likely to annoy modern critics trained to value ironies and complexities. It ends with a credo particularly trite by most contemporary standards: "Beauty is everlasting / and dust is for a time." But this confident declaration is prefaced immediately by three notably self-suspicious lines: "I would not believe it./ I inwardly did nothing. / O Iscariot-like crime!" Even this last apostrophe, the figure Jonathan Culler calls the most "pretentious and mystificatory in the lyric," cannot entirely dispel the humbling and demystifying force of the comparison of the self to Judas.[31] Before simply dismissing the final couplet, which reverts suddenly to traditional accentual meter instead of the pure syllabic verse Moore usually preferred, as sentimental and clishéd, we would do well to remember Jane Tompkins's warnings about the politics of those labels when they are applied to nineteenth-century popular novels, works whose function is "heuristic and didactic rather than mimetic" and which "do not attempt to transcribe in detail a parabola of events as they 'actually happen' in society": "What the word *sentimental* really means in this context is that the arena of human action . . . has been defined not as the world, but as the human soul. [Such works develop] a theory of power that stipulates that all true action is not material, but spiritual."[32] In "In Distrust," however, the spiritual cannot, except with difficulty and momentarily, supersede other theories of power; definitions of "the arena of human action" waver. In a variety of ways familiar to readers of modern poetry, the poem undercuts its own apparent anti-ironic commitment to the war well fought. Part of its force for its contemporary audience surely lay in its expression and partial resolution of conflicts between Christian typology and modernist suspicion.

The poem's shaky mixture of tempered heroic assertion and strong ironic contradiction guaranteed its great appeal for forties critics and anthologists, who, with the harsh memory inscribed in the antiwar soldier poetry of the last war behind them, faced the difficult task of reshaping a canon which could at once convey the war's brutality and represent its necessity, recognize both its justice and its meaninglessness. "In Distrust," which could be read as either an inconclusive or a conclusive "just war" plot, as patriotic or antipatriotic, satisfied their needs precisely. But Moore's most appreciative respondents tended to mute the conflicts in the poem in their public reviews, subsuming its self-fragmentations into a clear, single, reassuring spiritual quest narrative. Her own late description of the writing of the poem shares these critics' emphasis on authenticity of feeling—"It is sincere

. . . . Emotion overpowered me"—but her account emphasizes, much more than theirs, the presence of contradictory drives and inward disjunctions: "Haphazard; as form, what has it? It is just a protest—disjointed, exclamatory. Emotion over-powered me. First this thought and then that."³³ For Moore, as she looks back on "In Distrust," the major effect of the poem is that of breaks and outbreaks, a sense of unresolvable conflict.

In a 1945 issue of *Partisan Review*, shortly after "In Distrust" was published in the volume *Nevertheless* to wide acclaim, Randall Jarrell undertook a dissenting opinion. His review's opening lines manage at once to acknowledge and gently mock Moore's privileged position in the new canon of war poetry. Its closing lines, too, bow to Moore with respect, affection, and a trace of condescension. In between, Jarrell constructs an impassioned argument, one which forces its readers to grapple with some of the most powerful and intractable cruxes in the interpretation of modern war literature. At the same time, like the male reviewers with whom he argues over Marianne Moore, he systematically misreads her war poems, ignoring their dynamic processes, overemphasizing the static quality of images within them, and presenting Moore as exaggeratedly sanguine, stolid, and simpleminded.

From the start, his review of "In Distrust" introduces Moore's entire poetic project as a fussy exercise in formal tedium. Moore operates with "static particulars . . . at the farthest level of abstraction from the automatically dynamic generali-zations of the child or animal"; her lines merely fix "specimens on their slides"; her rhymes are the opposite of the kinesthesia of common English rhyme; "every-thing combines to make the poem's structure . . . a state rather than a process" ("PWP," pp. 127–28). Jarrell's emphasis, however disapproving, on the visual aspects of Moore's poetics, on the defamiliarizing textuality of her poetry, provides a useful corrective to readings such as Williams's or Eberhart's which treat the war poems as direct utterances from the heart. But his insistence on the sterile calm of the poems precludes assessment of the kind of flux and tension I have been describing in "In Distrust."

This initial suppression of the agonistic elements in Moore's entire body of work prepares for a more particular erasure of struggle in her war poems. With a fierce wit which suggests that there is a great deal at stake for him in this argument, Jarrell objects to Moore's *Nevertheless* on several grounds. She writes too much about inanimate or nonhuman characters (referring to the poem "Nevertheless," a parable which involves a regenerating strawberry, he asks dryly, "how can anything bad happen to a plant?" ["PWP," p. 128]). Her fables concerning things and animals evade the complexities of the human, of consciousness, and they evade hard facts of social and political relationship; what's more, they evade the presence of inexplicable violence in the world, as Jarrell illustrates with a fable of his own:

> The way of the little jerboa on the sands—at once True, Beautiful, and Good—she understands; but . . . the little larvae feeding on the still-living

> caterpillar their mother has paralyzed for them? We are surprised to find
> Nature, in Miss Moore's poll of it, so strongly in favor of Morality. . . . To
> us, as we look skyward to the bombers, . . . [she] calls *Culture and morals*
> *and Nature still have truth, seek shelter there,* and this is true; but we forget
> it beside the cultured, moral, and natural corpse . . . At Maidanek the mice
> had holes, but a million and a half people had none. ["PWP," p. 128]

It is worth noting the obvious, in the face of Jarrell's impressive appeal to the hard
facts about real nature (as opposed to what he defines as Moore's weak, selective
version): this is an unresolvable ideological quarrel. The slim grape tendril in
Moore's "Nevertheless," which represents how "the weak overcomes its / menace"
(*CP*, p. 126), bears no less and no more essential and immediate a relation to
human experience than Jarrell's caterpillar unable to escape from the sinister
larvae-mother, or than the mice at Maidanek who, serving a different rhetorical
purpose, *can* escape into a hole. Whether or not a reader can return to "Nevertheless" after hearing Jarrell's case out and find the poem of equal value will
depend on—among other things—the reader's assumptions about the efficacy or
the futility of individual human action, beliefs about what constitutes the self, and,
not least, predilections for or aversions to traditional forms of Christian verse such
as allegory or parable.

For at issue here are hard questions not only about what human nature "is,"
but also about how it should be represented. Should war and can war be depicted
by emblems, fables, moral allegories? Or is it incomparable, unrepeatable, irreducible, like each individual person lost to torture, or to genocide, or to battle,
or lost for no reason those who survive will ever know? Should this war, and can
it, be depicted at all, or does Maidanek, as Elie Wiesel has argued, negate "all
literature as it negates all theories and doctrines?"[34]

In the presence of the silent object of the corpse, Jarrell argues, linguistic and
symbolic orders collapse; the adjectives "cultured" and "moral" cannot adhere in
any meaningful way to a dead and tortured body which remains "natural" only in
the most literal sense we have for that word. Moore has made a similar point, in
her reading notes: "The difficulty is one of language." Yet Jarrell's corpse, whose
presence temporarily erases the memory of all reassuring symbolic order, is itself
a symbolic construction, placed "beside" us through a linguistic act, within a
cultural artifact which is also a moral argument about the truth of nature. Jarrell
does not elaborate on Maidanek's possible undoing of all poetry, his own as well
as Moore's. He seeks, provisionally, to affirm a notion of aesthetic decorum: that
the war demands literary treatment which, though always overtly acknowledging
language's difficulties, still represents itself as relatively literal, relatively rooted
in the external world of actual Second World War experience, in contrast to Moore's
obviously stylized and overtly figurative fables of inward warfare.

Underlying this aesthetic dictum is an implicit political aim. War is, in a word
which crops up repeatedly in Jarrell's reviews of this period, "incommensurable";
its dark realities resist easy simile or analogy; to openly imagine metaphors for

what happens to people in war—unless those metaphors refer eventually, emphatically, back to the suffering body—is, therefore, to participate directly in war's perpetuation by falsifying the truth. Jarrell implies that traditional literary techniques such as allegory or fable, which fail to satisfy strict standards of verisimilitude in their depiction of human pain and violence, carry with them a proclivity for, if not a necessary relationship to, warmongering since they do not show sufficiently the pressure of the literal. For Moore, as for Jarrell, a good war poem is an antiwar poem, but Moore assumes, with a strong tradition of Christian rhetoric and ethics behind her, that parables have special power, not only to comfort sufferers but to change behavior. Writing, however ironically, within that tradition, she is primarily interested in war's relation to the states of the cultured, moral, and supernatural *soul*. And indeed there is no clear evidence that Moore's work impressed her wide audience with the wrongness of war any less or any more than Jarrell's, or that the difficulty which was one of language was any less or more apparent to her readers.

Although gender seems to be of no concern in this discussion of the relation between literary technique and political values, Jarrell makes use of conventional formulations of sexual difference throughout as he shapes his terms and rhetorical strategies. He employs, for instance, an underlying image of an oblivious woman, "timid" and "private spirited" in her patterned garden while war rages around her, a figure whose presence pervades literature about women's role in wartime.[35] In order to carry off this reading of Moore, which demands that she be inert and impervious, Jarrell ignores moments in the war poems, such as those I have traced in "In Distrust," which suggest a troubled, conscious relation to her distance from direct conflict and suffering. In "In Distrust of Merits," for instance, he ignores most notably the moment of resistance to looking at the photograph of the dead soldier ("I cannot / look and yet I must"), a point at which Moore's poem itself enacts the fear which precedes the moment of forgetting all ethical consolations "beside the cultured, moral, and natural corpse."[36] Moore seems to demonstrate here, in fact, the very qualities Jarrell praises in Ernie Pyle, the legendary Second World War correspondent, who, Jarrell says, "knew to what degree experience . . . is 'seeing only faintly and not wanting to see at all.' "[37]

What distinguishes Pyle's sight and aversion to sight from Moore's is, of course, his eyewitness status; he, unlike Moore, has the right to claim the words from Whitman which Jarrell cites often: "I was the man, I suffered, I was there."[38] Jarrell's eulogy for Pyle, written a few months before his review of *Nevertheless*, provides an instructive contrast to his treatment of Moore's war poetry. Paradoxically, Pyle's open recognition of his inability to "see" or know war in some primary, unmediated way functions, for Jarrell, only to reconfirm the credibility of his testimony, to further authenticate his eye. In the Pyle piece, Jarrell shifts repeatedly, sometimes even instantaneously, between tributes to two contradictory principles, both part of the aesthetic which Second World War poets inherit from modernism: that authentic experience, felt beyond cliché, is vital ground for the work of art, and yet that all language is nonreferential and all experience is inseparable from already determined cultural and linguistic systems.[39] Or as Gertrude Stein writes in her *Wars I Have Seen*, a predictably playful critique of referentiality in war literature, "However near a war is it is not very near. Perhaps if one were a boy it would be different, but I do not think so."[40] Praising Ernie Pyle, Jarrell negotiates with great care between mythologizing and demythologizing the idea of transparent representation of direct experience. He begins a statement about Pyle, "What he cared about was the facts" but then adds "But facts are only facts as we see them, as we feel them"; he places "real and imaginary" in close proximity, following his phrase "the real war" with "that is, the people in it, all those private wars the imaginary sum of which is the public war" ("EP," p. 112). Still, despite the repeated, cautious moments in Jarrell's treatment of Pyle which emphasize the mediated and mediating aspects of Pyle's writing, it is Pyle's *nearness* to war—the nearness of what Stein calls "boys," a close masculine contact with literal combat—which finally, for Jarrell, renders his work of value.[41]

When Jarrell turns in his review of Moore to an angry, eloquent reading of "In Distrust of Merits," he once again identifies his own stance, with some careful qualification, as less mediated in relation to the real war than Moore's. Here again he partially misreads Moore, and does so eloquently, imaginatively, in the service of a landmark modern protest against war. Objecting to Moore's representation of warfare as heroic ("fighting," he writes, "is the major theme of the poem"), he chides her for her failure to understand and remember

> that [soldiers] are heroes in the sense that the chimney sweeps, the factory children in the blue books, were heroes: routine loss in the routine business of the world . . . that most of the people in a war never fight for even a minute—though they bear for years and die forever. They do not fight, but only starve, only suffer, only die: the sum of all this passive misery is that great activity, War. . . .
>
> Who is "taught to live" by cruelty, suffering, stupidity, and that occupational disease of soldiers, death? The moral equivalent of war! ["PWP," p. 129]

The sudden, sputtered interpolation of the famous title phrase of William James's "Moral Equivalent of War" points to implicit concerns which are at the heart of Jarrell's argument with "In Distrust of Merits." Jarrell rightly finds traces of James's influence on Moore's representations of war. Those echoes are complex enough to merit a detailed study in themselves, but what matter here are simpler questions: how does Jarrell read James's essay, and why does he cite it with such sardonic emphasis here?

James functions as a shorthand representative of several political and aesthetic evils with which Jarrell wishes to connect Moore's war work and from which he strongly wishes to differentiate his own. He objects, as I have said, to any process of image-making which attempts to find overt "equivalences" for war. He objects as strenuously to an idea of human nature which emphasizes what James calls "energies and hardihoods," or human intentionality, at the expense of ignoring or minimizing human dependence, powerlessness, and suffering. James proposes systems for developing, as a substitute for war, "toughness without callousness, authority with as little criminal cruelty as possible";[42] Jarrell would argue that there is no toughness without callousness, no authority without cruelty, and that most people are the subservient victims of both. Finally, and most radically, Jarrell objects to James's explicit and Moore's implicit constructions of the idea of masculinity in their arguments for positive and peaceful modes of combat. James's main argument—that military conflict will persist until antimilitarists find an adequate substitute (the "moral equivalent") for the central function of war, "preserving manliness of type"—is energized by a pervasive anxiety about constitutions of masculinity, a fear that martial experience alone can make a man.[43] Linking Moore's images of inward war to James's manly equivalents, Jarrell articulates his difference from both writers: where they see only the exemplary heroism of stalwart foot soldiers, he sees pernicious, exploitive myths of manhood, and his critique of "In Distrust" gathers force and turns to outrage as he seeks to undo what he perceives as deadly codes of masculine style.

Jarrell's challenge to social constructions of masculinity points to a paradox: how can his review, which Bonnie Costello describes as upholding "in clear sexual categories" a brutal "male vision of amoral nature," be written by the pacifist writer whom Sara Ruddick, the feminist pacifist, has cited as a " 'maternal' man" whose war work exemplifies the kind of "preservative love" generally taught to and practiced by women?[44] Why does Jarrell simultaneously *refer* to rigid distinctions of sexual difference, in his reading of Moore as a woman in a garden and in his own claim to the authority of a soldier, and *refuse* to accept conventional scripts for masculine soldierly behavior? How can he write at once like a man and like a woman, and at the same time criticize Moore both for writing like a woman (timidly, privately, obliviously) and writing like a man (glorifying intention, and Truth, and cause, and war)?

Ways of "writing like a woman" or "writing like a man," as J. Hillis Miller has suggested, often "tend to change places or values in the moment of being defined and enacted": "The male thinks he is writing constatively, but in fact his affirmations are groundless performatives. The woman writer knows there is no truth, no rhythm but the drumbeat of death, but this means that her broken, hesitant rhythms are in resonance with the truth that there is no truth."[45] In Jarrell's argument with Moore, it is the woman poet who is placed in the position of the "constative," "masculine" writer who actually produces "groundless performatives," and it is the male critic who places himself in the role of the feminine writer who knows no rhythm but the drumbeats of death. But if Moore and Jarrell do exchange "places and values" of masculinity and femininity, they do not do so randomly or idiosyncratically. Their shifting reenactments and redefinitions of selfhood have strong political motives and implications within the specific social context of the American Second World War home front.

"Dividing the protector from the protected, defender from defended, is the linchpin of masculinist as well as military ideology," Ruddick writes.[46] Both Moore's distrustful text and Jarrell's even more distrustful review of that text seem to circle around the same linchpin, at once overdetermined by structures of sexual difference in wartime and desperately evasive of those structures. Evasive and exaggerated in opposite directions: where Moore, the female civilian, attempts to imagine a world where everyone could be a soldier, Jarrell, the male soldier, attempts to imagine a world where everyone could be an innocent. We might say that Moore writes "In Distrust of Merits" as if to argue that everyone can act "like a man," and Jarrell his review as if to argue that everyone is passive "as a woman."

The tradition of ironic soldier poetry which has dominated critical discussion of war poems for most of this century encourages sensitive readings of Jarrell's project but not of Moore's. Another look at Jarrell's critique of Moore's images of war may help to explain this situation. "Most of the people in a war," Jarrell writes, "never fight for even a minute—though they bear for years and die forever" ("PWP," p. 129). "Bear for years" is a peculiar phrase—oddly abstract in the midst of a relatively concretizing series of passive verbs—and an apt one. The word "bear," though it does not necessarily signify a feminine condition (people of both genders bear burdens and bear pain), carries nonetheless a strong association with the female body. In our culture generally, as Margaret Homans has argued in her *Bearing the Word*, "the literal is associated with the feminine, the more highly valued figurative . . . with the masculine," and this "complex and troubling tradition" originates in a simple actuality: "that women bear children and men do not."[47] Jarrell's "bear" invokes an image of childbirth to redescribe war not just because childbearing is linked to pain or because it is associated with submission to the brunt of things, but because it represents a prolonged encounter with unmitigated, unmediated fact. Childbirth, in Homans's words, is inherently a structure of literalization, in which "something becomes real that did not exist before—or that existed as a word, a theory, or a 'conception' " and by which "the relatively figurative becomes the relatively literal."[48] Throughout his career, but particularly in the early forties, Jarrell strove to define a poetics of war which could adequately recognize that warfare itself is a "structure of literalization": "what in peace struggles below consciousness in the mind of an economist," he writes, "in war wipes out a division" ("EP," p. 113).

Valuing a war poetry which is rooted, as nearly as possible, in the concrete, the material, the "borne," Jarrell writes within a strong tradition of masculine antiwar protest in which the soldier becomes responsible for transcribing the literal. The more "literal" the representation of men's experience within this tradition of soldier poetry, the more feminized those men will appear, as their function shifts from "fighting" to "bearing." Thus, in Owen's classic, inaugural war poem "Dulce et Decorum Est," the depiction of gas warfare, which represents itself as starkly realistic in opposition to earlier clichés, begins with a description of the men as bent "like hags."[49] "Dulce" was originally titled "To A Certain Poetess" and written in angry response to Jessie Pope's metaphors of war as, among other things, football. In this tradition of soldier poetry which has dominated critical discussion of war poems for most of this century, men come to occupy the place of the literal *as well as women,* or to displace women entirely; the figurative, in turn, is associated especially with the feminine, with the abstract allegories and stylized banalities of "certain poetesses." And in this case, the text's commitment to "literal" representation, its firm alliance with an authority of male experience, makes it *especially* highly valued and qualifies it for inclusion in the ranks of canonical war poetry.[50]

I do not want to deny the importance, the potential efficacy, or the polemical brilliance of the appeal to literal experience in the modern tradition of war literature.[51] But when experience is privileged or even required as an aesthetic, political, and moral criterion for the proper war poem, the attendant dangers are several. Overvaluation of the concrete and particular may prevent recognition of war poems which have overtly given expression to significant ideological principles and conflicts—even when those poems, like Moore's "In Distrust," clearly speak in abstract terms which large audiences of contemporaries found compelling.[52] Where obviously stylized and didactic literary techniques such as Moore's allegory signal from the start both their literariness and their political and philosophical stakes, a more narrative war poem which refers more openly to real experience may not recognize the limits of what constitutes the "real" within it.[53] In American forties war poetry, for instance, "experience of war" was generally taken to comprehend the experience of the soldier but not generally, during the war itself, the experience of the Holocaust victim, the Japanese American in an internment camp, or a woman working in a defense plant. Finally, reading war poetry as we have so often been taught to read it—as a register of difference between and within men over the affairs of manhood, in which, say, the euphemisms of generals are broken open by the literalizing story of the soldier—we may once again be complicit in rendering women (who have also, always, had our say about war) silent and invisible and static, suppressing our own dynamic and complex relations to systems of warmaking. Rereading "In Distrust" in the context of a different set of texts—the body of highly abstract works by women which enact inward wars rooted in spiritual traditions, from Emily Dickinson's Civil War meditations to two of the most influential poems of the Second World War, Edith Sitwell's "Still Falls the Rain" and H.D.'s *Trilogy*—we may begin to understand not only the potential power of figurative models of representation and protest in war literature, but also how thoroughly and insistently Moore writes her war poems "like a woman."

In his *Complete Poems,* Jarrell's "Eighth Air Force" appears as the first poem of a section called "Bombers," a classic collection of soldier poems of the modern ironic type. Beginning with a detailed, mimetic representation of a tangible scene of soldiers' encampment—what tune the drunk sergeant whistles, what ordinary card games three soldiers play between missions—"Eighth Air Force" shifts quickly back and forth from literal narrative to tense, abstract meditation, till its original representational mode is replaced entirely by a lyric soliloquy spoken by Pilate at Christ's trial, or, more accurately, by a voice which sounds partly Pilate-like.

The poem is almost obsessively concerned not just with humanity but with masculinity—the speaker explicitly identifies himself as "a man, I," and the word "man" occurs, with heavy stress, at the end of over a third of the poem's lines and repeatedly within them. It therefore seems a culmination of and a self-reflexive commentary on the androcentric traditions of war poetry and warmaking. "Eighth Air Force" is, we might say, a poem about how a man looks at other men, and how he struggles to come to terms with what "manhood" means for himself in a culture at war. Yet the poem's first turn away from literal description and toward the abstract question of manhood, accomplished through an allusion to Plautus, suggests a more pressing intertextual relation to an influential contemporary text by a woman. " 'Man's wolf to man,' " Moore quotes Plautus's words in "In Distrust," "and we devour / ourselves." Jarrell writes: "shall I say that man / Is not as men have said: a wolf to man?"[54]

Other insistent connections between the two texts suggest that despite Jarrell's distaste for "In Distrust" in his review, the power of the poem was not so easily dismissed. The struggle with the meaning of manhood in "Eighth Air Force" may be read as energized not by the fellow soldier's sight of real men but by the fellow poet's reading of a civilian woman's work. Jarrell's poem, in a number of ways, deliberately retraverses Moore's terrain. Both poets, for instance, employ the traditional device of representing the soldier as Christ (a strategy used by patriotic and antiwar poets alike throughout this century); both poems focus inward, on the dilemma of the observer of the crucifixion. When placed within the context of the American literary culture which lauded Moore's war poetry during and immediately after the Second World War, Jarrell's portrayal of the Pilate-like observer, which might otherwise seem a meditation on enduring, universal questions about guilt, justice, and forgiveness, can now be understood as a specific, topical revision of Moore's influential representation of the self as Iscariot-like. His soldiers, half innocents and half murderers, bear, too, a direct revisionary relation to Moore's heroic, patient fighters.

Although Moore's uses of Plautus and New Testament narrative appear at first to be far more dogmatic than Jarrell's, in the context of "In Distrust" they are undercut as dramatically. It seems to me likely that whether Jarrell consciously recognized it or not, he found a model for the self-questioning, "disjointed, exclamatory" voice of "Eighth Air Force," one of the most significant "soldier poems" to come out of the Second World War, in the searching voice of "In Distrust of Merits." Jarrell comes to sound most like Moore in a poem which, more than any other of his war works, acknowledges that no poetic text can say with unequivocal, literal meaning, "I was the man, I suffered, I was there," and that all poetic representation must also take place, in part, from the position of Pilate, the implicated observer who says, "Behold the man!" If we are to understand better the relation of suffering to observing, "there" to "not there," front to sidelines in twentieth-century war and twentieth-century war poetry, present-day critics and anthologists must recognize that the discourse of war consists not just of "what men have said" but also of what women like Marianne Moore have written.

Notes

1. W. H. Auden, review of *Nevertheless*, by Marianne Moore, *New York Times*, 15 Oct. 1944, p. 20.

2. Randall Jarrell, "Poetry in War and Peace," *Partisan Review* (Winter 1945); reprinted in *Kipling, Auden and Co.: Essays and Reviews, 1935–1964* (New York: Farrar, Straus, and Giroux, 1980), p. 127. All further references to this essay, abbreviated "PWP," will be included in the text.

3. Robert Graves, "The Poets of World War II," *The Common Asphodel: Collected Essays on Poetry 1922–1949* (London: H. Hamilton, 1949), p. 308.

4. See Siegfried Sassoon, introduction to Wilfred Owen, *Poems* (London: Chatto and Windus, 1920).

5. Graves, "The Poets of World War II," p. 310.

6. Richard Eberhart, "Preface: Attitudes to War," in *War and the Poet: An Anthology of Poetry Expressing Man's Attitudes to War from Ancient Times to the Present*, ed. Eberhart and Selden Rodman (New York: Devin-Adair Co., 1945), pp. xv, xiii.

7. Eberhart, "Preface: Attitudes," p. xiii.

8. Oscar Williams, ed., *The War Poets: An Anthology of the War Poetry of the Twentieth Century* (New York: Day, 1945), p. 6.

9. Bonnie Costello, *Marianne Moore: Imaginary Possessions* (Cambridge, Mass: Harvard University Press, 1981), p. 110.

10. Elizabeth Bishop to Houghton Mifflin, 22 Jan. 1945, in *Elizabeth Bishop: A Bibliography, 1927–1979*, ed. Candace W. MacMahon (Charlottesville, VA: University of Virginia Press, 1980), p. 8.

11. Marianne Moore, "Interview with Donald Hall," in *A Marianne Moore Reader* (New York: Viking, 1961), p. 261.

12. See Laurence Stapleton, *Marianne Moore: The Poet's Advance* (Princeton, N.J.: Princeton University Press, 1978), p. 134.

13. Moore, "In Distrust of Merits," *The Complete Poems of Marianne Moore* (New York: Macmillan, 1967), pp. 136–38. Page references for other poems in this collection, abbreviated *CP*, will be included in the text.

14. Costello describes extensively how the emblems in Moore's poems of "a world already represented" draw "descriptions of the world into a private setting where the world might be brought under imaginary control," epitomizing Moore's method of "imaginary possession" (Costello, *Imaginary Possessions*, p. 6).

15. Costello, *Imaginary Possessions*, p. 38.

16. Quoted in Stapleton, *The Poet's Advance*, p. 130.

17. The quotations from Moore's unpublished material which follow are taken from conversation and reading notebooks in the Moore collection of the Philip H. and

A. S. W. Rosenbach Foundation, Philadelphia, Pennsylvania. Excerpts will be cited hereafter as "Rosenbach," followed by their file numbers. This entry is from Rosenbach 1251/1 (conversation notes 1938–1957), dated 10 June 1938.

18. Rosenbach 1251/12 (reading diary 1942–58), three entries: 23 July 1943; 22 Mar. 1943; undated.

19. For an excellent discussion of "images of sweetened combat" in Moore's work, see Costello, *Imaginary Possessions*, pp. 108–32.

20. Marianne Moore, "There Is a War That Never Ends," *Predilections* (New York: ,1955), p. 41.

21. Both entries are taken from Rosenbach 1251/1. On the Christian tradition of spiritual warfare narrative, see Sue Mansfield, *The Gestalts of War: An Inquiry into Its Origins and Meanings as a Social Institution* (New York: Dial, 1982), pp. 127–33.

22. Rosenbach 1251/1, dated 9 Aug. 1937; 1251/1, dated 23 Sept. 1940; 1251/12, undated.

23. Rosenbach 1251/12, dated 22 Mar. 1943.

24. John Ellis, "Victory of the Voice?" *Screen* 22, no. 2 (1981): 69.

25. Rosenbach 1251/2, dated 23 July 1942.

26. Rosenbach 1251/12, undated.

27. The feminist historian Susan M. Hartmann notes, "The global scope of American involvement, the increasing complexity of modern war, and the development of military technology had reduced the proportion of military personnel directly engaged in battle. During World War II 25 percent of military personnel never left the United States, and only about one in eight actually saw combat" (Hartmann, *The Home Front and Beyond: American Women in the 1940s*, American Women in the Twentieth Century [Boston: Twayne, 1982], p. 34).

28. Cynthia Enloe, *Does Khaki Become You? The Militarization of Women's Lives* (Boston: South End Press, 1983), p. 15.

29. Geoffrey Hartman, "Six Women Poets," *Easy Pieces* (New York: Columbia Univesity Press, 1985), p. 111.

30. Cary Nelson, *Our Last First Poets: Vision and History in Contemporary Poetry* (Urbana, Ill.: University of Illinois Press, 1981), p. 17.

31. Jonathan Culler, "Apostrophe," *Diacritics* 7 (Winter 1977): 60.

32. Jane Tompkins, *Sensational Designs: The Cultural Work of American Fiction 1790–1860* (New York: Oxford University Press, 1985), pp. xvii, 151. Paul Fussell discusses the metrical shift at the end of the poem in his *Poetic Meter and Poetic Form* (New York: Random House, 1965), pp. 8–9.

33. Moore, "Interview," p. 261.

34. Elie Wiesel, *A Jew Today*, trans. Marion Wiesel (New York: Random House, 1978); cited in Annette Insdorf, *Indelible Shadows: Film and the Holocaust* (New York, Random House, 1983), p. xi.

35. Perhaps the most famous text in the long tradition in which an overprotected, feminine *hortus conclusus* is opposed to masculine engagement in historical crisis is Ruskin's "Of Queen's Gardens," *Sesame and Lilies: Three Lectures* (Chicago: W. B. Conkey Co., 1890), pp. 72–101. In the Second World War period, see Arthur Koestler's Sylvia in "The Artist and Politics," *Saturday Review of Literature* 25 (31 Jan. 1942), pp. 3–4, 14–15; the

attack on American women for failing to prevent war in Philip Wylie's *Generation of Vipers* (New York: Farrar and Rinehart, 1942); Pearl Buck's chapter on women, domesticity, and war in *Of Men and Women* (New York: John Day Co., 1941); and Williams's image of American civilians protected by a wall of flesh, quoted earlier in this essay.

36. Bonnie Costello argues persuasively, in her discussion of Jarrell's review, that Moore's work not only is part of a tradition of domestic "feminine realism . . . which links observation to ethical generalization" in American women's poetry but also constitutes a transformation of that tradition: "All the poems follow a dictum of resistance even while they move through an apparent structure of observation-moral, for they continually propose definitions only to unravel them" (Costello, "The 'Feminine' Language of Marianne Moore," in *Women and Language in Literature and Society*, ed. Sally McConnell-Ginet, Ruth Borker, and Nelly Furman [New York, 1980], p. 235). Costello follows Emily Stipes Watt's work in *The Poetry of American Women from 1932 to 1945* (Austin, Tex., 1977).

37. Jarrell, "Ernie Pyle," *Kipling, Auden and Co.*, p. 112; all further references to this essay, abbreviated "EP," will be included in the text.

38. See, for instance, Jarrell's repeated quotations from Whitman in "These Are Not Psalms," *Kipling, Auden and Co.*, pp. 122–26.

39. I owe to conversation with Catherine Gallagher my formulation of this point.

40. Gertrude Stein, *Wars I Have Seen* (New York: Random House, 1945), p. 9.

41. A similar complex conflation of "real" and "imaginary" occurs in Jarrell's description of Owen as "a poet in the true sense of the word, someone who has shown to us one of those worlds which, after we have been shown it, we call the real world" (Jarrell, "The Profession of Poetry," *Kipling, Auden and Co.*, p. 169). Ernest Hemingway's introduction to his anthology of writing about war, *Men at War*, reveals identical ambivalence. On the one hand Hemingway, paying tribute to Stephen Crane's *Red Badge of Courage*, argues that the writer's imagination "should produce a truer account than anything factual can be. For facts can be observed badly." On the other hand, he praises Crane's depiction of a boy "facing *that thing which no one knows about who has not done it*" (Hemingway, intro., *Men at War: The Best War Stories of All Time* [New York: Crown, 1942], pp. xv, xviii; my italics). See also the strained arguments about experience in Williams's collection of prose statements by poets on poetry and war, part of his *War Poets*.

42. William James, "The Moral Equivalent of War," *Memories and Studies* (Westport, Conn., 1941), pp. 291–92.

43. James, "Moral Equivalent of War," p. 292.

44. Costello, "The 'Feminine' Language," p. 234; see Sara Ruddick, "Pacifying the Forces: Drafting Women in the Interests of Peace," *Signs* 8 (Spring 1983): 479.

45. J. Hillis Miller, "Mr. Carmichael and Lily Briscoe: The Rhythm of Creativity in *To the Lighthouse,*" in *Modernism Reconsidered*, ed. Robert Kiely (Cambridge, Mass: Harvard University Press, 1983), p. 188.

46. Ruddick, "Pacifying the Forces," p. 472.

47. Margaret Homans, *Bearing the Word: Language and Female Experience in Nineteenth-Century Women's Writing* (Chicago: University of Chicago Press, 1986), pp. 5, 88.

48. Homans, *Bearing the Word*, p. 26.

49. See Owen, "Dulce et Decorum Est," *Collected Poems*, ed. C. Day Lewis (London: Chatto, 1963), p. 55. For the Jessie Pope connection, see Day Lewis's notes on the manuscript variations on the same page. On the persistent analogy in Western culture between warmaking and childbearing, see Nancy Huston, "The Matrix of War: Mothers and Heroes," in *The*

Female Body in Western Culture, ed. Susan Rubin Suleiman (Cambridge, Mass.: Harvard University Press, 1986).

50.   Many of the essays in the "American Representations of Vietnam" issue of *Cultural Critique* 3 (Spring 1986) explore American culture's continuing myths of the special value of the soldier/veteran's experience. See especially Michael Clark, "Remembering Vietnam," pp. 46–78; Rick Berg, "Losing Vietnam: Covering the War in an Age of Technology," pp. 92–125; John Carlos Rowe, "Eye-Witness: Documentary Styles in the American Representation of Vietnam," pp. 126–50; Philip Francis Kuberski, "Genres of Vietnam," pp. 168–88.

51.   Nor do I mean to imply that women in American culture cannot and do not employ strategies of literalization in their representations of war. Elaine Scarry's recent, powerful treatment of "injury and the structure of war" in *The Body in Pain: The Making and Unmaking of the World* (New York: Oxford University Press, 1985), for instance, is very much within the tradition advocated and represented by Jarrell here.

52.   Tompkins discusses related problems in the evaluation of popular nineteenth-century works with "designs upon their audiences" in her introduction and throughout *Sensational Designs*.

53.   Homans notes this danger in myths of female experience (see *Bearing the Word*, p. 15), citing Jane Gallop on the inherently conservative nature of a "politics of experience." In her discussion of Irigaray's work on the female body, Gallop goes on, however, to warn at the same time against unproblematic *denials* of experience: "the gesture of a troubled but nonetheless insistent referentiality is essential" if one's aim is "*a poiésis* of experience, that attempts to reconstruct experience itself, to produce a remetaphorization . . . a salutary jolt out of the compulsive repetition of the same" (Gallop, "*Quand nos lèvres s'écrivent:* Irigaray's Body Politic," *Romanic Review* 74 [Jan. 1983]: 83). The most powerful "soldier poems" in the present canon of war poetry—Owen's "Dulce," for instance, or Jarrell's "Death of the Ball Turret Gunner"—certainly attempt to produce such salutary jolts, strongly revising the metaphors which formerly applied to the male body in war.

54.   Jarrell, "Eighth Air Force," *The Complete Poems* (New York: Farrar, Straus, and Giroux, 1969), p. 143.

Notes on Contributors

Carol L. Barash is Assistant Professor of English at Rutgers University. Her publications include *An Olive Schreiner Reader: Writing on Women and South Africa* and numerous articles about women writers and feminist theory. She is currently completing *English Women Writers and the Body of Monarchy, 1660–1720*, a study of gender, monarchy and literary authority; and, with historian Rachel Weil, *Sex and Social Order, 1660–1730*, an anthology of political and literary writings about the history of sexuality.

Christopher Craft is Assistant Professor of English at the University of California, Davis, where he is completing a study entitled *Another Kind of Love: Sodomy, Inversion, and Male Homosexual Desire in English Discourse, 1850–1920*. His essays have appeared in *Representations* and *Genders*.

Susan Stanford Friedman is Professor of English and Women's Studies at the University of Wisconsin-Madison. She is the author of *Psyche Reborn: The Emergence of H.D.*, co-author of *A Woman's Guide to Therapy*, and co-editor of *Contemporary Literature's H.D.: Centennial Issue*. She has also published articles on women's poetry, psychoanalysis and feminist criticism, women's education and feminist pedagogy. *Penelope's Web: H.D.'s Fictions and the Gendering of Modernism* is forthcoming.

Elliot L. Gilbert is Professor of English at the University of California, Davis. He has published books and articles on Kipling, Dickens, Carlyle, Tennyson, and Wilde among others. He is currently working on a book about the relationship between history and creativity in the nineteenth century. Gilbert also edits the *California Quarterly*, a literary magazine published at Davis.

Sandra M. Gilbert is Professor of English at Princeton University. She has most recently published *No Man's Land, Volume 1: The War of the Words*, coauthored with Susan Gubar. With Gubar, she has, in addition, coauthored *The Madwoman in the Attic: The Woman Writer and the Nineteenth Century Literary Imagination*, and coedited *The Norton Anthology of Literature by Women: The Tradition in*

English. She has also published three collections of poems with a fourth forthcoming.

Barbara Johnson teaches French and Comparative Literature at Harvard. She is the author of *Défigurations du langage poétique* (1979), *The Critical Difference* (1980), and *A World of Difference* (1987). She is the translator of Jacques Derrida's *Dissemination*.

David Leverenz, Professor of English at the University of Florida at Gainesville, is the author of *Manhood and the American Renaissance*, forthcoming. He has also written *The Language of Puritan Feeling* (1980), as well as various essays on American literature and psychoanalytic criticism.

D.A. Miller is Professor of English and Comparative Literature at the University of California, Berkeley. He is the author of *Narrative and its Discontents* and *The Novel and the Police*.

Phyllis Rackin teaches English at the University of Pennsylvania. Her publications include *Shakespeare's Tragedies* and numerous essays on Shakespeare and literary theory. She is presently completing a book on Shakespeare's English history plays and the Renaissance revolution in historiography. This essay grows out of her long-standing interest in gender construction in early modern England.

Patrocinio P. Schweickart is Associate Professor of English at the University of New Hampshire. She is the co-editor, with Elizabeth Flynn, of *Gender and Reading: Essays on Readers, Texts and Contexts*. Her essays on feminist criticism and gender and reading have appeared in *Signs*, *Canadian Journal of Political and Social Theory*, and *Reader*. She is currently working on a book on a feminist theory of discourse.

Susan Schweik is Assistant Professor of English at the University of California, Berkeley. She is currently completing a book, *A Gulf So Deeply Cut: American Women Poets and the Second World War*.

Peter Schwenger, Professor of English at Mount St. Vincent University in Halifax, Nova Scotia, is the author of *Phallic Critiques: Masculinity and Twentieth-Century Literature*. He is completing *Nuclear Narrative*, a study of narrative theory and the literature of nuclear holocaust.

Eve Kosofsky Sedgwick, Professor of English at Duke University, is the author of *The Coherence of Gothic Conventions* and *Between Men: English Literature and Male Homosocial Desire*. "The Beast in the Closet," which is part of a forthcoming book, *Epistemology of the Closet*, has been awarded the Crompton-Noll Prize in Gay Studies from the Modern Language Association.

Elaine Showalter is Professor of English at Princeton University. She is the author of *A Literature of Their Own* and *The Female Malady*, and has edited books on feminist criticism and women's writing. She is completing a book entitled *Borderlines: Men and Women at the Fin de Siècle*.

Valerie Smith is Associate Professor of English and Afro-American Studies at Princeton University. Author of *Self-Discovery and Authority in Afro-American Narrative*, she is at work on a study of black feminist literary theory.